DIFFICULT STUDENTS & DISRUPTIVE BEHAVIOR in the CLASSROOM

NORTON BOOKS IN EDUCATION

DIFFICULT STUDENTS & DISRUPTIVE BEHAVIOR in the CLASSROOM

TEACHER RESPONSES THAT WORK

Vance Austin & Daniel Sciarra

W. W. NORTON & COMPANY

independent publishers since 1923

NEW YORK • LONDON

Note to Readers: Models and/or techniques described in this volume are illustrative or are included for general informational purposes only; neither the publisher nor the author(s) can guarantee the efficacy or appropriateness of any particular recommendation in every circumstance.

For information about permission to reproduce selections from this book, write to Permissions, W. W. Norton & Company, Inc., 500 Fifth Avenue, New York, NY 10110

For information about special discounts for bulk purchases, please contact W. W. Norton Special Sales at specialsales@wwnorton.com or 800-233-4830

Manufacturing by Edwards Brothers Malloy
Production manager: Christine Critelli

Library of Congress Cataloging-in-Publication Data

Names: Austin, Vance
L., author. | Sciarra, Daniel T., author.
Title: Difficult students and
disruptive behavior in the classroom : teacher
   responses that work /
Vance Austin, Daniel Sciarra.
Description: First edition. | New York :
W.W. Norton & Company, 2016. |
   Series: Norton books in education | Includes
bibliographical references
   and index.
Identifiers: LCCN 2015047524 |
ISBN 9780393707540 (pbk.)
Subjects: LCSH: Classroom management—United
States. | Problem
   children—United States—Discipline. | School
discipline—United States.
Classification: LCC LB3013 .A87 2016 | DDC
371.102/4—dc23 LC record available at http://lccn.loc.gov/2015047524

ISBN: 978-0-393-70754-0 (pbk.)

W. W. Norton & Company, Inc., 500 Fifth Avenue, New York, N.Y. 10110
                    www.wwnorton.com
W. W. Norton & Company Ltd., Castle House, 75/76 Wells Street, London W1T 3QT

1 2 3 4 5 6 7 8 9 0

To my wife Theresa and son James who have given my
life meaning and fulfillment; to my brother, Tim, for loving
kindness that defies time and space, and to my mother, Lois,
for *everything*. . .
—VA

To the children of the Child Guidance Center of Southern
Connecticut whose lives taught me the importance of
attachment.
—DS

Contents

ACKNOWLEDGMENTS

We would like to thank Deborah Malmud, Vice President and Director of Norton Professional Books, for getting us started on this project and for her encouragement and support along the way. Likewise, we offer very special thanks to Ben Yarling, Associate Editor, Norton Professional Books, who was able to share our vision for this project and see beyond the developmental imperfections and appreciate its contribution to the field. Similarly, we would like to thank Alison Lewis, Marketing and Editorial Assistant at Norton Professional Books, whose patience, focus, and attention to detail helped us move more efficiently to production. Also, we would be remiss if we did not acknowledge the generous support provided by Elizabeth Baird, our Project Editor, as well as the exceptional work of our copy editor, Rebecca Caine, whose meticulous editing contributed significantly to the coherence and accuracy of our manuscript.

Finally, we would like to thank our family members, Brenda, Theresa, and James, whose unconditional love, patience, and encouragement made the completion of this project both possible and worthwhile.

As the inclusive classroom continues to develop into standard practice throughout the United States, classroom teachers can no longer claim that students with special needs and behavioral challenges are not their responsibility. Frequently, within the inclusion model, special and general educators are paired to serve students with a variety of needs—gifted, average, learning disabled, and emotionally disturbed—in a single classroom. As a result, all teachers must now acquire the skills and dispositions necessary to effectively teach students with a wide variety of needs. Teacher preparation programs and schools must find ways to ensure that preservice and novice teachers are prepared to address the increasingly diverse needs of all students assigned to their classrooms. As one step in the reflective process of teacher preparation and professional development practices, the effective behaviors of successful teachers need to be considered.

In discussing the needs of some of the most challenging students, Cavin encouraged teachers to "remember that these kids with all of their problems, their criminal records, their probation officers, their idiosyncrasies, their unlovable characteristics, and their strange families are still kids. They need someone to care. They need someone to accept them. They need to know they are somebody. If you are willing to provide these ideals, you can be the connection that bridges the gap from dropout to diploma" (1998, p. 10).

A further incentive to stay the course with challenging students was provided by a former colleague, who observed, "For some kids, these days in school may be the best of their lives: the safest, the happiest, and the most secure." We never forgot this insightful pronouncement, and it helped change our attitudes about teaching even the most oppositional, defiant students.

A final inducement to persevere with difficult students comes from recent data provided by the U.S. Office of Juvenile Justice. In 2010, according to their records, 70,792 juveniles were incarcerated in the United States—the greatest number worldwide. In fact, the incarceration rate for juveniles (school-age children) in the United States in 2002 was 336 for every 100,000 youth—compare that figure to the country with the next-highest rate, South Africa, with 69 of every 100,000 youth in detention (as cited in Mendel, 2011). In response to these abysmal statistics and his own extensive experience, DeMuro, the former commissioner of the Pennsylvania Juvenile Corrections system, described the current state of juvenile justice in the United States as "iatrogenic" (as cited in Mendel, 2011). Mendel (2011) noted further that while education and treatment at most juvenile detention facilities is nonexistent, the average annual cost to house an incarcerated youth in a detention facility is approximately $88,000, whereas the cost to provide that same individual with effective intervention services in a public or specialized school is approximately $10,000 to $15,000. Moreover, the recidivism rate for incarcerated youth in New York State three years or more after release ranges from 73% to 89% (Annie E. Casey Foundation, 2011).

Similarly, a 2006 investigation revealed that only 33% of youth who said they would return to school once released from a Pennsylvania corrections camp program actually did so (Hjalmarsson, 2008). Since there are, effectively, no rehabilitation programs in most juvenile corrections facilities, youths detained in them can actually become more antisocial and more inclined to engage in criminal behaviors after their release. Thus, the data clearly suggest that the last, best hope for most of these at-risk youth is in school—and perhaps the best models of prosocial behavior are their teachers.

A FRAMEWORK FOR GOOD TEACHING

After reviewing the relevant literature concerning the elements common to most good teachers, we have identified three fundamental factors: (1) relationship building, (2) pedagogical skills, and (3) subject knowledge, in that order.

Relationship Building

What is meant by *relationship* as it pertains to teachers and students? Simply put, the term refers to the rapport the teacher builds with the student—a connection that fosters trust and that facilitates learning. Truth be told, such meaningful and affirming relationships are the reasons most teachers want to teach in the first place. Good teacher–student and student–teacher relationships are often the reason that students choose to stay in school, acquire an affinity for a particular subject, feel good about their school experience, look forward to coming to class, and report feeling a sense of self-efficacy. Teacher–student relationships, like any other human relationship, can be either healthy and reciprocally validating or unhealthy and destructive. Boynton and Boynton (2005) note that students are more likely to do what teachers ask when they feel valued and cared for by them. Similarly, Thompson stated that "the most powerful weapon available to [teachers] who want to foster a favorable learning climate is a positive relationship with our students" (1998, p. 6), and Canter and Canter (1997) suggested that students who enjoy a positive relationship with their teachers will be more inclined to comply with their requests and work conscientiously on assignments.

Furthermore, Marzano (2003) suggested that students who feel genuinely cared for and respected by their teachers are less likely to pose discipline problems. In a similar way, Kohn asserted that "Children are more likely to be respectful when important adults in their lives respect them. They are more likely to care about others if they know they are cared about" (1996, p. 111). Likewise, Algozzine, Daunic, and Smith asserted that "Research has consistently shown that a positive relationship with an adult is a critical factor in preventing violence at school." They recommended, as a result, that schools provide opportunities for teachers and students to spend "quality" time together (2010, p. 215). Jones and Jones further posited that both academic achievement and behavior in the classroom are directly influenced by the "quality of the teacher–student relationship." (1981 p. 95). Important to that relationship, of course, is the passion that the teacher feels for her subject and enthusiastically imparts to her students. Indeed, in support of that, Rose observed that "It is what we are excited about that educates us." (2000, p. 106).

Similarly, in his investigation of teacher–student interactions at both the elementary and secondary levels, Hargreaves (2000) underscored the frequently unheralded importance of an emotional connection or relationship between teachers and students. In examining this critical aspect of good teaching, Hargreaves offered, "Teaching is an emotional practice. This use of emotion can be helpful or harmful, raising classroom standards or lowering them. . . . Emotions are located not just in the individual mind; they are embedded and expressed in human interactions and relationships" (p. 824). Lastly, Zehm and Kottler (1993) have suggested that students will *never* trust or truly attend to teachers without an established sense of mutual valuation and respect.

Additionally, it is vital that teachers integrate their personal and professional selves. It is important that they explore and reflect on their concepts of self and their beliefs about the essential qualities of good teaching, good teachers, and good character to cultivate an "integrated" self and thereby develop authentic relationships with students and colleagues.

Several relational theories have been found relevant to the field of education and teaching, such as mindfulness (Broderick, 2013), belongingness (Fiske, 2004), and classroom as community (Kohn, 1996); nonetheless, we have decided to focus on the importance of understanding attachment theory as described by Bowlby (1980) and, more recently, Ainsworth (1989). Simply put, Bowlby and Ainsworth posited that a child's behavior is heavily influenced by the quality and strength of the attachment bond with her or his parent figure. We posit that this phenomenon, in turn, affects the teacher and her or his ability to develop a therapeutic relationship with the student. Since the teacher has, ostensibly, developed an attachment bond of some form with her own parent, she should be aware of its influence on her interactions with the student. An example of the nexus of two antithetical forms of attachment, experienced by most teachers, is the student who seems to possess an uncanny ability to identify their vulnerabilities. In order to protect their bruised egos and regain control of the classroom, many teachers react impulsively and mete out a punitive consequence to the offending student, never acknowledging the influences of their own parent-bond. As a result, they create a relational schism between themselves and their antagonist, which makes relationship building with that student difficult, if not impossible. In subsequent chapters, we will discuss ways that teachers can understand their own predispositions relative to relationship building with difficult students, as well as the influences of their students' attachment experiences, to help them develop healthy, prosocial relationships with even their most challenging students.

Maya Angelou, the acclaimed poet, author, and solon, once wrote, "I've learned that people will forget what you said, people will forget what you did, but people will never forget how you made them feel" (n.d.). In a sense, the quality of a relationship is determined by the way those in that relationship *feel* about it. Thus, relationships, genuine and affirming, provide the foundation for everything else that teachers strive to do. Relationships open the doors of students' minds to learning, enticing them to see education as something worthwhile, to want to acquire the knowledge and skills that teachers want to impart. In short, without such quality relationships, there can be no real teaching and learning.

Pedagogical Skills

Similarly, good teachers must be steeped in the art and science of effective teaching—what we refer to as *pedagogical knowledge*. According to the Cambridge Dictionary Online (2012), the term *pedagogy* is defined as "the study of the methods and activities of teaching." There is no shortcut to attaining this vital skill set—it is honed and refined throughout the professional lifetime of the teacher. Frankly, if teachers do not know *how* to teach subject matter or impart knowledge about a topic or skill, it matters little that they have much to teach and possess a vast knowledge base. Many people who are recognized widely for their expertise in a particular area or subject simply do not possess the pedagogical skills to effectively impart that knowledge to others.

Undeniably, sound pedagogical skills must be acquired through effective training, reflective practice, and more reflective practice. As Loughran noted, "If learning through practice matters, then reflection on practice is crucial, and teacher preparation is the obvious place for it to be initiated and nurtured" (2002, p. 42). Ideally, the foundation of a sound pedagogy should be established in a reputable college-based teacher preparation program.

Cogill (2008) stated that pedagogy, as it pertains to the teaching profession, is multifaceted and thus difficult to simply define. Watkins and Mortimore described the term as "any conscious activity by one person designed to enhance the learning of another" (1999, p. 3). Alexander expanded on this definition by adding, "It is what one *needs* to know, and the *skills* one needs to command in order to make and justify the many different kinds of decisions of which teaching is constituted" (2004, p. 3). We find Shulman's (1987) seven categories of teacher knowledge to be a very helpful framework for understanding pedagogical skills, so we will list them here: (a) content knowledge, (b) general pedagogical knowledge (e.g., classroom control, group work), (c) pedagogical content knowledge (we refer to this simply as "content or subject knowledge"), (d) curriculum knowledge, which is more specific to instructional design, (e) knowledge of learners and their characteristics, (f) knowledge of educational contexts (e.g., schools and their communities), and (g) knowledge of education purposes and their values (for students) (as cited in Cogill, 2008, pp. 1–2). Simply put, pedagogy is the "how-to" in effectively imparting a skill to other people.

In a different vein, Korthagen (2004) posited a developmental model of pedagogical skills central to a good teacher. He refers to this model as "the onion" because the skills are equally important and interrelated. They flow from a central mission, through identity (of the teacher), beliefs (of the teacher), competencies (teaching), behaviors (relative to effective teaching), and, finally, the interaction of the teacher's environment with the teacher and her instruction. In line with his model, Korthagen proposed "a more holistic approach towards teacher development, in which competence is not equated with competencies" (p. 94). He further suggested that the educator who trains teachers should understand his own core qualities in order to more effectively and authentically promote them in his prospective teachers.

Subject Knowledge

Imparting subject knowledge to students is a teacher's professional raison d'etre. Relative to this assertion, Palmer described an unforgettable professor who defied "every rule of good teaching": "He lectured to such a degree and with such passion that he left little time for student questions, and he was not a good listener." What he did impart to Palmer was his love of learning and his passion for the subject knowledge—as well as the subject matter itself, of course. Palmer recalled, "It did not matter to me that he violated most rules of good group process and even some rules of considerate personal relations. What mattered was that he generously opened the life of his mind to me, giving full voice to the gift of thought" (1998, p. 22). He went on to say,

> Passion for the subject propels that subject, not the teacher, into the center of the learning circle—and when a great thing is in their midst, students have direct access to the energy of learning and of life. A subject-centered classroom is not one in which students are ignored. Such a classroom honors one of the most vital needs our students have: to be introduced to a world larger than their own experiences and egos, a world that expands their personal boundaries and enlarges their sense of community. . . . A subject-centered classroom also honors one of our most vital needs as teachers: to invigorate those connections between our subjects, our students, and our souls that help make us whole again and again. (p. 120)

While the instructional technology revolution has forever changed the way teachers present lessons in the classroom—for the better, in the opinion of most educators—the data suggest that the single most important aspect of classroom instruction is the quality of the teacher and her knowledge of the subject matter (Cochran-Smith & Zeichner, 2005; Croninger, Buese, & Larson, 2012; Darling-Hammond, 2006; Donovan & Bransford, 2005; Pantić & Wubbels, 2010). In response to this acknowledgment, Zimpher and Howey (2013) offered an exhortation to teacher preparation programs, school leaders, and future teachers:

> Teachers must be equipped to prepare students to meet the requirements and demands of the 21st Century workforce—but to do that

teachers and school leaders themselves need the right kind of rigorous, continuous education, in both pedagogy and content area expertise, in order to become the high-quality professionals students need. (p. 419)

A report commissioned by the U.S. Department of Education in 2001 summarized research on five key issues in teacher preparation: subject matter preparation, pedagogical preparation, clinical training, preservice teacher education policies, and alternative certification. The investigators conducted a meta-analysis of 57 studies that met specific research criteria and were published in peer-reviewed journals. Ultimately, they found a positive connection between teachers' preparation in the subject matter and their performance in the classroom (Wilson, Floden, & Ferrini-Mundy, 2001). Goldhaber and Brewer (2000) and Monk (1994) determined that not only was content preparation positively related to student achievement in subjects like math and science, but courses in methods of teaching, specific to subjects, also demonstrated a significant increase in student achievement.

Thus, based on the apparent paucity of subject knowledge evident in many preservice and novice teachers, Metzler and Woessmann (2010) suggested that a renewed emphasis on teacher subject knowledge must become an important component in hiring policies, teacher training practices, and compensation schemes.

We set out to provide the reader with a theoretical framework consisting of three elements of good teaching—relationship building, pedagogical skills, and subject knowledge—as well as a rationale for adopting this framework. Although there was some variation between studies in terms of the teacher skills and dispositions they considered to be *most* important, they all shared these three elements. Our extensive review of the literature on effective teacher qualities and behaviors has revealed that many of the skills heretofore considered intrinsic and therefore unteachable can, in fact, be taught to novice and developing teachers. The only two ineradicable traits that appear to defy transmission are a teacher's belief in his students' ability to learn and his unwavering commitment to that conviction. Indeed, the research clearly substantiates Dweck's assertion that "The great teachers believe in the growth of the intellect and talent and they are fascinated with the process of learning" (2008, p. 194).

Since providing the reader with the subject knowledge appropriate to her specific certification area is well beyond the scope of this book and the expertise of the authors, we have instead focused on the other two elements in our trifecta; namely, (a) the quality of the **teacher–student relationship**, best understood through attachment theory, and (b) the development of a sound **pedagogical schema**. This book provides the reader with a framework in both of these areas from which to address some of the most challenging student behaviors teachers typically encounter in the classroom. Armed with this knowledge, you will be a more effective teacher!

DIFFICULT STUDENTS & DISRUPTIVE BEHAVIOR in the CLASSROOM

CHAPTER 1

Attachment Theory and Its Application to Good Teaching

As stated in the Introduction, good teaching involves knowledge, pedagogy, and relationships. This last aspect, relationships, is often dealt with in teacher preparation programs through courses in classroom management techniques built upon the principles of contingency management. Teachers are taught to reinforce good behavior and punish bad behavior. We do not minimize the importance of such an approach, as we have found it effective in our work with students.

However, a relationship, even between student and teacher, involves a constant dynamic interplay of forces affecting the development of both the student and the teacher. We want to help teachers by increasing their knowledge of students' behavior as well as their own; in this sense, our approach can be understood as psychodynamics applied to the classroom. Taking a moment to reflect upon one's own behavior and that of another can reduce a teacher's impulse to behave reactively. In more traditional psychodynamic theory, the approach might be called the *transference and counter-transference* between students and teachers. Since teachers are authority figures, students can easily "transfer" their conflicts with authority from the past onto teachers and make them conform to how students think about their world. Teachers, on the other hand, also bring to the relationship their own unresolved conflicts and may distort a child's behavior based on previous unresolved conflicts and losses.

In this book, we have forsaken this traditional approach. Instead, we frame our discussion of teacher–student relationships on attachment theory, which originated from the work of John Bowlby (1958, 1969, 1973, 1980) and was further developed by Mary Ainsworth (1969, 1989) along with a host of others whose work will be cited in the following pages. Attachment theory suggests that from early experiences with the primary attachment figure, the child develops an attachment style. There is much discussion as to whether teachers can be considered attachment figures—a question that we will elaborate on later. It is clear, however, that children bring their attachment style into the classroom, and it interacts with the teacher's own attachment style to cause an interplay of relational dynamics that, if not properly understood, will only lead to poor classroom management. A premise of this book is that students' emotional and behavioral disorders, which cause them to display difficult behavior in the classroom, may have the child's attachment style as an underlying factor. Bowlby posited that significant disruptions in the mother–child relationship were a predictor for subsequent psychopathology. However, more than just understanding attachment styles and being better able to manage difficult behaviors, teachers may even be influential in changing the attachment styles of the children they interact with on a daily basis.

INTRODUCTION TO ATTACHMENT THEORY

Bowlby's theory of attachment has a biological basis, drawing on the evolutionary perspective of his time. Heavily influenced by Darwin, Bowlby understood attachment as resulting from the need for survival: Those young who were securely attached to their mothers were less likely to be in danger and more likely to survive. Since a mother's reactions are not set in stone, the child over time learns the most effective way to establish closeness to the mother, even in the face of abusive treatment. For example, if a child experiences her attachment-seeking behavior as not having the desired effect, she may resort to "deactivating strategies," whereby the attachment system shuts down (Cassidy and Kobak, 1988). She avoids or withdraws—but this is still an attempt to feel securely attached, because the perception of support is more important than actual support (Booth-LaForce, Rubin, Rose-Krasnor, & Burgess, 2005). We will have more to say about hyperactivating versus deactivating strategies later on in the chapter. For now, it is sufficient to understand that from early on, the infant is either securely or insecurely attached, based upon the infant's perception of the caregiver's availability and the organization of the infant's responses to that perception (Weinfield, Sroufe, Egeland, & Carlson, 2008). The goal of attachment-seeking behaviors is a state of sufficient proximity to the mother (Cassidy, 2008), and the child learns which ways are most effective in achieving this proximity.

According to Bowlby, attachment is related to other human systems necessary for survival: exploration, fear, socializing, and caregiving (Cassidy, 2008). Secure children operate from a secure base and can therefore explore—first through play with other children, and eventually in the larger environment. All children face fears, but when they have a secure base, their fears are not excessive; they know protection, when needed, is within close proximity (and as we will show later on, many anxiety disorders in children can be traced back to insecure attachment). Having good social support is necessary for survival—from an evolutionary perspective, animals that are alone are more likely to be killed by predators (Eisenberg, 1966); as well as for overall psychological health—secure children, when they explore, make friends and develop social supports that make them less likely, for example, to be victims of aggression and bullying from other students. Finally, a parent's caregiving style is closely linked to the child's attachment system. A parent who readily provides protection for the child causes the deactivation of attachment-seeking behaviors. Or when the child does seek protection and it is readily available, this also results in deactivation.

An important assertion of this book is that teachers, too, can be considered attachment figures, and the relationships between students and teachers can be considered attachment bonds. We will take up this discussion in a later section, but for now it is important to understand what is meant by *attachment bonds*. Ainsworth (1989) described the attachment bond as a tie that one individual has to another who is seen as stronger and able to provide protection and help in times of need. The clearest example of this is the bond that forms between infant and mother.

The attachment bond is a subset of a larger class of bonds that Bowlby and Ainsworth called *affectional bonds*. Humans form many different affectional bonds over the course of a lifetime that result from having warm and positive feelings toward one another. According to Ainsworth, affectional bonds have the following characteristics: (a) they are persistent, not transitory; (b) they involve a specific person; (c) they have emotional significance; (d) there is a desire to keep close contact with the other person; and (e) there exists discomfort upon separation.

A sixth characteristic distinguishes attachment bonds from affectional bonds: the seeking of security and comfort from the other person. The seeking of security—not the attainment of security—defines an attachment bond. The following sections will elaborate on the characteristics of secure versus insecure children, but first we will discuss the precursors of attachment security.

Much discussion has taken place around the etiology of a child's behavior; the nature-versus-nurture argument will always be with us. This discussion has been augmented, more recently, by an emphasis on the neurobiological, genetic bases of human behavior. Cynics will attribute that shift to Big Pharma. If one accepts that behavior is predominantly biologically based, then the only way to change difficult behaviors would be through psychopharmacological interventions. It should come as no surprise that attachment theory, in contrast, places more emphasis on the nurture part of behavioral development, especially on the attachment bond that forms between infant and mother.

Is the quality of the attachment bond determined more by the infant's behavior or the mother's? Ainsworth (1979) believed that the relationship was not totally determined by the mother but, at the same time, believed that the mother had greater influence than the child in shaping the quality of an attachment bond, given her relative power. One of the reasons we opted for using attachment theory as the basis for the teaching relationship is its emphasis on environment, context, and interaction with others in determining one's behaviors. Along with Ainsworth, we believe that more important than what a child says or does is the reaction of the parent. As the reader will see later on, we believe the same is true for teachers: More important than what a student says or does in the classroom is the reaction of the teacher, given the teacher's power and privilege.

Let's delve a bit further into the nature-versus-nurture argument as it relates to attachment theory. On the nature side, it can be argued that a child's genetically endowed temperament determines the quality of attachment, due to its effects on the mother (Belsky & Fearon, 2008). Therefore, a child with a very difficult temperament might very well compromise attachment—his unsettling nature may lead his mother to interact with him in such a way that does not provide protection and security. Obviously, the nurture side of the argument posits that temperament is not primary in determining the quality of the attachment bond, because a mother who provides sensitive and protective care will establish a secure attachment bond with even a difficult child.

So, what does the actual research say about all this? One thing safe to say is that temperament can and does change. There may very well be a genetic basis to temperament, but everyone can recall ways in which they acted with more intensity than they do now. For some, a change in temperament comes with age; for others, a different set of circumstances is responsible. Numerous studies have compared identical and fraternal sets of twins (see, for example, Bokhorst et al., 2003; O'Connor & Croft, 2001) and, according to Belsky and Fearon, "The cumulative picture is quite consistent, suggesting a significant role for shared and nonshared environmental effects and apparently little role for genetics" (2008, p. 297), at least in regard to attachment security. Some factors that have an effect upon attachment security include the mother's personality (Belsky & Jaffee, 2006), especially her capacity for empathy; a supportive relationship between parents when their child is an infant (Krishnakumar & Buehler, 2000); and social support beyond the mother's significant other (Cochran & Niego, 2002). These factors have all been shown to affect the way parents, and especially the primary attachment figure, interact with their children.

The fact that environmental effects are stronger than genetic effects on attachment security is very good news for the teachers of difficult students. If teachers can be considered attachment figures or, at the very least, can have an effect upon a student's attachment insecurity, then students with difficult behaviors pose an opportunity for teachers. By assuming the role of a secure attachment figure, teachers may find they can change their students' behavior.

THE EMERGENCE OF ATTACHMENT THEORY

Mary Ainsworth (née Salter) joined Bowlby's research team in 1950, concentrating on separation and reunification studies. In 1953, Ainsworth convinced the research team to move to Uganda following her husband's appointment to the East African Institute of Social Research. Informed by Bowlby's incipient ideas on attachment, Ainsworth began an observation study of infant–mother attachment among Ganda families. She recruited 26 families with babies ages 1 to 24 months whom she observed every two weeks for two hours over a period of nine months. The Ganda data revealed three distinct patterns of attachment: (a) infants who did not cry a lot and in the presence of their mothers explored easily, (b) infants who cried frequently even when held by their mothers and did little exploration, and (c) infants who showed indifferent behavior to their mothers.

In the early 1960s, Ainsworth conducted another observation study, this time in Baltimore, Maryland, with 26 families that included 18 four-hour home visits beginning in the first month the baby's birth and ending at 12 months. Ainsworth decided to employ the use of the Strange Situation (Ainsworth & Wittig, 1969) for the 1-year-olds from the Baltimore study. The Strange Situation is a 20-mintue drama intended to test an infant's attachment style. First, mother and infant are introduced to the playroom. They are joined by a strange female, who plays with the baby, while the mother leaves for a brief period. The mother returns, but then both she and the stranger leave, and the baby is alone. Finally, the stranger returns, followed by the mother. In general, Ainsworth found, the infants explored the playroom and toys more in the presence of their mothers than with the stranger or by themselves.

More interesting to Ainsworth, though, was the child's reaction upon reunification with the mother. A few of the infants were angry after the three-minute separation from the mother, evidenced by wanting contact, but not to cuddle—upon contact with mother, they would kick and scream. Ainsworth labeled this group *ambivalent*. Still another group seemed to actively avoid contact with the mother upon reunification in spite of looking for her when they were separated. Ainsworth labeled this group *avoidant*. The children who were labeled either avoidant or ambivalent toward their mothers in the Strange Situation had less harmonious relationships at home with their mothers than those children who sought proximity and interaction with their mothers upon reunification (Ainsworth, Bell, & Stayton, 1971.

Since the Strange Situation also brought into play parents' behaviors, Main and colleagues developed the Adult Attachment Interview (AAI; George, Kaplan, & Main, 1984, 1985, 1996) as a means of investigating and classifying attachment representation in adolescence and adulthood. The AAI consists of 20 questions designed for the interviewees to reflect on their own attachment histories and their possible impact on current behavior. Based on the subjects' ability to maintain coherence when speaking about their early attachment experiences and after analyzing thousands and thousands of transcripts, the AAI classification system was developed and consists of five patterns of response:

1. **Secure/Autonomous:** marked by coherent, collaborative discourse. The subject is remarkably consistent in talking about their attachment experience regardless of whether it was positive or negative. Little or no indication of defensiveness. Predictive of Secure in the Strange Situation.
2. **Dismissing:** not coherent. The subject's representation of positive attachment experience is either unsupported or contradicted. Responses deny anxiety and guilt. Tendency is to idealize or derogate one or both parents. Excessive

defensiveness and inconsistences pervade the narrative. Shown to be predictive of Avoidant in the Strange Situation.

3. **Preoccupied:** also not coherent but tend to relate attachment experience in long entangled, vague manner. Tend to appear angry or passive or fearful when talking about experiences of being parented. Also marked by high defensiveness and disappointment in connecting meaningfully with others. Shown to be predictive of Ambivalent/Resistant in the Strange Situation.

4. **Unorganized or Unclassifiable:** when talking about experiences of loss or abuse, they tend to have loose associations with lapses in reasoning. The narrative shifts back and forth from Dismissing to Preoccupied and is thus deemed Unclassifiable. They tend to escape into long silences or eulogistic speech. Often linked with past trauma or loss. (Adapted from Hesse, 2008; and Steele, Murphy, and Steele, 2015)

From the Baltimore study and its use of the Strange Situation originated Ainsworth's now well-known classification system on infant attachment: secure, avoidant, and ambivalent (later known as *anxious/resistant*). Main and Solomon (1990) added a fourth category, *disorganized/disoriented*, to describe those infants who manifested fearful, odd, conflicted behaviors such as falling huddled to the floor, covering their faces, and hunching their shoulders, or more disoriented behaviors such as freezing or acting like they were in a trance. The following sections describe in greater detail each of these attachment behaviors and how they play out in everyday life.

Secure Attachment

In the Strange Situation, secure children consistently display flexibility of attention (Ainsworth, Blehar, Waters, & Wall, 1978). They play and explore in the presence of the parent, change their focus to the parent upon separation, and seek contact with the parent upon reunification. Secure children will oscillate between exploration and checking back with the parent, show signs of missing the parent (e.g., crying) during separation, actively greet the parent and initiate physical contact upon reunification, but then will settle down and return to play. This child engages in "secure exploration," defined as confident, attentive, eager, and resourceful exploration of materials and tasks even in the face of disappointment (Grossmann, Grossmann, Kindler, & Zimmerman, 2008). Behavior in the Strange Situation reveals that the child feels he or she has a secure base (i.e., the mother) to return to when needed. Children who use their parents as a safe haven when distressed develop emotional regulation and can cope more effectively with stress. They know help is reliable and not far away.

Bowlby spent a good deal of his career researching attachment and loss, a focus that culminated in the publication of his landmark trilogy, *Attachment and Loss* (1980). How an individual deals with loss, especially the loss of an attachment figure, is crucial in personality development. Securely attached individuals can oscillate between deactivation and hyperactivation of the attachment system, which allows for reorganization, the key to healthy grieving and dealing with loss. They can think and feel deeply about the loss, but they do not ruminate or disengage, as insecurely attached individuals might. This is analogous to the way securely attached infants in the Strange Situation would resolve the separation from the parent by initiating contact (activation of the attachment system) but then return to exploration and play (deactivation of the attachment system).

It is only through exploration that mastery of the environment and self-confidence can be achieved, and exploration is only possible when the child sees the parent or caregiver as a source of comfort and protection (Weinfield et al., 2008). Because of their early experience, securely attached children have a mental representation of the attachment figure as available and responsive when necessary (Cassidy, 2008). This is in contrast to insecurely attached children, who do not achieve mastery or self-confidence, because they cannot explore without worry. Maternal characteristics that result in attachment security include prompt responsiveness to stress, moderate and appropriate stimulation, harmonious interaction with the child, warmth, and involvement. Overall, the most important characteristic is maternal sensitivity, which allows the caregiver to intuit the child's needs and desires and respond appropriately while at the same time allows the child freedom to explore.

Resistant Attachment

These children in the Strange Situation show little flexibility of attention, and their focus is mostly on the parent throughout the minidrama. They often appear distressed even prior to separation from the mother, and their preoccupation with the parent, which prevents them from exploring and playing, can be either passive or angry. These children can either internalize or externalize their anger and anxiety. Even upon reunification, they do not take comfort in their parent's return and often show signs of anger, yet their efforts at contact with the parent are relatively weak.

In general, resistant children are characterized by a hyperactivation of the attachment system. They seek contact but are not comforted; they tend to be demanding, clingy, dependent, and helpless (Bergin & Bergin, 2009). Their hyperactivating strategies result in preoccupied attachments, and they are quick to reduce any interpersonal distance they might feel (Skourteli & Lennie, 2011). With an excessive reliance on feelings, resistant children have exaggerated intimacy and dependency needs and will often appear cute, babyish, or even angry (Moss, St-Laurent, Dubois-Comtois, & Cyr, 2005). As they grow older, they tend to have boundary issues such as crowding others, touching too much, or always sitting next to an adult like a counselor or teacher (Sroufe, Egeland, Carlson, & Collins, 2005). General petulance is one way to describe this population—their constant contact seeking is often mixed with angry rejection (hence Ainsworth's term "ambivalent").

The Strange Situation is very revealing: Resistant children seek constant contact with the attachment figure but are not comforted by the contact; the connection seems to always be threatened and never secured. Therefore, these children cannot explore without worry and will not achieve the level of self-confidence and mastery of the environment more characteristic of secure children. The exploratory system and the attachment system are inversely related. An increasingly activated attachment system will result in an increasingly deactivated exploratory system.

As adults, they are hypervigilant, overly dependent, have lower self-ratings on job performance and an overall negative view of self (Richards & Schat, 2011), and are constantly anxious that their partner will not be available to them (Fraley & Shaver, 2008). Furthermore, these children, even as adults, will have difficulty with bereavement and loss. As mentioned previously, reorganization is the key for healthy resolution of loss by maintaining functional bonds with the deceased, and it requires oscillation between hyperactivation and deactivation of the attachment system. Resistantly attached individuals cannot oscillate, because they cannot deactivate the attachment system. Only through a certain amount of deactivation can things get done, and this includes everything from exploration of the environment to resolution of loss.

Avoidant Attachment

In contrast to children with a resistant attachment style, who are prone to hyperactivating strategies to achieve security, those who are avoidant employ deactivating strategies. In the Strange Situation, avoidant infants, similar to resistant infants, show little flexibility of attention; but in contrast to resistant infants, whose primary focus is on the parent, avoidant infants' focus is on the toys and the playroom, not on the mother, regardless of whether she is present, departing, or returning. Avoidant infants do not appear distressed upon separation from the parent and tend to treat the stranger in the Strange Situation in the same way as the parent—sometimes, they can be even more responsive to the stranger (Weinfield et al., 2008). Their tendency is to look away rather than seek contact.

The deactivation of the attachment system is the result of lost hope for responsiveness from the primary caretaker, whom the child experiences as underinvolved. Put another way, the avoidance is an organized defense against anger toward the attachment figure for being unavailable. Since the child is not allowed to express this anger, he or she suppresses emotion so as to avoid rejection by the attachment figure, rather than face shame and humiliation (Bergin & Bergin, 2009). In the Adult Attachment Interview (AAI)—where parents are asked to describe their attachment-related experiences—parents of children classified as Avoidant tend to fall into the *dismissing* category, characterized by idealization, lack of memory, or outright derogatory dismissal of their attachment history (George, Kaplan, & Main, 1996).

As they mature, children with an avoidant style continue to employ deactivating and distancing strategies in dealing with others and the world around them. They tend to have a negative view of others, difficultly trusting others, excessive reliance on rational thought, and low levels of dependence. They avoid intimacy. In school, these children will tend to sit by themselves, and if there is contact, it is usually initiated by adults. With lower levels of self-efficacy, these children don't do as well in class (Sroufe et al., 2005). As a result of their early attachment history, marked by a lack of responsiveness from the attachment figure, children with an avoidant attachment style expect rejection from others, which leads to withdrawal—or even aggression, resulting from the suppression of anger from chronic rejection. They are more likely to victimize others with a neutral coolness (Moss et al., 2005; Weinfield et al., 2008).

Disorganized Attachment

Once they had established the three attachment patterns (secure, resistant, and avoidant), researchers began to observe that some infants, particularly those from high-risk environments, did not fit into any of the three categories—they lacked an organized attachment strategy. Unlike children with resistant and avoidant strategies, these children had "fear without solution" (Main & Solomon, 1990). The researchers classified these infants as "disorganized." In the Strange Situation, these infants evidence a collapse of any behavioral strategy: becoming frozen or trancelike, falling down and huddling on the floor, clinging to the parent while crying effusively, or leaning away with their eyes averted from the parent. Main (1999) proposed that the disorganized strategy results from experiencing the attachment figure as frightening, with behaviors such as looming in the child's face, approaching the child aggressively, handling the child as if he or she were an inanimate object, or manifesting fearful facial expressions. The conflict is severe for these children, because the person whom they expect to be responsible for their safety is actually frightening them, and this results in an irreconcilable split where the attachment figure is seen as both rescuer and persecutor.

Children with a disorganized strategy have been found to comprise up to 70% of clinical samples, compared to 15% of nonclinical samples (Bergin & Bergin, 2009; Liotti, 2011), and meta-analysis found that the percentage increased to 24% in low SES samples (van Ijzendoorn, Schuengel, & Bakermans-Kranenburg, 1999). Disorganization has been found to predict the more severe forms of psychopathology such as disassociation and borderline personality disorder (Lyons-Ruth & Jacobvitz, 2008; Sroufe, et al., 2005). Disorganized children tend to have the worst outcomes in treatment (Bergin & Bergin, 2009) and score the lowest on formal measures of academic performance in addition to generally getting low grades in school (Kerns, 2008). We will have more to say about attachment style and psychopathology later on in this chapter.

Main and Solomon (1990) listed the following behaviors that disorganized children might exhibit in the Strange Situation:

- A display of contradictory behaviors that could alternate between a strong attachment behavior and one marked by avoidance, freezing, or being dazed.
- Contradictory behaviors that might include strong avoidance followed by behaviors that are contact seeking, distressed, or angered.
- Movements and expressions that are undirected, misdirected, incomplete,

and interrupted that often include expressions of distress along with movements away from, rather than toward the attachment figure.

- Movements that are stereotyped, asymmetrical and mistimed away from rather than toward the attachment figure and abnormal postures such as stumbling for no reason solely in the presence of the parent.
- Movements and expressions that resemble freezing, stilling, and as if one were swimming underwater.
- Signs of apprehension toward the parent, for example, hunched shoulders or facial expressions that suggest fear.
- Signs of disorganization and disorientation that include wandering without direction, facial expressions that are dazed and confused, or labile changes in affect.

Although they lack an organized attachment style, disorganized children nevertheless employ coping mechanisms. Main and Solomon (1990) reported that there are two types of disorganized patterns of attachment: punitive-controlling and caregiving-controlling. Infants in the first subgroup are more externalized and engage in hostile and aggressive interactions with the parent, perhaps with the hope of humiliating the parent into submission. Infants in the second subgroup are more internalized and are motivated to protect the parent by being overly cheery, polite, or helpful (Moss et al., 2005). The majority appear to be the controlling type. They can employ extreme fight-or-flight defenses and alternate between severe aggression and withdrawal as means of reducing the demands of the relationship. It is important to remember that these children feel helpless in the face of frightening events, and their extreme behaviors results from trying to cope with the fright because they cannot rely on the attachment figure to provide protection.

As you might intuit at this point, children with a disorganized attachment style have garnered a great deal of attention over the years, most likely because this attachment style in infants has a predictive relationship with children being difficult in school and later developing the more severe forms of pathology.

What are some of the risk factors for infants who exhibit disorganized behavior? Studies of genetic effects (see, for example, the review by Swanson et al., 2000) and hormonal levels have found that infants with disorganized attachment styles have higher cortisol levels upon separation from the parent (Hertsgaard, Gunnar, Erickson, & Nachmias, 1995; Spangler & Grossmann, 1993). More attention has been paid to family correlates of disorganized attachment behavior. Depression, borderline personality disorder, substance abuse, and anxiety in mothers have all been found to correlate with disorganized behavior in their infants. Manassis, Bradley, Goldberg, Hood, and Swinson (1994) found that 78% of anxiety-disordered mothers were classified as *unresolved* on the AAI—that is, during discussion of loss or abuse, they would evidence signs of disorientation like lapses in memory, long silences, or unexpected eulogistic speech—and 65% of these mothers had children classified as disorganized. (Lyons-Ruth & Jacobvitz, 2008). From behavior on the AAI, Main and Hesse (1990) hypothesized that the attachment figures' frightening or frightened behavior in interactions with their children could be explained by unresolved trauma. This would explain the children's often disrupted and contradictory forms of communication around their need for safety and security, to the extent that more organized strategies (i.e., resistant and avoidant) are not sufficient to maintain protection (Lyons-Ruth, Bronfman, & Parsons, 1999).

In order to delineate more clearly the parental state of mind behind the disorganized child, Hesse and Main (2006) developed six subtypes of frightened or frightening behavior:

1. **Threatening.** Marked by aggressive postures, facial expressions, and movements such as sudden movements into the infant's face and eyes.
2. **Frightened.** Behaviors that suggest the attachment figure is frightened without explanation such as sudden retreat from the infant.
3. **Dissociative.** Behaviors that indicate an altered state of consciousness manifested by trance-like or haunted voice tones.
4. **Timid or deferential.** Submissive parental behaviors that could include a timid or obsequious handling of the infant.
5. **Spousal or intimate.** For example, a touching or fondling of the infant that is excessively intimate or sexualized.
6. **Disorganized.** Here, parental behaviors resemble those of infant disorganized and disoriented behaviors. (Lyons-Ruth & Jacobvitz, 2008)

Studies seem to support the bidimensionality of the parents' frightening behaviors, relating them to both the children's disorganized behavior and their own unresolved state of mind (Abrams, Rifkin, & Hesse, 2006; Tomlinson, Cooper, & Murray, 2005). Other parental behaviors not included in the Main and Hesse typology that correlate with disorganized infant behavior are mocking or teasing the infant, silent interactions with the infant, contradictory cues of nonresponse such as inviting the infant to come close and then distancing themselves, and unusual changes in tone or volume of voice (e.g., yelling) when interacting with the infant (Lyons-Ruth, Bronfman, & Parsons, 1999). Studies have also shown a gender difference in infants' responses to parental frightening or withdrawal behaviors. Female infants tended to approach the mother at reunion and were less likely to engage in disorganized behaviors, in contrast to male infants, who showed more disorganized behaviors and withdrawal in response to frightening behaviors.

Disorganized attachment is a strong predictor of later psychopathology, including both internalizing and externalizing behaviors in school-aged children. We will have much more to say about school behavior and attachment in later sections.

INTERNAL WORKING MODELS

Bowlby (1969/1982) theorized that from the quality of the early attachment relationship, children begin to have expectations about how the world—and other people—will treat them. Bowlby believed that these expectations were the result of internal working models (IWMs), which function as internalizations of the attachment relationship. IWMs are the foundation for expectations of the self and for later relationships with caregivers and noncaregivers (e.g., teachers). IWMs are a general construct, not limited to attachment theory—we all "represent" to ourselves in relationships or interactions with others based on previous experiences with them, and we plan for future interactions based on that representation. In Bowlby's theory, IWMs are relationship specific. According to Bowlby, the child, based on the attachment experience with the primary caregiver,

> is busy constructing working models of how the physical world may be expected to behave, how his mother and other significant persons may be expected to behave, how he himself may be expected to behave, and how each interacts with the other. Within the framework of these working models, he evaluates his situation and makes his plans (Bowlby, 1969/1982, p. 354).

Bergin and Bergin (2009) described three components of IWMs: (a) a model of others as trustworthy, (b) a model of the self as valuable, and (c) a model of the self as effective when interacting with others. For example, a child with a secure attachment history, where the attachment figure has provided comfort and protection while recognizing the child's need for independence and exploration, will develop an IWM of herself as valuable and self-reliant. On the other hand, a child whose attempts for comfort and exploration have been rejected will most likely develop an IWM of himself as unworthy and incompetent (Bretherton & Munholland, 2008).

At the risk of oversimplifying, in the world of attachment theory, it comes down to this: A responsive parent leads to a more effective child. Children with secure attachment histories grow up to see the world as safe, good, and responsive, and see themselves as worthy of being treated in a consistently sensitive manner. In contrast, those with insecure histories, marked by harsh or erratic treatment, will grow up to see the world as unpredictable and insensitive and view themselves as not worthy of much more (Weinfield et al., 2008). IWMs guide children's future expectations, especially in regard to other attachment figures, and shape the behaviors that result from these expectations.

An important question arises in relation to IWMs: how malleable are they? Can they change, and if so, what factors contribute to that change? The simple answer to this question is yes, but it can be difficult. Bowlby (1969/1982) articulated three reasons why IWMs are seemingly immutable. First is the process of assimilation, a concept Bowlby borrowed from Piaget (1952), whereby we adapt to learning new information by reinterpreting it to make sense with information we already know—so a child's lack of confidence in the attachment figure is not likely to change by an occasional show of caregiver sensitivity. Second is that relationships are a dynamic process, and for real change to take place, both individuals in the relationship have to be willing to change. For example, one member of the dyad might try out new behaviors, but the other member resists the change, and the old pattern is maintained. Third is habituation, where behaviors become so automated that little attention is paid to possibly revising the working model based on new evidence (Bretherton & Munholland, 2008).

Bowlby (1988) believed that securely attached children were more apt to revise IWMs and overcome the stabilizing processes mentioned above. Secure children as they grow older are treated differently by their parents, who gradually update their models to allow their children to be more functional in an ever-changing world.

Insecurely attached children's IWMs, however, may be significantly more difficult to change. Bowlby (1973, 1980, 1988) introduced the idea of *defensive processes*, whereby very emotionally charged material is excluded from consciousness in order to avoid conflict. In the case of a child who was sexually abused by a parent and the parent denies the behavior, the child is forced to exclude either the abuse or the denial to avoid a psychologically intolerable conflict. In most cases, the fact that the abuse occurred is excluded, and what remains available to consciousness is what the parent wants the child to believe. Defensive exclusion, according to Bowlby, is a necessary adaptation and causes a change in IWMs, because the child is forced to change his internal representation of the parent. IWMs that develop from defensive exclusion are very resistant to change, even when circumstances improve dramatically in the developing child's life.

The concept of defensive exclusion is another way to explain what happens in attachment trauma, where memories of the trauma are stored differently—in episodic memory, rather than in semantic memory where it would be much more available to consciousness. In other words, what the parent wants the child to believe is stored in semantic memory, but actual memory of the trauma is stored in episodic memory.

If secure children derive their security from having been given the freedom to explore, it stands to reason that they are more open to revising their IWMs, because their revision requires continued openness to exploration of the inner self and the world around them. Bowlby believed that one of the best ways parents could contribute to helping their children develop revisable and more adaptive IWMs was through open communication about relationships. Humans are meaning-making animals, and in the world of attachment theory, IWMs are the brain's mechanism for making meaning of ourselves, others, and the world around us.

Neuroimaging studies have identified regions in the brain's prefrontal cortex that are responsible for flexible thinking and generating alternative courses of action, which can offer clues about the biological basis for people's ability to alter their IWMs. Studies have shown that adults with weaknesses in the orbital frontal cortex lack the capacity for flexible evaluation and tend to make poor decisions (Damasio, 1999), and infants with brain damage in this area have difficulty understanding social rules and the violations of those rules(Anderson, Bechara, Damasio, Tranel, & Damasio, 1999). In other words, they lack the capacity to entertain revisions of IWM's that are necessary to consider and evaluate alternative course of actions. The quality of the parent-child bond can affect the capacity for executive functioning. A secure attachment provides a safe environment where children can learn to master self-regulated thoughts and actions that define executive functioning located in the pre-frontal cortex (Lewis & Carpendale, 2014). Without getting overly technical, suffice it to say that areas of the brain that would be responsible for evaluating, revising, and updating IWMs may very well be compromised in insecure children Attachment theory would have one believe that these children were not born like that, but their early attachment figures behaved in ways that did not allow for the full development of these prefrontal regions. Analysis of findings from the AAI indicate that parents tend to "induct their infants into a way of relating that is consistent with their own secure or conflicted/defensive models of self in relationships" (Bretherton & Munholland, 2008, p. 118).

If IWMs are revisable, can others—such as teachers—contribute to those revisions? Yes! Studies have shown that other close relationships, such as those with teachers and even friends, can contribute to the development of a secure relational self (Simpson, Collins, Tran, & Haydon, 2007; Sroufe et al., 2005). As a matter of fact, the AAI has a category of *earned secure*, given to parents who attained a secure self through the revision of insecure IWMs. Losses, traumas, and new attachments are the most likely ways to alter IWMs. In a later section, we will deal more extensively with how other relationships, especially those with teachers, can influence and perhaps even change IWMs.

ATTACHMENT THEORY AND DEVELOPMENT

According to Weinfield et al. (2008) there are four explanations as to how early attachment experiences affect later development: (a) Early attachment relationships have an effect on the developing brain; (b) early attachment relationships are the foundation for self-regulation, the ability to control emotional responses; (c) observation of the attachment figure allows the child to learn how to behave in relationships; and (d) early attachment relationships, as we have pointed out above, determine IWMs. Anxiety or anger is often the reaction to an unavailable caregiver, and these traits become part of a child's life well beyond infancy. Likewise, the capacity for empathy, enabled through being cared for and responded to, is carried into relationships later on. Simply put, developmental outcomes are the result of early attachment interacting with subsequent experiences (Thompson, 2008).

During middle childhood, children continue to rely heavily on the attachment figure for security and as a base for exploration, but they also begin to use other adults (e.g., teachers, grandparents, siblings) and even peers. Children at this age look for the attachment figure to be available, rather than in close proximity, as is the case in infancy and early childhood. This is the stage of development where changes in IWMs are most likely to take place; solid IWMs often do not form until adolescence (Kerns, 2008). If, on the other hand, attachment experiences during this time are consistent, then a more enduring IWM can take hold in middle childhood.

It is not clear whether peers at this stage of development can be considered attachment figures. Kerns, Tomich, and Kim (2006) found that children continue to show a strong preference for parents over peers, but they may exhibit attachment behavior toward peers. For example, they might confide certain secrets or rely on peers for protection, support, companionship, responsiveness, and help in resolving conflicts. If the quality of the peer relationships is consistent with early attachment experiences, the processes underlying the IWMs will be strengthened.

During adolescence, a developmental period marked by greater cognitive complexity, the individual begins to reflect upon his or her attachment experience and develops "states of mind," the result of formal operational thinking, that allow the adolescent to adopt "a more integrated and generalized stance toward attachment experiences" (Allen, 2008, p. 420). The adolescent is capable of reflecting upon and modifying these states of mind. For those with a secure attachment history, they will begin to understand their parents in more realistic terms—neither idealizing nor demonizing them (Steinberg, 2005). They avoid the "splitting" mechanism typical of those with certain forms of psychopathology, such as borderline personality disorder, who tend to see others as all good or all bad. The more secure adolescent will reflect and think something like the following: "My parents weren't perfect; they had both good and bad, but in the end they were good enough."

During this period, the IWMs, more solidified, serve as an organizational construct for incoming information about relationships. Let's take as an example an adolescent classified as Avoidant based on her early attachment experiences. Since she tends to avoid closeness, she will more likely be pursued rather than pursue when it comes to relationships. The avoidant adolescent who experiences someone wanting to be close to her might organize the information in such a way as to say to herself: "This person seems nice, but it is better not to get too close, since I will only get hurt in the long run."

A common preoccupation of adolescence is establishing autonomy, often understood as seeking independence and being true to one's identity (Erikson, 1964). Attachment theory sees the task of adolescence as balancing the need for autonomy and attachment. Parents and teachers alike have to respect the adolescent's need for autonomy and also be willing to maintain the relationship even in rebellious moments.

As stated earlier, parental sensitivity is the key ingredient for secure attachment in childhood. In adolescence, parental sensitivity can result in the secure adolescents' ability to openly communicate with their parents (Allen, 2008). Many parents' main complaint about their adolescents is that they lie. But for adolescents, lying is protection; in their minds, the benefit of lying outweighs the cost of telling the truth. The fact that the children fear telling the truth means they are not secure in their relationship with their parents.

Adolescents classified as *preoccupied* on the AAI (i.e., they have a hyperactivation of the attachment system) reported the presence of symptoms at levels higher than those reported by teachers and parents (Berger, Jodl, Allen, McElhaney, & Kuperminc, 2005). Simply put, their cries for help were not being heard, an experience most likely consistent with their insecure attachment as children. The exact cause for this lack of communication during adolescence is not known. Reasons could include parent insensitivity, poor communication by the adolescent, peers who are not receptive, or a combination of these (Allen, 2008).

Academic Development

This section deals with research about attachment security as it relates to children's academic achievement. In general, secure children have the best academic outcomes; disorganized children have the worst outcomes; and resistant children are in between (Bergin & Bergin, 2009). In perhaps the most well-known study on attachment and development, the Minnesota Study of Risk and Adaptation from Birth to Adulthood, Sroufe et al. (2005) followed 180 children born into poverty from birth until age 28 and found five characteristics related to attachment that indirectly affected school outcomes: (a) the ability to accept challenges and independence, (b) social competence, (c) emotional regulation, (d) attention deficits and hyperactivity, and (e) psychopathology and delinquency.

Secure children tend to be more cognitively engaged and have higher levels of mastery motivation (Moss et al., 2005). They have a greater sense of self-esteem, confidence, and agency that is tied to both academic and social outcomes (Sroufe et al., 2005). Students who are prosocial are more engaged in school, and this, in turn, increases their academic achievement, indicated by higher test scores and higher grades (Miles & Stipek, 2006).

As mentioned previously, insecure children have difficulty with emotional regulation, a key ingredient to school success. Resistant children are especially vulnerable to poor emotional regulation because their anxiety interferes with learning. Rather than focusing on what the teacher is saying, these children are preoccupied with their safety and potential threats to their safety (Bergin & Bergin, 2009). There is a link between insecure attachment and ADHD, but the exact cause is not known. Resistant children are more likely to be diagnosed with ADHD. One hypothesis is that parent intrusiveness, where the parent directs the child's behavior according to the parent's agenda, is responsible for a high level of frustration, hyperactivity, and attention deficits in preschoolers as well as elementary school children (Sroufe, 1996; Sroufe et al., 2005).

It is also important to note that children with secure attachment histories attend school more regularly than those with insecure histories, and school attendance is an obvious contributor to positive academic outcomes. This may explain why Sroufe et al. (2005) found that attachment history was related to math and reading scores but not to IQ. Some insecure students may have high aptitude but, because of the factors listed above, are underachievers.

On a final note, studies have shown that children with learning disabilities have lower rates of secure attachment (Al-Yagon, 2007, 2010). It is possible that poor quality of care can result in deficits of sociocognitive processing, but the reverse is also possible—that the deficits for those with learning disabilities affect the quality of care, causing the parent to have more difficulty understanding the child's needs for comfort and exploration. For example, the parent of a child with a learning disability may have reservations about the child's decision-making and judgment, and this, in turn, might make him reluctant to allow the child the necessary space for exploration. And in a more recent study, Al-Yagon (2012) found that adolescents with learning disabilities experienced their teachers as more rejecting when compared to typically developing peers. This is somewhat disconcerting, especially in light of the findings from the Minnesota study (Sroufe et al., 2005), where the participants who graduated from high school were more likely to report having had a teacher who was "special" to them.

Social Development

We have already made quite clear that children with secure attachment histories are more socially competent. This section attempts a bit more specificity in regard to both pro- and antisocial behaviors. For example, in the case of bullying, avoidant children were found more often to be perpetrators, resistant children more often to be victims, and secure children more often not to be involved at all in such relationships (Kurth, 2013). And Sroufe et al. (2005) found that adolescents with secure histories had greater capacity for negotiating group relations during summer camp than those with resistant histories. They also drew the attention of others in more positive ways and were more likely to be elected as a spokesperson for the group. In terms of more intimate relationships (i.e., dating) during adolescence, those with secure and avoidant histories had more experience than those with resistant histories by the age of 16. However, the secure teens differed from the avoidant teens in the longevity of their relationships. Those with secure histories were much more likely to have relationships of more than three months, while the relationships of those with avoidant histories were much shorter (Sroufe et al., 2005). As far as sexual activity, adolescents with insecure histories had more sexual partners and less frequent use of contraception, and those classified as preoccupied on the AAI were more likely to engage in early sexual activity, especially if they had mothers who were focused on their own autonomy (Marsh, McFarland, Allen, Boykin McElhaney, & Land, 2003).

Development of Psychopathology

Attachment theory originated in Bowlby's early focus on disruption in the attachment bond; he believed that the parent–child bond is necessary for healthy emotional development and not easily replaceable (Kobak & Madsen, 2008). Bowlby found that children's reactions to separation had two phases: protest followed by despair. Protest is marked by crying with the hope that the attachment figure will return, and despair is marked by withdrawal upon the realization that the situation is hopeless. With the advent of the Strange Situation, researchers were able to study in greater detail the reactions of children to separation and loss. For example, the withdrawal behaviors noted early on by Bowlby were further delineated as the fearful and freezing behaviors of the disorganized child.

Children who have experienced trauma and loss do not see attachment figures as potential sources of security, but quite the opposite—as potential sources of danger. The fear, anger, and sadness associated with such trauma and loss are contributing factors to the development of psychopathology later in life. Sometimes children deal with these emotions by detaching (in the example of the avoidant child); if this is not successful in defending against painful emotions, they may instead direct intense hatred toward the parent and parent-like figures (Kobak & Madsen, 2008). It is important to keep this in mind when dealing with difficult students who exhibit externalized anger and hate. Their behavior may stem from despair, due to withdrawal, or perhaps hope, an attempt to make contact with an inaccessible parent (Johnson, 2008).

The pathway to the development of psychopathology in childhood cannot be reduced to a single factor. A poor attachment bond is considered one risk factor among others such as poverty, family violence, and parental psychopathology. Risk factors exist on multiple levels: the individual, the family, and the broader environment (Kobak, Cassidy, Lyons-Ruth, & Ziv, 2006), and they have differential significance according to the developmental level during which they occur (Fraley, 2002). For example, a child with a secure early attachment history will most likely fare better experiencing a loss than a child with an insecure history will. And attachment security is just one of many protective factors—such as temperament, intelligence, school quality, neighborhood safety, and quality of peer attachments—that can reduce the likelihood that risk factors will lead to psychopathology.

Though we consider the quality of the attachment bond only one of many factors in the development of childhood psychopathology, its significance increases because of its direct link to mechanisms that determine maladaptation. These mechanisms include inability to control emotional responses, exhibiting disruptive behaviors, maintaining social cognitions (i.e., IWMs) that create negative expectations, and having poor social skills (DeKlyen & Greenberg, 2008).

Sroufe et al. (2005) used the concept of *continuity* to explain insecure attachment as a predictor of psychopathology. As an example, consider an infant who is resistant, where there is hyperactivation of the attachment system. This child is prone to outbursts and tantrums; therefore, what he needs are firm, consistent limits. The issue is that parents of resistant children are usually not capable of providing such limits, so these problem behaviors are carried forward into the school years, because the child has an IWM that makes him think the world is not safe and those responsible for him will not provide safety. He will tend to isolate himself, as he does not trust the interest and responsiveness of others, or he will behave in such a way as to elicit reactions from others that confirm the way he thinks about himself and the world. Isolation and rejection serve to heighten his anxiety; such children are at risk for developing anxiety and depressive disorders.

In the world of attachment theory, pathological disturbance is more predominantly caused by interactions and transactions between people and their environment than by disease-causing agents within the individual. In other words, disturbance is the result of a dynamic process where brain chemistry and environment interact with each other (Sroufe et al., 2005). The same can be said for resilience, a protective factor against the development of psychopathology. Rather than an inherited, immutable trait, resilience is the result of developmental systems that provide support and resources, especially during times of stress. Even people with insecure attachment histories can become more resilient through experience with other caregivers, school supports, and even teachers who provide them with an experience antithetical to what they have come to expect as a result of their attachment history. What happens, however, is that patterns develop that determine later behavior, and, like anything else, the longer those patterns are in place, the harder they are to change. Now let's take a look at some specific forms of psychopathology as they relate to attachment history.

Mood disorders. Bowlby (1980) posited three events in the developing child's life that would be predictive of later depression: (a) the death of a parent that results in feelings of hopelessness and despair, (b) the child's inability to form secure and stable relationships with caregivers that results in feelings of failure, and (c) the child receiving consistent messages that he is unlovable and therefore coming to regard himself as unlovable and others as unloving (Bretherton, 1985).

Resistant and avoidant attachment histories have both been found to correlate with depression, but for different reasons. In resistant children, the depression results from feelings of helplessness, while in avoidant children, the depression results from feelings of alienation (Sroufe et al., 2005). The Minnesota study also found that the single strongest predictor of childhood depression was some form of early abuse followed by maternal depression, both of which have a negative impact upon attachment security. These same factors were also the strongest predictors of adolescent depression.

In addition, adolescents with depression tended to classify as preoccupied on the AAI (Fonagy et al., 1996; Rosenstein & Horowitz, 1996). Other studies have found adult depression to be correlated with a classification of dismissing on the AAI (Patrick, Hobson, Castle, Howard, & Maughan, 1994). This is not surprising, since parents with preoccupied and dismissing classifications on the AAI are more likely to see resistant and avoidant attachment styles in their children, both of which are associated with adolescent depression. Numerous studies have also found adult depression to be correlated with a classification of unresolved on the AAI (Fonagy et al., 1996; Patrick et al., 1994; Rosenstein & Horowitz, 1996). Adults with bipolar disorders were classified more often as dismissing on the AAI (Fonagy, et al., 1996; Dozier, Lomax, Tyrell, & Lee, 2001). Research seems to suggest that those with mood disorders can classify differently on the AAI.

Anxiety disorders. As the reader might expect, there is a clear link between resistant attachment and anxiety disorders; resistant attachment is a strong predictor of the child developing an anxiety disorder by age 17 (Sroufe et al., 2005). Some studies have also found a relationship between anxiety and disorganized or avoidant attachment among preschool children (see, for example, Shamir-Essakow, Ungerer, & Rapee, 2005), but it may be that in very young children, these types of insecure attachment are manifested as anxiety, and only later on do the symptoms become more externalized and disruptive.

More specifically, agoraphobia in children has been related to early separation from the mother, parental divorce, early separation anxiety, and parents low on affection and high on overprotection (de Ruiter & van IJzendoorn, 1992). And post-traumatic stress disorder (PTSD) was more likely to be found among parents classified as unresolved on the AAI rather than preoccupied, even though PTSD has been considered an anxiety disorder.

Eating disorders. Cole-Detke and Kobak (1996) hypothesized that those who develop eating disorders are trying to control their world through eating behaviors and thus direct attention away from their own feelings. Such a hypothesis would suggest that eating disorders are associated with avoidant attachment style. Research shows that those with anorexia nervosa often describe their parents negatively (Rowa, Kerig, & Geller, 2001; Wade, Treloar, & Martin, 2001; Woodside et al., 2002)—their fathers as being emotionally unavailable and mothers as domineering, overprotective, and perfectionistic (Woodside et al., 2002). On the AAI, adults with eating disorders were mostly classified as dismissing (Cole-Detke & Kobak, 1996) but if combined with depression they were more likely to be classified as preoccupied (Wade et al., 2001).

Disruptive behavior disorders. ADHD, oppositional defiant disorder, and conduct disorder are often grouped together under the category of disruptive behavior disorders because they have in common, in some cases, externalized hostility and aggression. The Minnesota study, which looked at children born into poverty, found that the strongest predictor of adolescent externalization was a disruptive male presence in the home, and direct support of the child by available men predicted lower externalization throughout the childhood and adolescent years (Sroufe et al., 2005). The same study found a gender difference, where externalization for boys was highest when living with their mothers alone and for girls highest when living in a stepfamily during their early years. It also found that single status of the mother when her child was born was the strongest predictor of ADHD, drug and alcohol problems, and risky sexual activity in her child. Single mothers in poverty live under stressful circumstances, and this stress is often related to insecure attachment.

Both avoidant and disorganized attachment have been shown to relate to externalization—these children often have a history of rejection, which results in anger, which results in externalization. And because of overstimulation, even resistant children have been known to exhibit restlessness, impulsivity, and low frustration tolerance (DeKlyen & Greenberg, 2008). To be clear, in avoidant children the hostility is result of the attachment figure's lack of availability; in resistant children it is the result of the attachment figure's overstimulation; and in disorganized children it is the result of the attachment figure being a source of fright rather than a source of safety.

In regard to children who show more serious externalization behaviors, such as those diagnosed with conduct disorder—the precursor of antisocial personality disorder—Fonagy, Target, Steele, & Steele (1997) hypothesized that parent–child attachment bonds are reconfigured toward institutions (e.g., schools) and those who represent them (e.g., teachers). The serious deficits in early bonding are carried forward and result in little or no school bonding along with an inability to consider the needs and feelings of others. Empathy, reciprocity, mutuality, and sensitivity, all learned early on through the relationship with a responsive and caring attachment figure, are absent, which allows the child and adolescent to engage in criminal acts without remorse. Factors in the development of antisocial personality disorder (known also as *sociopathy*) include prolonged separations from the attachment figure, deviant fathers, unaffectionate mothers, and physical abuse (Dozier, Stovall-McClough, & Albus, 2008). On the AAI, those diagnosed with either conduct disorder or antisocial personality disorder tend to classify as either unresolved or dismissing with derogation, meaning that their early experiences with caregivers are remembered very negatively.

Finally, a word about borderline personality disorder, since children with this disorder can be explosive and disruptive. The label originally came from considering this population as being on the "border" between psychosis and neurosis. An unstable sense of self and others is the defining characteristic of those who receive this diagnosis. In an attempt to derive a stable sense of self, those with borderline personality disorder alternate between idealization and demonization of others—people are all good or all bad, and things can change on a dime. Because of the unstable sense of self, they live in constant fear of abandonment. In terms of attachment theory, they report long periods of separation from the attachment figure during childhood (Zanarini, Gunderson, Marino, Schwartz, & Frankenburg, 1989). One hypothesis held that disorganized children, who do not develop an integrated sense of self and others due to the frightening or frightened behaviors of their caretakers, would be at risk for developing borderline personalities. However, Lyons-Ruth, Yellin, Melnick, and Atwood (2005) found that disorganization did not predict developing the disorder, but early maltreatment and abuse along with disrupted communication between parents and children did increase the chances. On the AAI, those with borderline personality disorder tend to classify as either preoccupied or unresolved (Barone, 2003; Fonagy et al., 1996).

Dissociative disorders. In contrast to the findings about borderline personalities, disorganization appears highly predictive of dissociative disorders such as trance-like states, multiple personality disorder, depersonalization, and derealization (Carlson, Armstrong, Loewenstein, & Roth, 1998; Sroufe et al., 2005). Frequently found in those who have suffered severe trauma, these disorders have in common the individual's need to "dissociate" (i.e., remove from consciousness) the psychic pain that is too overwhelming. However, complete dissociation is not possible; therefore, the person lives with the painful memory's sporadic intrusion into consciousness. For children who have suffered a traumatic event (e.g., severe abuse or loss), dissociation is not inevitable. Those children who receive sensitive caretaking and protection in the aftermath of trauma will most likely not experience what Main and Hesse (1990) called "fright without solution" (p.163). On the other hand, if the child does not receive protection, or the person designated to protect them is the actual abuser, then dissociation is a likely outcome.

Summary. We have tried in this section to look at the relationships between specific forms of psychopathology and attachment. While there are some inconsistent findings, it is safe to say that psychiatric disorders are associated with insecure forms of attachment. Unresolved is the most represented state of mind on the AAI, and this is often related to loss and trauma. Dismissing states of mind on the AAI are associated with minimizing attachment needs; therefore, the disorders that result from this state of mind turn attention away from the self (e.g., antisocial personality disorder, externalized forms of depression and anxiety, eating disorders, and substance abuse). On the other hand, preoccupied states of mind lead to overfocusing on the self and result in internalized forms of anxiety and depression (Dozier et al., 2008).

ATTACHMENT AND OTHER RELATIONSHIPS

We have come to the point in our journey on attachment and the teaching of difficult students where we wish to examine more closely the role and effect of other caretakers, with a particular eye on teachers. We have established that to develop in a healthy psychological fashion, children need to operate from a secure base. We have also made clear that secure children have the self-confidence to meet the inevitable challenges they face—be they academic or relational. However, this book is about teaching difficult students, and we have also established in the above section that the difficult ones will most likely be those students with insecure histories of attachment.

Bowlby (1969) very early on believed that the primary attachment figure could be replaced not only by another person but also by an institution:

> During adolescence and adult life a measure of attachment behavior is commonly directed not only towards persons outside the family but also towards groups and institutions other than the family. A school or college, a work group, a religious group or a political group can come to constitute for many people a subordinate attachment "figure," and for some people a principal attachment figure. In such cases, it seems probable, the development of attachment to a group is mediated, at least initially, by attachment to a person holding a prominent position within that group (p. 207).

Schools and teachers within those schools can be subordinate attachment figures. We will see later on how teachers can deal more effectively with insecure students in the classroom. First, however, is the task of examining teachers as substitute caregivers and attachment figures.

We made the case earlier that IWMs are open to revisions, especially in the preschool and elementary school years, but even beyond. This is based on the high importance that attachment theory gives to the affective quality of teacher–child relationships (Verschueren & Koomen, 2012). More specifically, this affective quality has been understood as having three relational dimensions: closeness, conflict, and dependency, which can be assessed using the Student-Teacher Relationship Scale (STRS) (Koomen, Verschueren, van Schooten, Jak, & Pianta, 2012). The STRS was originally developed from attachment theory and tries to examine the quality of the teacher's relationship with the child, the behavior of the child toward the teacher, and the feelings and thoughts that the teacher and child have about each other. In terms of attachment theory, *closeness* refers to the level to which the child sees the teacher as a safe haven; *conflict* refers to resistance and disharmony in the teacher–child relationship; and *dependency* refers to the child's inability to use the teacher as a safe haven for exploration (Verschueren & Koomen, 2012).

Not all teacher–student relationships can be placed in the category of attachment, but they may be "attachmentlike." Sometimes, there is insufficient interaction between the student and teacher, or the teacher is unresponsive and prevents an attachment bond from taking place (Bergin & Bergin, 2009). Perhaps it is better to understand the teacher–student relationship along an attachment continuum, with many of the relationships having some but not all of the characteristics of an attachment relationship.

Waters and Cummings (2000) coined the phrase "secure-base figures of convenience" to refer to teachers as attachment figures for children as they pass through school from year to year. The connotation of the phrase is fluidity. Since most student–teacher relationships are time limited, children can use them conveniently—as needed, not forever. As mentioned earlier, closeness to teachers can serve as a protective factor in the development of pathology, and closeness is an obvious outcome of teacher sensitivity.

Much has been written about the concordance between relationships with parents and teachers. In general, research supports that children's security with parents is related to security with teachers and other caregivers, especially in early childhood. One study found that the concordance between a student's relationship with his parents and with his teachers was especially high when teachers were less sensitive—insecure children continued to have less close relationships to teachers when teacher sensitivity was low—but when teacher sensitivity was high, children with insecure attachment histories were no less likely than secure children to develop close relationships with teachers (Buyse, Verschueren, & Doumen, 2011).

Classroom Dynamics Based on Attachment Theory

Howes and Ritchie (1999) studied the attachment behaviors of over 3,000 predominantly poor preschoolers and developed the following parallel typology for parent–child attachment:

- "*Avoidant* children were more interested in classroom materials than in the teacher or other children. They did not approach the teacher, so the teacher easily lost track of them. When the teacher approached, they acted as if they did not hear or notice the teacher. If requested to come to the teacher, they did so, but quickly left. They did not call out to the teacher to show something.

When hurt or upset they did not seek the teacher, or even moved away if the teacher tried to comfort them.

- *Resistant* children were irritable and fussy with the teacher for no apparent reason. They often cried and were difficult to console. They resisted classroom routines like cleaning up. They clung to the teacher and cried if the teacher left the room. Every bump or scratch brought tears. They were easily frustrated by difficult tasks. They were demanding and impatient with the teacher and not satisfied with the teacher's attempt to respond to them.
- *Secure* children accepted comfort if hurt or upset, molding their bodies to the teacher if held. They spontaneously hugged the teacher. They touched the teacher gently during play. They readily shared their activities with the teacher, showing things and welcoming entrance into play. They asked for help if they needed it. They read the teacher's face for information. They easily followed directives, and acted sorry if the teacher spoke firmly to them. They made transitions smoothly. They were glad to see the teacher at the beginning of the day.
- *Near secure* children displayed moderate avoidant behaviors and some secure behaviors. They distrusted their teachers, but conformed readily to classroom procedures, such that teachers did not perceive a problem in their relationships. This category could be thought of as 'attachment in the making.'" (From Bergin & Bergin, 2009, p. 151, used with permission)

The above typology indicates that some students will be "difficult" and therefore pose a challenge for teachers looking to develop a sensitive and caring relationship. Insecure students often behave in ways that make it hard for teachers to form an attachment relationship. Longitudinal research indicates quite convincingly that a negative student–teacher relationship as early as kindergarten predicted lower grades and test scores and inferior work habits all through the elementary school years, resulting in lower academic achievement at the eighth-grade level (Hamre & Pianta, 2001). Positive student–teacher relationships are a developmental asset. Studies have shown that students who have closer relationships with their teachers evidence better social skills and academic performance and less externalizing behavior (Crosnoe, Johnson, & Elder, 2004; Ladd & Burgess, 2001; Pianta & Stuhlman, 2004).

The challenges for teachers in developing positive relationships with insecure children can be understood through the psychodynamic concept of *parallel process*. When applied to attachment theory, parallel process means that children will tend to recreate the same kind of relationship (i.e., a parallel relationship) with attachmentlike figures (i.e., teachers) that they have had with their primary attachment figure. Simply put, the dynamics and quality of the mother–child relationship influence the teacher–child relationship (Howes, Matheson, & Hamilton, 1994), as does the early attachment with other caretakers. For example, Howes and Tonyan (2000) found that attachment security with early childcare providers was the strongest predictor for teacher–child attachment security. Insecure children with a history of neglect and abuse from the relationship with their primary caregiver behave in such a way as to recreate interactions with teachers that parallel their maladjusted histories (Lynch & Cicchetti, 1992; O'Connor, Collins, & Supplee, 2012). This all relates back to IWMs. Based on their internalized models, children apply their early attachment experiences to teachers and therefore behave to elicit the same responses they received from the primary attachment figure. Simply put, schools are the primary place where children reenact and recreate their childhood memories.

The response of teachers. Teaching involves a dynamic, interactive relationship between student and teacher. Up to this point, we have utilized attachment theory to understand what students bring to the relationship based on past experiences with attachment figures. In this section, we not only examine what can be the appropriate responses of the teacher to the different types of insecure children but also help teachers understand how their own attachment history might be affecting their behavior.

Nothing is better than a secure teacher! Secure teachers transform their classrooms into bases for exploration where students challenge themselves, ask questions, are not afraid to make mistakes, and increase their self-confidence and self-efficacy. While it is natural to like some students more than others, secure teachers treat everyone fairly and do not rely on their students for affective fulfillment. It is only human to enjoy positive feedback and dislike negative feedback. Teachers would much prefer to hear positive comments from students rather than negative ones. The secure teacher, however, does not take either personally and does not rely on students for self-definition. This is important especially when working with students with insecure attachment histories, as they tend to respond in less gratifying ways to the teacher's efforts than secure children. Secure teachers have better caretaking, listening, and responding patterns (Posada, Waters, Crowell, & Lay, 1995).

How teachers deal with insecure children can have an effect upon the students' socialization. For example, Taylor (1989) found that when teachers evidenced acceptance of a peer-rejected child, the child was less likely to be rejected in the future. Even with a disorganized child, teachers who provided security, safety, and support had a positive impact on the student's later school performance and aggressive behaviors (Ladd & Burgess, 2001). Children can change, and teacher behavior can be a significant factor in that change. Supportive student–teacher relationships encourage more positive behaviors, manifested as less aggression, internalization, and withdrawal (Buyse, Verschueren, Verachtert, & Van Damme, 2009; Mufson & Dorta, 2003).

How do teachers tend to react to secure versus insecure children? The Sroufe et al. (2005) Minnesota Study rated teachers' behaviors toward secure, resistant, and avoidant children along seven scales: engagement, affection, control, anger, nurturance/support, tolerance, and expectations for compliance. *Nurturance* refers to providing comfort and taking care of the child's physical and emotional needs.

Tolerance refers to making allowances for the child, such as permitting immature behavior and violations of rules. *Expectations for compliance* refers to how much teachers follow up after giving directions: If teachers were to give a directive and immediately turn to other business, they would be rated high on expectations for compliance because they expect the child to comply. In contrast, teachers who repeat directions or give any other reinforcing actions would be rated low on expectations for compliance.

The results were interesting. Teachers rated secure children high on expectations for compliance and low on control, anger, nurturance/caregiving, and tolerance. This means they held high standards for these children. Teachers rated resistant children as low on expectations for compliance and high on nurturance, tolerance, and control. This means they tended to treat these children as if they were younger. And teachers rated avoidant children high on control and low on expectations for compliance, tolerance, and nurturance/caregiving. The avoidant group was the one most likely to elicit anger from the teachers, who wanted to remove them from the classroom. Remember, avoidant children can do hurtful things to other children, which often makes the teacher angry, resulting in rejection not only by other students but also by the teacher. Having suffered rejection in their early attachment histories, avoidant children will elicit the same response from other attachment figures, thus replicating the pathology in their attachment history.

Any adult in a helping relationship with a child who creates a secure base for that child to explore is giving a wonderful gift. This is what makes a teacher such an important figure in the life of a child. Secure teachers are more likely to do this than insecure teachers. We urge teachers to reflect upon their own attachment histories. How might a teacher with an avoidant attachment style behave in the classroom? It's more than likely that this teacher's relationship with students would be characterized by a lack of warmth, trust, and sensitivity. Any overtures by a student for a closer relationship would most likely be met with distance and coldness. Remember those with avoidant histories have learned to be very independent and self-reliant, which could result in unrealistic expectations in regard to students' maturity and independence (Kennedy & Kennedy, 2004). Such teachers' preferred mode of classroom management is punishment of observable behaviors, and they will rarely take the time to understand the underlying causes of the misbehavior or how their own behavior might be a contributing factor.

While teachers with an avoidant attachment history run the risk of emotional underinvolvement in the relationship with their students, teachers with a preoccupied attachment history risk the opposite: becoming emotionally overinvolved in the lives of their students. In contrast to the rigid boundaries that rule the relationship of the avoidant group, diffuse boundaries typify the relationship for the preoccupied group. Preoccupied teachers may rely too much on their students and go out of their way to make sure their students like them. They constantly need and seek support from other staff and run the risk of also seeking support from their students, in contrast to avoidant teachers, who will often deny the need for help.

Preoccupied teachers will suffer from hyperactivation of the attachment system; avoidant teachers suffer from deactivation of the attachment system.

Mentalization for teachers. Main (1991) used the term *metacognitive monitoring* to refer to the state of mind for those classified as secure-autonomous on the AAI. They have the ability to think about their thinking, evidenced by finding contradictions in their own description of their attachment history or wondering out loud what made them say a particular statement. This reflective capacity of the secure state of mind came to be known more commonly as the capacity for *mentalization* as defined by Slade (2008).

> Mentalization refers to the capacity to envision mental states in oneself and another, and to understand one's own and another's behavior in terms of underlying mental states and intentions. Inherent in high-level mentalizing is the capacity to regulate and envision negative and disruptive mental states, as well as to appreciate the interpersonal, intrapersonal, causal, and dynamic aspects of mental states. (p. 764)

Wow! That sounds like a mouthful, so let's see if we can understand mentalization in more applied terms. Affect regulation, empathy, and productive social relationships are all a result of mentalization (Fonagy, Gergely, Jurist, & Target, 2002). Why? Because mentalization allows one to understand one's own behavior in relation to another's behavior and vice versa. Mentalization is the opposite of being reactive. Let's take as an example someone who makes an angry, hostile, abrupt, insulting remark. A reactive response would be to say something in kind. People who mentalize, however, ask themselves first: *What made this person say that? Is it something internal to him? Maybe he has a good deal of self-hate, and his comment to me is simply a splitting off and projection of his own self-hate. Or maybe the vicious comment is the result of something going on between the two of us? Maybe it is linked to something in our past that has never been dealt with.* These questions attempt to distinguish what is internal to the self, internal to the other, or—as is more often the case—an interaction between the two. With mentalization, a teacher's responses are not dictated by another but by reflection and control, allowing him to take ownership and responsibility of his behavior rather than feeling that his behavior just seems to happen (Allen & Munich, 2003). In fact, a lack of mentalization has been linked to more severe forms of psychopathology (Fonagy et al., 2002), and there is a strong correlation between secure attachment and mentalization (Fonagy, 2006).

ATTACHMENT THEORY AND TEACHING DIFFICULT STUDENTS

So, what does all this talk about mentalization have to do with teaching difficult students? Plenty! Difficult students bring their attachment histories into the classroom and direct their feelings toward the teacher as an attachment figure, even though the teacher is not the one originally responsible for the difficult behavior. How the teacher responds to the difficult behavior will make all the difference in the world. Secure teachers will be more likely to mentalize; insecure teachers will be more likely to react. Sroufe et al. described mentalizing as the ability to "see, think about, and understand one's self and others in terms of inner states" (2005, p. 280), and it is the result of having caregivers who were emotionally attuned to their child's inner states. When confronted with a student's difficult behavior, teachers who mentalize will ask themselves: *What is this behavior about? Does it appear to be the result of anger, anxiety, deactivation of the attachment system, hyperactivation of the attachment system? What, if anything, have I done to make the interaction better or worse? What is my first internal response? Do I want to rescue this highly anxious student? Do I want to run away from this encounter with an angry, hostile student?* Like a good caregiver, teachers who mentalize use the feelings that students' behavior provokes in them as a window into their inner states. Thus, instead of rescuing the needy child, which would only reinforce the child's difficult behavior, the teacher may provide an unexpected response, such as: "I am not able to help you right now, but I also trust that you can do this on your own. As soon as you do it, I will be glad to take a look and go over it with you." Not only does such a response empower the child, it also rewards him or her with teacher contact—but only after the child has completed the assignment.

Avoidant students can be a real challenge, because they warm slowly, if at all, to a relationship with a teacher. A preoccupied teacher and an avoidant student can be a toxic combination. The teacher may go out of her way to help the student, only to have the student adopt a rejecting and dismissive attitude. The teacher maximizes affect; the student minimizes it. A secure teacher who mentalizes will intuit the inner state of the student by sensing the rejection and not be upset that the student's response to the teacher's help is anything but gratifying. Teachers often get upset over how much they reached out to a student and tried to help, only to have the student be unresponsive or even outwardly dismissive. Secure students, on the other hand, are comfortable seeking and receiving help.

Then there are the disorganized students, perhaps the most challenging of all because of their emotional dysregulation and frightening behaviors. While resistant students will often create feelings of annoyance and avoidant students feelings of anger, there is something peculiar about the feelings generated by the disorganized student because of the level of pathology. Their dysregulation may create fear in the teacher, and the disassociation a feeling of befuddlement and worry about the student's level of stability. The teacher's first reaction may be a desire to run away. Secure teachers who mentalize, however, will allow these extreme feelings to help them understand the inner state of the disorganized student—one of extreme pain and trauma. Remember, mentalization allows for empathy, and that is what is called for even in the face of such difficult and unregulated behaviors. Know there is pain behind the student's behavior. Trying to reason with these students when they are manifesting their pain in such provocative ways will do little good. A simple comment that emanates from the teacher's own feeling will do: "Now is not the time for us to discuss your behavior, but we both know something is very wrong, and perhaps with time we can figure it out. But if it's OK with you, I'd like your help to get back to teaching." Dysregulated students will tend to dysregulate others, including the teacher. What's called for is an antithetical response! No matter how odd or how disturbing the behavior may look, the response should be measured and calm. It is the only chance to create a secure base for students with this type of attachment history. The following chapters will incorporate a good deal of composite case material about students with different disorders and describe how best to work with these students in the classroom—trying to understand the behavior of both the student and the teacher through the lens of attachment theory and pedagogical style.

CHAPTER 2

Principles of Pedagogy for Teachers of Students with Challenging Behaviors

Give a man a fish and you feed him for a day; teach a man to fish and you feed him for a lifetime.
—Maimonides

IS TEACHING (PEDAGOGY) AN ART, A SCIENCE, A CRAFT, OR AN AMALGAM OF ALL THREE?

This question raises the specter of a very old debate, effectively described in N. L. Gage's book *The Scientific Basis of the Art of Teaching* (1978). In that book, Gage defined *teaching* (pedagogy) as "any activity on the part of one person intended to facilitate learning on the part of another" (p. 14). Of course, given the focus of this book, which concerns the education of "difficult" students in today's K–12 schools, we need a more inclusive description of pedagogy. Teaching has been transformed in the 21st century to incorporate a more expansive job description—one that acknowledges that, in addition to facilitating learning, today's teacher serves as a role model for prosocial behavior, provides examples of civil discourse, and in some cases even acts as a surrogate parent. What has precipitated this revolutionary change? One needs only to examine the changing social structure that surrounds students; specifically, the volatile economy, which has caused a radical increase in the number of hours people spend working, and, as a result, has all but eradicated the luxury of the stay-at-home parent. Without parental guidance, many American students have found themselves without the traditional role models who once taught and reinforced prosocial behaviors and discouraged antisocial ones.

In a different tack, Palmer (1998) asserted that "good teaching cannot be reduced to techniques; good teaching comes from the identity and integrity of the teacher" (p. 10). As we noted in the introduction, effective teachers must know themselves both as persons and professionals and understand their role in the classroom—this is the essence of what we referred to earlier as "pedagogical knowledge." The "art and science" aspects of sound teaching that we also discussed at the outset of the book develop over years of practice in the crucible of the classroom. The message we want to impart to teachers is the importance of the "how" and "why" of instruction. *How* we convey information to our students reflects our unique perception of the lesson, the subject, and, ultimately, our world view. We suggest that it is important for teachers to understand and acknowledge the factors that influenced these perceptions and be willing to accommodate new perspectives and interpretations. *Why* we teach a particular lesson requires thoughtful assessment, during which we might ask ourselves the following questions: Is the information we are providing meaningful for these students? Is it essential to their growth as scholars and as members of the larger community and the world? Will it help to prepare them for the next phase of their intellectual and moral development? Or, as Kohn (1996) suggests, we might ask ourselves where we would like to see each of our students in ten years and what we would like them to have achieved, in a broader sense than simply success in school or employment.

A New Paradigm of Teacher Pedagogy: "New Wine in New Wineskins"

As noted in our introduction, Cogill (2008) suggests that teacher knowledge is integral to pedagogy and cites Shulman's (1987) seven categories as a schema for understanding the nuanced term. We think this "framework" is very helpful in understanding pedagogical skills as they pertain to the teaching profession. It might be instructive to list them here: (a) content knowledge, (b) general pedagogical knowledge (e.g., classroom control, group work), (c) pedagogical content knowledge (we refer to this simply as "content or subject knowledge"), (d) curriculum knowledge, which is more specific to instructional design, (e) knowledge of learners and their characteristics, (f) knowledge of educational contexts (e.g., schools and their communities), and (g) knowledge of education purposes and their values (for students) (as cited in Cogill, 2008, pp. 1–2). Simply put, pedagogy is the "how to" in effectively imparting a skill to another.

Ostensibly, these prospective teachers would reciprocate in reflecting on their "core qualities" and values to encourage the development of these qualities within their own students. In a similar vein, Palmer (1998) insisted that good teachers know themselves (i.e., "identity") and are honest with themselves and others, unafraid to show their students and colleagues who they really are (i.e., "integrity"). Loughran (1997) added that teaching, in its highest form, requires an understanding of oneself and others and is predicated on the quality of relationship between the teacher and student. Many students with behavioral challenges have had to acquire a heightened sensitivity to hypocrisy and disingenuity, for the preservation of their emotional and sometimes physical well-being. These students prefer teachers who are consistent, fair, and authentic, and thus such teachers are more apt to achieve success in teaching them (Austin, Barowsky, Malow, & Gomez, 2011).

Furthermore, sound teacher pedagogy requires a purpose, which establishes the starting point for learning. Thus, the most effective teacher pedagogies involve the modeling of a desired skill, behavior, or disposition by a capable teacher to demonstrate the "why" or purpose of teaching a desired skill or conveying information. However, Loughran (1997) asserted that knowing *why* we teach must be linked to knowing *how* we teach.

Northfield and Gunstone (1997) articulated six recommendations for the development of a sound pedagogy that are especially relevant to preservice teachers: (a) prospective teachers have needs that must be considered in planning and implementing a program, and these needs change through their preservice development; (b) the transition from learner to teacher is difficult but is aided by working closely with one's peers; (c) the student teacher is a learner who is actively constructing views of teaching and learning based on personal experiences strongly shaped by perceptions held before entering the program; (d) the approaches to teaching and learning advocated in the program should be modeled by the teacher educators in their own practice; (e) student teachers should see the preservice program as an educational experience of worth; and (f) preservice education programs are inevitably inadequate—they mark the start of a teacher's career, which will involve appreciably more learning over time.

Schön's (1983) conception of the "reflective practitioner" is an essential notion for those who teach in a preservice program, as well as for those learning to teach. In support of this contention, Sellar noted, "reflection is very broadly able to be defined as the deliberate, purposeful, metacognitive thinking and/or action in which educators engage in order to improve their professional practice" (2013, p. 2). Similarly, Russell (1997) stressed that an important aspect of sound pedagogy is self-reflection; that is, reflecting on one's teaching.

Furthermore, Smith (2012) asserted that pedagogy is a process that consists of accompanying learners, caring for and about them, and bringing learning into their lives. Sound pedagogy, he continued, induces change in the learner and, ultimately, in the world. Similarly, Noddings stated that caring relations are a foundation for pedagogical activity (2005). Thus emerges the notion of "social pedagogy" in Watkins and Mortimore's revised definition, suggested in the introduction: "Any conscious activity by one person designed to enhance learning in another" (p. 3). The authors add that teachers (and their pedagogies) are influenced by their contexts—students' learning differences and preparedness; the subject matter; teachers' prejudices and predispositions, likes and dislikes. They must present their curriculums in different ways to address the social-emotional makeup of the class, sequence of lessons, and knowledge of both learning groups and individuals. Teachers, as pedagogues, help students see themselves as active agents contributing to their own learning, members of a community of learners engaged in the generation and evaluation of knowledge alongside the teacher (Watkins & Mortimore, 1999).

Freire (1970) and later Bruner (1996) insisted that to truly develop an effective pedagogical framework, the teacher must understand her cultural context as well as the cultural contexts of her students and be cognizant of how culture influences how and what she teaches. Furthermore, Alexander (2004) stated that teacher pedagogy may be understood as (a) what we need to know, (b) the skills needed to impart that knowledge, and (c) the commitment we need to display in order to make the many different kinds of decisions required of a teacher each day. Children are engaged from very early on in a mission to make sense of their world. The teacher's pedagogical imperative is to facilitate that natural process by helping children and adolescents make connections between new and familiar situations, directing student focus, piquing the interest and curiosity of the child, supporting any and all attempts to learn, structuring students' experiences, regulating levels of complexity and difficulty for them, and motivating them through success and acceptance. Expert teachers know the structure of their disciplines, and this knowledge intersects with and enhances their pedagogical skills (Alexander, 2004).

Mascolo (2009) offered that there are many heuristic ways that teachers can develop their pedagogical skills—through their own practice, through collaboration with colleagues, through professional development opportunities, and from the various extracurricular roles they play (e.g., youth group worker, coach, parent, community club organizer).

As far back as 1896, a didactic model of teaching was encouraged: the heretofore-revolutionary idea that teachers should share their knowledge with everyone (Comenius as cited in Gundem, 1992). Furthermore, Alexander (2004) contended that teacher pedagogues reflect on fundamental questions of life such as: How should one live one's life? What is the right way to act in a given situation? What does happiness consist of for me and others? How should I relate to others? And, what sort of society should I be working towards? (p. 11).

What Do We Know About Effective Pedagogy?

According to Ireson, Mortimore, and Hallam (1999), an effective teacher pedagogy should (a) be clear about its goals, (b) have high expectations for students and provide them with motivation to learn, (c) incorporate beneficial technologies, and (d) be grounded in a well-tested theory that inspires innovative practices. The authors also cited Vygotsky's (1987) notion of "cultural tools" and proposed that these tools might be relevant to one's understanding of a "pedagogical framework." To that end, they suggested six fundamental ideas. We will briefly discuss them here.

First, they asserted that the term *pedagogy* is seldom clearly defined or understood (as this chapter's lengthy discussion of the term illustrates). We have attempted to define it so that it comports with our proposed framework and is therefore more useful to teachers.

Second, the authors contend that there is no "one-size-fits-all" teacher pedagogy. We agree that many authors of books on pedagogy have misinterpreted the term and have confused it with teaching techniques, of which there are legions, many of which are effective given the right contexts and students. However, we have defined teacher pedagogy in much broader, philosophical terms. To us, it is a way of thinking about teaching and learning that involves self-reflection on the part of the teacher and a willingness to learn about, care for, and connect with students. Thus, rather than a "toolbox" of teaching strategies, our approach has been to suggest a pedagogical framework, which can be applied broadly to enhance the effectiveness of any teaching initiative.

Third, teachers are important. We wholeheartedly agree with this pronouncement. In fact, we would advance this assertion by suggesting that teachers—good teachers, empowered by a sound pedagogy—are essential in inspiring learners to want to learn and in building their self-efficacy. We believe that until this truth becomes self-evident, teaching will continue to be regarded by most as just another occupation.

Fourth, context matters. We also support this notion for reasons that we have discussed throughout this chapter. As Bolles (2015) notably described in his book, *What Color is Your Parachute?*, transferable skills—those that are invaluable to the individual regardless of the context—are critical to students' success in school and in later life. Examples of these include what we refer to generally as social skills, like knowing how to begin and end a conversation, how to be courteous and considerate of others' feelings, when to be silent and when to speak up, how to identify the "hidden curriculum" in a new social milieu, and so on. In short, our pedagogy must acknowledge the importance of providing real-world instruction in authentic contexts.

Fifth, the authors offered some pedagogical principles gleaned from an analysis of many related articles on the subject. These principles include the following:

- Be clear about your goals and ensure that your students know them.
- Plan, organize, and manage your teaching effectively.
- Hold your students accountable to the highest expectations appropriate for them as individuals.
- Provide positive formative feedback to all your students.
- Address individual differences and needs in the inclusive classroom.
- Provide meaningful learning tasks that are informed by good assessment procedures.
- Teach transferable skills to all your students.
- Make your rules explicit and meaningful, and don't forget to teach students how to acquire the "hidden curriculum" embedded in all social contexts.
- Teach students to identify their strengths and weaknesses as a means of empowerment and to take increasing responsibility for their own learning.
- Motivate and enthuse learners.

In concert with these principles, Tompkins (1999) stated,

> My chief concern is that our educational system does not focus on the inner lives of students or help them to acquire the self-understand-

ing that is the basis for a satisfying life. Nor, by and large, does it provide the safe and nurturing environment that people need in order to grow. . . . What was lacking in me—respect for the whole human organism, emotions, body, and spirit, as well as mind—is what is lacking in American education as well. (p. xii)

And further, Tompkins went on to assert, "A holistic approach to education would recognize that a person must learn how to be with other people, how to love, how to take criticism, how to grieve, how to have fun, as well as how to add and subtract, multiply and divide" (1996, p. xvi). Unfortunately, for many students, the following assessment rings true: "School, by its existence, militates against the very thing that education is for—the development of the individual" (p. xix).

And finally, sixth, remember to acknowledge the fact that teachers are learners, too! Cultivate a love of learning and bring your enthusiasm and passion for learning into the classroom. As Plutarch once wrote, "Education is not the filling of a pail, but the lighting of a fire" (as cited in Waterfield, 1992), and teachers can "light a fire" in their students by modeling their own passion for teaching and learning. In support of this exhortation, Tompkins (1996) noted, "The teachers who made the most difference to me were the ones who loved their subjects and didn't hide it" (p. 61).

INCLUSION, "DIFFERENCE," AND A RELEVANT PEDAGOGICAL SCHEMA

In another area, teacher pedagogy for those who teach students with disabilities is centrally about the relevance of teaching to difference and diversity (Corbett & Norwich, 1999). Corbett and Norwich (1999) insisted that teaching students with special education needs requires the adoption of a "connective pedagogy"—relating to these learners individually, with an acute awareness of and connection to their social context. The authors further contended that differences between children might call for differences in the pedagogical style employed by these teachers. They continued that the teacher's pedagogy should be considered in terms of relationships and balances between practices that are (a) common to all students, (b) specific to some, and (c) unique to individuals. The authors addressed the question of why a teacher would feel called to become a "special educator." They suggested that it might be because the teacher relates to the students' vulnerabilities by connecting them to the teacher's own. Thus, these special educators may possess an innate "caring pedagogy," which is more individually sensitive. Finally, Corbett and Norwich challenged teachers of students with special education needs, especially those working in the increasingly popular inclusive classrooms, to employ what they described as a "connective pedagogy" to facilitate the development of a rapport with these students and help them develop a sense of belongingness with their classmates.

The teaching model known as inclusion requires the collaboration of both special and general educators and the ability to accommodate and provide services for diverse classroom populations. For many teachers this popular model will require a willingness to work with students who are ethnically, culturally, and linguistically diverse. This new and transformed classroom will also include students with exceptional needs.

One sub-group of this latter category that elicits concern, especially in novice teachers, are those students diagnosed with emotional and behavioral disorders. In recent years, school districts across the country have reported an increased number of students classified with emotional and behavioral disorders (U.S. Department of Education, 2008). To remain current and viable, teacher preparation programs and professional development staff in schools must begin to evaluate the qualities that effective classroom teachers demonstrate, even when confronted by the most challenging students, and consider which of these identified qualities the less skilled or experienced teachers could acquire.

The concepts of effective teaching behaviors and teacher quality have proven difficult to define, so much so that the terms are frequently rendered useless (Kennedy, 2008). One framework that appears to be more useful is Kennedy's (2008) categorization of effective teaching behaviors: "(a) personal resources—the qualities that the teacher brings to the job, (b) teacher performance—teachers' everyday practices that occur in and out of the classroom, and (c) teacher effectiveness—the relational teacher qualities that influence students" (p. 60). Utilizing these categories suggests a schema from which to discuss the qualities of teacher effectiveness. (Adapted from Austin et al. (2011) with permission of the Editor, *JAASEP*.).

Personal Resources

Kennedy (2008) described personal resources as traits such as beliefs, attitudes, values, knowledge, skill, and expertise. His research found four basic personal qualities to be effective: knowledge in the subject area, respect toward students, reflection about teaching, and being active in one's professional growth.

Effective teachers in general education are highly qualified teachers who possess a strong knowledge and certification in their content area (Helm, 2007; Mowrer-Reynolds, 2008; Polk, 2006). Stough and Palmer (2003) reported that knowledge of individual students' needs is a central tenet of effective teaching.

Teachers who are effective believe in the potential of all children to learn. This belief is translated by demonstrating respect for students (Mowrer-Reynolds, 2008), their families (Woolfolk, 2004), and student differences (Imber, 2006). Similarly, dispositions of caring, concern for children, and empathy should be encouraged for teachers to be effective (Helm, 2007; Imber, 2006). Elementary students preferred teachers who showed that they truly cared for the well-being of each of their students (Pratt, 2008).

Teaching effectively is linked to a willingness to continuously develop as a professional (Harris, 1998). Helterbran (2008) noted that students defined good teachers as ones who are never satisfied with their teaching but are always eager to stretch, grow, and refine their teaching skills and subject knowledge. To remain effective, teachers self-develop or participate in lifelong learning (Polk, 2006) that should include growth in their own self-awareness in regard to the relationships they form with their students. The avenue to continued professional development is self-reflection and inquiry (Harris, 1998). Topping and Ferguson recommended that all teachers should "have access to opportunities to monitor and reflect upon teaching behaviors they use and do not use, in different contexts" to enhance teaching efficacy (2005, p. 141). In a study on special education instruction, Stough and Palmer found that reflection and "concerned responsiveness of teacher to individual students" were central to effective teaching (2003, p. 220). The challenge is to develop an assessment system that transfers newly acquired skills to the classroom so that the quality of teaching and student behavior can be improved (Bracey, 2009).

Teacher Performance

Performance qualities are teacher practices that occur daily, such as learning activities, actions that foster student learning, and motivating students (Kennedy, 2008). For learning to take place, students need a safe and stimulating learning climate maintained through efficient classroom management (van de Grift, 2007). One aspect of classroom management is clear communication. Effective teaching is highly dependent on the teacher's ability to communicate the instructional objectives well (Harris, 1998; Polk, 2006; van de Grift, 2007). Other behaviors of effective teachers are recognizing and using teachable moments (Woolfolk, 2004) and modeling concepts in their content area (Polk, 2006).

Highlighted in the research is the necessity for flexibility in teaching methodology. Teachers need a repertoire of more than one style to be maximally effective in their teaching (Harris, 1998). Effective teachers exercise creativity to adapt their teaching and use of teaching-learning strategies to match the needs of different students (Rosenfeld & Rosenfeld, 2004; van de Grift, 2007; Woolfolk, 2004). Additionally, Rosenfeld and Rosenfeld (2004) reported sensitivity to individual learning differences as an integral component of effective teaching when working with students with special needs.

It is difficult to find research that distinguishes the universally recognized characteristics of a "master teacher." Most of what we read in journals, online mailing lists, and blogs simply reflects the subjective opinions or insights of the author with very little, if any, scientific bases. This may be due to the fact that the characteristics of acknowledged "master teachers" are germane to each. Therefore, absent a scientific criteria, we offer several lists of behaviors displayed by most teachers who are recognized as exemplary, including those effective teacher behaviors identified in our own research. In addition, we encourage teachers who wish to achieve this status to be patient and observant of colleagues who are acknowledged as models of exceptional teaching. For example, Couros (2010) has suggested that the behaviors that master teachers evidence include: knowing each student and her interests; differentiating instruction; preparing students for life, not just for tests; enticing students to want to learn by helping them discover their passions; modeling a love of learning; being a reflective practitioner; teaching with passion and zeal (and being passionate about their subject); incorporating character education as an integral part of their curriculum; educating all students and thus influencing school culture; and communicating frequently and effectively with colleagues and parents.

Similarly, Jackson posits that some important characteristics of master teaching invariably include: (a) start where your students are; (b) know where your students are going; (c) expect to get students to their goal; (d) support students along the way; (e) use feedback; (f) focus on quality, not quantity; and—perhaps surprising—(g) never work harder than your students (2012).

In 2002, Buskist, Sikorsky, Buckley, and Saville surveyed 916 undergraduates about the qualities of master teaching and found the following ten to be perceived as the most representative (in order of importance): (1) has realistic expectations and is fair, (2) knowledgeable about the topic, (3) understanding, (4) personable, (5) respectful, (6) creative and interesting, (7) positive and humorous, (8) encourages and cares for students, (9) flexible and open-minded, (10) enthusiastic about teaching. Simultaneously, the researchers presented the same list of qualities to 118 faculty members, and a comparison of the results showed that, though there was no hierarchical consensus among the two groups, the faculty participants included six of the students' top ten qualities in their own lists. Specifically, the faculty members valued, in order: (1) knowledgeable about the topic, (2) enthusiastic about teaching, (3) approachable and personable, (4) respectful, (5) creative and interesting, and (6) has realistic expectations and is fair. Clearly, some of these qualities could be considered pedagogical skills, and others appear relevant to relationship building.

Teacher Effectiveness Based on the Authors' Investigation

Recently, we and fellow researchers designed a study to investigate the practice of teachers qualified as "very effective," according to a rigorous, evidence-based protocol (Austin et al., 2011). We employed a mixed-methods approach, which included interviews, videotaped observations of practice, and student feedback via survey. The results reflected the findings of several similar studies but also revealed a few surprises.

Kennedy (2008) considers effective teacher qualities to be those that influence students. One way that effectiveness can be identified is by questioning students. Pratt (2008) and Biddulph and Adey (2004) studied the topic of teacher efficacy from the perspective of the student. Biddulph and Adey (2004) found that it was not the content of the curriculum that piqued students' interest in a subject; rather, it was the quality of the teaching and meaningfulness of the learning activities that influenced students' opinions about a teacher and the subject area. Pratt (2008) noted that elementary-level students preferred teachers who made them feel like they were an important part or member of a community, provided choices in learning activities, allowed for cooperative projects, made learning seem fun, and used authentic and meaningful assessments.

Other researchers also reported qualities related to humor as effective traits of teachers. Mowrer-Reynolds (2008) found that using humor and being entertaining ranked highly as exemplary teacher characteristics. In addition to being humorous, teachers who were easy to talk to, approachable, and provided outside help were often considered exemplary (Mowrer-Reynolds, 2008).

These teacher performance qualities are observable characteristics of teachers—what they do in a classroom. All three data sources in our study found strong evidence that the behaviors represented in this category are exhibited by the highly qualified teachers, which speaks to the importance of these characteristics. Furthermore, students find these behaviors desirable in general and acknowledge them in their teachers.

Within this category, it is important to note that the four videotaped teachers in our study (Austin et al., 2011) did not exhibit the same teaching style, nor was it necessary that they do so. One of the teacher participants best represented this perspective in her interview response, noting that "A mixture of teaching approaches and strategies are most effective," and that she purposely changes her approach every "20 minutes or so" to keep students focused and interested. Additionally, she notes that having the ability to "read a student and know how to change one's strategy if it's ineffective" is an essential skill that can be taught to novice teachers (Austin et al., 2011).

Qualities of interpersonal behavior have been identified as important in teacher effectiveness (e.g., Goldhaber & Hansen, 2010; Kyriakides, 2005). The highly qualified teachers of students with emotional and behavioral challenges included in this investigation evidenced strong interpersonal behaviors in all three ways we measured them. Specifically, it was interesting to hear all four teachers strongly endorse forming relationships with students in order to promote their well-being both academically and personally. Finally, effective teachers understand that the teacher–student relationship can be difficult (Austin et al., 2011).

To summarize, as described in a recent study conducted by the authors and colleagues (Austin et al., 2011):

> [T]he research objectives of the authors' investigation were to examine the effective teaching behaviors of highly qualified teacher participants who taught, primarily, students with emotional and behavioral problems, and to identify those behaviors deemed teachable for future inclusion in teacher preparation and in-service professional development programs. In the course of the research, the behaviors of four highly qualified teachers were observed. After analyzing the data from the videotapes, interviews, and student surveys, the researchers identified effective teaching behaviors. The importance of Kennedy's (2008) framework for breaking effective teaching behaviors into teachable components for general educators was supported and was demonstrated to be applicable to teachers of students with emotional and behavioral disorders as well as for general education teachers. The effective behaviors of highly qualified experienced teachers of difficult students fell within the three categories framed by Kennedy (2008) for general education teachers. In particular, the performance category presents teachable instructional and interpersonal behaviors. These

included strategies such as awareness of body language, flexibility in accommodating different learning styles, active listening techniques, the use of eye contact, teacher availability, and incorporating a variety of teaching methodologies. (pp. 15-16)

Two Strategic Interventions Relevant to Our Pedagogical Framework

The work of Redl (1966), which addresses behavioral and emotional crises in school and in the classroom, can be quite helpful here, especially the elements of the Life Space Interview (LSI), which consists of both immediate "emotional first aid on the spot" as well as some "after-action" teacher guidance. The Life Space Interview is a crisis-intervention technique in which a teacher discusses a student's behavior with her or him immediately at the time of the problem's occurrence. There are two types of LSI; both are "here-and-now" reactions to an event or experience in a student's life. The first, emotional first aid on the spot, is used when the teacher wishes to help defuse the problem quickly and reintegrate the student back into the scheduled program. The second, clinical exploitation of life events, is a debriefing technique in which the teacher helps the student to gain insight into his or her behavior and change maladaptive responses to behavioral triggers.

There are five discrete interventions associated with providing emotional first aid on the spot, described by Redl (1966) as: allowing students that are upset or agitated to simply vent, helping students sort through troubling feelings and thoughts, keeping the lines of communication open, applying school and classroom rules in a consistent and fair manner, and settling student conflicts impartially and equitably. Similarly, the five elements of the clinical exploitation of life events, as described by Redl (1966), consist of reaffirming shared values, reminding students of past successes in employing problem-solving strategies and applying them in new situations, helping students gain objectivity and reevaluate a volatile situation or conflict from a more balanced perspective, respecting the autonomy and rights of others, and helping students to view their behavior from others' perceptions.

The process of implementing any of the Life Space Interviewing techniques involves first, intervening; second, listening to all parties involved in a nonjudgmental manner; third, analyzing the situation to determine whether the behavior is acute (an atypical or episodic occurrence) or chronic (frequently recurring); fourth, selecting a specific LSI approach; fifth, implementing the approach or approaches in a respectful, attentive, and professional manner; and finally, combining or modifying the relevant approach or approaches as required by the circumstance.

Three other simple, evidenced-based interventions that might prove helpful to teachers working with students who display challenging behaviors are:

1. **"Behavior-specific praise,"** which is predicated on four principles; namely, that the praise must be immediate, it must also be specific and must include details that describe the acknowledged prosocial behavior, it must be offered

contingent, exclusively, on the presentation of the desired behavior, and it must be frequent (e.g., Conroy, Sutherland, Snyder, Al-Hendawi, & Vo, 2009).

2. **"Behavior momentum,"** which involves the following four steps: (a) identify problem tasks (those that are most onerous to the student), (b) identify easy tasks (those the student is likely to complete because they are easily performed), (c) collect data to validate both the 'problem' and 'easy' tasks, and (d) implement the intervention by first asking the student to complete 'easy' tasks, with a high probability of complicity, then introduce a 'problem' task (one with a lower probability of completion). The research suggests that by introducing a student to 'easy' tasks first, there is a greater likelihood that the student will be more predisposed to completing the 'problem' or hard task (e.g., Lee, Belfiore, & Budin, 2008).

3. **"Implementing choice," a behavioral approach that consists of the following four stages:** (a) identify problem activities or contexts, (b) identify choices that might be afforded in each context, (c) implement 'choice' in one context at a time, and (d) if effective, implement the 'choice' in different contexts or circumstances. For example, a student might be provided options or choices relative to the order of assignment completion, the type of assignment (e.g., portfolio, essay, report), where to work on the assigned task (e.g., classroom, library, outdoors, at a desk, table, or on the floor), and the type of reward or reinforcement the student can earn upon successful completion of the assignment that are desirable to the student and reasonable to the teacher. Finally, of course, the 'choice' must produce measurable benefit relative to the student's behavior (e.g., Kern & Parks, 2012). (Adapted from Landrum & Sweigart, 2014)

A USEFUL FRAMEWORK TO CONSTRUCT AN EFFECTIVE TEACHER PEDAGOGY

This might be a good time to review for the reader what our study of effective teaching and sound pedagogy has revealed. First, to revisit our discussion of the old debate about the essence of good teaching—Is it properly considered an art, a science, or a craft?—we suggest that it is properly considered an amalgam of all three.

As stated in the introduction, the term "pedagogy" can be simply and effectively defined as "any conscious activity by one person designed to enhance the learning of another" (Watkins & Mortimore, 1999). Alexander (2004) expanded on this definition of pedagogy by adding that, to be considered useful and effective, it must provide students with what they need to know, it must evidence the skills needed to impart that knowledge, and it must demonstrate the commitment necessary to make the daily decisions about instruction and learning required of an effective teacher. Further, Palmer (1998) and Loughran (1997) asserted that good teachers take the time to really know themselves, strive to be honest with themselves about who they are and what they know and believe, and be courageous in that revelation (i.e., the pursuit of the "identity" and "integrity" of the teacher). Similarly, researchers (e.g., Austin et al., 2011; Korthagen, 2004; Loughran, 1997) proposed the authenticity of self as a tenet of effective teacher pedagogy. As Loughran (1997) affirmed, *why* we teach affects *how* we teach.

In addition to these pedagogical characteristics, Russell (1997), Schön (1983), and Sellar (2013) encouraged "self-reflection" as another important aspect of sound pedagogy. In a similar way, Noddings (2005) and Smith (2012) extolled the importance of developing caring teacher–student relationships as vital to any notion of pedagogy. And, of course, Freire (1970) and Bruner (1996) stressed the importance of understanding the teacher's culture and its relevance to the classroom, as well as the cultures of her students.

Nonetheless, as we developed our own pedagogical framework, we were inspired by the work of Ireson, Mortimore, and Hallam (1999) to identify six critical elements.

- The first of these is the requirement that such a pedagogical schema be clearly understood and operationally defined.
- Second, our framework cannot consist of faddish techniques—it is not a toolbox of instructional strategies; rather, it should offer teachers a theoretical foundation upon which to build a contextually and culturally viable pedagogy.
- Third, our pedagogical framework is predicated on the value of teachers— teachers need to see their worth to their students, their profession, and their society. They need to develop their identities as professionals and ultimately must, as Stout exhorts, cultivate "certainty, positivity, and the unity of self and moral goals" (2005, p. 194). Accordingly, teachers should be able to say, without reservation, "Who I am is what I want to do and what I am doing" (p. 195). In other words, teachers should be persons of integrity.
- Fourth, context matters in the development of a sound pedagogical framework. Specifically, teachers must be able to impart an understanding of social cues and an understanding of the value of cultural nuance as well as the "hidden curriculums" of social structures.
- Fifth, a sound pedagogy must empower students to identify their strengths and weaknesses, and take responsibility for their own learning. Teachers who possess such a pedagogical foundation should motivate and entice learners, help them learn how to be with others, how to love, take criticism, grieve, and have fun (Tompkins, 1996).
- Lastly, our pedagogical framework acknowledges and celebrates the notion that teachers are learners, too—to be relevant and effective, they must cultivate a love of learning and bring their passion for learning into the classroom every day!

A final recommendation from Smith (1994) is instructive as it relates to the development of a pedagogical framework. Smith suggests three elements that he considers vital to a sound pedagogy: animation, reflection, and action. By *animation*, he is referring to "bringing life into situations and introducing students to new experiences." He describes *reflection* as "creating moments and spaces to explore lived experiences." Lastly, he defines *action* to mean "working with people so that they are able to make changes in their lives" (p. 10).

We hope that our suggested pedagogical framework provides a useful schema for our readers to further develop ones that are contextually viable for their specific teaching experiences.

LOOKING FORWARD

In this book, we strive to impart knowledge to enable the reader to become a master teacher. The qualities and behaviors described in this chapter will surely facilitate that process, but nothing can compensate for time in the classroom and the opportunity to continually hone one's craft through sustained professional development and the emulation of successful colleagues.

In the subsequent chapters of this book, our intention is to enable teachers to work effectively and confidently with the most challenging students; simply put, to become good at their calling. We intend to do this by providing valuable information about these students as well as research-based approaches to help the teacher address the students' learning and behavior challenges. In addition, we will consistently relate these approaches, skills, and strategies to our perennial two elements of good teaching: relationship building, which we discuss through the lens of attachment theory, and a sound pedagogy that is built on a well-designed and theoretically solid framework.

Each chapters focuses on specific challenges—from disruptive behaviors to anxiety disorders. The emphasis of this book is principally to empower teachers by providing them with knowledge and understanding, while encouraging them to find their passion and soar. Admittedly, this book has a grander motive: to turn everyone into good teachers. Palmer (1998) and others have said that the greatest gift society can give a child, besides unconditional love, is a good teacher—one who is passionate and knowledgeable about her subject, her craft, and her students. If you want to be that kind of teacher, read on!

CHAPTER 3

Teaching Students with Disruptive Disorders

Student Vignette: "Marcus"

Marcus, at 6' 2" and weighing 215 lbs, is an intimidating guy—even more so since he is a sixteen-year-old high school sophomore. Marcus's family is very dysfunctional. His father, Jace, is on parole from the city jail and has been required to enroll in an outpatient rehabilitation program for substance abusers and to attend mandated anger management sessions with a family counselor.

Citing spousal and child abuse, Marcus's mother, Miriam, obtained a divorce from Jace and achieved sole custody of both of her children. In addition, Miriam recently sued for child support, which she despairs of ever receiving. Marcus says he "hates" his father and occasionally intimidates his mother, Miriam, when she does not accede to his wishes.

At school, Marcus has been suspended many times for fighting and threatening classmates. He is seemingly unconcerned about the suspensions, taking them in stride, and he appears very proud of his reputation as a fighter. He usually emerges the winner from these bloody contests.

In class, Marcus is generally very diffident, almost brooding at times. When confronted by a teacher or administrator and accused of some misdemeanor, Marcus becomes defiant and adversarial, inviting a more serious consequence. He is generally very uncooperative with teachers and their demands and regularly shirks school and classroom rules. Recently, Marcus has begun to escalate his insubordinate behavior to the point of physically intimidating his teachers.

A recent example of this behavior occurred when Mr. Malone, the 10th-grade

*science teacher, engaged him in a power struggle, which ended with Marcus chal-
lenging the much smaller teacher to a fistfight, from which Mr. Malone backed
down, bestowing Marcus with instant power and instilling fear in both teachers and
students.*

*A bigger student once challenged Marcus in the hallway, during the transition
between classes. Marcus chose not to respond in that moment but waited for his
opponent after school and jumped him when they were no longer on school property,
administering a vicious beating that resulted in several lacerations, which required
stitches. Because the fight occurred off grounds, Marcus was not suspended, but the
boy's parents pressed charges, and Marcus was remanded to juvenile court. He was
sentenced to probation and was required to perform 20 hours of community service
and attend 10 hours of anger management therapy sessions.*

*On another occasion, several teachers' cars were keyed after they assigned Mar-
cus afterschool detentions. They suspected Marcus of causing the damage but could
not prove he did, so the matter was dropped. Similarly, Marcus remarked to a new
female teacher, Mrs. Burns, that if she knew some of the things he did in and out of
school, she would be very afraid and might consider transferring to another school.
She petitioned the principal to have him removed from her English class. She told
the principal that she really was afraid of Marcus!*

*The final straw occurred last spring, when Marcus sent a threatening text mes-
sage to one of his classmates who liked a girl Marcus admired. When confronted
about this behavior in the principal's office, Marcus remarked that they had all
better watch their backs, since he knew where they lived! In response to this latest
threat, a superintendent's hearing was scheduled for the summer, and the school
district administrators will review the evidence and decide whether to require a
special residential treatment placement for Marcus or expel him from the district. A
few teachers and an administrator even recommended that the school district press
criminal charges against Marcus for verbal assault.*

WHY DOES THE TEACHER NEED TO KNOW ABOUT CONDUCT-DISORDERED BEHAVIORS?

As we are acutely aware, with the proliferation of inclusion in most schools, teachers are encountering students who exhibit disruptive behaviors such as conduct
disorders, oppositional defiant disorders, and attention deficit hyperactivity disorders, especially those presenting predominantly hyperactive impulsive behaviors. Many teachers may not be familiar with the causes of these disorders or the
most effective interventions used to address them in the classroom; nevertheless,
most are acquainted with their characteristic behaviors since, according to several researchers, these behaviors constitute the primary reason cited for teacher
attrition (e.g., Kopkowski, 2008; Simon & Johnson, 2015; National Commission on
Teaching America's Future, 2005).

While the classroom teacher is not expected to study clinical psychology, limited
access to a school psychologist necessitates that teachers possess a working knowledge of the causes, characteristics, and recommended interventions that will most

certainly affect the quality of the teacher's interactions with these students. Likewise, if teachers learn and acknowledge that, in many cases, antisocial and acutely disruptive behaviors are symptomatic of chronic neurological disorders that have been exacerbated by the affected student's environment, they may be more tolerant of the student's behavior. Most teachers are more inclined to help such students if they understand that these difficult behaviors are not intended to disrupt lessons, prevent other students from learning, or cast aspersions on the quality of the teaching; they are, in fact, symptoms of a deep-seated disorder that is beyond the student's power to control.

The following information will help teachers become better prepared to effectively address disruptive behaviors when they occur in their classrooms.

WHAT THE TEACHER SHOULD KNOW ABOUT CONDUCT-DISORDERED BEHAVIORS

Students with serious conduct problems unquestionably represent a challenge to all teachers. They are often narcissistic, unpleasant to deal with, and disruptive to the lesson. However, contrary to the predictions of some, these students are not lost causes, nor should we simply try to bravely teach over, around, or in spite of them, as other teachers have suggested. One hypothesis is that these children present such behaviors in the classroom because they feel "safe" to act out the accumulated frustrations acquired at home. They may think that most teachers typically will not react violently or, conversely, provide inconsistent discipline, as their parent might.

The *Diagnostic and Statistical Manual of Mental Disorders* (5th ed.; *DSM-5*; American Psychiatric Association [APA], 2013) has maintained two distinct types of disruptive behavior disorder: oppositional defiant disorder and conduct disorder, but some think that oppositional defiance might be a precursor to conduct disorder. Research has been inconclusive as to whether the two disorders should be considered separately or together (Frick & Nigg, 2012). What is clear, however, is that not all children and adolescents who are diagnosed with oppositional defiant disorder progress to conduct disorders—only about one third do (Biederman et al., 1996; Hinshaw & Simmel, 1994). Furthermore, adolescents can develop conduct disorders without having had an earlier diagnosis of oppositional defiant disorder (Rowe, Costello, Angold, Copeland, & Maughan, 2010). The progression from oppositional defiance to conduct disorder appears to depend on three classes of risk factors: child characteristics, parenting practices, and family organization problems (Lehmann & Dangel, 1998; Behan & Carr, 2000). Early onset, greater severity, frequent physical fighting, parental substance abuse, and low socioeconomic status all increase the risk (Loeber & Burke, 2011).

Characteristics and Symptoms of Oppositional Defiant Disorder

As the diagnostic label suggests, the defining characteristics of oppositional defiant disorder are opposition and defiance, with a pattern of developmentally inappropriate behavior and high levels of negativistic, disobedient, and hostile behavior, especially toward authority figures. This disorder has three major characteristics: angry or irritable mood, argumentative or defiant behavior, and vindictiveness. To make a diagnosis, at least four of the following symptoms must be present for a minimum of six months and directed to an individual other than a sibling: frequent loss of temper, touchy or easily annoyed, often angry and resentful, often argues with authority, often deliberately annoys others, often blames other for mistakes or misbehaviors, and has been spiteful or vindictive at least two times within six months (American Psychiatric Association, 2013). The question arises as to what "often" means. For children younger than five, the *DSM-5* indicates that the behavior should occur on most days for a period of six months; for those older than five, the behavior should occur at least once per week.

To distinguish oppositional defiant disorder from a mood disorder (especially disruptive mood dysregulation disorder), the symptoms are more behavioral in nature and go beyond angry and irritable mood. Furthermore, the *DSM-5* points out that those with disruptive mood dysregulation disorder have more frequent and more severe temper outbursts without the vindictive and defiant behaviors. Another distinguishing feature is that those with oppositional defiant disorder do not experience their symptoms as problematic but often see their behavior as justified in response to unreasonable demands placed upon them by adults and especially authority figures. It must also be noted that for a diagnosis of oppositional defiant disorder to be made, the symptoms do *not* have to cross settings, allowing a child, for example, to be oppositional at home but not at school, or vice versa.

Differentiating oppositional defiance from ADHD and conduct disorder can be helpful. While some symptoms of ADHD (e.g., interrupting others, blurting out) may overlap with oppositional defiant disorder, the distinction lies in the purposefulness of the behavior. Such behaviors in children with ADHD result from restlessness and are by and large unintentional, as opposed to children with oppositional defiant disorder, in whom the behavior is more purposeful (Becker, Luebbe, Fite, Greening, & Stoppelbein, 2013). These children tend to have a hostile attribution bias that causes them to react aggressively to otherwise neutral environmental stimuli. Their aggression associated with oppositional defiant disorder is often the result of a perceived threat or provocation. In contrast, the aggression associated with conduct disorder is more proactive (Frick, Blair, & Castellanos, 2013)—that is, it anticipates a reward. Furthermore, social problems in children with oppositional defiant disorder are, for the most part, with authority figures and other adults, whereas children with ADHD and conduct disorder have more generalized social problems.

Prevalence rates for oppositional defiant disorder range anywhere from 1% to 11% (APA, 2013). This wide range is due to the historical lack of precision in diagnosing the disorder and the difficulty in distinguishing mild forms of the disorder (e.g., tantrums, crying, screaming) from normal, developmentally appropriate behavior (Greene, 2006). Oppositional defiant disorder is twice as common in males as in females, and it is most frequently diagnosed in children under 8. It rarely exists alone and is highly comorbid with ADHD and, to a lesser extent, with anxiety and mood disorders.

Causal Factors in the Development of Oppositional Defiant Disorder

Etiological factors in the development of oppositional defiant disorder are biological underpinnings, parenting and familial factors, and the child's social-cognitive processes. Most studies suggest that genetic factors interact with psychosocial and environmental factors to produce a diagnosis in the realm of disruptive behavior disorders, with special attention to the additive effect of adrenergic genes (Yang et al., 2013). The explanation is the same for hormonal factors and their effect upon adolescent behavior.

In general, studies on **biological** factors have found hormone levels, particularly high levels of testosterone and its derivatives such as dehydroepiandrosterone (DHEAS; also found in boys with conduct disorder), to be associated with conduct problems (Shenk et al., 2012). Studies have examined the role of neurotransmitter dysfunction in the development of aggression in children, adolescents, and adults. Abnormal function of serotonin—the neurotransmitter implicated in the expression and regulation of affect—has been found to play a role in aggression and lack of impulse control, as have low levels of 5-hydroxyindoleacetic acid in the cerebrospinal fluid (Moberg et al., 2011). Minor neurological deficits also seem to correlate with conduct problems. For example, studies have shown a consistent association between low IQ and disruptive behavior (Loeber et al., 2012). Few studies have examined the role of neurological deficits specifically in the case of oppositional defiant disorder. The focus has been mostly on conduct disorder, where studies have shown a relationship between neurological deficits and reduced temporal lobe volume, resulting in deficits of executive function and inhibition (Rubia, 2011a; Rubia, Halari, Mohammad, Taylor, & Brammer, 2011). Studies have shown that prenatal toxins, such as nicotine and alcohol, are associated with disruptive behavior (Latimer et al., 2012). In conclusion, few studies have examined the biological bases of oppositional defiant disorder specifically, but many of the biological bases for conduct disorder apply here as well.

Studies on **environmental** factors have consistently established a link between parenting and familial characteristics and the development of oppositional defiant disorder. Family dysfunction, lower levels of family income, higher levels of authoritarian parenting, lower levels of parental warmth and supervision, and inconsistent discipline are all implicated in the disorder's development. In addition, insecure attachment to the primary caregiver has also been associated with oppositional defiance (Fearon, Bakermans-Kranenburg, van IJzendoorn, Lapsley, & Roisman, 2010). Inconsistent, irritable, explosive, inflexible, and rigid discipline along with low parental supervision and involvement are thought to play a role as well (Kimonis & Frick, 2011).

Some experts have emphasized the need to pay greater attention to **child characteristics** such as the capacity for emotional regulation, frustration tolerance, adaptation, and problem-solving skills (Cavanagh, Quinn, Duncan, Graham, & Balbuena, 2014; Greene, 2006). The failure to possess such skills results in a lack of compliance, defined as the ability to delay one's own needs and wants in deference to those of an authority figure. If compliance is the result of having learned a complex set of social-cognitive skills, oppositional behavior (understood as a lack of compliance) can be understood as the child having a learning disability—that is, an inability to learn the skills needed for compliance (Greene, 2006; Matthys, Vanderschuren, Schutter, & Lochman, 2012). This lack of executive skills is also present in the psychiatric disorder most comorbid with oppositional defiant disorder—namely, ADHD—leading to the conjecture that ADHD may "set the stage" for the disorder. The child is not able to learn from past events nor anticipate the consequences of his or her actions (working memory), responds with a high level of emotion such as screaming or swearing (emotional regulation), has trouble responding immediately to adults' requests (shifting cognitive set), and is limited in the repertoire of alternate responses (problem-solving skills) available to him (Greene, 2006; Matthys et al., 2012; Rhodes, Park, Seth, & Coghill, 2012).

Children with oppositional defiant disorder have trouble encoding social cues, generating alternative solutions, and choosing among the most appropriate solutions. Their preferred means of solving conflicts is through aggression, because cognitively it is the only means available to them.

In summary, research has investigated the etiological component of oppositional defiant disorder through two dimensions—parent or family characteristics and child characteristics—though researchers disagree over which dimension is the primary one. Do child characteristics associated with oppositional defiant disorder result from certain parenting practices, or is the reverse true? The most likely explanation is that there is an interaction effect between child and parent, where the parent's response to a lack of compliance can serve to increase frustration and arousal in the child (Kochanska, Kim, Boldt, & Yoon, 2013).

Recommended Treatments for Oppositional Defiant Disorder

The three most popular treatment programs for oppositional defiant disorder are parent–child interaction therapy (McNeil & Hembree-Kigin, 2010), problem-solving skills training together with parent management training (Kazdin, 2010), and the Incredible Years training series (IYTS) (Webster-Stratton, 2011). While all three programs enjoy empirical support, the IYTS is perhaps the most well-known and has the most empirical support. Its use of videotaped modeling has proven especially effective, and the fact that it has a teacher-training component makes it especially attractive to those who work in schools with young children, particularly ages 6 through 10, for whom the program was designed. It can be adapted, however, to older children. The IYTS has three different types of programs: one for parents, one for children, and one for teachers.

The teacher component consists of a four-day (32-hour) training appropriate for teachers, school counselors, and psychologists. The goals of the training are to increase teachers' use of effective classroom management strategies for dealing with disruptive behaviors, promote positive relationships with difficult students, strengthen social skills in the classroom and beyond, and strengthen collaboration between teachers and parents (Webster-Stratton, Reid, & Beauchaine, 2011). School personnel learn effective problem-solving strategies to help children with oppositional defiant disorder improve their peer relationships and, at the same time, help their peers respond more effectively to them.

All three training programs are video based, a unique aspect of the IYTS, and research supports its effectiveness. Models used in the videotapes reflect a diversity of age, culture, socioeconomic status, and temperament. Models are often unrehearsed and show both the right and wrong approaches to interacting effectively with children with oppositional defiant disorder. Focused discussions, designed to promote learning and mutual support among members in the group, follow all presentations of videotaped vignettes. The inclusion of training for different constituencies (parents, children, and teachers) results from the premise that the origin of oppositional defiant disorder and its maintenance are the result of a complex interaction where outcome is dependent upon the interrelationships between children, parents, teachers, and peers (Webster-Stratton, Reid, & Beauchaine, 2011).

Characteristics and Symptoms of Conduct Disorder

According to the *DSM-5* (APA, 2013), conduct disorder is "a repetitive and persistent pattern of behavior in which the basic rights of others or major age-appropriate societal norms or rules are violated" (p. 469). The *DSM-5* distinguishes two subtypes based on age (childhood-onset type and adolescent-onset type) and three levels of severity based on the number of conduct problems presented (mild, moderate, and severe). Age of onset is a significant factor in determining the future course of conduct disorder. The adolescent type develops after age 10, usually with the onset of puberty. Well over 50% of those with early-onset conduct disorder (before age 8) continue with serious problems into adulthood, marked by disrupted and violent relationships, vocational problems, and substance abuse; anywhere from 25% to 40% develop adult antisocial personality disorder. They are more likely to drop out of school. On the contrary, about 85% of those with adolescent-onset type show an absence of antisocial behaviors by their early 20s (Pardini & Frick, 2013).

Among community samples, the prevalence rate for conduct disorder is between 2% and 4%. The ratio of prevalence, boys to girls, ranges from 2:1 to 4:1. Childhood-onset conduct disorder is more common among boys; however, before the age of 5, rates are more or less equivalent for both sexes (Merikangas et al., 2010). Researchers have found significant differences in rates of conduct disorder among ethnic groups. African American youth, compared to White youth, have higher rates. Such differences might be contextual, because a greater percentage of children of color live in neighborhoods with higher rates of crime, poverty, and violence. Evaluator bias can also play a role in assessing clients of color more or less severely (Gushue, 2004; Gushue, Constantine, & Sciarra, 2008).

Children and adolescents with conduct disorder often suffer from other disorders, the most frequent of which are ADHD, learning disability, anxiety, and depression. ADHD is the most highly comorbid disorder. ADHD is more frequent among those diagnosed with childhood-onset conduct disorder, and this subgroup tends to display more chronic delinquency and more severely aggressive acts during adolescence and more violent offenses in adulthood. Children with conduct disorder have high rates of anxiety and depression. Estimations are that anywhere from 15% to 31% of children with conduct disorder have depression and anxiety (Beauchaine, Hinshaw, & Pang, 2010; Polier, Vloet, Herpertz-Dahlmann, Laurens, & Hodgins, 2012). Those who are depressed are at an increased risk for suicidal ideation. Since children with conduct disorder have pervasive relationship problems, the high rates of anxiety and depression can also be the result of interpersonal conflicts.

Additional subtypes of conduct problems include aggressive versus nonaggressive behaviors, overt versus relational aggression, and reactive versus proactive aggression (Kimonis & Frick, 2006). Nonaggressive behaviors such as being stubborn, angry, defiant, and touchy are more appropriate of oppositional defiant disorder; whereas bullying, fighting, property violations such as vandalism, cruelty to animals, and setting things on fire are more indicative of conduct disorder. Overt aggression involves hitting, pushing, kicking, and threatening, in contrast to relational aggression, which is designed to damage relationships and peer group affiliations through gossiping and spreading rumors (Kimonis & Frick, 2006; Marsee et al., 2011).

Children evidence either reactive or proactive aggression. Proactive aggression is carefully planned and designed with a clear purpose in mind—for example, to obtain some material benefit (robbery), to hold power over others (bullying), or to increase one's social status such as through risk-taking behaviors (Kimonis & Frick, 2006). Reactive aggression, on the other hand, is retaliatory and based on real or perceived threats (Kimonis & Frick, 2006); these children evidence deficits in social information processing with a tendency to employ a hostile attribution bias to ambiguous situations (Lochman, Powell, Whidby, & Fitzgerald, 2006). A reactively aggressive child can turn a neutral encounter into a fight, often with deleterious consequences.

A final subtype of children with conduct-disordered behaviors is termed *callous and unemotional*. They tend to be more proactive in their aggression, suffer from an absence of guilt, like to participate in novel and exciting risk-taking behaviors, and are by and large insensitive to punitive consequences for their behaviors (Kimonis et al., 2014).

Causal Factors in the Development of Conduct Disorder

In general, the literature has divided the risk factors for developing conduct disorder into three categories: biological, psychological, and social. Multiple risk factors play a role in the development of conduct disorder. Kimonis and Frick (2011) suggested three methods for understanding the way multiple risk factors influence each other: cumulative, interactionist, and multiple pathways. The *cumulative* method is concerned simply with the number of risk factors—the more risk factors one has, the more likely one is to development conduct disorder. The *interactionist* perspective emphasizes the significance of certain risk factors interacting with others, and it is the combination rather than the accumulation of factors that results in conduct disorder. The *multiple-pathway* method suggests that different causal processes are involved in the development of conduct disorder, and each involves a different set of risk factors.

Biological factors are divided into genetics, hormones, neurotransmitter dysfunction, neurological issues, and prenatal toxin exposure (Hendren & Mullen, 2006). The most recent twin studies have examined the different subtypes of conduct disorder. Among people with adolescent-onset conduct disorder, family environment had more of an impact, in contrast to younger children with the disorder and comorbid ADHD, where the genetic influence was a more significant factor (Boden, Fergusson, & Horwood, 2010). Numerous studies have supported a strong association between preadolescent onset and parental antisocial behavior (Silberg, Maes, & Eaves, 2012) as well as parental psychopathology such as mothers with substance abuse, anxiety, or depression (Rowe et al., 2010). Some studies have also found hormone levels—particularly, high levels of testosterone and its derivatives—to be associated with conduct disorder (Matthys, Vanderschuren, & Schutter, 2013). Relatively new research in neuroanatomy has consistently shown frontal lobe damage in subjects prone to violence and aggression. Underarousal of the autonomic nervous system (i.e., lower heart rate) is associated with adolescent antisocial behavior and later criminality (Fahim et al., 2011). Prenatal and perinatal complications and maternal smoking or substance abuse during pregnancy have also been associated with behavioral problems. Finally, exposure to environmental toxins, such as lead, is also associated with delinquency and aggression (Marceau et al., 2013). There also exist a host of biological factors for which empirical research has established a link not with conduct disorder specifically but with violence and aggression—the prominent characteristics of the disorder—in general. A combination of these biological factors is more likely to contribute to a diagnosis of conduct disorder than any one factor alone.

In regard to **psychological factors**, the more consistent and stronger associations with conduct disorder are neuropsychological deficits, especially in the area of executive functioning; low achievement and school failure; and reading problems. In general, these children have lower-than-average IQs, particularly verbal IQ. Studies have also shown impairment in executive functions—concentration, attention, planning sequencing, and inhibition (Rubia, 2011b), along with deficits in reading (Hyatt, Haney-Caron, & Stevens, 2012).

The most significant **psychosocial factors** in the development of conduct disorder are abusive parenting practices, peer effects, and neighborhood or socioeconomic determinants. Poor family management (i.e., inconsistent and severe discipline, poor supervision, and failure to set clear expectations) is among the most powerful predictors of later delinquency (Henggeler & Sheidow, 2012). Another pathway to conduct disturbance seems evident: Children whose parents are hostile, negative, and neglectful are at risk for developing all sorts of mental health problems which in turn lead to patterns of antisocial and violent behavior

(Harold, Elam, Lewis, Rice, & Thapar, 2012). Undoubtedly, when children experience violence in the home, they come to understand violence as an acceptable way of dealing with conflict and solving problems. Exposure to high levels of family and marital conflict increase the risk for later violence (Ehrensaft & Cohen, 2012). Peer-related factors in predicting conduct problems are having delinquent siblings, delinquent peers, and gang memberships (Bierman & Sasser, 2014). Neighborhood and socioeconomic factors that contribute to the disorder in youth are poverty, community disorganization, availability of drugs and firearms, and neighborhood adults involved in crime (Frick, 2012). The greater the number of risk factors, the more likely a youth will have a diagnosis of conduct disorder.

Recommended Treatments for Conduct Disorder

There are four effective treatment strategies for conduct disorder: individual cognitive behavioral, family based, multisystemic, and psychopharmacological.

Cognitive-behavioral treatment focuses primarily on thought processes and employs behavioral techniques to change those processes seen as responsible for problematic behavior. The helper attempts to engage the student in new ways of thinking that will result in new ways of feeling and behaving. Since aggressive children tend to perceive neutral acts by others as hostile, the helper can work with them around their perceptions and change some of their faulty thinking (Beck, 2011). The teaching of problem-solving skills and relaxation training can also form part of the treatment. Empirical studies over the years have found cognitive-behavioral treatment to be moderately effective in treating conduct disorder, though less effective than family-based and multisystemic treatments (Kazdin, 2011).

Family-based interventions fall into two categories: those that focus on parenting and work exclusively with the primary caregivers in terms of parent management training and those that work with the entire family system. Parent management training is primarily for preschool and elementary school children who are evidencing conduct problems. The theoretical basis is the assumption that conduct problems are developed and sustained in the home by maladaptive parent–child interactions (Kazdin, 2010). The trainer works with the parents to alter their interaction with the child by teaching them to give clear rules and commands, positive reinforcement for compliance, time-outs and loss of privileges for noncompliance, negotiation, and contingency contracting with consistent consequences for unwanted behavior (Hagen, Ogden, & Bjørnebekk, 2011). Numerous studies have shown parent management training to be effective in both the short and long term. However, parental resistance and psychopathology are impediments to treatment.

Family systems therapy treats the entire family (defined as those living together) and results from the notion that the symptoms of conduct disorder may serve a function in the family system. For example, a family counselor might view conduct disorder as the family's need for avoiding interpersonal contact or as a way of distracting a child's mother and father from their own relationship problems. Functional family therapy consists of three phases: engagement and enactment, behavioral change, and generalization (Alexander & Robbins, 2011). During the first phase, the counselor meets with the family, knowing that within a short period the family will demonstrate its familiar ways of behaving. The counselor is alert to patterns of communication, coalition, and boundaries being either too diffuse or too rigid. In the second phase, the counselor begins to interrupt these familiar patterns and restore power and authority to the executive subsystem. In the third phase, the counselor teaches the family to apply its new learning by anticipating problems and practicing interventions to prevent them from relapsing into old and familiar ways of relating. The advantage of functional family therapy is its short-term focus—anywhere from 6 to 12 sessions. Two disadvantages are the difficulty of engaging the entire family system and the lack of helpers sufficiently trained to work confidently with the entire family. However, there is some empirical support for its effectiveness (Henggeler & Sheidow, 2012).

More recently, **multisystemic treatment** for conduct disorder has shown the greatest success. This treatment goes beyond family treatment because it considers the family system as important but only one of a number of systems in which a child is embedded (Henggeler & Sheidow, 2012). These other systems include peers, school, and the neighborhood. Research has shown that not only family relations but also involvement with deviant peers, school difficulties, and neighborhood or community factors are strong contributors to delinquency. At the family level, multisystemic treatment will employ some form of functional family therapy outlined above. At the peer level, interventions attempt to diminish the association with deviant peers and replace those relationships with more positive ones by facilitating membership in organized athletics, afterschool activities, and church youth groups (Borduin, Munschy, Wagner, & Taylor, 2011). At the school level, the provider develops strategies to help parents monitor school performance by opening lines of communication between parents and teachers and structuring time at home to go over homework and other school-related activities. If biological factors are involved, multisystemic treatment employs the use of psychopharmacology, an intervention discussed below. Multisystemic treatment is broad-based and flexible, attempting to consider and deal with any factors contributing to conduct disorder. For example, the provider would also address a parent's stress resulting from unemployment that complicates the task of effective parenting. In spite of its documented success, multisystemic treatment is not always the preferred mode of treatment for conduct disorder. One disadvantage is that it is time-consuming, and practical concerns like insurance reimbursement for a provider's time spent outside the traditional therapeutic encounter make it difficult for some clinics and programs to implement this treatment.

Recent literature has established a genetic and neurobiological link in the development of conduct disorder. This has led to an increased consideration of **psychopharmacological intervention** with this population. The most prescribed medications for conduct problems are stimulants, especially methylphenidate (Ritalin being the most popular). Since conduct disorder is highly comorbid with ADHD, stimulants known to be effective in reducing the impulsivity associated with ADHD have reduced conduct problems in children with both conduct disorder and ADHD (Matthys et al., 2012). While there is some evidence for the effectiveness of several medications for reducing the symptoms of conduct disorder, the support is far from conclusive. At most, medications are partially helpful, and results that are more effective require the need for complementary treatment modalities. When psychosocial treatment is combined with medication therapy for conduct problems, the rate of improvement tends to be greater (Farmer et al., 2011).

In spite of studies showing the effectiveness for different interventions for conduct disorder, a number of challenges and limitations exist in achieving success with this population. A significant number of children do not improve. Improvement is difficult to sustain over time and across settings, and rarely does a child with conduct disorder reduce behaviors to a normative level. Children under the age of 8 show the greatest improvement, which emphasizes the need for early intervention, and suggests that interventions with older children and adolescents are less effective (Kimonis & Frick, 2006). Because they work with children on a daily basis, schools that have developed school-based intervention programs for children with conduct disorder have the greatest chances of success in reducing aggressive behaviors.

UNDERSTANDING THE CONDUCT-DISORDERED STUDENT FROM AN ATTACHMENT PERSPECTIVE

The details of the vignette indicate that Marcus quite clearly meets the diagnostic criteria of conduct disorder, and his severe forms of externalizing behaviors suggest a disorganized attachment style. The reader will remember that a disorganized attachment style results primarily from experiencing the attachment figure as frightening or frightened, in contrast to an avoidant style, which results from the primary attachment figure being unavailable. Based on his family's dysfunction, Marcus's disorganized style is no surprise. His father was mostly likely a very frightening figure with his own externalizing behaviors, most importantly in the form of spousal and child abuse. It is very likely that Marcus's mother, the victim of a male batterer, suffers from unresolved trauma that has prevented her from providing a secure attachment experience for her son. Disorganized attachment style and an attachment figure who suffers from unresolved trauma are highly correlated. The two most important figures in Marcus's life charged with protecting him and providing security are frightening. All children experience fear, but the disorganized child experiences fear without solution and therefore employs the psychological defense of fight or flight. Marcus prefers to fight, which takes the form of severe externalized aggression. There are two types of disorganized attachment style: punitive controlling, manifested by hostility and aggression toward the parent, or caregiver controlling, manifested by trying to protect the parent. Marcus's style is clearly the former, where he intimidates his mother and other attachment figures like teachers as well as his peers. Let's be honest— Marcus is not a very likable character. However, it may help to understand that his severe externalization, which takes the form of threats and fights, are really ways of coping with his own fright that results from his inability to rely on attachment figures, an experience that he carries into institutions like school.

The disorganized child has the most difficulties in school, both academically and socially. Social bonding is either completely absent or very low, which raises concerns about the potential for large-scale violence—something Marcus has threatened to do. Empathy, reciprocity, mutuality, and sensitivity (all learned from a caring and responsive attachment figure) are lacking in Marcus. The reader may remember that the Minnesota study (Sroufe et al., 2005) found that the strongest predictor of externalization was a disruptive male presence in the home. Marcus's father was undoubtedly that and most likely exposed Marcus to traumatizing domestic violence. Marcus grew up with a frightening or frightened attachment figure, and he developed a defense of extreme externalization in the form of unmitigated aggression toward others. Working with and trying to help Marcus will not be easy, and the prognosis for him to turn his life around is not good. However, certain responses by the school can ameliorate Marcus's situation, while others may worsen it.

UNDERSTANDING TEACHER INTERVENTIONS FOR THE CONDUCT-DISORDERED STUDENT FROM BOTH ATTACHMENT AND PEDAGOGICAL PERSPECTIVES

Mr. Malone, the science teacher to whom Marcus is assigned, has a very "traditional" view of discipline: the "authoritarian" model, which might not be effective with a student with a conduct disorder, like Marcus.

Mr. Malone: "Removing a Bad Seed"

Mr. Malone, Marcus's science teacher, feels that the only kind of intervention Marcus understands and responds to is a kind of "quid pro quo" social justice. In the staff room, he recounts an article in the New York Times *in which the "broken windows" approach to policing and punishment was extolled. "The only thing Marcus understands and his misbehavior warrants is punishment, swift and severe!" he remarks to colleagues. Indeed, it would appear that Mr. Malone has given up on any attempt at developing a rapport with Marcus and is determined to write him up whenever his behavior violates a school rule. He seems to be intent on getting Marcus expelled from the school district, or, at minimum, suspended.*

Whenever Marcus is in his science class, Mr. Malone avoids making eye contact and never calls on him to answer a question or engage in discussion. A few of Mr. Malone's students have actually noticed that he rarely focuses his attention on the side of the classroom where Marcus sits. In response, it appears to the students that Marcus plays on Mr. Malone's fear of him and deliberately lingers after the bell, almost daring Mr. Malone to confront him or threaten him with consequences. Perhaps to compensate for his fear of Marcus and to mitigate his self-deprecation at being intimidated by a student, Mr. Malone has begun a campaign of vilification. He seems determined to enlist the support of other teachers in an effort to collect sufficient evidence to have Marcus removed from the school.

Mr. Malone from an Attachment Perspective

Mr. Malone's approach to dealing with Marcus is a popular one and may even have some validity. Simply put, this approach says that if you commit the crime, you pay the fine! The teacher feels that the only way for Marcus to change his ways is for him to suffer the appropriate consequences of his actions. The "broken windows" approach espoused by Mr. Malone suggests that making Marcus pay for his minor acts of violence now will prevent him from committing crimes that are more serious in the future. Like many teachers, Mr. Malone seems to have taken Marcus's behavior personally, since he "has given up on any attempts at developing a rapport with Marcus." This implies that in the past, he has tried to establish rapport with Marcus, and perhaps met only with rejection and hostility. This would bother almost any teacher, except one who mentalizes and is able to get beyond the actual behavior and see the story behind it. Maybe Mr. Malone, for whatever reason, reminds Marcus of his father.

Cognitive Behavior Therapy (CBT) uses the triangle of human behavior. At the top point of the triangle are thoughts, and the two bottom points represent feelings and behaviors (see Figure 3.1). Teachers who mentalize use all three points of the triangle. What may be driving Marcus's behavior are thoughts and feelings about his father. From an attachment perspective, we could say that Marcus's behaviors are designed to provoke rejection, and this is exactly what Mr. Malone does. The interactions between Marcus and Mr. Malone parallel the interactions between Marcus and his father, who rejected him. The solution, from an attachment perspective, would be to give Marcus a reaction that he least expects—one of empathy and understanding and acceptance—with the hopeful goal of changing the student's IWM of a world that is frightening and cannot be trusted. In Marcus's world, the best way to deal with his own fright is to frighten. So what is preventing Mr. Malone from offering an alternative reaction that does not reinforce Marcus's IWM?

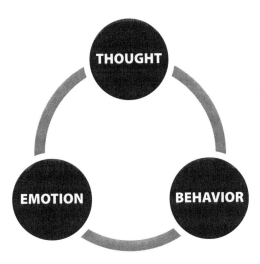

Figure 3.1: The Tri-partite framework of human behavior

The answer is a bit tricky. We have already suggested that one reason could be the teacher's inability to mentalize, the result of an insecure attachment style that would explain why he takes Marcus's behavior so personally. The fact that Mr. Malone is determined to serve Marcus the appropriate punishment suggests a power struggle between the student and the teacher's own understanding of authority. Mr. Malone may very well be classified as dismissing on the AAI, which would suggest an avoidant attachment style as a child, causing Mr. Malone to display low sensitivity. For Mr. Malone, adding emotion and empathy into the equation with Marcus is a sign of weakness. The only way to deal with a tough person like Marcus is through being tougher and not letting Marcus take advantage of others—least of all teachers!

The question remains whether Marcus is capable of a genuine relationship. At age 16 with many symptoms of conduct disorder, and perhaps well on his way to a diagnosis of antisocial personality disorder, he will take advantage of and manipulate even those who show him kindness, understanding, and empathy. We know Mr. Malone's answer to this question: Marcus is a "bad seed" who cannot be trusted; the only thing he will understand is swift and severe punishment. Remember that the hallmark of the sociopath is a lack of capacity for empathy. Mr. Malone's position indicates that he considers Marcus a bona fide sociopath.

The other school of thought is that Marcus is the way he is because he was never shown empathy, reciprocity, mutuality, and genuineness, and this led to a disorganized attachment style. If he is shown these qualities in a substitute attachment relationship, such as that with a teacher, Marcus will be able to change his IWM and become more capable of a genuine relationship. The following teacher vignette involving Mr. Gruener represents this alternate approach.

Mr. Malone from a Pedagogical Perspective

Mr. Malone, like many teachers, believes in an intractable interpretation and consistent application of the rules. While the principles of effective pedagogy encourage the fair and consistent application of rules, this should be tempered by an appreciation for the learning and behavioral differences inherent in the student. Sound pedagogy requires that the teacher learn as much as he can about his students and himself, since we know from research (e.g., Austin et al., 2011) that challenging students require a sense of belongingness and acceptance before they can learn in the classroom. This can only be achieved through the formation of a positive teacher–student relationship, as recommended by Noddings (2005) and Smith (2012).

Mr. Malone seems unwilling to pursue such a relationship with Marcus at present, and his negative predisposition is the antithesis of effective pedagogy. By avoiding Marcus, even at the expense of other students' learning, Mr. Malone is actually becoming less effective as a teacher. He has allowed his fear and disdain for a student to influence his teaching, and he is unable to perceive the effect of this conflict on his other students.

According to the principles of sound pedagogy outlined in Chapter 2, Mr. Malone first needs to summon the courage to examine his own teaching style, the "self-reflection" advocated by Russell (1997), Schön (1983), and Sellar (2013), and obtain the insights of colleagues he respects who evidence successful teaching. He would also benefit from student feedback regarding their perceptions of his teaching. Finally, he might heed another principle of sound pedagogy: to develop prosocial relationships with each of his students. Again, researchers suggest that students appreciate and respond to the genuine efforts of teachers to learn about their lives outside the four walls of the classroom—their "extracurricular" lives (e.g., Austin et al., 2011). He might find that as he seeks to understand Marcus and the family and environmental dynamics that affect Marcus's life in and out of school, he will gain a greater appreciation for Marcus's challenges and, ultimately, develop compassion toward this troubled youth. Indeed, the work of both Freire (1970) and Bruner (1996) emphasized how important it is to understand how the nexus of the student's and the teacher's cultures affect each other. Furthermore, according to Smith (2012) and Tompkins (1996), Mr. Malone should "motivate and entice" students like Marcus to want to learn. This is not to suggest that he will succeed in establishing a rapport with Marcus or effect positive behavioral change—and certainly this cannot be accomplished if Marcus feels ostracized and rejected; however, by incorporating some of the components of the framework described above, Mr. Malone will most certainly improve his pedagogical skills and grow as a teacher.

Mr. Gruener: "Extending a Friendly Hand"

Mr. Gruener, Marcus's math teacher and the school's ice hockey coach, seems to have developed a very positive rapport with Marcus, despite the persistent urging of colleagues to be cautious around him and avoid forming a relationship since "Marcus can't be trusted." Mr. Gruener ignored their pleas and continued to befriend Marcus, listening sympathetically to his concerns, worries, and fears about his father and about his future—that he seemed destined, like his father, for a life in constant conflict with the law and the establishment. Mr. Gruener invited Marcus to come to his home, meet his family, and share a meal, but while Marcus seemed to appreciate the gesture, he never actually took Mr. Gruener up on the offer. Unlike other teachers and the school administrators, Mr. Gruener was never condescending to Marcus and was always encouraging—even inviting him to come to the practice sessions of the hockey team and join in on scrimmages. Since ice hockey was Marcus's passion, he availed himself of this opportunity. He seemed to be another person on the ice. Even team members who heard that Marcus was a fighter and troublemaker, and were anticipating problems, found him to be a very talented player and a decent person.

On one occasion, Mr. Malone approached Mr. Gruener to discuss his very negative experiences with Marcus and to warn him about Marcus's potential for violence. Mr. Gruener listened politely, then shared a bit of Marcus's family history as well as his successful social experience when scrimmaging with the ice hockey team. He also encouraged Mr. Malone to give Marcus a chance and try to provide positive reinforcement whenever possible. Mr. Malone's response revealed his dis-

like for Marcus. "He's a real bad seed," Mr. Malone said. "He's headed for a tough life. I could easily see him hurting someone, or worse, and ending up behind bars for a very long time. Give him a wide berth!"

Mr. Gruener from an Attachment Perspective

Mr. Gruener's approach to Marcus represents the second school of thought to dealing with a student whose attachment style is disorganized and who exhibits antisocial behaviors. Mr. Gruener's success with Marcus did not happen magically. Rather, Marcus tested Mr. Gruener in the same ways that he tests all teachers: by frightening and threatening. The difference most likely was that Mr. Gruener responded to Marcus's externalizing behaviors in ways that were unlike most teachers' reactions. He did not take Marcus's behaviors personally and understood that behind those behaviors was a history of deep hurt and fear. This allowed Mr. Gruener to get beyond Marcus's manifested behavior to the feelings and thoughts driving such behaviors.

Essentially, Mr. Gruener mentalizes and represents how a teacher with a secure attachment style can be so much more effective with even the most difficult students. Comments from other teachers for Mr. Gruener to be cautious are interesting. We would posit that Mr. Gruener, by mentalizing, *was* being cautious, because he was not simply reacting to Marcus. Not being cautious leads to pure reaction by teachers, which would reinforce Marcus's IWM and his own insecure relationship with his parents.

When reading the part where Marcus expresses his "concerns, worries, and fears about his father" to Mr. Gruener, one cannot help but wonder if this is just another form of manipulation by this budding sociopath, designed to get the teacher to feel sorry for him and then to take advantage of that feeling. It is clear how Mr. Malone would answer this question. Yet one of the theses of this book is that high-sensitivity teachers can change IWMs and can form attachment bonds even with the most difficult of students. Mr. Gruener seems to be doing exactly that and more. Getting Marcus involved with the ice hockey team is textbook intervention for several reasons. First, it serves as a healthy outlet for Marcus's aggression; second, it foments school bonding; and third, it helps to develop positive peer relations. Alfred Adler (1964) believed that all misbehavior results from feelings of not belonging that originate from one's early family life and then carry over into the school. Marcus did not feel he belonged in his family, which resulted in low or no school bonding. Adler, however, also believed that schools can provide a corrective experience for those students who suffered from a lack of belongingness. Schools are rife with opportunities for helping students find some activity or group that will ameliorate feelings of alienation. Mr. Gruener, by involving Marcus in the ice hockey team, is doing exactly that. Will it work in the end? No one is sure except for Mr. Malone; he is convinced that Marcus is "headed for a tough life."

Finally, we would like to address Mr. Gruener's inviting Marcus to his house for dinner. One can sense that the teacher hopes to accentuate the bonding with Marcus and provide him with a corrective paternal and family experience, but this is a risky intervention for several reasons. First, it blurs the boundary between student and teacher; second, it could have an inadvertently negative effect, in that Marcus will see a family very different from his own; and third, the experience may be too overwhelming and confusing to Marcus. We do not know why Marcus never did go to the teacher's house. It may be that at some level even Marcus knew this was not a good idea. The whole experience does bring up the issue of proper boundaries around helping. Mr. Gruener probably wanted to do everything possible to help and save Marcus from a "tough life." Yet he must recognize there is a limit to what he can do, and the ultimate outcome for Marcus is not totally within his control. His secure attachment style should allow him to recognize this. He is to be commended for taking such a different approach from the rest of the teachers, but he should not, as some teachers are wont to do, fall into the role of savior rather than helper.

Mr. Gruener from a Pedagogical Perspective

In sharp contrast to Mr. Malone, Mr. Gruener embodies many of the most salient principles of pedagogy outlined in Chapter 2. First, he appears to know himself and his teaching strengths and seems very comfortable with his identity both as a person and as a teacher (Loughran, 1997; Palmer, 1998). In support of this perception, as noted in the previous section, Mr. Gruener did not take Marcus's behavior personally and tried to understand the feelings and thoughts underlying such behaviors. Similarly, through his treatment of Marcus, Mr. Gruener appears to possess the "certainty, positivity, and the unity of self and moral goals" extolled by Stout (2005, p. 195), which is a tenet of our recommended pedagogical framework described in detail in Chapter 2.

Moreover, Mr. Gruener seems determined to accept Marcus and allow him to reveal himself, without the influence of prejudice based on Marcus's past behaviors and hearsay. Mr. Gruener clearly understands the effects of Marcus's cultural milieu on his social conduct (Bruner, 1996; Freire, 1970). In response to this knowledge, Mr. Gruener makes every effort to include Marcus and affords him the trust and opportunity to make responsible choices, which few if any adults have offered in the past. Again, one of the key principles of effective pedagogy is the willingness of the teacher to reveal himself appropriately to his students. This modeling by the teacher creates the climate of trust that gives his students permission to do likewise, thus helping to build healthy, prosocial teacher–student bonds (Noddings, 2005; Smith, 2012). In addition, Mr. Gruener seems to demonstrate Smith's (2012) three key elements of effective pedagogy: animation, reflection, and action. By *animation*, Smith means "bringing life into situations and introducing students to new experiences." In his unequivocal acceptance of Marcus, Mr. Gruener is certainly providing him with a new experience. Smith describes *reflection* as "creating moments and spaces to explore lived experiences." One senses that Mr. Gruener will provide such an opportunity for reflection as he works with Marcus. Further, Smith defines *action* to mean "working with people so that they are able to make changes in their lives" (2012, p. 10). Clearly, Mr. Gruener has facilitated such an opportunity for Marcus. Finally, as Maslow (1954) first identified, individuals need to feel that they belong in order to flourish in a community. Mr. Gruener has encouraged and accepted Marcus as a member of his ice hockey team, and Marcus has responded positively, flourishing in such an affirming, inclusive social environment. Here, accepted and not judged based on his past behaviors, Marcus is finally free to become the productive young man he has always yearned to be. Mr. Gruener's pedagogical skills have facilitated this social and behavioral transformation. Moreover, the journey to self-awareness is just beginning for Marcus.

This section offered a detailed analysis of Marcus's case from both an attachment and pedagogical perspective. Because disruptive disorders manifest similarly in terms of observable classroom behaviors, the following section presents vignettes about oppositional defiant disorder.

STUDENT VIGNETTE: "MICHELLE" (OPPOSITIONAL DEFIANT DISORDER)

Michelle, a student in Mrs. Barnette's sixth-grade class, has become very defiant and oppositional of late. Despite Mrs. Barnette's best efforts to ameliorate the situation by speaking with Michelle after class and providing positive reinforcement for even minimal compliance with classroom rules, Michelle's defiant behaviors have escalated. Her comments are negatively affecting the climate in Mrs. Barnette's classroom as well as her quality of instruction. For example, the other day, when Mrs. Barnette asked Michelle to stop talking during her lesson, Michelle retorted, "We were talking about the assignment; I thought you wanted us to do that. I guess you just want good little boys and girls with no minds of their own. Mrs. Glazer lets us talk."—And as an aside to the class—"She's a real teacher!" A few of the other students suppress laughter, and several applaud her audacity. To be sure, Michelle occasionally exhibits defiant behavior in Mrs. Glazer's class as well; however, Mrs. Glazer manages to redirect Michelle and help her to de-escalate the behavior before it reaches the level of insubordination, a misbehavior addressed under the school's new "zero-tolerance" policy, which demands a call home, an office referral, and an afterschool detention. Mrs. Barnette seems to be fearful of the power wielded by her petite charge, Michelle, and is somewhat reluctant to impose punitive consequences—possibly because Michelle's father, a successful politician, is also a member of the school board! Mrs. Glazer has made some inquiries about the possible cause of Michelle's recent behavioral changes and has learned that Michelle's parents are in the midst of a divorce and are engaged in a bitter dispute over child custody.

Michelle from an Attachment Perspective

As written, Michelle would not fit the criteria for oppositional defiant disorder due to the behavior's recent onset and the implication that her oppositional qualities are more a reaction to her parents' divorce. Her more appropriate diagnosis might be adjustment disorder with disturbance of conduct. For a diagnosis of oppositional defiant disorder, the oppositionality would need to have been present prior to sixth grade and exist in a variety of contexts toward authority figures. In any event, it is possible to examine Michelle's behavior from an attachment perspective, because opposition and defiance are often the result of insecure attachment (Lavigne, Gouze, Hopkins, Bryant, & LeBailly, 2012).

Little is known about Michelle's attachment history, but once again, she is an example of how a contextual event like divorce can change a student's behavior, especially when the event heightens a sense of insecurity. Custody battles tend to be ugly, and children often find themselves caught in the middle, needing to choose one parent over another—something most children do not want to do. Furthermore, Michelle's fate seems to be in the hands of family court and beyond her control. Oppositional behaviors are designed to take control away from authority figures. Michelle's actions in the classroom are both punitive and rejecting, especially toward Mrs. Barnette. Michelle's invalidation of her teacher is most likely the result of her own feeling of invalidation in light of the custody battle and her parents' divorce. Behaviors such as Michelle's can be extremely disruptive to the classroom environment. If a teacher were to take these attacks on her integrity personally, chances are she would overact or enter into a power struggle with the student. Both of these reactions would only escalate an already difficult situation.

Mrs. Barnette: "Michelle Is a Different Person, so Unlike Who She Was Last Year!"

Mrs. Barnette is having a very difficult time understanding what has happened to cause such a drastic change in Michelle's behavior. She remembers a different Michelle in years past—a kind, respectful, conscientious student who was the epitome of a well-behaved, cooperative young woman, one who always seemed eager to learn. Mrs. Barnette wonders if she is doing something differently in class or if she has in some way offended Michelle; Michelle really seems to have a vendetta against her. To further complicate things, Michelle's father is a very influential man in the town and is currently serving on the school board. As a teacher in a union-free school district, Mrs. Barnette is acutely aware of his ability to influence the board's decision regarding her tenure and award of merit pay. Mrs. Barnette feels she has been blindsided by this angry and adversarial student, whom she used to enjoy teaching. Though she keeps reminding herself that the issue is really Michelle's, her self-efficacy has been shaken, and she wonders whether Michelle is right about her pedagogical skills—perhaps Mrs. Glazer is a better teacher!

Mrs. Glazer: "The Disruptions at Home Are the Likely Cause of Michelle's Recent Defiance"

Mrs. Glazer, voted the school district and regional teacher of the year twice in the last decade, knows she can teach her subjects and teach them well! She is, therefore, unflappable when challenged by Michelle's defiant attitude. Understanding Michelle's current troubles at home, Mrs. Glazer is determined to provide positive behavioral interventions and supports for her rather than impose the requisite penalties for insubordination in accordance with the school's "zero-tolerance" policy. Mrs. Glazer knows that once the issues affecting her family are resolved, Michelle's behavior will invariably improve. She knows how to re-engage and entice Michelle to want to learn new things. This success with Michelle is largely due to her highly developed pedagogical skills and the fact that she truly cares about Michelle's well-being and success in school.

Mrs. Barnette and Mrs. Glazer from an Attachment Perspective

There is a discrepancy between the two teacher vignettes in regard to the information that each teacher possesses. The second vignette makes clear that Mrs. Glazer knows about Michelle's troubles at home, while the first vignette with Mrs. Barnette makes no mention of such troubles. Information about a student's background always helps to understand that student and allows the teacher to mentalize and consider all the factors that might be responsible for a student's behavior. It is quite realistic that one teacher might know something about a particular student that another teacher might not know due to issues of confidentiality. This might be the fine line between Mrs. Glazer and Mrs. Barnett; Mrs. Barnett's lack of information about Michelle's family situation makes it harder for her not to take the student's attacks personally. She reminds herself that the issue is Michelle's, but she does not possess the same security as Mrs. Glazer. While Mrs. Glazer seems to focus more on what is the best way to intervene with Michelle, Mrs. Barnett focuses the attention onto herself, which often occurs when insecurity is present. It is hard not to feel a certain amount of compassion for Mrs. Barnett, because she feels her job could be in jeopardy due to Michelle's father being an influential school board member. This limits her effectiveness in dealing with Michelle and results in a preoccupied state of mind. Mrs. Glazer, in contrast, appears to operate from a more secure-autonomous state of mind that prevents her from taking Michelle's behaviors personally and allows her to search for creative ways to engage the student. In general, it is best to avoid getting into a power struggle with students who exhibit oppositional qualities. Their behaviors may seduce teachers into such a struggle, but the students usually win that battle. A better intervention is to allow the student to feel she has some control. In the case of Michelle, where she might feel that her life is out of control due to the divorce and custody battle, a teacher might give her prosocial responsibilities in and out of the classroom to make her feel that she is in charge to some degree.

Mrs. Barnette and Mrs. Glazer from a Pedagogical Perspective

According to Palmer (1998) and Loughran (1997), teachers really need to strive to be honest with themselves about who they are and what they know and believe, and be courageous in that revelation—in other words, they need to know their "identity" and possess "integrity." Mrs. Barnette seems to be experiencing self-doubt because of the insinuations of a defiant, oppositional sixth grader and has seen her identity and integrity challenged. Likewise, while she has noted the sudden change in Michelle's demeanor, she does not appear to have taken the time to investigate its possible cause. Instead, Mrs. Barnette seems to be taking Michelle's insults personally, ascribing far too much power and control to an 11-year-old girl, and abdicating her responsibility to request collegial support. Furthermore, as Alexander (2004) noted, sound pedagogy "must demonstrate the commitment necessary to make daily decisions about instruction and learning" (p. 11); however, Mrs. Barnette seems frozen in indecision caused by self-doubt and the fear of recrimination. As a result, Mrs. Barnette is unable to work with Michelle in a way that enables her to change Michelle's behavior (Smith, 2012).

In sharp contrast to Mrs. Barnette, Mrs. Glazer enjoys a clear knowledge of herself and her competencies as a teacher. She appears to identify as a good teacher, one who possesses sound pedagogical skill. Furthermore, she has taken the time to investigate the possible cause of Michelle's dramatic change in disposition, which has likely prompted a sympathetic appreciation of Michelle's difficult family circumstances and their inevitable effects on her demeanor. Finally, in concert with her exceptional pedagogical skills, Mrs. Glazer knows how to "motivate and entice" Michelle to want to re-engage with her studies (Tompkins, 1996, p. xvi), and to eventually be able to change her behavior from oppositional to prosocial (Smith, 2012).

EFFECTIVE TEACHER RESPONSES

For students with a conduct disorder, like Marcus:

- Build a sense of community and belonging that includes every student in your classroom.
- Establish rules of conduct for the class and include yourself and their expectations of you in the discussion.
- Provide for choices—meaningful and appropriate ones.
- Triage the crises; some, like a fistfight, require immediate attention; others, such as an epithet uttered under the breath, do not.
- Provide meaningful praise and positive reinforcement. Connect the praise to a discrete accomplishment or behavior, not to some vague or future possibility.
- Find a reason to appreciate every student in your class. There must be some quality the student possesses that can be viewed as a strength.
- Get to know the likes and dislikes, the hobbies and pastimes, the passions and dreams of these students—it will help build relationships, and a teacher cannot truly provide help outside of one. Likewise, a teacher cannot be simultaneously uncaring and effective—not with a student with a conduct disorder.
- Provide meaningful learning experiences for these students; connect the lesson to real-life applications.
- Ignore small annoyances and disruptions. Students with conduct disorders are going to try to provoke the teacher—they expect to be disliked. Try not to fall prey to their contest of wills.
- Be consistent and fair with each student. Treating each student fairly, especially those with conduct disorders, does not mean treating each student the

same. Would it be fair to expect a student with cerebral palsy to run competitively in a race with physically able students? Essentially, being consistent with rewards and consequences means just that (Cavin, 1998).

For students with oppositional defiant disorder, like Michelle:

- Do not allow the child to draw you into an argument that can escalate. Likewise, be careful not to use ultimatums (e.g., "If you say one more word, I will assign you a 30-minute detention," or "Get up out of your seat and leave the room at once—I want you out of here!"). These kinds of responses often force the child to choose between compliance (sometimes viewed as a sign of weakness) and insubordination that will invariably result in punishment.
- Plan a regular conference time for the student during which her comments and expressed feelings are not subject to censure or sanctions. This will teach the student that there are socially appropriate times and places for expressing anger and frustration.
- Investigate the causes of the student's agitation. Take immediate steps to provide relief from the source and help the student select a more appropriate behavioral approach.
- Praise the student frequently for making appropriate behavioral choices. Remind the individual that, ultimately, she is responsible for both the good and bad ones.
- Become an expert in identifying the verbal and nonverbal signals characteristic to the individual that precede a behavioral incident.
- Say what you mean, and mean what you say! In other words, if you must give the student a warning or an ultimatum, make sure that you follow through. Sometimes teachers feel compelled to give the student an "if–then" condition: "If you do this, or if you don't do that, then . . . [name a consequence]." Occasionally, such an admonition is a reaction to what is perceived as outrageous behavior; frequently, it is simply a human response to what ostensibly is disrespect. Nevertheless, if you do assign a consequence, then you are duty bound to deliver. The same is true in the case of the promise of a reward. Students with oppositional defiant disorder are used to inconsistency in dealings with authority figures and the meting out of consequences, good or bad. This inconsistent treatment is often a factor in the development of their defiant behavior (Patterson, Reid, & Dishion, 1992; Chamberlain & Patterson, 1995).
- Set boundaries around the inappropriate behavior. Speak privately with the child and, keeping in mind that defiance of authority is a sign not of strength but of a fragile ego, establish yourself as a benevolent authority. Explain that although you understand that the child may have underlying issues and that you will help her try to understand them, you will not tolerate her inappropriate behavior. Stress the seriousness of the situation and the consequences if it persists (Pierangelo & Giuliani, 2001).

- Try to help the student understand why she is defiant. Encourage her to verbalize what she is feeling or why she does what she does. If she cannot give voice to her feelings, you may want to provide her with some descriptors. For example, you may want to say that you have seen other students defy authority because they felt they were not doing well in school, had problems at home, or felt rejected by peers (Pierangelo & Giuliani, 2001).

- If the defiant behavior follows a consistent pattern, confer with the student's parents to obtain information about any issues at home. Consult with the school counseling or social-work staff or the school psychologist about developing a behavioral contract for the student. Parent involvement will be important. Finally, if the problem is severe and persists, consult the school's pupil personnel or child study team (Pierangelo & Giuliani, 2001).

- Arrange for a safe and supervised "time-out" or "chill space." The purpose of such a place is to provide a neutral site for the student to cool off when she becomes aware that she is about to lose it. Give her a laminated "chill pass" to show you before she leaves the room. Praise her for her self-awareness and good choice in removing herself from the classroom and taking a positive time-out rather than succumbing to her volatile and unpredictable emotions. If the student seems to abuse this privilege, discuss your concerns in a private conference and negotiate the number of times she may use the pass, encouraging her to reduce the frequency of its use as she learns to employ more appropriate coping strategies. Suggestion: Because students who exhibit defiance disorders often prefer to receive praise or criticism in private, avoid publicly spotlighting them with public displays of praise and criticism. (Pierangelo & Giuliani, 2001)

Concluding Thoughts

This chapter discussed the two most commonly identified disruptive disorders: namely, oppositional defiant disorder and conduct disorder. While some researchers believe that oppositional defiant disorder is a precursor to conduct disorder, many maintain that the two are distinctly different disorders. Those who support this contention suggest that students with oppositional defiant disorder do not exhibit physical aggression, whereas students with conduct disorder clearly do. Likewise, the etiologies of the two disorders are very different. For example, students with oppositional defiance typically have parental caregivers or models who are either lax and permissive or authoritarian and repressive. On the other hand, students identified with conduct disorder tend to come from disorganized, dysfunctional homes in which one or both of the parental caregivers are abusive, life is chaotic, and parental behavior is unpredictable.

We also discussed some best-practice interventions that have demonstrated positive results in reducing maladaptive and antisocial behaviors in students with both oppositional defiant disorder and conduct disorder. As noted in the beginning of the chapter, the three most popular treatment programs for oppositional defiant disorder are parent-child interaction therapy, problem-solving skills training along with parent management training, and the Incredible Years training series. Of these three, the IYTS is perhaps the most popular and appears to be the most successful. For children and adolescents diagnosed with conduct disorder, multi-systemic treatment has shown the greatest success. This treatment goes beyond family treatment, considering a number of other systems as well—including peers, school, and neighborhood—that influence the affected child's treatment prognosis.

Finally, we reiterated the importance of reflecting on the influences of one's own parental caregivers as well as the caregivers of the student with oppositional defiant disorder or conduct disorder. Remember that, unaware of these influences, teachers can react in nontherapeutic ways to students' maladaptive behaviors. Teachers should reflect unequivocally on their teaching styles, with an eye to self-improvement and a determination to understand and include every child as a valued constituent of the class. This is the mission of purposeful teachers!

In the next chapter, we turn our attention to another set of challenging students: those who display high anxiety and, in turn, create anxiety in us!

CHAPTER 4

Teaching Students with Anxiety Disorders

STUDENT VIGNETTE: "VALERIE" (SEPARATION ANXIETY)

According to her mother, Valerie enjoyed going to school until the end of winter recess in eleventh grade. At the conclusion of the holidays, Valerie appeared increasingly despondent and experienced frequent sleeplessness and nausea prior to returning to school for the third quarter. Her mother, Miriam, reported that she had, herself, experienced a real sense of loss when her daughter returned to school after the holidays. When Valerie began to complain of an upset stomach one morning, Mrs. V. suggested that she stay home and recuperate. However, this behavior persisted for weeks, and Mr. V., a corporate executive, began to insist that his daughter return to school, suggesting to his wife that Valerie was "fine" and Mrs. V. was simply exacerbating the situation by permitting her daughter to miss school.

The situation worsened when Mr. V., together with his wife, drove Valerie to school in spite of her protests. When Mr. V. attempted to drop Valerie at the appropriate school entrance, Valerie screamed that she was really sick and fainted on the sidewalk, at which point Mrs. V. intervened and ordered Mr. V. to put Valerie back in the car and return home. Valerie's parents are both very influential community members, and Mrs. V. is a member of the school board. As a result of their influence, they were able to obtain a home tutor for Valerie. Valerie responded very well to this accommodation; however, after a few months, the school psychologist expressed concern that Valerie was not really addressing her separation anxiety issues and that they might worsen over time. Mr. V. asked her for suggestions, and the school psychologist recommended a residential placement to facilitate consistent school attendance and reduce the reinforcement of school avoidance by well-meaning caregivers, specifically Valerie's mother.

After several trials, each of which was compromised by Valerie's mother, who insisted that Valerie return home at the first sign of discomfort, Valerie was finally able to remain in the residence school for an extended period of time without recourse to a home visit.

WHY DOES THE TEACHER NEED TO KNOW ABOUT ANXIETY DISORDERS?

The first and most apparent reason is that, as classrooms become more inclusive of students with learning, behavioral, cultural, and linguistic differences, the greater the chance that every teacher will, at some point in her career, encounter students who evidence chronic or acute anxiety. Since most school districts are experiencing severe budget cuts, it is very unlikely that every school within a district has a psychologist on staff. Therefore, it is incumbent on teachers to be familiar with the behaviors associated with anxiety disorders as well as a few techniques to provide "emotional first aid" to help mitigate the anxiety and keep the student safe in the classroom until professional assistance can be afforded. Van Acker lamented that since many states are adopting noncategorical certifications for teachers, the knowledge base about disabilities is becoming a "thin veneer" and is thus doing these students a real disservice. He asserted that "There is a depth of knowledge you have to have to work effectively with this population" (as cited in Zabel, Kaff, & Teagarden, 2014, p. 35). The following information will help teachers become better prepared to effectively address such behaviors if and when they occur and affect students in their classrooms.

WHAT THE TEACHER SHOULD KNOW ABOUT ANXIETY DISORDERS

Anxiety disorders in general are marked by fear and avoidance. When fear predominates, the symptoms are more internalized; when avoidance predominates, the symptoms are more externalized (Dozier et al., 2008). However, fear and avoidance work together, because the autonomic solution to reduce or eliminate the fear is to avoid the feared stimulus. From a behavioral learning perspective, the avoidance is reinforced by the consequential removal of fear. Another distinction is between fear and anxiety. Fear is normally the response to a perceived imminent threat, while anxiety results from the anticipation of a future threat (APA, 2013). All children have fears and anxiety; therefore, the challenge becomes to distinguish between normal developmental fears and disordered fears. When the symptoms are persistent, excessive, and interfere with the child's functioning, a disorder is present (Kendall & Suveg, 2006). The cause of anxiety disorders is commonly thought to be multifactorial—resulting from innate temperament, early stressful life events such as loss and trauma, and early socialization experiences. From an attachment perspective, anxiety is related to the attachment figure's availability. The three most common anxiety disorders in children and adolescents are specific phobia, social anxiety, and separation anxiety disorder.

Specific Phobia

Specific phobia "is marked fear or anxiety about a specific object or situation (e.g., flying, heights, animals, receiving an injection, seeing blood)," according to the *DSM-5* (APA, 2013, p. 197). It rarely exists in isolation and is highly comorbid with other anxiety disorders, depressive disorders, and disruptive disorders. It is important to distinguish specific phobia from normal fear, since all children have fears, and fear is considered part of the normal developmental process. There are four distinguishing characteristics of a phobia: (a) It is out of proportion to the demands of the situation, (b) cannot be explained or reasoned away, (c) is beyond voluntary control, and (d) leads to avoidance of the feared situation (James, Cowdrey, & James, 2012).

The most common behavioral manifestation of specific phobia in children is avoidance of the feared stimulus. Some examples might include:

- avoiding or escaping certain situations, such as feared places in the home (e.g., the basement),
- keeping the light on when sleeping or insisting on sleeping with parents to escape the darkness,
- avoiding eating for fear of choking,
- refusing to attend a doctor's appointment for fear of a needle.

Cognitive responses usually include scary thoughts ("I'm afraid"), negative self-statements ("I can't do it"), and the expectation of some catastrophic result ("I'm going to die from the lightning"). Physiological responses include sweating, an upset stomach, dry mouth, increased heart rate, shakiness, muscles tension, and even fainting in the case of the blood/injection/injury type of specific phobia (APA, 2013; Ginsburg & Walkup, 2004). Developmentally, specific phobias are known to occur before the age of 7, especially those related to animals, darkness, insects, and blood or injury, whereas those of the natural-environment type have a more common onset around ages 11 or 12.

The cause of childhood fears is not completely understood at the present time, since not all fears, as previously thought, can be accounted for through an individual's learning history, and other factors (e.g., biological and parenting influences) must also be considered in the causality of specific phobia.

The earliest thinking about the development of phobias concentrated on aversive **classical conditioning**. A child would experience a trauma around a certain stimulus and then associate the same trauma with any future experience of the same stimulus. Though the experience of trauma can certainly be the cause of a phobia, it is not the only learning pathway to developing a phobia. Social learning factors can also play a part. A child may observe a phobic reaction in someone else (e.g., another child) or learn about the phobic reaction of others through reading and various media outlets (Davis & Ollendick, 2011). Rarely is only one factor responsible for the development of the fear, and in most cases there seems to be an interaction between classical conditioning and vicarious conditioning.

The role of **genetics** also appears to be related to an individual's propensity to fear, and environmental factors play the part of manifesting this propensity in the form of a specific fear. Certain **temperamental** characteristics (e.g., shyness, introversion, withdrawal) are thought to play a role in the development of childhood fears. Differences in the sympathetic nervous system activation responses of behaviorally inhibited children lend support to the neuropsychological bases of anxiety disorders in general and phobic disorders in particular (Strawn, Wehry, DelBello, Rynn, & Strakowski, 2012).

Increased rates of behaviorally inhibited children born to parents with anxiety and phobic disorders raise the question not only of a genetic connection but also an **environmental** one. Children constantly exposed to the influence of anxiety-disordered parents might develop behaviorally inhibited characteristics such as cautiousness, uncertainty, and fearfulness in new and different situations (Pereira, Barros, Mendonça, & Muris, 2014). Phobic parents might model avoidant behaviors, thwart any risk-taking behavior, and discourage exploration in their children. Direct behavioral observations of the interaction between parent and child in stressful or difficult situations confirm that fearful parents tend to use insulating and protective behaviors (Rapee, 2012).

Social Anxiety

The child who suffers from social anxiety typically may be referred to as "shy." Much of the research on social phobia has been done with adults. Approximately 1% of the adult population is diagnosed with social phobia, and most experts agree that social phobia has its precursors in childhood, where the prevalence rate is likely the same or higher. The most common age of onset for social phobia is adolescence, particularly early to middle adolescence. The most difficult situations for those with social phobia are reading in front of the class, musical or athletic performance, joining in on a conversation, speaking to adults, and starting a conversation (Mesa, Beidel, & Bunnell, 2014).

Approximately 60% of socially distressing events occur at school. When distressed, children with social phobia manifest physical symptoms such as heart palpitations, shakiness, flushes, chills, sweating, and nausea. The socially anxious child wants to engage socially and feels distressed at not being able to. In adolescence, the disorder may take the additional forms of poor social networks, underachievement in school and work, and poor social skills. Age of onset appears to be the strongest predictor of recovery from social anxiety—the later the age of onset, the greater the chance of recovery.

The development of social anxiety disorder is multifactorial. Factors include behavioral inhibition as a child, a history of parental separation and divorce, early pubertal maturation in females, and exposure to maternal stress during infancy. **Behavior inhibition** as a child appears to be the strongest predictor (Essex, Klein, Slattery, Goldsmith, & Kalin, 2010). **Having a parent who is shy**, reticent, or avoidant of social situations is also considered a risk factor, due to the modeling and social learning it provides to the child (Bögels & Perotti, 2011) along with family communication patterns where the child may have received messages emphasizing shame or an exaggerated concern about the opinion of others (Kim, Thibodeau, & Jorgensen, 2011). As is the case in other anxiety disorders, genetic disposition and temperament is thought to play a role in the development of social anxiety. Many experts believe there is an interaction effect between biological and environmental factors. If a child by temperament is behaviorally inhibited, a parent may feel compelled to protect the child from challenging social situations and therefore reinforce the child's genetic predisposition.

Separation Anxiety Disorder

The focal point for symptoms of separation anxiety disorder is children's excessive fear and anxiety related to being away from home or attachment figures, and tremendous worry that harm will come to themselves or their parents while they are separated. Many children have fears of separation; therefore, it is important to distinguish between normal separation anxiety and that which constitutes a disorder. The differential diagnosis is made according to the type, severity, duration, and impact of symptoms upon the child's functioning.

In regard to age of onset, most children develop symptoms of separation anxiety disorder between the ages of 8 and 12. Symptom expression differs across age groups. Adolescents with the disorder tend to report physical complaints on schools days; older children (ages 9–12) tend to report excessive distress upon separation; and young children (ages 5–8) tend to report nightmares about separations.

With the proper interventions, the prognosis is very good. In a few cases, separation anxiety disorder in children can persist into adulthood, but this is rare. Such persistence is most likely the result of biological factors and the experience of continued insecurities in primary attachments (Silove & Manicavasagar, 2013). Separation anxiety is one of the most common anxiety disorders among children, estimated to constitute about a third of all anxiety disorders. Prevalence rates are estimated to be between 3% and 5% in children and adolescents.

Silverman and Dick-Niederhauser (2004) identified six developmental pathways for this disorder: biological factors, cognitive factors, family processes, parental anxiety or depression, and caregiver stress. Overall, **genes** appear to play less of a role in the development of separation anxiety than environment does. In general, children with anxiety disorders manifest more **negative thinking** than nonanxious comparison groups, and children with separation anxiety disorder are no exception. Since this book focuses on attachment issues and their relevance in the classroom, we will concentrate on family processes to which parental anxiety and depression and caregiver stress are related.

For a long time, **family dynamics** and parenting styles have been examined as a factor in the development of separation anxiety disorder. One long-standing consideration has been an enmeshed relationship between mother and child, the result of a dysfunctional marital relationship in which a coalition is formed between the two against the father. Other psychodynamic explanations include the sexually inhibited mother who prefers the affective fulfillment she receives from the relationship with her child to that provided by her spouse. The lack of research to support such hypotheses has turned attention away from psychodynamic explanations and led the focus more to the investigation of attachment styles.

Two possible parenting pathways can lead to the development of separation anxiety disorder (Manassis & Wilansky-Traynor, 2013). The first is the pairing of a difficult child with an ambivalent caregiver who is sporadically available to the child. This heightens the child's insecurity, and he then seeks to attach himself to his mother in order to attain comfort. This exaggerated effort to seek comfort from the parent reduces the possibility of the child's exploration, and the child becomes unaccustomed to dealing with new and different situations. In addition, the parent becomes anxious in dealing with the difficult child; the child picks up on this anxiety and seeks to comfort the parent by attaching himself to her; this increases the **parent's anxiety**—setting up a cycle of reinforcement for attachment behaviors.

The second pathway proposed is the parent's inability to provide a consistent model for **dealing with stress**. Often, these parents are ill, and the child becomes preoccupied with the health and well-being of the parent and eventually develops separation anxiety disorder. This may be related to another pathway, parental anxiety and depression. Children with separation anxiety disorder are known to come from families with a high incidence of anxiety disorders and depression. And caregiver stress, be it caused by the marital relationship or something extrafamilial, is known to result in insecure attachment between parents and their children. Parent background variables (age, degree of support, education) are more predictive of anxiety in mothers than employment status. Mothers who were younger, less educated, and received less support were found to be more anxious and have more insecure attachment styles (Aber, 2012).

For separation anxiety disorder, as with many of the other anxiety disorders in children, training in contingency management for parents and school personnel is also necessary. Attachment figures must eliminate reinforcement for the disorder's symptoms and reserve reinforcement for the successful management of anxious feelings.

Understanding the Anxious Student from an Attachment Perspective

Quite obviously, Valerie has an insecure attachment style that can be classified as resistant (refer to Chapter 1). Separation anxiety results from the hyperactivation of the attachment system and causes the exploratory system to shut down. In behavioral terms, this means the child stays close to home and avoids school, the natural place of exploration.

It will come as no surprise that adults who suffered from anxiety disorders in general and separation anxiety disorder in particular are mostly classified as preoccupied on the AAI. Valerie's mother, quite possibly, may have a history of anxiety that contributes to the separation disorder. A significant detail in the vignette is that Miriam experienced a sense of loss when her daughter returned to school. Valerie most likely senses this loss, since it is probably communicated to her in subtle ways, and may feel the need to remain home and accompany her mother.

Family dysfunction is suggested by the fact that Valerie's parents are at odds with one another over their daughter's school refusal, which allows the mother and daughter to establish a coalition against the father. The vignette does not speak about the quality of the marital bond between Valerie's parents, but the closeness that her mother seeks from her daughter may substitute for the affective fulfillment lacking in the relationship with her husband. A family systems therapist would be quick to assess the quality of the marital bond and entertain the hypothesis that Valerie's separation anxiety is simply the expression of some kind of failure in the executive subsystem.

The causes of separation anxiety disorder often go beyond the individual child and more often result from the interaction between the child and the primary attachment figures. By staying home from school, Valerie gets what she wants, and so does her mother—which can make her disorder very resistant to intervention, as the vignette suggests.

We mentioned above the developmental pathways commonly thought to contribute to separation anxiety disorder. However, this disorder is particularly vulnerable to issues of attachment, and this can make it very difficult to treat. In fact, we would venture to say that no treatment will be successful without involving the primary attachment figures. In the case of Valerie, her mother appears to play an integral part in the separation anxiety. Parents should never need their children to the extent of not allowing them to separate and explore. No doubt, Miriam felt she was acting in her daughter's best interests. Counseling, however, might help her to see that she was also acting in her own interests. Yes, all children have some separation anxiety, but remember that those children who have secure attachment histories do not hyperactivate; they deal with their anxiety in a more moderate fashion that allows them to explore the world beyond the attachment dyad.

For school refusal in general, teachers and other school personnel can play a significant role in helping the family get the student to school. Often accommodations have to be made. In the case of separation anxiety disorder, things can get a little tricky, especially in a case like Valerie's where the parent is colluding in the school avoidance. An earlier chapter explained how teachers can be substitute attachment figures and provide the necessary security for students with insecure attachment histories. From an attachment perspective, the solution would be to pair Valerie with someone who could provide that security. However, Miriam might be an obstacle in allowing such substitute security to take place. In fact, she may even see a secure relationship with a teacher as a threat to her own relationship with Valerie. Insecure parenting results in insecure attachment.

In a case like this, any intervention by the school would have to treat the relationship with Miriam in delicate fashion. For example, the school should exaggerate the importance that Miriam has in Valerie's life and reassure her that no one could ever pretend to equal her in importance. The first step would be engaging the mother in a plan to get Valerie to school. Changing the message from the mother to Valerie is crucial. Presently, it is thought that Valerie's separation anxiety results from needing to take care of her mother by staying home and mitigating her mother's sense of loss. The helper working with Miriam has to get her to say, "I am your mother—I take care of you; you don't take care of me. I love you, and because I love you, I don't need you all the time in my life. Part of my job as mother is to help you explore a life and relationships that go beyond you and me."

Once Miriam is on board with helping her daughter, the school can work with her and make some accommodations to ease Valerie back into the routine of going to school every day. The problem with school refusal is that the longer it goes on, the harder it is to resolve. At the beginning, the only goal should be getting Valerie inside the school building. For each step she takes toward having a complete day at school, she can be rewarded through the development of a contingency management plan. Right now, she is being rewarded for staying home from school by maintaining a close relationship with her mother. The message from her mother has to be: If you stay home from school, there will be no relationship with me. Encouragement from the mother to allow relationships with her teachers to flourish will also help. School refusers can be very frustrating to teachers who want to help. Family therapy and parental guidance in conjunction with the school doing everything possible to make the student feel safe and secure is most likely the only chance of success in a case like Valerie's.

Understanding Teacher Interventions for the Anxious Student from Both Attachment and Pedagogical Perspectives

Mr. Richie: "We Are Reinforcing Valerie's Need for Attention"

The school's principal, in collaboration with the recommendations of the school psychologist, shared a behavioral intervention plan with her teachers that would help Valerie feel welcome and supported in her classes. The plan required that her teachers utilize a meaningful point system that would reward her for attendance and participation in the full class period. The plan also provided for an "emergency" backup in the event that Valerie refused to remain in class and attempted to contact her mother or father via cell phone, requesting to go home. Teachers were directed to contact a crisis care counselor to provide close and continuous support and supervision of Valerie while she was out of the program.

Mr. Richie, her eleventh grade science teacher, regarded these instructions with some disdain, stating that Valerie was just behaving immaturely to garner attention. He felt she just wanted to be the "star of the show," and he was loath to comply with a plan that he considered to be reinforcing her noncompliance. For example, on one occasion, he physically restrained her and refused to let her leave his classroom. When other staff investigated the commotion caused by his preventive actions, he told the crisis counselors that he had "everything under control" and urged them not to "coddle" Valerie by acceding to her attempt to leave the classroom. One of the counselors left and alerted the principal, who came to the classroom and demanded that Mr. Richie let Valerie leave under escort, and he reluctantly complied. As Valerie left the room, she hurled invectives at Mr. Richie, promising to call her parents and have him fired.

Mr. Richie from an Attachment Perspective

The school's behavioral intervention plan contains many indicated elements for getting Valerie to attend school. The first goal for a school refuser is to get her inside the school with whatever accommodations may be necessary to reduce her anxiety, with the eventual goal of having her last the entire day and attend all classes. Mr. Richie, however, does not agree with this plan, which he sees as pandering to Valerie's manipulations. He makes his own behavioral analysis: By giving Valerie such accommodations, the school is only reinforcing her bad behavior by making her out to be so special—"the star of the show." He may have a point. The only way to decide would be from the results. If the school's behavioral intervention plan achieves the desired outcome of getting Valerie to school, then Mr. Richie's opposition to the plan would lack validation. He is the type of teacher who objects to behavioral intervention plans by saying something like, "Why should she be rewarded for something she is supposed to do, like going to school?" The answer is simple: The student has a disorder! She needs accommodations to overcome the obstacles caused by the disorder.

Since this book is about attachment style and effective teaching, what can we infer about Mr. Richie? Mr. Richie would most likely be classified as dismissing. What are the predominating attitudes toward attachment for adults classified as dismissing on the AAI? Hesse (2008), summarizing Main, Goldwyn, and Hesse (2003), wrote the following about those classified as dismissing:

> Self positively described as being strong, independent, or normal. Little or no articulation of hurt, distress, or feelings of needing or depending on others. Minimizes or downplays description of negative experiences; may interpret such experiences positively, in that they have made the self stronger. May emphasize fun or activities with parents, or presents and other material objects. Attention is inflexibly focused away from discussion of attachment history and/or its implications. May express contempt for other person(s), or, relatedly for events usually considered sorrowful (e.g., loss or funerals). (p. 568)

A dismissing state of mind is highly correlated with avoidant in the Strange Situation. Mr. Richie may very well have had an avoidant attachment style as a child. Since avoidant can be considered somewhat the antithesis of resistant, the reader can begin to see that the teacher, Mr. Richie, and the student, Valerie, are like oil and water. The following graphic illustrates how they are opposites:

Valerie	Mr. Richie
Hyperactivating strategies	Deactivating strategies
Exaggerated emotion	Suppresses emotion
Seeks closeness/intimacy	Avoids closeness/intimacy
High level of dependence	High level of independence
Highly anxious	Highly stoic
Poor, diffuse boundaries	Strict, rigid boundaries

Mr. Richie has very little empathy for Valerie's situation, and one could imagine him saying, "Stop being a baby; grow up. All you need is good kick in the pants." The fact that the teacher resorted to force in trying to prevent Valerie from leaving the classroom indicates that he will have none of this babylike behavior—at least, not in his class! And if Mr. Richie were told that consideration must be given to Valerie because she has a disorder, his response might be something like: "That's a lot of crap. She's just a baby, and your way of doing things is making her more of a baby." Unfortunately, Mr. Richie is not alone in some of his opinions.

It will not be easy to work with Mr. Richie in getting him to empathize with Valerie's situation and comply with the behavioral intervention plan. The school psychologist, working with Mr. Richie, should first validate his approach as effective in working with *some* students, and validate that part of his thinking is correct and that Valerie may indeed be highly manipulative. His style, however, will not work with all students. The psychologist might even suggest to him that he had a much different upbringing compared to Valerie, and that it is clear his parents did not baby him but dealt with him in such a way as to make him the strong, independent person he is today. Valerie could learn a lot from him. Only after such validation can Mr. Richie be challenged to work more effectively with Valerie, perhaps by first getting him to understand the dynamics between him and Valerie. By complying with the behavioral intervention plan, he is not giving in to Valerie but modifying his style to get the student to come to school on a regular basis. This will not be easy, because those with a dismissing state of mind are not flexible in their approach and can believe that "one size fits all." Remember, if indeed Mr. Richie as a child had an avoidant attachment style, he learned to survive by taking emotion and closeness out of the equation in his relationship with his own parents. The fact of the matter is that his style (similar to Valerie's father) has not worked—so why not try something else? Valerie's mother is most likely the antithesis of Mr. Richie's own primary attachment figure, and he may unconsciously resent this. She may even represent something that, on another level, Mr. Richie wishes he had—a closer and more nurturing relationship. The psychologist might even say to Mr. Richie that Valerie's mother could learn from him, but he must also be willing to learn from others who represent a different way of relating to students. After all, if it works, it works!

Mr. Richie from a Pedagogical Perspective

It seems clear from his unsuccessful approach to Valerie's separation anxiety that Mr. Richie has adopted a very adversarial stance in response to his interpretation of her demands. He seems to take her insistence on being able to leave his room as an affront to his teaching ability and, perhaps, as a threat to his authority in the classroom. This teacher-centric perspective appears to be at odds with Palmer's (1998) insistence that a key underpinning of sound pedagogy is the integrity of the teacher; the courage and resolve of the teacher to know him or herself—"warts and all." This analysis is further supported by Mr. Richie's attempt to physically restrain Valerie as she attempts to leave his classroom, prompting the principal's admonishment and intervention. Mr. Richie may know his subject and be able to impart that knowledge to his students, but he does not seem to understand the importance of relationship building to effective teaching, as emphasized by Noddings (2005) and Smith (2012).

Likewise, it is important that teachers develop an attitude of caring for each of their students, according to Smith (1994) and Smith (2012). Although it may be unrealistic to expect that they will care equally for their students on a consistent basis, there is always something an effective teacher can identify in each of his students that makes teaching with them worthwhile. This student-centered focus, as espoused by Palmer (1998), can help the teacher transcend the temptation to react to disruptive, defiant behaviors as though they were a personal disparagement. Mr. Richie is encouraged to employ this approach with Valerie and other students he finds challenging and therefore difficult to work with. At least in this instance, he has missed an opportunity to establish a prosocial rapport with Valerie, and it seems unlikely that he will easily establish one with her in the future.

In addition, Mr. Richie is encouraged to employ a few of the pedagogical tools recommended in Chapter 2 of this book; specifically, the use of "behavior-specific praise," "behavior momentum," and "implementing choice" (Landrum & Sweigart, 2014). For example, he might offer positive reinforcement in the form of praise for any effort Valerie makes to stay in class, or to at least request a few minutes outside (ostensibly with supervision). Likewise, Mr. Richie could develop a graduated "seat time" plan with Valerie and her therapist that might require that she remain in class during tasks that she finds engaging, but would be permitted to go to an alternate location, accompanied by her one-to-one aide, to complete more onerous tasks. Lastly, Mr. Richie needs to consider the value of providing choices for Valerie with respect to (a) types of assignments (e.g., a report, portfolio, or essay), and (b) the environment in which the assignment can be completed (e.g., outdoors, in the library, in the cottage, at a desk or table or on the floor) (Landrum & Sweigart, 2014).

Finally, it is very important that Mr. Richie understand his culture and context as well as Valerie's. This is addressed in greater detail in the attachment sections;

however, it might help Mr. Richie understand the possible causes of Valerie's behavior if he takes the time to investigate her anxiety disorder and its perceived causes. The school counselor would be an invaluable resource in this endeavor. Learning a bit about Valerie's family and home life might provide insights relative to the onset and exacerbation of her anxious behaviors, as well.

Ms. Ellsworth: "Valerie Is Part of Our Classroom Community"

When Valerie returned to school the next week, she was provided with a one-to-one aide, who accompanied her to each of her classes. Her homeroom teacher, Mrs. Ellsworth, welcomed her back and assured her that she would not be forced to attend any class, and that if she began to feel overwhelmed and anxious about her parents, she could always leave the room, escorted by her aide, and with the permission of her social worker, call home to speak with her parents. Mrs. Ellsworth also reminded Valerie that she and Valerie's classmates considered Valerie a valued member of the class, and she fully appreciated that every student in the class had some challenge that she or he needed help in overcoming. As a class, they affirmed that everyone belonged and was a member of the classroom community. Mrs. Ellsworth pointed out the class motto, which stated: "Everyone you meet is fighting battles you know nothing about; therefore, be kind to everyone!" Valerie seemed encouraged by Mrs. Ellsworth's reassurances and was able to attend and remain in every class for its duration for the first time in months. Clearly, she and Mrs. Ellsworth had established a positive rapport, predicated on mutual respect and genuine caring.

Mrs. Ellsworth from an Attachment Perspective

Mrs. Ellsworth's approach to dealing with Valerie is antithetical to Mr. Richie's. Reading the vignette, one could only imagine Mr. Richie's reaction: "You are overindulging this child! What are the other students going to think? Now they, too, will want special attention!" Mrs. Ellsworth's approach, however, does answer Mr. Richie's concerns: Everyone belongs, but everyone belongs in a different way. Therefore, we have to make accommodations. Her treatment is not necessarily overindulging; it is helping someone belong who heretofore has had trouble belonging to the school environment.

Mrs. Ellsworth's classroom motto makes it clear that her attachment state of mind would classify as secure. A secure adult state of mind manifests itself on the AAI as recognizing the need for dependence on others, but with an openness and willingness to explore different options and a flexibility of attention. At ease with the imperfection in their own selves, adults with a secure state of mind are characterized by forgiveness and compassion. They are not locked into a certain view of a person or event but can change their views as things progress and new data are available. They reveal a sense of balance, proportion, and even humor (Hesse, 2008).

The reader begins to see that the teacher's secure state of mind is the perfect antidote to the student's resistant attachment style. One can infer from the vignette that the more anxious Valerie becomes, the more calm and reassuring Mrs. Ellsworth will become. In contrast to Mr. Richie's thinking, Mrs. Ellsworth, by accommodating Valerie, does not cede power and control to Valerie but gains that power and control through establishing rapport. Mr. Richie's approach for establishing control was to force Valerie into conformity—"You will not be given special treatment"—the opposite of Mrs. Ellsworth, who recognizes that every student in the class has some challenges that can prevent them from feeling that they truly belong in the learning environment. The flexibility resulting from a secure state of mind allows Mrs. Ellsworth to employ different strategies to establish an attachment bond with a diverse student body.

The vignette does not mention the actions or reactions of Valerie's mother but implies that she does not sabotage the efforts of Mrs. Ellsworth and the school, since her daughter has been able to attend school on a consistent basis. With students diagnosed with separation anxiety disorder, schools must also engage and work with the parents. For whatever reason, Mrs. Ellsworth has been able to form a close bond with Valerie that does not threaten or substitute for Valerie's close relationship with her mother. In the real world, this is not an easy feat. Valerie's success was probably accomplished with the help of outside family therapy, whose goal was getting Valerie's parents to work together as a team in allowing their child to become more securely attached, therefore allowing their daughter to activate the exploratory system and develop as a normal child, attending school and establishing new friendships.

Mrs. Ellsworth from a Pedagogical Perspective

Mrs. Ellsworth appears to demonstrate the principles suggested by Palmer (1998) and especially Loughran (1997), who points to the importance of the quality of the teacher–student relationship. Mrs. Ellsworth takes the time to reassure Valerie, acknowledging her separation anxiety and, consequently, her need to communicate frequently with her parents. She doesn't feel slighted by the concessions to accommodate the needs of this student, as does Mr. Richie. Similarly, in accordance with the work of Shulman (1987), Mrs. Ellsworth seems to be clear about her identity, as a teacher of students with disabilities, and seems confident in her pedagogical practice, as evident in her effective interaction with Valerie after her return to the classroom. Also, Mrs. Ellsworth demonstrates the pedagogical values espoused by Korthagen (2004), who cites knowledge of learners and their characteristics, knowledge of educational contexts, and knowledge of education purposes and their values for students as critical elements of a sound pedagogy. Mrs. Ellsworth's unequivocal acceptance of Valerie and her willingness to appropriately accommodate Valerie's perceived needs resonates with the principles of effective pedagogy recommended by each of the theorists cited above.

Mrs. Ellsworth's supportive pedagogical approach in working with Valerie appears to reflect one or two of these recommended strategies. Clearly, treating Valerie's separation anxiety as a very credible issue by listening to her concerns would allow Valerie the opportunity to express her fears and feelings, which might help de-escalate the intensity of her feelings and reduce the chance that she might engage in more externalizing and potentially unsafe behaviors (i.e., "drain off frustration acidity," as discussed in Chapter 2). Moreover, Mrs. Ellsworth clearly employs "support for the management of emotions" (see Chapter 2) when she reassures Valerie and provides a contingency plan should Valerie need to contact her parents during the school day.

Most relevant to Valerie's condition, as described earlier in the chapter, would be "reality rub" and "new-tool salesmanship" (refer to Chapter 2). Although these are not employed by Mrs. Ellsworth in the brief behavioral vignette provided, one could presume that they might be utilized at a later date, to help Valerie feel included and accepted as a member of the class. For instance, at times Valerie becomes anxious about being separated from her parents and obsessively worries about possible worst-case scenarios, such as a foreboding about her parents' safety and the chance that they might have been injured in an automobile accident. The teacher might provide reassurance by refuting each unrealistic assumption ("reality rub") and reminding Valerie to repeat a mantra or affirmation (as described in Chapter 2) to mitigate her intrusive morbid thoughts ("new-tool salesmanship"). For example, when Valerie feels a compulsion to perseverate about her parents' safety, she might think: "My parents are safely at work right now. There is nothing that can harm them in their respective workplaces. If there was an emergency, I would be informed, and the appropriate professionals would be immediately dispatched. I can call my parents at the end of the school day to ensure that all is well with them."

When Valerie successfully employs this mantra and reduces her anxiety, Mrs. Ellsworth would say, "Valerie, I'm so pleased that you were able to use your affirmation, [restates the agreed-upon affirmation], to help you overcome those persistent thoughts that make you so fearful—you must be feeling very good about yourself right now!"

In Valerie's case, when she insists that she must leave the classroom and call her mother, Mrs. Ellsworth would acknowledge her anxiety about being apart from her mother, but might ask her to complete one more math problem, write two more sentences in response to a discussion question, or remain in class for five more minutes. Over time, Valerie would be asked to remain in class and on-task for a full period of instruction, with the ultimate goal of a full day of classroom participation.

Again, relative to Valerie's situation, the short-term goal is to have Valerie stay in class, engaged, for the entire period. Ultimately, of course, the objective is to enable Valerie to remain engaged for an entire school day. Mrs. Ellsworth might offer preferred choices in the classroom, such as working on an audiovisual presentation rather than one exclusively typewritten. She might also consider proposing a different venue in which to work on the presentation assignment, such as the library, perhaps with a friend or Valerie's one-to-one aide. The "reward" for successful completion of the assignment might be permission to call home and speak with her mother for five minutes during lunch.

Valerie's case provided a detailed analysis of separation anxiety disorder from both attachment and pedagogical perspectives. Other anxiety disorders manifest similarly in terms of observable classroom behaviors. Therefore, we will now provide two brief student vignettes specific to social anxiety disorder and specific phobia, as well as representative helpful and unhelpful teacher responses and a concise analysis for both of these infrequently encountered subtypes.

Student Vignette: "Gabriella" (Social Anxiety)

Gabriella, a 14-year-old Latina, has recently developed a generalized fear of public exposure that involves speaking, reading, or performing in front of a large group of people—even engaging in a conversation with two or more people. Her parents recently divorced after 14 years of marriage, but her mother insists that was not a factor in the development of Gabriella's social anxiety disorder.

The implications of this phobia as it affects Gabriella's ability to engage with others in social settings are profound and far-reaching. Gabriella was previously very active in the high school marching band as well as the youth choir in her church. She is unable to participate in these activities as a result of her social phobia. Likewise, Gabriella, usually very gregarious in school, has become almost reclusive, preferring solitary activities to group ones. Her best friends report really missing their once-personable friend's contributions to their social activities. Gabriella had been a very popular student, and she has been elected class representative to the student government associations for the past two years.

Gabriella's mother revealed to the school psychologist that the family had moved seven times in the last 12 years because Gabriella's father is a professional musician who has played in several traveling bands in different regions of the country. Gabriella seemed to adjust well to the new environments and schools until recently. Her mother also reported that Gabriella hit puberty early, and the experience was a difficult one for her.

Her teachers are very concerned about her recent withdrawal from activities and people she used to love; this reticence is clearly affecting her school performance. They want to be supportive and sensitive to her needs, but they are not sure what to do to help her regain her former confidence and reverse her academic downturn.

Gabriella from an Attachment Perspective

Most noteworthy about Gabriella is that she was not always a shy person; her social phobia is a more recent development. She was even able to sustain the many moves and changes of schools, leaving only the consideration of her parents' divorce and going through puberty. Her mother denies that the divorce is responsible for her daughter's recent withdrawal; however, we do not know this for sure. Gabriella has seemingly gone from secure to insecure. The reader should remember that contextual events, such as divorce or entrance into adolescence, can alter attachment styles. However, it is also assumed that individuals operating from a secure attachment base established in early infancy and childhood will be able to successfully weather and overcome those events that instill a sense of insecurity. If her teachers and the school environment can provide a renewed sense of security, the prognosis for Gabriella overcoming her social anxiety ought to be good.

Mr. Lane: A Man on a Mission

Mr. Lane, the band director and student council faculty advisor, simply cannot fathom that his drum major and class president could become so reticent and withdrawn seemingly overnight! A natural optimist and student activity enthusiast, Mr. Lane has been persistent in his efforts to get Gabriella to "snap out of her funk." He seems convinced that Gabriella's sudden disinterest in what were her passions a few weeks ago is simply a temporary condition, probably caused by physical exhaustion or perhaps an acute medical condition such as mononucleosis. Despite Gabriella's insistence that she was simply unable and unwilling to continue in these very social activities, Mr. Lane has decided that she is his latest "challenge," and he is determined to see her lead the band and student council once again!

Mrs. Nash: Wants to Respond to Gabriella's Needs

Mrs. Nash, Gabriella's living environments teacher, is equally concerned about the sudden and dramatic change in her behavior; however, she senses that Gabriella is truly fragile at this point and wants to provide whatever support she needs to feel secure and to be successful in school. To ensure that she is providing the right kind of assistance to Gabriella, Mrs. Nash approaches the school counselor, Dr. Sanders after dismissal and asks him what she can do, as a classroom teacher, to help Gabriella. Dr. Sanders is delighted to offer a few strategies for Mrs. Nash to try and suggests that they meet again in a week to discuss Gabriella's response to the recommended interventions. On the suggestion of Dr. Sanders, Mrs. Nash also contacts Gabriella's parents to let them know she is available to discuss Gabriella's progress anytime, and that she will do whatever she can to support Gabriella's treatment plan and provide the necessary classroom accommodations.

Mr. Lane and Mrs. Nash from an Attachment Perspective

Mr. Lane and Mrs. Nash represent two different approaches to Gabriella. The first is rooted in an "I know best" attitude, while the second is rooted in "I don't know what's best" and therefore creates the need to consult with others who might know more, such as the school counselor. At first glance, it may appear that Mr. Lane is the more secure of the two, since he is convinced he has the capability of getting Gabriella to "snap out of it." Mrs. Nash, on the other hand, does not know what to do, and could be accused of lacking self-confidence and therefore being insecure.

From an attachment perspective, the opposite is true. It is often the secure person who admits to herself that she does not know something and needs consultation. There is research to support that more experienced teachers are more open to consultation than inexperienced ones, precisely because the experienced teachers are more secure. The vignette implies that Mr. Lane takes Gabriella's behavior personally, indicating that he cannot fathom losing his drum major. This is not uncommon in schools where teachers, coaches, and other adults base their relationships on the students serving the adults' needs, when it really should be the opposite. When a professional sees the people he is helping as serving his own needs, it almost always indicates an insecure attachment style. Mr. Lane may need Gabriella more than Gabriella needs Mr. Lane. His band may not be as good without Gabriella—but so what? The important question is not what is best for Mr. Lane but what is best for Gabriella. Once students sense an agenda from a teacher where the teacher's needs are primary, any hope of building a workable, trusting, secure relationship with that student is almost surely doomed.

Mr. Lane and Mrs. Nash from a Pedagogical Perspective

Mr. Lane and Mrs. Nash present contrasting pedagogical styles in addressing the needs of their student, Gabriella. Mr. Lane, although he means well, is nonetheless insensitive to Gabriella's new circumstances—she is not suffering from some transitory malady; she has a chronic disorder that, with effective treatment, may diminish in intensity over time. Meanwhile, she needs Mr. Lane to accept her condition and the social limitations that it imposes. Mr. Lane should follow Mrs. Nash's lead and learn how he can best support Gabriella and her parents, but he is impelled by his behavioral imperative to restore Gabriella's self-confidence.

In contrast, Mrs. Nash is aware that she is unfamiliar with Gabriella's recently identified disorder and is therefore unable to effectively support her in the classroom. As part of her teaching pedagogy, Mrs. Nash reflects on what she needs to do to truly assist Gabriella (Sellar, 2013). In doing so, she also evidences the "caring teacher–student relationship" that Noddings (2005) and Smith (2012) advocate as a critical component of any sound teacher pedagogy. She demonstrates these tenets when she seeks the advice of the school counselor and implements his suggestions.

STUDENT VIGNETTE: "BILLY" (SPECIFIC PHOBIA)

Billy is a fifteen-year-old boy currently attending a public high school. His case file provides a description of his presenting emotional/behavioral disorder; namely, specific phobia. His symptoms first emerged five years ago, at age 10, shortly after a group of four older neighborhood boys invited him to join their "secret club" and informed him that in order to be admitted as a member, he would need to participate in an initiation. The initiation that the boys conceived was for Billy to spend several hours in a trunk that the boys described as a "coffin." The old steamer trunk the boys selected had a few holes drilled in its lid, which permitted airflow. The space, as Billy described it, was just large enough to allow him to lie down with his knees drawn up to his chest. After an hour of suffering extreme discomfort, Billy began to reconsider his decision and first asked, then pleaded to be let out. The older boys refused and began to deride him for his cowardice, insisting that each of them had endured the same initiation without complaint. After another hour of confinement, the boys decided to let Billy out, since they hadn't heard further complaints. Upon opening the trunk, the boys discovered that Billy was "in a bad way." He continued to remain in a fetal position, with his legs drawn up, refusing to be consoled or to snap out of his bizarre, trancelike behavior. One of the boys panicked and called his parents who, in turn, called the police.

Since the incident and subsequent counseling sessions, Billy appears to have made a full recovery from the initial trauma produced by the event; however, his life has been affected by the residual effects of the episode. For instance, since the event, Billy has been unable to enter small, enclosed spaces, such as elevators, cars, buses, small rooms, and even classrooms, especially ones that are locked or windowless. That means that Billy is unable to attend some of his classes and must be accommodated in special classroom with windows and open spaces. He is also very uncomfortable being in locked facilities; however, recent school policies require that all doors in the school be locked to prevent unauthorized entry. While Billy is a very good student, who enjoys his teachers and classmates, he has recently refused to attend school on several occasions, citing his fear of being "locked up" in school and being unable to "escape" should the need arise. Billy was encouraged to continue seeing a psychologist who specializes in treating phobias in children and adolescents. After a thorough evaluation, a treatment plan was developed that would be implemented both at home and in school.

Billy from an Attachment Perspective

Billy is yet another example of a boy who has a seemingly normal, secure life, but suffered a contextual event that resulted in prolonged fear associated with the traumatic event of being locked in an enclosed space for an inordinate amount of time. He is an adolescent, when the need to belong is perhaps most intense and allowed Billy to acquiesce to the demands for initiation into a "secret club." We know nothing about Billy's early years and the kind of parenting that he received. However, it can be safely said that children and adolescents who operate from a secure base are more open to exploration, but at the same time will exercise better judgment; they do not need to comply with peer demands at any cost. Secure children are able to say no when they do not feel comfortable with peer demands, since peer acceptance is not the ultimate criteria for their self-worth. One has to wonder, in the case of Billy, if an insecure attachment style is responsible for his willingness to satisfy his older peers. Ultimately, the question has to be asked: Why was their acceptance so important to him as to make him do something so dangerous? While we do not know the answer to this question, we do know that schools, and teachers in particular, can help students feel more secure, so as to mitigate the ill-advised demands of peers.

Mrs. Watchorn: "Perhaps It's Time to Retire!"

Mrs. Watchorn, Billy's homeroom teacher and a local union rep, is acutely aware of the legal implications of failing to provide Billy with the services and supports to which he is entitled. Fully apprised of Billy's special-education services and related accommodations, she responds immediately to his requests for help. As a result of her preoccupation with Billy and his learning and emotional needs, she neglects several other students who, although not classified with a disorder, are clearly at risk of school failure. Billy has quickly learned that he can obtain whatever help or accommodation he requests from Mrs. Watchorn, and he is taking full advantage of his newfound "power." To raise the stakes, Billy's mother is a special-education advocate in the school district and has acquired a reputation as someone who gets what she wants from the school district; she has even hastened the firing of a couple of her son's teachers who failed to provide the quality services she demands for her son and other students with disabilities! Mrs. Watchorn, a veteran teacher with 28 years' experience in the classroom, is finding her job less satisfying this year, due in part to the pressure and scrutiny imposed by Billy's mother. Perhaps this would be a good year to retire, she ponders.

Ms. Santorelli: "I Will Ensure Billy Receives Appropriate Accommodations"

Ms. Santorelli, on the other hand, has conferred with the child study team, which includes the school psychologist in this instance, and has helped develop a behavior intervention plan that effectively addresses Billy's needs. She appreciates Billy's resilience in the face of his intense fear of enclosures and the courage he displays every time he comes to school—and she shares this with him, as appropriate. However, Ms. Santorelli is very knowledgeable about the provisions afforded by the Individuals with Disabilities Education Act (IDEA; 2004) and does not allow Billy's demands to monopolize her attention, nor does she feel intimidated by Billy's mother. Ms. Santorelli is confident because she possesses sound pedagogical skills and, as her principal has observed on more than one occasion, "She knows her stuff!"

Mrs. Watchorn and Ms. Santorelli from an Attachment Perspective

The teacher vignettes offer more insight not only into the challenges facing Billy but also into the issues presented by his mother, an influential figure in the school district who reportedly has contributed to the end of several teachers' tenure. No one should criticize a parent who advocates for her child. However, when the parent's approach is more adversarial and perhaps controlling rather than collaborative, as may be the case with Billy's mother, teacher reactions to dealing with such a parent take on a great deal of importance. Mrs. Watchorn and Ms. Santorelli represent two different attachment states of mind. The former operates from a more insecure base that leads to possible withdrawal ("Maybe it's time to retire") and overindulgence of the student in question ("I'd better not do anything to get this mother mad at me, or I might lose my job"). What really has been lost is the teacher's leverage to enter into a collaborative relationship with the mother, and as a result, the mother calls all the shots. Previously mentioned was the fact that controlling people are insecure people. If Billy's mom fits such a profile, then an insecure teacher's reaction to Billy's mother will diminish her ability to teach all students effectively. As the vignette points out, Mrs. Watchorn has neglected her other students in her desire to attend to Billy and placate his mother.

Ms. Santorelli represents a more leveraged, secure reaction to Billy's needs and his mother's supposed influence in the school district. Once again, a good teacher is able to enter into collaboration with the child study team and implement the plan designed for Billy—no more, no less. This gives Ms. Santorelli leverage, as she is following the guidance of the child study team, and any complaints or further demands by Billy's mother will have to be referred to them. The vignette makes clear that the teacher does not fear Billy's mother, and this in turn will garner the mother's respect. Of course, the principal's respect for Ms. Santorelli is huge in allowing her to proceed with confidence in dealing with a child whose mother has a reputation for making trouble. Needless to say, an insecure principal or one who was not supportive to her would diminish and challenge the teacher's leverage.

Mrs. Watchorn and Ms. Santorelli from a Pedagogical Perspective

It is apparent that Mrs. Watchorn lacks the confidence that comes from a sense of self-efficacy. As we learned in Chapter 2, according to Palmer (1998) and Loughran (1997), good teachers strive to be honest with themselves about who they are and what they know and believe, and to be courageous in revealing those truths to students, parents, and colleagues. Mrs. Watchorn seems to lack this assurance, and Billy and his mother are taking advantage of her insecurity. Similarly, consistent with Alexander's recommendation about the tenets of good teaching, Mrs. Watchorn must "demonstrate the commitment necessary to make the daily decisions about instruction and learning required of an effective teacher" (2004, p. 11). Clearly, by simply accommodating Billy's every demand, Mrs. Watchorn is not fulfilling that pedagogical mandate.

Conversely, Ms. Santorelli exudes confidence, the kind of self-assurance that arises from a sound pedagogy. Evidence in support of this contention is her consultation with the members of the child study team, as well as her own professional knowledge and solid understanding of the legislation that is the foundation of her field, special education. Ms. Santorelli also displays evidence of the fifth element in our pedagogical framework—specifically, that a sound pedagogy must empower students to identify their strengths and weaknesses and take responsibility for their own learning. She demonstrates this tenet when she provides Billy with appropriate accommodations, encourages his attendance, and does not cater to his whims.

EFFECTIVE TEACHER RESPONSES

For students with an anxiety disorder (general suggestions):

- Consult with the school psychologist in developing the behavioral assessment and intervention plan, and apply the latter conscientiously.
- Always provide the affected student in your class with a safe, structured environment in which to learn.
- Provide consistent praise and positive reinforcement for every effort the student makes to control the targeted behaviors.
- Never demean or disparage a student for expressing "unreasonable" fears.
- Get to know *each* of your students. Building positive relationships with your students is the single most important step in the development of an effective school-based intervention plan.
- Read the student's case file and become knowledgeable about the behavioral and academic goals described in the student's individualized education plan.

For students with a separation anxiety disorder, like Valerie:

- Show support and encouragement and provide positive reinforcement for even small achievements, such as going through the school day without a panic attack, emotional outburst, or request to call home.
- Maintain a firm position relative to the child's requests to call a parent or be sent home. She will begin to accept school attendance as compulsory only if there are no alternatives.
- Give the child encouragement; let her know you truly care about her and are committed to her success in school. Help her feel valued and a sense of belonging.
- Encourage the child with SAD to make friends in class. Provide cooperative learning opportunities; consider pairing the student with a peer tutor or study buddy.
- If the student is absent for any reason, let her know she was truly missed upon her return. You may also call home to let the child know you missed her and want her to return as soon as possible.
- Never shame or punish the child for an emotional outburst. Instead, try to comfort the student and isolate her until she can regain her composure.
- Hold the student accountable for all missed work due to absence; the student must take responsibility for her school performance.
- Ensure that you understand the behavioral intervention plan instituted for this child, and participate in it as directed. For example, if the key intervention is cognitive-behavioral treatment, know the self-statements or prompts and encourage the student to use them; provide reinforcement where possible.
- Develop an effective rapport with the child's parents or guardians to enhance collaboration and facilitate the exchange of relevant information concerning the student's target behavior.
- Speak to your students before the child with separation anxiety returns to your classroom in order to help them understand their classmate's challenges and solicit their support.
- Perhaps most important to the success of a school-based intervention is the individualization of treatment. For the teacher, this means making a special effort to develop a positive relationship with the child. Research supports the importance of this individualized approach in the reduction of separation anxiety behaviors (Ollendick & King, 1998).

For students with a social phobia, like Gabriella:

- Assign the student a study buddy to help her with coursework and projects.
- Encourage the student to participate in small group discussions of 4 to 6 students.
- Encourage the individual to find outlets for nonacademic skills and interests

that will typically involve membership in afterschool programs and extracurricular activities.

- Make a point of speaking to the student every day in both academic and social contexts in order to desensitize her and demystify the experience of speaking with an adult or authority figure.
- Help the student identify school- or community-based clubs that help individuals who are socially withdrawn or "shy" gain self-confidence and poise (e.g., the toastmasters club; the school debate society; the speakers bureau). (Reprinted from Austin & Sciarra (2010), with permission, Pearson Education)

Furthermore, teachers might consider presenting a unit or a series of lessons on verbal and nonverbal communication skills that would benefit all students in the class, especially a student with social phobia. Finally, teachers should avoid embarrassing the student or inadvertently creating anxiety by arbitrarily calling on her without advance notice. The teacher should consider "rehearsing" a planned question with the student before class to allow her to prepare and then be able to respond with confidence. Likewise, the teacher and student might identify an established nonverbal cue that can signal the teacher's intention to call on the student. The student could then signal her willingness to do so, or decline surreptitiously and thereby avoid embarrassment. (adapted with permission from Austin & Sciarra, 2010).

For students with a specific phobia, like Billy:

- Don't allow the student to perseverate about his fear.
- Don't allow the student to monopolize your attention with his fearful obsession; instead, reinforce the prescribed intervention plan or use "planned ignoring."
- Avoid deviating from the treatment plan by acceding to the student's requests to call home.
- Provide established prompts if the student appears fearful or mentions feeling afraid.
- Immediately change the subject if the affected student becomes preoccupied with his phobia.
- Be prepared to provide a rational explanation to help allay the child's fear. (Reprinted from Austin & Sciarra (2010), with permission, Pearson Education)

CONCLUDING THOUGHTS

To be sure, there are many "Valeries" out there—students who, because of their chronic anxieties, confound and frustrate teachers. Each one expresses an anxiety with different features and causes; some will display seemingly baseless fears of "trivial" things. Others may display obsessions with germs, resulting in compulsive cleaning rituals. Still others may become traumatized by horrific real-world events that, although they occurred years before, are incessantly relived by the child as though they happened yesterday.

The teacher is neither equipped nor expected to provide the therapeutic interventions of a clinical psychologist or behavioral therapist, but that doesn't mean she isn't responsible for keeping the anxious student safe and ensuring that he learns. It is also important that the teacher help students who express chronic anxieties—ones that affect the quality of their lives—feel accepted and included as valued constituents in the classroom.

Rather than providing a list of interventions de rigueur—which can be rather faddish and promote a very prescriptive, knee-jerk response to the anxious behaviors presented by students in their classes—we contend that teachers who possess a sound pedagogical foundation; have invested time in understanding themselves and their teaching purposes or philosophies; and can step back from the anxious behavior and be mindful of their own prejudices, fears, and assumptions before offering an intervention will have a far better chance of success in relating to and understanding the child who exhibits these challenging behaviors.

Every child and every situation is unique and presents a very different context with many different variables. Thus, a one-size-fits-all approach will likely prove fruitless. Our intention, in this book, is to provide every teacher with a framework from which to purposefully and effectively address both the child and the anxious behavior. This chapter has provided the teacher with a research-based schema from which to do just that.

CHAPTER 5

Teaching Students with Mood Disorders

Student Vignette: "Emily" (Depression)

Emily had always been "daddy's little girl." Everyone close to her family noted the bond established between Emily and her father; her mother admits to having been envious of their relationship. At school, Emily performed well, scoring in the 90th percentile and above on most tests and exams. She was also very active in school and extracurricular activities such as concert band and the science club. Similarly, Emily was a proficient soccer player as well as a talented first-base player in the girls' softball league. Neighbors and teachers remember her as an energetic, gregarious child who was always smiling. That all changed during seventh grade, the year her father and "best friend" was diagnosed with pancreatic cancer.

As treatment after treatment proved unsuccessful in slowing the disease, and her father's prognosis was assessed as grave, a change became evident in Emily. She stopped eating, her demeanor changed from ebullient to somber, her grades declined precipitously, she lost interest in her many school and extracurricular activities, and she withdrew socially. These profound behavioral changes climaxed with the death of her father in February of seventh grade. Her mother notes that at the funeral she seemed emotionally detached, and she subsequently withdrew from all social activities, finding even attending school an arduous task.

Family members remarked at the fact that, despite the close relationship between father and daughter, they never observed Emily displaying emotion over her father's death. Her mother and relatives consigned this lack of emotional response to Emily's grief process and were sure that, in due time, she would rebound and return to the Emily that they all knew and loved. However, things did not change; in fact, they seemed to worsen. As the months wore on, Emily began to withdraw more and more, as if she were retreating into some dark tunnel in which she felt safe and secure. When, a year after her father's death, Emily's emotional state remained unchanged, Mrs. Helm, Emily's mother, contacted the school's psychologist who, in turn, referred her to a psychiatrist who specializes in cases involving children and adolescents with mood disorders. This clinician diagnosed Emily with major depression and prescribed a multimodal treatment regimen consisting of cognitive behavioral therapy, medication, and family therapy.

WHY DOES THE TEACHER NEED TO KNOW ABOUT MOOD DISORDERS?

One of the most frequent emotional problems encountered by teachers in today's classrooms are what we refer to generally as mood disorders, typically qualified as depression or bipolar disorder (Kochanek, Murphy, Xu, & Arias, 2013). Of course, teachers are not therapists, as we have repeatedly pointed out; nonetheless, because 95% of child and adolescent suicides are thought to have been committed by students diagnosed with a mental illness, most frequently a mood disorder, and since suicide is the third leading cause of death for people age 15 to 24, it is vital that all teachers learn about the characteristics, causes, and preventive steps that help to reduce the incidence of these tragedies (New York State Department of Health, 2011)

Once again, it is important to remind the reader that with the increased popularity of the inclusion model in schools, most teachers are routinely assigned to inclusive classrooms, wherein they are expected to work effectively with students with learning differences and emotional and behavioral challenges. In fact, as of 2010, 95% of students with disabilities were receiving most of their education in inclusive classrooms (National Center for Education Statistics, 2013). Indeed, as the incidence of identified mental disorders in children and adolescents is increasing, including depression and bipolar disorder, teachers face a greater likelihood that they will have several students affected by these disorders in their classes (Clinical Advisor, 2013). We know that students who experience these disorders often struggle academically and may also display behavioral problems, despite the popular misconception suggesting that students who are depressed are typically withdrawn and lethargic. We will provide some important information about mood disorders in the next section.

WHAT THE TEACHER SHOULD KNOW ABOUT MOOD DISORDERS

The diagnosis of major depressive disorder in Emily's case appears accurate, given the length and severity of her symptoms. Interestingly, the *DSM-5* (APA, 2013) eliminated the bereavement exclusion that prevented the diagnosis of major depressive disorder for symptoms lasting less than two months after the death of a loved one. Critics argued that this gave the impression that bereavement should last only two months, something most experts would disagree with—bereavement lasts anywhere from one to two years. The second reason for the removal of the bereavement exclusion was the recognition that the death of a loved one is a major psychosocial stressor that can easily precipitate the onset of depression soon after the loss, especially with a vulnerable individual, as might be the case with Emily. While she may not exhibit all the signs of depression, Emily certainly has some of them: depressed mood, diminished interest in activities that previously were pleasurable, social withdrawal, constricted or even dissociated affect. Other symptoms that could be present would include problems with sleeping and eating, suicidal ideation, impairment in concentration, feelings of worthlessness, psychomotor agitation or retardation, fatigue or loss of energy, and recurrent thoughts of death.

Mood disorders, also known as *affective disorders*, are abnormalities and disturbances in the regulation of mood. There are two types of mood disorders: depressive disorders, characterized by periods of sadness, and bipolar disorders, characterized by alternating moods of sadness and mania. Depression exists across the life span, but its diagnosis requires the age-level consideration, since symptom manifestation will be different for different age groups.

The highs rates of comorbidity with externalizing disorders (Oppositional Defiant Disorder and Conduct Disorder), anxiety disorders, and ADHD for children and adolescents with major depressive disorder raises the question as to whether this high rate "is the result of the lack of a well-developed exclusionary criteria in this age group or whether it represents true comorbid disorders" (Kowatch, Emslie, Wilkaitis, & Dingle, 2005, p. 144). There are many psychiatric disorders (e.g., anxiety, learning disabilities, personality disorders, substance abuse, eating disorders, and disruptive disorders) that have symptoms that overlap with major depressive disorder but do not meet the full criteria. In order to address some of these concerns, the *DSM-5* added some new depressive disorders, most notably disruptive mood dysregulation disorder for children up to age 18 who present with persistent irritability and frequent episodes of behavior dyscontrol (APA, 2013).

DEPRESSIVE DISORDERS

Major depression occurs in approximately 2% of children and between 5% and 8% of adolescents (Rohde, Lewinsohn, Klein, Seeley, & Gau, 2013). In childhood, girls and boys are equally likely to be diagnosed with depression, but by adolescence girls are twice as likely to become depressed. There are gender differences in regard to symptom presentation: Girls have more mood symptoms, such as feeling sad and depressed, whereas boys have higher rates of irritability (Weller, Weller, & Danielyan, 2004).

Most experts believe that depression in childhood and adolescence is underdiagnosed, and there are several reasons for this. As mentioned previously, the manifestation of symptoms can be different than what is typically thought of as depression (e.g., vegetative states of psychomotor retardation, loss of appetite, excessive sleep). Another factor is that children do not have the capacity to express in verbal terms their emotions and may present with dubious symptoms, such as irritability and boredom. Since it is highly comorbid with other disorders, underlying depression may often be overlooked.

According to the *DSM-5*, a child or adolescent diagnosed with major depressive disorder will manifest five or more of the following in the same two-week period: depressed mood (feeling sad, empty, or hopeless), loss of interest or pleasure, significant weight loss or gain, insomnia or hypersomnia, psychomotor agitation or retardation, fatigue or loss of energy, feelings of worthlessness, impairment of concentration, and recurrent thoughts of death. At least one of the symptoms must be depressed mood or loss of interest or pleasure (also known as *anhedonia*). Major depressive disorder is an episodic condition that can recur, and children and adolescents have high rates of relapse (Curry et al., 2011). Comorbid diagnoses among children and adolescents with mood disorders are more the rule than the exception, and some studies reveal that anywhere from 40% to 70% of depressed children and adolescents have a comorbid psychiatric disorder (Thapar, Collishaw, Pine, & Thapar, 2012). In addition, there are a variety of medical conditions that can produce symptoms of depression. These include malignancy, brain injury, infection, endocrine disorders, metabolic abnormalities, AIDS, multiple sclerosis, and chronic fatigue syndrome. The most common comorbid diagnoses are dysthymic disorder, anxiety disorders, personality disorders, disruptive behavior disorders, and substance abuse. Anxiety and depression are highly comorbid even among adult samples. It may be difficult at times to decide on a primary diagnosis, and individuals can become depressed over their anxiety or vice versa.

Depressed adolescents tend to have an earlier onset of substance abuse than those substance abusers without a history of major depressive disorder (McCarty et al., 2012). It is quite possible that adolescents turn to drugs in order to self-medicate for their depression. One must also not rule out a substance-induced depression, where the use of substances has actually caused the depression. This differential diagnosis is made by taking a careful history and assuring that no depressive episodes occurred before the use of substances. A substance-induced mood disorder usually results from long-term abuse.

Persistent depressive disorder occurs in approximately 2% of children and as high as 8% of adolescents (Zalaquett & Sanders, 2010). High rates of comorbidity between persistent depressive disorder and major depressive disorder have led some to question whether these are two distinct disorders. Early onset of persistent depressive disorder is considered a gateway to the occurrence and reoccurrence of other mood disorders. Persistent depressive disorder is less intense and more prolonged than major depressive disorder. For a diagnosis to be made, symptoms of depression must have persisted for at least one year in children, evidenced by at least two of the following: poor appetite or overeating, insomnia or hypersomnia, low energy or fatigue, low self-esteem, poor concentration, or feelings of hopelessness (APA, 2013). Children with persistent depressive disorder "characteristically have good days and bad days, or they may have many mixed days, but they do not have good weeks" (Kowatch et al., 2005, p. 135).

As mentioned previously, in order to deal with how depressed children and adolescents can differ in their clinical presentation, the *DSM-5* developed a new diagnosis called **disruptive mood dysregulation disorder**, the core feature of which is chronic, severe, and persistent irritability (APA, 2013). The irritability must be manifested both by temper tantrums occurring at least three times per week and irritable or angry mood most of the day every day during at least a 12-month period. The symptoms have to cross at least two of three settings: home, school, or peers.

Causal Factors of Depression

There is no one specific cause of major depressive disorder. A number of interacting factors can result in a child or adolescent suffering from depression. **Biological models** of depression are of two types: genetic and biochemical (McWhirter, McWhirter, Hart, & Gat, 2000). The genetic model derives from research that found that genetic factors account for approximately 50% of the variance in mood disorders (Scharinger, Rabl, Sitte, & Pezawas, 2010). Biochemical models explain depression as a hormonal imbalance, and there is some evidence that depressed children and adolescents have a hyposecretion of growth hormone (Wong et al., 2014). On the other hand, some have argued that biochemical imbalances may be less the cause and more the result of depression and early environmental stressors related to attachment issues (Sroufe et al., 2005).

Psychoanalytic theory described depression as anger turned inward, toward the self, connected to a judging and controlling superego. More recent psychodynamic models describe depression among the young in terms of a loss that stems from childhood helplessness and the disruption of emotional bonding with the primary caregiver. The result is a loss of self-esteem. The child or adolescent has no internal sense of self-worth, relying instead on external sources for confirmation of his or her self-worth; when those external sources are lost, the child or adolescent becomes depressed (Dozier et al., 2008).

Behaviorists argue that depression is produced by the lack of positive reinforcement for behaviors that are considered more normal. As time goes on, the depressed youngster manifests behaviors that are less likely to elicit positive reinforcement but draw attention to the child and bestow a sense of control. The symptoms of depression, then, are both cause and consequence of the lack of positive reinforcement. The key for helpers is not to reinforce the depressed behaviors but to reserve praise and encouragement for those behaviors that show improvement in both task and social functioning (Manos, Kanter, & Busch, 2010).

M. E. P. Seligman's (1974) **learned-helplessness model** of depression is based directly on research with behavioral reinforcement. Learned helplessness is a response to a series of failures to solve a problem or to improve a situation. In time, the individual becomes convinced that nothing he or she does or tries makes a difference. People with learned helplessness have an external locus of control (their life is controlled by outside forces) and an internal locus of responsibility (they blame themselves). Their feelings of hopelessness generalize to most of life's situations. For children and adolescents, learned helplessness often revolves around schoolwork: The student has made numerous attempts and tried numerous means to improve his or her schoolwork without success. So the student gives up, and depression sets in.

Cognitive models understand depression as the direct result of negative or irrational thoughts. Beck (1967) was the first to develop a cognitive theory of depression; some years later, he and his colleagues described a cognitive triad that they believed was characteristic of people who are depressed (Beck, Rush, Shaw, & Emery, 1979). The triad consists of three negative thought patterns: of oneself, of the world, and of the future. Over time, these thought patterns develop into schemas—frameworks so much a part of the individual's cognitive makeup that they are like personality traits. Environmental stimuli are filtered through these schemas and distorted to conform to the individual's negative view of his self, world, and future. Even the most positive experiences are distorted. For example, a depressed child might respond to praise for a good grade with "The teacher probably felt sorry for me." Depressed children often making negative comments about themselves: "I always fail," "I'm not good at anything," "No one likes me."

Family systems theorists believe that children's behavior—even behavior that is symptomatic of depression—maintains balance (homeostasis) in the family system. Family systems theorists would not approve of treating just the child; they would argue that the family must be treated. For example, a child's illness allows parents to focus their psychic energy on the child instead of on other difficulties they should be resolving. If there is evidence that the child's depression is serving some function in the family, the school should facilitate a referral for family counseling.

Treatments for Children and Adolescents with Depression

The treatment of depressive disorders can be divided into two basic categories: psychopharmacological and psychosocial. Psychosocial treatments include cognitive-behavioral, interpersonal, and family therapy.

In the cognitive model, the first step in helping a student who is depressed is to teach the student to use positive self-talk for negative self-statements. The helper usually gives the student a homework assignment: "Every time you say to yourself, 'I'm a bad person,' I want you to correct that statement by saying, 'I'm a good person.'" Other school-based interventions include guidance lessons that teach the relationship between thoughts and feelings and role-play activities that focus on the problems and symptoms of childhood depression (peer rejection, feelings of guilt and failure).

Interpersonal psychotherapy treats depression through improving interpersonal functioning and enhancing communication skills in relationships with significant others. Interpersonal psychotherapy addresses four areas of interpersonal functioning: interpersonal deficits, interpersonal role conflicts, abnormal grief, and difficult role transitions. Parents are involved in all phases of the treatment.

Family counseling is also recommended for the treatment of depression in children and adolescents. Based on the structural model of family therapy, Minuchin (1974) hypothesized that enmeshed relationships between children and parents were responsible for depression, since they prevented appropriate levels of attachment and separation. Many individual approaches to depression with adolescents include a parent-education component.

As far as psychopharmacological treatments, over the years a number of medications have been used to treat depression in children and adolescents. These fall into three groups: selective serotonin reuptake inhibitors (SSRIs), tricyclic antidepressants, and monoamine oxidase inhibitors. Today, without a doubt, SSRIs are the first-line pharmacological treatment for depression. While popular, SSRIs are prescribed to children and adolescents with caution due to some evidence of an increased rate of suicidality (Bridge et al., 2007; Olfson, Marcus, & Shaffer, 2006).

BIPOLAR DISORDERS

Bipolar disorders are typically characterized by the alternating presence of depressed and euphoric moods. The *DSM-5* distinguishes three types of bipolar disorders: bipolar I, bipolar II, and cyclothymic disorder. Difficulties in diagnosis make it challenging to report accurate prevalence rates. It is widely accepted that bipolar disorders occur in about a little less than 2% of children (Van Meter, Moreira, & Youngstrom, 2011). Peak onset appears to be between 15 and 19 years of age (Wicks-Nelson & Israel, 2003).

The diagnosis of **bipolar I** disorder requires the presence of a manic episode that may be followed by a hypomanic or depressive episode. A manic episode is marked by at least three of the following during a one-week period: grandiosity; decreased need for sleep; being more talkative than usual; flight of ideas; distractibility; increase in goal-directed activity; and excessive involvement in high-risk activities, such as spending sprees, sexual indiscretions, or foolish investment (APA, 2013). *Hypomania* is defined as a distinct period of persistently elevated, expansive, or irritable mood that is not as severe as mania and lasts at least four consecutive days. If hypomania occurs with evidence of only a depressive episode, the diagnosis is **bipolar II** disorder. Bipolar II is two to three times more common in children and adolescents than bipolar I (Kowatch et al., 2005). If hypomania insufficient to meet the criteria for a hypomanic episode occurs in conjunction with periods of depressive symptoms insufficient to meet the criteria for major depressive episode during the course of two years (one year in children and adolescents), the diagnosis is **cyclothymic disorder**.

Understanding bipolar disorder is complicated by two factors: the first is high rates of comorbidity; the second is the difficulty of distinguishing manic and hypomanic symptoms from typical childhood behaviors. ADHD is by far the most common comorbid disorder, with some studies estimating the rate to be as high as 98% (S. Miller, Chang, & Ketter, 2013). Furthermore, the symptoms of ADHD (distractibility, irritability, increased talkativeness, and risk-taking behaviors) can mimic those of mania. A differential diagnosis would be based on severity, occurrence, and age of onset. The symptoms of mania are more severe, occur episodically, and more often occur after the onset of puberty. The symptoms of ADHD are less severe, chronic, and begin typically in the preschool age or early elementary school years (i.e., before the age of 7). The child with ADHD may have difficulty sleeping, but the child with mania has less of a need for sleep. The overactive child with mania is goal directed, in contrast to the child with ADHD, where the overactivity is often disorganized and haphazard (Skirrow, Hosang, Farmer, & Asherson, 2012). Adolescents with bipolar disorder are five times more likely to develop a substance abuse problem (Miklowitz, 2012). Though many adolescents are sexually active, the hypersexuality that accompanies a manic episode can lead to risky sexual behaviors. Often not in control of their thoughts and actions, hypersexualized adolescents with bipolar disorder will not take the necessary precautions to avoid sexually transmitted diseases. Bipolar adolescents are also at increased risk for suicide.

Treatment for Bipolar Disorders

The recommended treatment for bipolar disorder is pharmacological. Lithium, anticonvulsants, and atypical antipsychotics have all been used in the treatment of children and adolescents with bipolar disorder. Lithium is the first-line medication for bipolar disorder and the only one approved by the FDA for the treatment of bipolar disorder in adolescents, ages 12 to 18. Two anticonvulsants, sodium divalproex acid and carbamazepine, have been used to treat mania in children and adolescents, especially for cases of mixed states and rapid-cycling bipolar disorders. In recent years, antipsychotics have been extensively used for the treatment of bipolar disorder in adults, and there is evidence to suggest they may be equally effective in treating children and adolescents.

UNDERSTANDING THE DEPRESSED STUDENT FROM AN ATTACHMENT PERSPECTIVE

Emily's case is intriguing because the details about her suggest that she went from secure to insecure after her father's death and that she had a closer relationship with her father than with her mother. The vignette highlights that her mother was jealous of the close relationship between Emily and her father. It is possible that Emily was secure more because of her relationship with her father than with her mother. (The chapter on attachment theory made clear that a child can derive attachment security from other adult figures besides the mother.) After her father's death, Emily employs deactivating strategies that result in withdrawal and avoidance as a way of feeling secure by remaining closely attached to her father in her internal world. Her deactivation of relationships in the real world allows for a hyperactivation in her internal world and maintains the relationship with her father. Emily's exploratory system has shut down, and the only way to feel secure is to avoid contact with people who are alive. Prior to her father's death, Emily presented as the ideal child—performed at a high academic level, was well liked and socially connected, and participated successfully in numerous extracurricular activities. It is quite possible that this "ideal" child shaped the bond with her father.

Recall the discussion from Chapter 1 about Bowlby's work on attachment and loss, where healthy grieving involves oscillation or alternation between hyperactivating and deactivating strategies, which eventually leads to reorganization. Emily cannot oscillate; she remains deactivated, the result of which is rumination and disengagement. We would need to know more about the relationship between Emily and her mother; Bowlby believed that an inability to oscillate was related to a lack of maternal sensitivity. Emily's mother is dealing with her own grief, perhaps making it difficult to empathize with her daughter, and it is also possible that her mother may have some unresolved anger over the relationship between Emily and her father, which appears to have been so close that it effectively excluded the mother.

Remember that an avoidant attachment style is an organized defense against anger. The child learns to suppress emotion to avoid rejection and hurt. At this point in time, Emily cannot allow herself closeness with another adult—it's too risky! We can speculate that given the tragic and premature death of her father, Emily's IWMs underwent a dramatic shift—she went from experiencing her world as basically safe to seeing it as unpredictable. Since the world is not safe, it is better to isolate and be detached rather than attached. The concept of defensive exclusion can help one understand Emily's withdrawal as the result of attachment trauma. She cannot accept that her "best friend" abandoned her and therefore is forced to exclude such an experience of her father. The avoidance allows her to withdraw into a world where she can still have her best friend. Can Emily's IWMs undergo further revision? Yes, but according to Bowlby, the best way for that to happen is through open communication with a parent—something that appears remote in the case of Emily and her mother. The idealized relationship between Emily and her father precludes the reworking of IWMs. The cost of idealization is that no one else can measure up, least of all Emily's mother. That makes the bond between Emily and her father irreplaceable, and the result is avoidance and feelings of alienation. One of her teachers, Mrs. Schwartz, has tried hard to help Emily overcome her feelings of alienation and wants to help make her more resilient. So, let's examine that teacher's response also through an attachment perspective.

UNDERSTANDING TEACHER INTERVENTIONS FOR THE DEPRESSED STUDENT FROM BOTH ATTACHMENT AND PEDAGOGICAL PERSPECTIVES

Mrs. Schwartz: "I Have Close Bonds with My Students"

One of Emily's teachers, Mrs. Schwartz, who teaches Global I and tends to develop very close bonds with her students, was determined to help Emily deal with the grief of her loss. When Emily would come to her class, Mrs. Schwartz seemed to hover near her desk and was instantly responsive to any of Emily's requests. Known to be an "amateur psychoanalyst," Mrs. Schwartz would often invite Emily to stop by her room after school to share her feelings and listen to her teacher's extensive list of suggested remedies for her depression. Some of Mrs. Schwartz's recommendations involved developing friendships and socializing with both male and female students, joining clubs, and generally doing things to stay busy and "keep your mind from dwelling on the unfortunate events of the past." She opined on one occasion, "You've simply got to think about positive things and count your blessings when you're tempted to dwell on your father's passing, honey."

It was clear to everyone in the school except Mrs. Schwartz that Emily did not appreciate her intrusive suggestions and comments. Although her actions were well intended, Mrs. Schwartz's hyperattention to Emily was actually causing Emily to withdraw from people and find ways to avoid attending her class.

Mrs. Schwartz from an Attachment Perspective

Mrs. Schwartz is described as having "very close bonds" with her students, and this most likely informs her approach to helping. Most likely classified as having a preoccupied attachment style on the AAI—the precursor for which is a resistant attachment style as a child—Mrs. Schwartz is quick to want to reduce any interpersonal distance between herself and her students. Emily's withdrawal and isolation is particularly challenging for the teacher who is prescriptive in her approach and offers lots of solutions. A preoccupied style usually involves the hyperactivation of the attachment system, evidenced by Mrs. Schwartz's need to hover near Emily's desk. The teacher knows Emily is in pain, or at least has shut down emotionally in order not to feel her pain. To experience Emily in this way is most likely very painful for Mrs. Schwartz, and her "quick tips" for Emily to move forward may result from her own difficulty at seeing the formerly high-functioning student in such a depressed state. In this regard, Mrs. Schwartz appears more reactive and less prone to mentalize, whereby she could reflect and understand better her own behavior. A preoccupied style is quick to want to "rescue" someone perceived as needy rather than use her own feelings to understand someone else's internal state.

A preoccupied adult with an avoidant child is a particularly difficult combination. The preoccupied attachment figure seeks closeness, while the avoidant child seeks distance. The more Mrs. Schwartz pursues Emily, the more likely she is to withdraw. Earlier, the closeness of the teacher–student relationship was defined by the degree to which the child sees the teacher as a safe haven. If Mrs. Schwartz represents an attachment figure for Emily, getting close to her does not represent safety—quite the opposite. Because of the death of her father, closeness for Emily represents risk, abandonment, and hurt. To put it simply, Emily sees Mrs. Schwartz as a source of danger. Closeness results from the attachment figure's sensitivity, and Mrs. Schwartz is not being sensitive by forcing herself upon Emily. There is no easy route for Emily to heal. It will take lots of time and patience, because insecure children behave in ways that make it difficult for teachers to form attachment relationships. It is only a matter of time before Mrs. Schwartz becomes frustrated with Emily, since none of her proposed solutions are taking effect. What the teacher fails to understand is that in a case like Emily's, less is more.

Mrs. Schwartz from a Pedagogical Perspective

According to Palmer (1998), good teachers share two traits: identity and integrity. To know who you are as a teacher requires that you know who you are as a person; in other words, you strive to understand yourself and your students. The teacher–student relationship—and this goes to the heart of sound pedagogy—is founded on trust and is manifested in the teacher's responsiveness to the needs of the student.

Such student–teacher trust is not possible if the teacher is the "expert." Good teaching begins with good listening—when the teacher really *listens* to the student's message (Loughran, 1997).

Integrity, or the adherence to a set of personal values (Cambridge Online Dictionary, 2012)), is evident in a teacher when she seeks to truly understand her students and their individual needs, and she resists the temptation to compromise her values—for example, by inflating student grades to improve her perceived effectiveness, or by forming inappropriately close relationships with students and thus achieve popularity. Indeed, as we noted in Chapter 2, Greene (1978) asserted that:

> If teachers are to initiate students into an ethical existence, they themselves must attend more fully . . . to their own lives and its requirements; they have to break with the mechanical life, to overcome their own submergence in the habitual, even in what they conceive to be virtuous, and ask the "Why?" with which learning and moral reasoning begin. (p. 46)

Finally, Hruska (2007) suggested that teachers need a philosophy of pedagogy that incorporates three seemingly dichotomous principles: (a) directivity and receptivity, (b) discipline and spontaneity, and (c) conviction and openness.

We will now discuss Mrs. Schwartz's pedagogical style relative to these three principles. Based on her response to Emily's withdrawal, it appears that Mrs. Schwartz does assume the role of a diagnostician, but there is little evidence that she has actually invested time in understanding Emily's perspectives and needs by truly *listening* to her. Loughran (1997) notes that student–teacher trust is not possible if the teacher presents herself as the "expert." Similarly, Palmer (1998) exhorted the teacher to "know herself" and learn her identity as a developmental component of her own integrity. Mrs. Schwartz's overbearing, hyperattentive approach to her students suggests that she isn't sensitive to their individual needs and differences, which may mean that she is unaware of this behavior and the purpose it serves in her own life.

Furthermore, Mrs. Schwartz doesn't seem to be aware of Emily's needs and is therefore unable to respond to them in a meaningful way. Indeed, her intrusive and maternal style might actually instigate the very behavior she wants to impede; namely, Emily's further alienation.

Mrs. Collier: "Being Is More Important than Doing"

After the school psychologist met with Emily's teachers and school administrators to explain the treatment process—the relevant aspects of the cognitive-behavioral therapy and the beneficial and adverse effects of the medication prescribed—several of her teachers discussed ways they could appropriately support the treatment plan. Mrs. Collier, a relative newcomer to the school, disclosed that her son was similarly diagnosed with a mood disorder and shared some ways that his teachers were working with his school psychologist to address related concerns in their class-

rooms. One thing Mrs. Collier stressed was the importance of really listening to the student and being attentive and alert to sudden changes in behavior, but avoiding the temptation to offer advice and "I know how you must be feeling" sympathies. She also suggested that it might be helpful to keep an anecdotal record of unusual or atypical behaviors and report any concerns immediately to the school counselor and the administration. "It's also OK to let Emily know that you care and are concerned, without imposing on her personal space or causing her embarrassment."

Mrs. Collier from an Attachment Perspective

No doubt, Emily presents with a challenging attachment style. As mentioned previously, those with an avoidant style want to avoid those who seek them out. Since her avoidance is the result of her father's traumatic death, it is easy to feel sorry for her and offer trite empathic remarks such as "I know how you are feeling." But the fact of the matter is no one really knows how Emily is feeling. Based on attachment theory, however, we can intuit that Emily's avoidance is, paradoxically, keeping her safe. Being with someone who has suffered traumatic loss poses a challenge as to the best way to be with that person psychologically. Human nature dictates action—the need to do something, to fix it—and this was exemplified in the approach taken by Mrs. Schwartz. Words are almost superfluous, and genuine empathy may involve just being with the person and being available to him or her when the moment arrives. Unfortunately, we do not know when that moment is, and there may only be subtle signs that it has arrived. Traumatic memories are stored differently, in a way that enables the original experience to be recreated. Emily was not given a diagnosis of PTSD, and she may not meet all the diagnostic criteria for it, but she may still suffer from situational accessible memories (SAMs). SAMs are not consciously accessible, but they erupt when the traumatized individual encounters a situation that reminds her of the traumatic event. Verbally accessible memories (VAMs), by contrast, are conscious representations of the traumatic event, whereby cognitive meaning is given to the event—in other words, a person can understand and talk about her physiological and emotional reactions. The goal of therapy is to help SAMs becomes VAMs. In the case of Emily, SAMs may be in the form of caring adults, a situation that reminds her of her father. Mrs. Schwartz and perhaps others in the school are not aware of or cannot fathom how their very presence could create a SAM and cause Emily to withdraw even further, the result of hyperarousal and re-experiencing. Emily is simply trying to avoid SAMs. Lacking verbal ability and emotional regulation to process SAMs, children may retain stable PTSD symptoms for a long period of time.

Mrs. Collier's more minimalist approach involves simply listening and observing Emily, rather than being intrusive, as is the case with Mrs. Schwartz. Emily is a bereaved trauma survivor, which puts her more at risk than trauma survivors who are not bereaved. Boys with traumatic grief tend to exhibit more aggression, whereas girls typically exhibit more anxiety and depression. In traumatic grief, an important variable in the child's return to normalcy is the functioning of the surviving parent. The school psychologist and Emily's outside therapist (if she has one) would do well to evaluate her mother, both alone and in interactions with her daughter. Emily's mother is concerned about her daughter, but we also know that she is jealous of Emily's relationship with her father. We do not know the attachment style of Emily's mother, but jealousy is often associated with anger and is more indicative of a preoccupied attachment style on the AAI. Like Mrs. Schwartz, Emily's mother may be intent on helping her daughter and is anxious that Emily overcome her avoidance and get on with her life. This may lead to inappropriate responses, similar to the approach taken by Mrs. Schwartz. In fact, Emily's response to her father's death may further intensify her mother's anger by reminding her of the close relationship she had with her father and not with her mother. In the end, the school and those who care for Emily will have to be patient and simply stand by her in this process. Her dissociation from affect is bound to erupt at some point, albeit in subtle ways. When that happens, the caring adults in her life need to facilitate further exploration. Although Emily might be considered old for play therapy, her regression also makes it a treatment of choice, given her lack of verbal communication at this point. There is no evidence at present that Emily is suicidal, but it cannot be ruled out, and the school should be vigilant of any signs of suicidality.

Mrs. Collier from a Pedagogical Perspective

Unlike Mrs. Schwartz, Mrs. Collier seems to embody some of the important principles of pedagogy espoused by Palmer (1998), Loughran (1997), Greene (1978), and Hruska (2007). She seems responsive and caring, but she is not compelled to act without understanding. Perhaps she might consider employing the "emergency first aid on the spot" technique of "communication maintenance" recommended in the work of Redl (1966) to encourage Emily to voice her feelings and concerns as she feels comfortable to do so. Mrs. Collier's "listening and observing" approach to Emily suggests that she understands her own identity, both as a human being and as a teacher, and this self-knowledge has helped her to develop confidence and self-efficacy. This self-assurance allows her to adopt a mindful state that gives her some perspective in understanding Emily and her issues, without compelling her to intervene without cause.

Indeed, as Greene (1978), Russell (1997), Schön (1983), and Sellar (2013) have encouraged, Mrs. Collier is able to contemplate her interactions with Emily and work on improving their relationship. In this state of reflection, she can decide which of Hruska's (2007) principles to employ in order to work more effectively with Emily. In a similar way, Mrs. Collier can employ Smith's (1994) pedagogical elements; specifically, animation: "bringing life into situations and introducing students to new experiences," reflection: "creating moments and spaces to explore lived experiences," and action: "working with people so that they are able to make changes in their lives" (p. 10). With her patient manner and genuine caring attitude toward Emily, she may be successful in enticing Emily to try new things and engage in novel learning experiences. Similarly, given her understanding of Emily and her willingness to learn more about her, Mrs. Collier will conceivably be able to help Emily create and explore long-remembered moments, and, most importantly, it would seem likely that, as her trust in Mrs. Collier grows, Emily will feel empowered sufficiently to make healthy, prosocial changes in her life.

This section provided a detailed analysis of Emily's case from both an attachment and pedagogical perspective. Mood disorders—depression and bipolar disorder—manifest similarly in terms of observable classroom behaviors; therefore, the next section provides a brief student vignette as well as some ways teachers might deal with bipolar disorder.

Student Vignette: "Chaim" (Bipolar Disorder)

Chaim is a fifteen-year-old high school sophomore who is active in the band and the drama club. He has recently been referred to a psychologist for evaluation for bipolar disorder. His mother and an aunt both have been diagnosed with the disorder.

Chaim began to exhibit the behavioral symptoms of bipolar disorder at the onset of puberty, about the time he turned thirteen. Family members and close friends noted that Chaim appeared to be uncharacteristically overbearing in social interactions and more egocentric in his conversations. Moreover, his parents noticed that he began staying up later, despite their protests, but was still able to get up at the usual time in the morning. He would also perseverate about an idea, seeming to have a one-track mind about whatever served as his current passion. These periods of frenetic activity would last for three to four days, after which he would appear to lose some of his initial enthusiasm and seem a bit depressed and somewhat depleted, as though he were "low on fuel."

These behaviors seemed to steadily intensify through eighth grade, culminating in several bizarre episodes. The first of these occurred early in ninth grade, when Chaim was selected to play a major role in the high school's fall production of Our Town. *Although he found the role quite challenging, and on top of that still had responsibilities as a member of the high school marching band, he entered a local "def poetry jam" competition that would most certainly consume all his remaining free time. Despite warnings from his parents, teachers, and friends, Chaim pushed himself to persevere in all three activities. Unfortunately, as a result of his overinvolvement in these extracurricular activities, his grades began to falter. Similarly, in English, Chaim offered to be the team leader for an important and challenging term project. Once again, as the deadline loomed and the pressure to complete the project mounted, Chaim succumbed, stating he felt overwhelmed, and had to pass the leadership role on to another student. After a year of this cycling behavior, alternating between periods of euphoria and depression, Chaim's parents and teachers requested a formal evaluation to determine the cause and develop a treatment plan.*

Chaim from an Attachment Perspective

Chaim presents with almost textbook symptoms of bipolar disorder. Mood disorders in general are highly hereditary, and bipolar disorder runs in his family. There is little research on attachment states of mind and bipolar disorder, though some studies have shown that adults with bipolar disorder tend to be classified as dismissing on the AAI (Fonagy et al., 1996). The reader will remember that the precursor to dismissing is generally an avoidant attachment style in childhood. In an avoidant style, the attention is always away from the primary caretaker, and the individual tends to employ relational strategies that put distance between himself and others. This would make sense for someone with bipolar disorder, since both mania and depression prevent others from getting close. In the manic stage, there may be lots of romantic activity, but on a very superficial level; while in the depressed stage the individual is equally incapable of intimacy. Working with students with bipolar disorder will always be a challenge, since their presentation can vary from one extreme to another. Let's look at how two teachers might see a student with bipolar disorder.

Mrs. Yost: "Chaim Is a Prodigy and Simply Needs to Hone His Time-Management Skills"

Mrs. Yost has taught Chaim English and drama in both ninth and 10th grade and is convinced his frenetic activity is evidence of his great "stage energy" and a natural gift for acting. She dismisses the concerns expressed by his other teachers, reminding them that "Sir Laurence Olivier suffered bouts of melancholia before and after some of his greatest performances!" She believes that as a young actor with nascent skills, Chaim simply needs to manage his time more efficiently. Also, Mrs. Yost has a nephew who exhibits behavior similar to Chaim's. Her nephew was evaluated by a psychiatrist and, a year after taking the medications prescribed by the doctor, "He has lost his creative spark," which she considers a great tragedy. Her nephew's experience has caused her to be very suspicious of the mental health profession. She feels psychiatrists tend to misunderstand idiosyncratic behavior and construe it as an "illness."

Mrs. Nevins: "Chaim Is Truly a Student at Risk Who Needs Help"

Mrs. Nevins, Chaim's guidance counselor, has known Chaim and his family for years. She was one of the first school professionals to raise concerns about Chaim's mental health. "He's never exhibited these behaviors before, and I've known him for most of his fifteen years," she says. "He's a young man at risk, and we need to develop an intervention plan that will address his mood swings and help reduce the stress caused by his frenetic behavior." Mrs. Nevins has initiated a multidisciplinary team meeting (that includes the school psychologist) to address Chaim's at-risk behavior and issues of real concern to his parents. The plan will likely involve prescribing appropriate medication to help moderate his dramatic mood swings, but it will ultimately comprise a multisystemic therapeutic approach that will involve Chaim's teachers, parents, and other school professionals.

Mrs. Yost and Mrs. Nevins from an Attachment Perspective

The two different views of Chaim espoused by Mrs. Yost and Mrs. Nevins remind one of the old arguments about normalcy—Is there such thing as mental illness? The reader might remember Thomas Szasz's classic book, *The Myth of Mental Illness*

(Szasz, 1974), where he argues that mental illness doesn't really exist, since it is only defined by what psychiatrists say it is. Mrs. Yost is not alone in her distrust of the mental health profession, and she may have good reason to be. It may not be fair to classify her as dismissing since, like many individuals in the manic stage, Chaim has shown her his creative qualities, which are highly admirable. One would need to know more about Mrs. Yost to determine if she does have a dismissing style, tending to downplay negative experiences. She wants to focus on the positive aspects of Chaim's behavior, but it is possible that her dismissing state of mind in combination with Chaim's avoidant style allows her to disregard the interference in Chaim's functioning.

Mrs. Nevins represents a more functional approach. As a trained counselor, she does not minimize the observed and drastic change in Chaim's behavior. Operating perhaps from a more autonomous state of mind, Mrs. Nevins might be seeing Chaim more objectively, and her desire for both behavioral and pharmacological interventions is rooted in the fact that Chaim's behavior is seriously interfering with his functioning. To answer, then, the question about the myth of mental illness, it is perhaps better to ask the question: To what degree does this student's behavior interfere with his functioning in school and relationships? This question can also be employed to guide the need for medication. If she operates from a secure-autonomous state of mind, Mrs. Nevins will be well equipped to handle the criticism from Mrs. Yost about the mental health profession. It is not uncommon for teachers to be critical of support staff, often claiming that they don't understand the realities of the classroom. The ultimate goal will be for Mrs. Yost and Mrs. Nevins to collaborate in helping Chaim, but this will be a process. Mrs. Yost does not trust counselors, and only by listening to her criticism and not becoming defensive will Mrs. Nevins be able to make progress in forming a collaborative bond with the teacher. The key, once again, to this relationship will be the counselor's ability to relate to Mrs. Yost from secure-autonomous state of mind.

Mrs. Yost and Mrs. Nevins from a Pedagogical Perspective

As Smith (2012) and others have observed, "Teachers are learners, too!" In her insistence that Chaim's frenetic behaviors are simply manifestations of his great "stage energy" that may herald a brilliant acting career, Mrs. Yost seems oblivious of the potential harm that these atypical behaviors portend. Likewise, as Bruner (1996) and Freire (1970) have both urged, the teacher must acknowledge her culture and its influence in the way she interacts with her students. In this instance, Mrs. Yost appears to be projecting her passion for the stage onto the behaviors of her student, Chaim. In doing so, she is unable to distinguish what she describes as "stage energy" from the behaviors that characterize a potentially serious mood disorder.

On the other hand, Mrs. Nevins's extensive knowledge of Chaim's typical behavior and her concern for his well-being allow her to accurately detect an aberration (Noddings, 2005; Smith, 2012). She responds in a professional manner, initiating a multidisciplinary meeting to address her concerns about Chaim's bizarre behaviors. Finally, as advocated by Stout, Mrs. Nevins demonstrates "certainty, positivity, and the unity of self and moral goals" (2005, p. 194) when she responsibly advocates for Chaim by sharing her concerns with the other professionals and caregivers.

Effective Teacher Responses

- Become thoroughly familiar with the characteristics, assessment procedures, and recommended interventions for students suspected to have or diagnosed with a mood disorder.
- Maintain accurate and detailed anecdotal records about any student in your class diagnosed with a mood disorder. This information will be invaluable in helping the clinician determine the effects of prescribed medication and other cognitive and behavioral interventions employed.
- Provide a structured curriculum and establish a predictable classroom routine for students diagnosed with a mood disorder. Stability that comes from routine is comforting to students who may be experiencing mood cycles, dysthymia, or a depressive episode. Their world may seem out of control, but your classroom may provide a safe haven of predictability, understanding, and support.
- Don't try to "make it all better" or cheer up a student who is depressed. Provide encouragement and support and alert parents, clinical professionals, and administrators if significant changes in behavior are observed.
- Avoid looking for causes for the student's depressed state. Usually the student does not understand the reason for her depression—it may be biochemical and therefore beyond anyone's power to "cure."
- Most importantly, be firm, but compassionately firm. Don't accept the student's depression as an excuse for not trying or completing an assignment. Of course, teachers need to be flexible and accommodating if the student has been absent due to treatment or hospitalization for depression, but it is important to help the student return to a sense of normalcy and routine as quickly as possible.
- If the student's depression is associated with a trigger or precipitating event, try to structure the classroom environment and activities so as to avoid exposing her to evocative stimuli.
- Consider reducing the student's workload. For example, provide fewer problems on a test or reduce the number of questions to be answered on a homework assignment. Similarly, provide alternative projects or assessments, and give the student a choice. Finally, give the student and extension for the due date of an assignment, because many students with mood disorders have difficulty with organizational tasks and meeting stringent deadlines. In other words, try to be flexible!
- Provide the student with a peer tutor. This can serve two purposes; specifically, (a) providing needed social interaction, and (b) helping the student stay on task and not feel overwhelmed with the demands of the curriculum. Finally, always include the student who is depressed in all classroom activities

and ensure he knows that he is a valued member of the classroom community. (Reprinted from Austin & Sciarra, 2010 with permission, Pearson Education)

Concluding Thoughts

In this chapter, we have addressed the topic of mood disorders, their characteristic behaviors, and their effects on students in the classroom. In concert with our themes of relationship and pedagogy—the pillars of effective teaching—we provided real-life case studies as exemplars of the behaviors that are common in adolescents with mood disorders and then described two examples of teacher responses to a student displaying such behaviors. Then we discussed the two contrasting teacher responses, as well as the student's behavior, relative to the theory of attachment and its influence on teacher and student behavior. Moreover, we examined both teacher responses through the lens of applicable teaching pedagogies to provide the reader with an understanding of the teachers' critical role in facilitating effective teaching and learning.

Mood disorders are fast becoming more prevalent diagnoses for older children and adolescents in the United States. Some researchers suggest that the cause for this increased identification might be due, in part, to environmental stressors, poor diet, family dysfunction, or genetic predisposition. Regardless of these speculations, the etiology of mood disorders is not well understood by the medical community. Nevertheless, as teachers, we will invariably encounter students in our classes who have been so diagnosed. Therefore, it is vital that we acquire the information provided in this chapter. The need for teachers' understanding of the characteristics of depression is made more urgent by the fact that the majority of suicide victims had or were suspected of having a mood disorder. We know that, as teachers, our professional obligations and code of ethics far exceeds that of simply providing instruction: we want to ensure our students' safety, to the extent possible, and improve the quality of their lives because we truly care for each of them.

We hope that you take what you have learned from this chapter about working with students in your classroom who have a mood disorder and may be at risk for suicide and apply it to your teaching pedagogy and your relationships with your students. Our goal is to help you become a better teacher and work more effectively with students who present the most challenging behaviors, and no issues pose a greater threat to the safety and well-being of these students than those addressed in this chapter.

In the next chapter, we will learn about a growing problem among children and adolescents, male and female, that teachers must be prepared to address: the challenges presented by students with eating disorders.

CHAPTER 6

Teaching Students with Eating-Disordered Behavior

STUDENT VIGNETTE: "ANNA" (BULIMIA)

Anna was the girl every other girl in the high school wanted to emulate—so together, so smart, and so pretty! Anna's father was the pastor of a local congregation, and Anna, a talented musician in her own right, frequently helped out in the choir and occasionally provided piano accompaniment for the hymns and choruses sung during the services. Most of the folks in her sleepy little prairie town secretly wished Anna were their daughter, or sister, or girlfriend. She just seemed so perfect, as did her life!

So it came as a great shock to her teachers when, on a sunny day in mid-April of her senior year, Anna disclosed to the school counselor that she was struggling with a dark secret: She felt she had an eating disorder. After further evaluation, the counselor confirmed her suspicions. Anna revealed to her counselor that she spent about half of her weekly paycheck from her job as a cashier at the local IGA Foodliner on junk food, which she concealed in the trunk of her car. Late at night, after everyone in her house had retired, she snuck out to her car and then stealthily returned to her bedroom, where she would binge on snack foods such as Twinkies, potato chips, candy bars, cookies, cheese spread and crackers, cinnamon buns, and peanut butter sandwiches. She would furtively gorge on these foods, consuming entire boxes of cookies and bags of chips, washed down with a two-liter bottle of Coke, allowed herself about 10 minutes to savor these guilty pleasures, and then surreptitiously make her way to the small bathroom in the basement—the one with the locking door—a can of air freshener in one hand and a small vial of ipecac in the other.

Once she had finished purging, she would return to her room, vowing to end this terrible cycle, but after an hour or so would begin to binge once more, the cycle repeating several times until, exhausted, she succumbed to the need for sleep. Anna was trapped in this cycle for several years.

Her disclosure to the counselor was prompted by some of the distressing side effects of her condition: the loss of tooth enamel, bloodshot eyes, and gastrointestinal complications.

As part of the therapeutic process, her parents and teachers were informed of her condition, and a behavioral intervention plan was prepared and implemented for the duration of Anna's school day. One component of the plan was close and continuous supervision, which involved Anna's teachers, and was met with stiff resistance from Anna. Nonetheless, thus far, the plan appears to be working, and Anna's parents report initial success at home.

WHY DOES THE TEACHER NEED TO KNOW ABOUT EATING DISORDERS?

A brief review of national statistics on eating disorders as well as their effects on students will provide the reader with a rationale for the value of this information for teachers.

First, our best estimates regarding the prevalence of eating disorders among men and women in the United States suggest that as many as 20 million women and 10 million men are currently diagnosed with these disorders, which have been increasing in number since 1950 (Wade, Keski-Rahkonen, & Hudson, 2011). Similarly, there has been a significant rise in the incidence of anorexia in young women, ages 15 to 19, in each decade since 1930; and the incidence of bulimia in girls and women, ages 10 to 39, tripled from 1988 to 1993 (Hoek & van Hoeken, 2003). Of the estimated number of women identified, 90% were between the ages of 12 and 25 (Department of Health and Human Services, n.d.). Furthermore, it is estimated that 11% of high school students have been diagnosed with an eating disorder (National Association of Anorexia Nervosa and Associated Disorders, 2015). In addition to these statistics, 42% of first- to third-grade girls have expressed that they want to be thinner (Collins, 1991), and 46% of 9- to 11-year-olds were "sometimes" or "very often" on diets (Gustafson-Larson & Terry, 1992). Finally, anorexia is the third most common chronic illness among adolescents (Eating Disorder Information Sheet, 2000).

The potential for catastrophic outcomes as a result of engaging in these disordered behaviors is very real, as researchers report based on recent investigations. For example, Harrop and Marlatt (2010) noted that students with an eating disorder were four times more likely to engage in alcohol and substance abuse than their peers without such a disorder. Likewise, students with an eating disorder are, not surprisingly, more likely to develop a mood or anxiety disorder, such as major depressive disorder or obsessive-compulsive disorder (OCD), as compared with their unaffected peers (Altman & Shankman, 2009; McElroy, Kotwal, Keck, & Akiskal, 2005). Finally, and most disturbingly, students with eating disorders have the highest mortality rate of any mental illness; it is estimated that a young woman with anorexia is 12 times more likely to die than other women of the same age who do not have anorexia (Sullivan, 2002). Moreover, estimates show that 5%–10% of individuals diagnosed with an eating disorder will die within 10 years of onset and 18%–20% will die within 20 years of onset unless effectively treated (Sullivan, 2002).

Nahas (n.d.) has developed an Eating Disorder Fact Sheet for Educators, which provides further support for our rationale. In it she notes that because teachers and other educators are in close contact with students at the ages that eating disorders typically emerge, they are uniquely positioned to identify at-risk students and take the appropriate preventive measures. She goes on to acknowledge that although teachers cannot provide clinical intervention, they can reach out to school clinicians, health-care professionals, and administrators for support and alert them to their concerns. As noted by the National Eating Disorders Association in its "Toolkit for Educators," invariably, as the eating disorder progresses, it will negatively affect both academic performance and social-emotional development due to the effects of malnutrition on attention and cognitive function and physical health. Frequently, Section 504 plans or special education services might be a necessary recourse to ensure that affected students receive the academic, medical, and psychological support they need in order to be successful in school.

WHAT THE TEACHER SHOULD KNOW ABOUT EATING DISORDERS

Since the 1970s, eating disorders have come to the forefront of emotional and psychological concerns facing a school-aged adolescent population. It was during that time that clinical studies resulted in a reexamination of eating disorders away from unconscious conflict based on psychoanalytic thought toward a more developmental, family, and socio-environmental perspective. More recently, studies have examined biological factors in the causality of eating disorders. In the 1970s, clinicians also began to make a distinction between different kinds of eating disorders, namely anorexia nervosa and bulimia nervosa. In addition to anorexia and bulimia, the *DSM-5* has added binge eating disorder.

The Core Characteristics of Anorexia Nervosa

The core symptom of anorexia is a drive for thinness and fear of becoming fat. It is common for those with anorexia to insist they are too fat even when they are dangerously underweight. This distorted body image interferes with body sensations. The individual may never feel hungry or may feel completely satiated with just a morsel of food. Excessive amounts of exercise and purging may also be part of the symptomatic picture. In fact, the *DSM-5* classifies anorexia into two types: the binge eating–purging type and the restricting type, the classic form of the disorder. The bulimic features of the former type are associated with longer-term negative outcomes and demand a different treatment approach (Forman, Yager, & Solomon, 2012). Anorexia tends to begin in adolescence between the ages of 14 and 18. Anorexia is evidenced by significantly low weight, an intense fear of gaining weight or becoming fat, undue influence of body weight or shape or self-evalua-tion, and a persistent lack of recognition of the seriousness of the current low body weight (APA, 2013).

The Core Characteristics of Bulimia Nervosa

The core characteristic of bulimia is a recurrent, out-of-control pattern of binge-eat-ing episodes characterized by the consumption of large quantities of food. The eating episodes occur in conjunction with compensatory behaviors, either of the purging or nonpurging type. It is often the case that those with bulimia present with a history of anorexia, and vice versa. The current preference is to understand eating disorders as existing along a continuum and not as mutually exclusive categories (Schwitzer, 2012). The onset of bulimia is usually in late adolescence or early adulthood. Those with bulimia can be either underweight or overweight; however, males with bulimia often have a history of overweight or obesity (K. L. Allen, Byrne, & Crosby, 2014). The classic symptoms for bulimia are recurrent episodes of binge eating and recur-rent inappropriate compensatory behavior in order to prevent weight gain, such as self-induced vomiting; misuse of laxatives, diuretics, enemas, or other medications; fasting; or excessive exercise (American Psychological Association, 2013). For a diag-nosis of bulimia, these behaviors must occur at least once a week for three months.

The Core Characteristics of Binge Eating Disorder

Binge eating disorder appears to be a common phenomenon in people who are obese and have little or no concern about their weight, in contrast to those with anorexia and bulimia. Similar to bulimia, the core characteristic of binge eating is eating an excessive amount of highly caloric food within a short period. What dis-tinguishes binge eating from bulimia is the lack of compensatory behaviors. There are recurrent episodes of binge eating along with a sense of lack of control over eat-ing during the episode. The binge-eating episodes are associated with eating much more rapidly than normal; eating until feeling uncomfortably full; eating large amounts of food when not feeling physically hungry; eating alone due to embar-rassment about how much one is eating; feeling disgusted with oneself, depressed, or very guilty after overeating (APA, 2013). The person usually feels distressed over eating so much, and the behavior occurs on average once a week for a period of at least three months.

In summary, all individuals with eating disorders share a common set of charac-teristics useful for understanding eating disorders in adolescents:

- "an abnormal attitude or set of beliefs about food, weight, and/or shape;
- a degree of emotional, social, or behavioral dysfunction that results from these behaviors and attitudes (significant problems with school, work, social, or familial functioning); and
- evidence that these behaviors and attitudes are unlikely to change without intervention" (Lock & le Grange, 2006, p. 486).

Prevalence of Eating Disorders

Most studies estimate the point prevalence rate for anorexia in adolescent girls to be about 0.5% (APA, 2013). Incidence rates for anorexia have risen continuously, and the increase has eliminated social class as a major predictor. Prevalence rates for bulimia are higher, estimated to be anywhere from 1% to 1.5% (APA, 2013). Subclinical cases of bulimia are considerably higher. Estimates are that anywhere from 4% to 19% of young women may engage in less severe bulimic-type behaviors. Bulimia is also on the rise, especially among younger age groups. Adult women, however, have the highest prevalence rate of clinical cases, estimated to be about 2% to 3% (Swanson, Crow, Le Grange, Swendsen, & Merikangas, 2011).

Epidemiological data for binge eating is rather scant, given the definition of this disorder and its recent status as a diagnostic category. Preliminary estimates of the prevalence rate for binge eating are 1.6% for females and 0.8% for males (APA, 2013). In regard to gender, all three eating disorders have higher prevalence rates for females than males. For anorexia, the prevalence rate is 19:2 female to male, and for bulimia it is 58:2 (Swanson et al., 2011). In general, adolescent and adult males comprise approximately 10% of clinically diagnosed cases of eating disorders (APA, 2013). Some people believe that eating disorders are significantly underdiagnosed in males because of a prevailing bias to see such disorders as strictly female. In addition, some symptoms, such as binge eating, may be more socially accepted in men than in women, and men may be less likely than women to seek clinical intervention for their disordered eating. Anorexia and bulimia appear to have different developmental courses, with the former being the more serious in regard to morbidity and mortality (Le Grange & Lock, 2011) .

Developmental Course of Eating Disorders

Anorexia typically develops in early adolescence, around the ages of 13–14, with the individual beginning a diet to lose weight, eat healthier, or improve performance in some activity like sports or dancing. The dieting usually begins with cutting out a small number of foods, such as desserts, but as time goes on the food choices become more narrowed, with an emphasis on consuming smaller quantities. Food preparation can become quite elaborate, accompanied by an obsession over not consuming a morsel of food that is "not allowed." Often, the individual will prefer to eat by herself. As food consumption decreases, rigid adherence to an exercise regimen increases. Through self-induced vomiting, the individual progresses to purging herself of even a small quantity of consumed food and may also resort to diet pills and laxatives. At some point during the process, as body fat declines, menstruation ceases in postmenarcheal females, though this will vary according to the individual—for some this happens early in the process, while others continue to menstruate in spite of having very low weight (Le Grange & Lock, 2011). As malnutrition sets in, a number of medical problems begin to develop, which can include lowered body temperature, decrease in blood pressure and heart rate, changes in skin and hair texture including lanugo (the development of fine body hair), hypogonadism, cardiac dysfunction, brain abnormalities, and gastrointestinal difficulties (Le Grange & Lock, 2011).

Outcomes for those with anorexia vary; some people make a complete recovery, while others suffer from long-term weight gains and losses that may lead to the development of bulimia. Less than one third of those with anorexia develop bulimia. Some never recover and follow a deteriorating course that can result in death. Mortality rates for those with anorexia range from 3% to 10%; half of these are the result of suicide, while the rest are from medical complications (Arcelus, Mitchell, Wales, & Nielsen, 2011). The aggregated mortality rate of anorexia is estimated at 6.5% per decade, higher than the mortality rate for any other psychiatric disorder (Franko et al., 2013). The longer the illness lasts, the greater the chance of mortality.

In comparison to anorexia, bulimia develops later, with most cases beginning around the age of 18. Prior to developing the disorder, these individuals typically have a history of weight preoccupation, and many of them suffered from mild to moderate obesity in childhood (Le Grange & Lock, 2011). Their histories often include failed attempts at weight reduction, and many report that their binge eating is the result of denying themselves food through fasting and dieting. The cycle includes guilt over binging and the consequential purging to avoid gaining weight. The most common form of purging is vomiting, but the use of laxatives, diuretics, and exercise is also common. As the illness progresses, these individuals will organize their lives around opportunities to binge. Since binging is done in private, they may withdraw from family and friends, decline in their schoolwork, and suffer from depressed mood. In addition to binging, those with bulimia may participate in other impulsive behaviors, such as drug use and stealing (Le Grange & Lock, 2011). While the weight of those with bulimia may fluctuate rather significantly, it rarely approaches the dangerously low levels of those with anorexia. Common medical problems, mostly the result of purging, include low potassium levels, tears in the esophagus, gastric abnormalities, dehydration, and severe changes in heart rate and blood pressure. Without treatment, bulimics can sustain a regimen of binging and purging for many years. Many patients are treated successfully, with about 50% becoming asymptomatic and another 20% significantly improved (Smink, van Hoeken, & Hoek, 2013).

Comorbidity

Conditions comorbid with eating disorders can be both psychological and medical. The most common *DSM-5* disorders comorbid with eating disorders are mood disorders, anxiety disorders, substance use, and personality disorders (APA, 2013).

Due to starvation, an individual with anorexia may exhibit many symptoms of depression (e.g., insomnia, irritability, fatigue, dysphoria, psychomotor retardation, and social withdrawal; Gauthier et al., 2014). When weight is restored, many of these symptoms tend to disappear. The most frequent personality disorders associated with restricting-type anorexia are obsessive-compulsive (22%), avoidant (19%), and borderline or dependent (10%). In contrast, the most frequent personality disorders in those with binge eating–purging type of anorexia are borderline (25%), avoidant or dependent (15%), and histrionic (10%). Borderline is also the most frequent comorbid personality disorder for those with bulimia (28%), followed by dependent and histrionic (both 20%; Sansone & Sansone, 2011).

One of the more difficult differential diagnoses is between anorexia and OCD. Those with anorexia limit their obsessive-compulsiveness to food and weight. For full-blown OCD to exist, the obsessive-compulsiveness would have to include aspects of one's life beyond food and weight. While anxiety disorders coexist with eating disorders, anorexia in particular, the drive for thinness and the extreme fear of becoming fat should not be confused with phobias and other anxiety disorders (Lawson et al., 2013). The high comorbidity between eating disorders and depression should be a major concern. Overeating can be a symptom of depressive disorders; it is distinguished from overeating in bulimia by the absence of compensatory behaviors (Mischoulon et al., 2011). Similarly, weight loss associated with depression is not accompanied by the intense fear of becoming fat, a critical sign of anorexia (APA, 2013). The same is true for body dysmorphic disorder, characterized by an excessive preoccupation with defects in one's general appearance, not limited to body shape and size or the fear of becoming fat.

Medical conditions comorbid with eating disorders are numerous. They can include neurological, dental and dermatological, endocrinological, gynecological, and gastrointestinal abnormalities (Terre, Poston, & Foreyt, 2006). Most of these medical conditions will subside with an increase in nutrition, but some (e.g., growth stunting and long-term fracture risk) may persist even after a return to average weight (Piran, Levine, & Steiner-Adair, 2013).

Etiological factors in the development of eating disorders include biological, psychological, familial, and sociocultural factors.

Research has investigated **genetics** as a cause of eating disorders, and studies have found higher rates of both anorexia and bulimia in first-degree relatives. Twin studies have revealed higher concordance rates among monozygotic twins than dizygotic twins—50% as compared to 14% (Trace, Baker, Peñas-Lledó, & Bulik, 2013). The unraveling of shared and nonshared environments in the causality of eating disorders remains a work in progress, and the contribution of genetic versus environmental influences remains unclear. The lack of longitudinal studies also complicates the etiological picture. Furthermore, while some genetic influence may be apparent, it is not clear exactly what is being genetically transmitted. For example, is a genetically inherited temperament or personality trait responsible for the development of an eating disorder? The answer to this question is not really known. The safest thing that can be said about the role of genetics in the causation of eating disorders is that girls, especially, who grow up in families with either the mother, father, or sister having an eating disorder are very much at risk for developing an eating disorder of their own (Easter, 2012).

Investigators have also considered the role of **neurobiological factors**, especially differences in serotonin activity, among people with eating disorders. Low levels of serotonin have been found in those with bulimia; antidepressants that increase levels of serotonin have proven effective in the treatment of bulimia (Pichika et al., 2012). If binge eating plays a role in mood regulation (i.e., by increasing levels of serotonin), then an antidepressant regimen may very well decrease the desire for such foods. In contrast, it is hypothesized that that those with anorexia may suffer from an overactivity of serotonin, which would decrease the desire for food intake (Bailer et al., 2013). Though studies have shown an association between serotonin activity and eating disorders, a definite causal link has not been established (Thornton, Mazzeo, & Bulik, 2011). It is possible that the differing levels of serotonin could also be the result of an eating disorder, rather than the cause. Since serotonin activity seems to play a role in numerous other disorders, it may be a common pathway rather than a specific link to eating disorders.

More recently, research has investigated **prenatal, perinatal, and early childhood complications** as possibly having a role in the development of eating disorders (Raevuori, Linna, & Keski-Rahkonen, 2014). Perinatal factors in the development of anorexia include preterm birth (less than 32 weeks), low birth weight, birth trauma, and pediatric infectious disease. To date, few of these findings have been replicated, and they should be regarded as tentative.

For many years, experts have considered **personality patterns** an important factor in the development of eating disorders. People with anorexia often exhibit personality patterns of compliance, perfectionism, dependence, social inhibition, emotional restraint, obsession, and self-hate guilt (Amianto, Abbate-Daga, Morando, Sobrero, & Fassino, 2011). Other studies have found those with anorexia to be low in novelty seeking, high in harm avoidance, and high in reward dependence (Taborelli et al., 2013). Personality patterns among those with bulimia are less consistent. Depression, poor impulse control, acting-out behaviors, low frustration tolerance, volatile emotions, difficult temperament, and inhibition have all been posited as personality traits common in those with bulimia.

Another line of research in the development of eating disorders is the **experiencing of early trauma** in the form of separation and loss, family discord and divorce, parental death, dysfunctional parental behavior, and parental illness, along with other types of family difficulties (Tasca et al., 2013). Childhood sexual abuse has received special attention as an etiological factor, but studies have produced mixed results. The greatest continuity has been between sexual abuse and bulimia (Dworkin, Javdani, Verona, & Campbell, 2014). The relationship between traumatic events and eating disorders has extended to sexual harassment, and studies have found a significant relationship between disordered eating and the experience of sexual harassment (Petersen & Hyde, 2013).

Adolescent developmental patterns are also thought to play a major role in the development of eating disorders. Adolescence can be a time of great insecurity, especially around one's physical appearance. Pubertal changes, particularly those that result in weight gain, can leave some adolescents feeling negatively about their bodies. Some are victims of teasing. This can create a desire to be thin, especially in light of the fashion world. An exaggerated focus on weight and shape may lead some adolescents to engage in various weight-loss measures (Le Grange & Lock,

2011). Engaging in measures that are extreme and harmful is a significant risk factor in the development of an eating disorder (Linville, Stice, Gau, & O'Neil, 2011).

For many years, **Western society's pressure for thinness** has been held responsible for the development of eating disorders. Its connection between fashion, success, and beauty is constantly reflected in the media and, most especially, in magazines and television shows that are popular among adolescents. Body size defines femininity and self-worth. This bombardment can easily result in some adolescents resorting to extreme weight-loss measures. For males, the media's portrayal of muscularity and low body fat as an indication of real manhood can contribute to body dissatisfaction and increased weight concerns (Calzo, Corliss, Blood, Field, & Austin, 2013). Those who come to Western countries from other cultures are also at risk. In an effort to increase their acculturation and social acceptance to their new environment, they may internalize Western cultural messages about weight, which could result in disordered eating (Lopez, Corona, & Halfond, 2013).

Family dysfunction has garnered a lot of attention as a possible cause of eating disorders. Those with eating disorders have been found to come from families that are enmeshed, conflict avoidant, inflexible, controlling (in cases of anorexia), chaotic, or critical and conflicted (in cases of bulimia) (Lyke & Matsen, 2013). High incidences of weight problems, eating disorders, physical illness, affective disorders, OCD, and alcoholism in families have all been considered risk factors in the development of eating disorders (Kluck et al., 2014). Two things must be said about these kinds of family dysfunction and eating disorders. First, not all people with eating disorders come from families with these kinds of dysfunction. Second, these types of family dysfunction have also been linked to numerous other emotional disorders. Therefore, it is difficult to isolate family factors as having a direct etiological link to eating disorders. At best, such factors may play an indirect role as part of the pathway to the development of an eating disorder. Parents and family members who tend to tease, criticize, and offer weight-loss advice to a family member can contribute to negative body image and unhealthy weight-control measures (Eisenberg, Berge, Fulkerson, & Neumark-Sztainer, 2012).

The etiology of eating disorders is multidetermined, and antecedents to the disorder will vary from one individual to another. There has been, in recent years, a bias in favor of biological and genetic factors. Eating disorders are most likely the result of a genetic predisposition to the disorder that interacts with a number of cognitive, psychological, and environmental variables to result in symptoms as outlined in the *DSM-5*.

Recommended Treatments for Eating Disorders

Depending on the need for hospitalization, treatment for eating disorders will differ according to where the treatment takes place. **Inpatient treatment** is typically multidisciplinary, with the goal of restoring the patient to a noncritical weight.

A typical inpatient team will include a psychiatrist, psychologist, medical consultant, and dietician or nutritionist. The primary goal of inpatient treatment is refeeding, with an initial goal of 1,000–1,600 calories per day, eventually increased to 3,000–3,600 calories per day (deGraft-Johnson, Fisher, Rosen, Napolitano, & Laskin, 2013). Along with the goals for caloric intake, there are also goals for weight gain, anywhere from 1 to 3 pounds per week. Denial, comorbid condition (e.g., depression and other medical problems), and feeling a loss of control inherent in any hospitalization may all delay or hinder successful inpatient treatment (Terre et al., 2006). In some programs, patients transition to less intensive care before they are fully discharged.

Individual counseling approaches to those with eating disorders have included behavioral, cognitive-behavioral, and interpersonal therapy. **Behavioral techniques** used to treat eating disorders include response prevention, operant conditioning, response delay, self-monitoring techniques, and stimulus control. In response prevention, the individual is prevented from vomiting. Since vomiting reduces anxiety, the hypothesis is that those with eating disorders would not binge if they were prevented from vomiting. Operant conditioning (the use of positive and negative environmental contingencies) has been used primarily in inpatient settings. Response delay is designed to have the client delay the impulse to binge by participating, for example, in an alternate activity. The technique is based on the hypothesis that if the response can be delayed, the sequence of events can be altered (Shingleton, Richards, & Thompson-Brenner, 2013). Response delay is a commonly used and well-accepted technique in the treatment of eating disorders in spite of an absence of studies to support its effectiveness. Self-monitoring requires careful monitoring by the individual of her thoughts, feelings, and behaviors both before and after the problematic behavior. The counselor uses this information with the goal of manipulating the antecedents that have led to the behavior. Stimulus control involves environmental engineering to remove or reduce the opportunities to participate in problematic eating. For example, favorite high-calorie foods, the preference of many binge-eaters, are not in the house. Replacement strategies might include removing all candy and substituting fresh fruit.

Cognitive-behavioral approaches employ techniques to restructure an individual's distorted cognitions about body image and her faulty beliefs that equate thinness with worth, strength, and success (Abbott & Goodheart, 2011) in conjunction with some of the behavioral techniques described above.

Interpersonal counseling focuses on the client's relationships based on the hypothesis that maladaptive relationships have either a direct or an indirect effect in the development of eating disorders.

Based on the hypothesis that maladaptive patterns of family interaction play an important role in the etiology of eating disorders, **family counseling** has long been a preferred mode of treatment. Family counseling is often a component of a comprehensive treatment package. Interventions range from simply providing education to the family about the disorder to changing a family's structural patterns. The latter approach is based on structural family therapy (see Minuchin, Rosman, & Baker, 1978) and results from the hypothesis that those with eating disorders come from families that are overly enmeshed, overprotected, and conflict avoidant (Lock & Le Grange, 2012). The goal of counseling, then, is to make a gradual disengagement from the family that allows the adolescent appropriate separation and autonomy. Families learn to establish boundaries that are neither too rigid nor too diffuse. A different approach utilizes the family as a resource in the treatment by eliciting their help in refeeding, consistent application of eating patterns, and meeting the developmental challenges of adolescence (Lock & Le Grange, 2012). In some ways, the family's role is similar to that of a nurse; and parental control over eating continues until the adolescent is able to maintain consistent and appropriate eating by herself. Seen separately or together with their adolescent son or daughter, parents need to be involved in the treatment of eating disorders, and this is especially true for adolescents who develop eating problems at a younger age.

Over the years, **group counseling** has been used more with bulimia and binge eating, and to a lesser degree with anorexia. Until the adolescent is medically stabilized, group work is not recommended for anorexia. Group interventions commonly employ either a feminist or a psychoeducational perspective. In the former, participants have the opportunity to discuss the conflicting demands placed upon women. They learn not to turn over their self-definition as women to the sexist elements of society. The psychoeducational approach provides information about the disorder, and the group members act as coaches and sources of support for each other. While it is not for everyone, the psychoeducational group approach offers an efficient and cost-effective treatment.

The use of **psychotropic medication** for those with eating disorders is based on the belief that that certain medications can help to stimulate appetite; however, clinicians have argued that lack of appetite is rarely the cause, for example, of anorexia. In cases of comorbidity with OCD and depression, the use of an SSRI should be considered (Hay & Claudino, 2012). The use of SSRIs and other antidepressants has been more common in treating bulimia, based on the theory that the disorder is the result of decreased levels of serotonin in the brain. The use of antidepressants are considered useful for the short-term treatment of bulimia, but medication alone is associated with more relapse and less overall effectiveness than when it is combined with cognitive-behavioral therapy (Tortorella, Fabrazzo, Monteleone, Steardo, & Monteleone, 2014).

Understanding the Student with an Eating Disorder from an Attachment Perspective

Anna presents with several risk factors for developing an eating disorder, most notably a tendency toward perfectionism. Being a senior in high school also elevates the risk; many eating disorders result from stressful transitions, such as the one from high school to the postsecondary world. The appearance of being perfect is a defense against insecurity and suggests that Anna has an insecure attachment style. Research seems to indicate that women with eating disorders are classified as either dismissing or preoccupied on the AAI, which suggests avoidant or resistant attachment styles as children and adolescents. Those with noncomorbid eating disorders are more frequently classified as dismissing, and those with eating disorders plus depression, for example, are more often classified as preoccupied. Since the vignette does not suggest comorbidity, we will consider Anna's eating disorder the result of an avoidant attachment style.

We know little about Anna's father and nothing about her mother, which leaves a lot of the attachment history to speculation. The research into family patterns of those with eating disorders has often portrayed a father who is unavailable and rejecting and a mother who is domineering, perfectionistic, and overprotective. This results in a daughter who feels rejected, controlled, and inadequate. The one detail we have about Anna's father is that he is a pastor of a church. If the church practices a more conservative, rule-oriented style of religion, perhaps her father is authoritarian, and in this sense, emotionally unavailable to Anna. However, we do not know this for sure, and there are many different types of churches and pastors, ranging from very liberal to very conservative. If we were to assume that Anna's mother fits the profile of the mother of a child with disordered eating, it would make sense that Anna would struggle with issues of autonomy that have come to light as she approaches graduation from high school. Her mother may not be supportive of her independence, which could result in an internal conflict over which Anna feels she has little control.

The hypothesis that those with eating disorders are trying to control the world around them through their eating behaviors is well established. This would make sense from an avoidant attachment perspective. The reader will remember that those with an avoidant attachment style use avoidant strategies to deal with their distress. These strategies can result in internalizing or externalizing symptoms. In the case of Anna, her eating disorder is the result of externalization. She does not have the psychological security to examine and talk about her own internal conflict and has decided to cope with her distress by diverting it onto her own body in the form of an eating disorder. Here, the eating disorder is understood as a deactivating strategy typical of an avoidant attachment style, because it allows for the suppression of anger toward the attachment figure but results in the externalization of that anger in the form of an eating disorder. We have to infer that Anna does not have the capacity to sit down and talk honestly with her mother about her fears of transitioning from high school and the lack of support she may feel from her mother. Rather than attempt a change in the attachment-related issue, Anna finds it easier and less intimidating to effect a more external change in regard to her body.

As mentioned in the psychological overview, eating disorders can be very resistant to treatment. Let us examine how teachers can be either a hindrance or a help to students with eating disorders based on the teacher's own attachment style.

Understanding Teacher Interventions for the Student with an Eating Disorder from Both Attachment and Pedagogical Perspectives

Mrs. Ballantine: "Not My Job"

Mrs. Ballantine insists that she should not be required to regulate Anna's lunch choices and portion sizes. She states that it is an unfair use of her time to have to supervise Anna's restroom visits. Mrs. Ballantine has remarked several times pub-

licly, "These requests are not part of my contractual obligations as a teacher." She further shared with teachers in the teachers' lounge that "Dealing with emotional issues is the school counselor's job—I shouldn't have to worry about what a student does or does not eat, and certainly should not be required to supervise the bathroom visits of a seventeen-year-old girl!"

Furthermore, Mrs. Ballantine has communicated to a few of her colleagues that she believes "Anna is just looking for attention—perhaps the attention she's not receiving at home! She's a bit of an actress, anyway, and she seems to like the melodrama she's created." Mrs. Ballantine has made it very clear to her fellow teachers, administrators, and even her students that she will not "babysit" a senior in high school, especially one whose looks and school performance mark her for a successful future. She has remarked to colleagues on several occasions that she does not consider Anna to have any real problems beyond which prestigious college to attend after graduation!

Finally, Mrs. Ballantine has made it very clear to her students, colleagues, and administrators that she believes that students are not in a position to choose what is best for them, relative to the curriculum. "That's why we are their teachers," she asserts. "High school students are in our classes to learn what they don't know, and they need to learn to conform to prescribed rules to attain the requisite knowledge and skills—they must acquire the mental discipline to do so. You do them a disservice if you let them choose the easy way out!"

Mrs. Ballantine from an Attachment Perspective

Mrs. Ballantine is opposed to collaborating with the school's intervention plan of close and continuous supervision. The plan is based on the behavioral principles of response prevention, response delay, and stimulus control, explained in the previous sections of this chapter. If, for example, the school can prevent Anna from vomiting, theory suggests that she will not engage in binge eating, knowing that she cannot purge. Such a plan is not easy to implement and requires the cooperation of everyone in Anna's life. People with eating disorders are quite adept at finding ways to conceal their habits and alternate ways of purging once those habits are discovered. Mrs. Ballantine has made her position clear: She is not willing to cooperate in the plan to help Anna. This will compromise the effectiveness of Anna's treatment plan.

The teacher's resistance is based on two popular arguments: "It's not my job" and "It's not fair." Both of these require some discussion, since Mrs. Ballantine is probably not alone in how she feels. Mrs. Ballantine from a contractual point of view may be right. Her job description probably does not include having to monitor what a student eats. However, the key to understanding Mrs. Ballantine's position from an attachment perspective may be her assertion that "Dealing with emotional issues is the school counselor's job." Mrs. Ballantine represents the antithesis of the mentalization approach for teachers. She wants to take emotion out of the equation in the relationship with her student rather than allow the student's presentation to affect her. Remember, mentalizing means to "see, think about, and understand one's self and others in terms of inner states" (Sroufe et al., 2005, p. 280). If Mrs. Ballantine had a more secure attachment style, she would be able to examine her reactions to gain greater understanding of her own self and her resistance to helping Anna. The teacher represents a more dismissing attachment style, the precursor of which is an avoidant style as a child. The hallmark of this style is to employ deactivating strategies when relationships become emotionally charged. Survival is best accomplished by distancing. What Anna needs are role models who allow for frank and open communication of emotional conflicts in order to minimize the tendency to displace her distress onto her body and gain control through disordered eating. An avoidant student and a dismissing teacher are not a good mix, and this very likely explains Mrs. Ballantine's strong negative reaction to the school's plan for Anna.

The teacher's second argument is heard all too frequently: "It's not fair." This allows Mrs. Ballantine to describe Anna in some very negative terms, including melodramatic, attention-seeking, and spoiled. The teacher describes her with almost borderline qualities, and she minimizes Anna's disorder, saying that she has no real problems besides what college she is getting into. Her reaction is strong. However, if Mrs. Ballantine were secure, she would recognize the strength of her reaction as an opportunity to learn something about herself. *Why am I reacting so strongly to this student? What in my history or the presentation of this student prevents me from acting as a secure container for this student's emotional difficulties?* Teachers who have learned to mentalize do exactly that.

Remember, those with avoidant histories often have learned to deal with their caretaker being emotionally unavailable by becoming self-reliant. We know nothing about Mrs. Ballantine's relationship history, but based on how she describes Anna, one can infer that she may have had a challenging upbringing and learned to survive by becoming self-reliant. This would explain her reaction to Anna, whom she sees as "having it all," and her feeling that the school is making a big mistake by feeding into Anna's perceived selfishness. One can imagine Mrs. Ballantine saying, "Anna does not know what a tough life is." The best way to help Anna, according to Mrs. Ballantine, is to make her learn to conform to the rules, and the school is doing this "baby" a disservice by making exceptions for her. All of these reactions can be explained from a dismissing position that, in the end, is usually a denial of the need for help.

Mrs. Ballantine from a Pedagogical Perspective

Mrs. Ballantine has clearly adopted a very judgmental attitude toward Anna and her eating disorder. She has publicly stated her views about Anna's treatment plan, and they reveal a teacher who appears judicious and rule bound. Her views and pedagogical style oppose those expressed in our pedagogical framework; specifically, the notion of a student-centered focus (Palmer, 1998; Loughran, 1997) as well as the development of a caring teacher–student relationship as advocated by Noddings (2015) and Smith (2012). We suggest that Mrs. Ballantine would develop a much better rapport with Anna and her parents if she adopted these pedagogical tenets. As it stands, she is really blaming the victim by asserting that "Anna is just looking for attention—perhaps the attention she's not receiving at home!" and claiming that Anna likes melodrama. Perhaps if Mrs. Ballantine attended to the recommendations provided by Freire (1970) and Bruner (1996) in learning about the student's culture—in this case, Anna's background that includes the development of her eating disorder—she might find that she is better able to empathize and develop a rapport with Anna.

Furthermore, Mrs. Ballantine's rather inflexible insistence that Anna "conform to prescribed rules to attain the requisite knowledge and skills" represents another roadblock in the development of a caring relationship with Anna and, perhaps, her other students. Mrs. Ballantine might also benefit from the adoption of our fifth pedagogical tenet: that teachers should strive to empower their students to "identify their strengths and weaknesses" and to "motivate and entice learners" (Tompkins, 1996, p. xvi). It would seem that, at least as it affects Anna, Mrs. Ballantine has abdicated a responsibility and an opportunity to empower and motivate Anna, which would theoretically have helped in the development of a caring teacher–student relationship. Lastly, Mrs. Ballantine's pedagogical perspective might be improved with the adoption of Smith's three elements, especially the third element, action, which encourages teachers to work with students "so they are able to make [positive] changes in their lives" (1994, p. 10).

If Mrs. Ballantine wanted to address the situation with Anna in a more helpful manner, she could consider consider (a) helping to create a school environment in which all students can feel safe from harassment and deprecation, (b) ensuring that school lunches and vending machines provide healthy selections, (c) certifying that participation in school and extracurricular activities is not limited by physical attributes or other restrictions, and (d) supporting the development of effective procedures to alert appropriate professionals in suspected cases of an eating disorder and providing information to affected students about school and community supports and resources (Nahas, n.d.).

In addition, Mrs. Ballantine can ensure that any personal disclosures by Anna relative to her eating disorder be conducted in a discreet setting, to protect her privacy. Mrs. Ballantine should also always express appreciation when a student shares very personal issues related to her eating disorder, acknowledging the courage required to reveal such sensitive information. Finally, if Mrs. Ballantine finds herself in this situation again, she should always inquire privately of an affected student how she would like teachers and other educational professionals to respond when asked how she is progressing in regard to her nutritional issues.

Ms. Gillespie: "Anna Needs a Role Model"

Mrs. Gillespie, Anna's English teacher, is determined to support Anna as she struggles with her desire to binge and purge. Mrs. Gillespie has a daughter who has also been diagnosed with an eating disorder, and she knows that the incidence of these disorders is increasing every year. One of the requested behavioral interventions is to ensure that Anna is accompanied to the restroom if she asks to use it immediately following lunch. Mrs. Gillespie has recruited a good friend of Anna's, Elizabeth, to ensure Anna isn't alone in the restroom and to discourage her from the temptation to purge after eating her lunch.

Furthermore, Mrs. Gillespie has educated herself about the characteristics, etiology, and treatment options pertinent to eating disorders, having spoken with several psychologists who specialize in working with individuals diagnosed with this disorder. She has learned that a frequent cause of eating disorders is the need for control on the part of the affected individual and her feeling of the loss of control relative to the choices in her life. Mrs. Gillespie is invested in understanding the disorder, having a daughter diagnosed with bulimia, and she is very careful to ensure that Anna feels empowered to make decisions regarding optional choices in her class. Accordingly, she provides all her students with optional assignments, assessments, and the ability to assign weight to each of the chosen assessments.

Also, Mrs. Gillespie models healthy food choices by bringing in nutritious snacks, such as carrot and celery sticks, for her students. She also demonstrates healthy meal selections in her own lunch, bringing vegetable soups and tossed salads with a little chicken or tuna added, along with a piece of fresh fruit for dessert and water as a beverage, and she tends to eat smaller but still satisfying portions.

Mrs. Gillespie from an Attachment Perspective

Mrs. Gillespie is participating in the behavioral intervention plan for Anna primarily by doing what she can for response prevention. She has asked Anna's good friend to accompany her to the bathroom with the goal of preventing her from purging. Adolescents are more likely to heed advice from their friends than from the adults in their lives. This friend should be secure and not overly concerned about her own weight in order to be a good role model for Anna.

The impetus for Mrs. Gillespie's determination to help Anna is having a daughter with an eating disorder. This allows for a certain identification with and empathy for Anna. The teacher, however, must be careful not to overidentify with Anna, since no two cases are exactly alike. Research shows that some identification with the person one is trying to help can be effective, but there comes a point where too much identification is counterproductive. If she can keep an appropriate boundary around the desire to help Anna, Mrs. Gillespie will be effective.

Mrs. Gillespie also employs psychoeducation by taking it upon herself to learn as much as she can about eating disorders to understand and help Anna. Like most dedicated teachers, Mrs. Gillespie is probably a busy person, and having to learn about eating disorders is certainly not in her job description. While it is not a contractual obligation, once could argue that it is an ethical one. If a teacher has a student from another culture, and she knows little about that culture, doesn't she try to learn something about the culture to understand and help the student learn better? The teacher would also need this information to establish a more effective relationship with the student's parents. The same is true for a student with a disability, and an eating disorder is a disability. Therefore, Mrs. Gillespie wants to know as much as she can. Her actions offer a glimpse into the attachment style of this teacher, classified as autonomous-secure. She is not afraid of admitting that her ignorance of certain issues hinders her ability to help some students, and she recognizes the need for more knowledge.

However, a clearer window into Mrs. Gillespie's attachment style emerges from her allowing Anna to make decisions regarding options in class. The intervention is psychologically astute. If Anna's eating disorder results from feeling a lack of control over her life, then giving her choices might help to diminish the student's externally oriented control that diverts her feelings of powerlessness onto her own body. Once again, we see a teacher who understands that by ceding some appropriate control to a student, one loses nothing and stands to gain trust and admiration. Only a secure-autonomous teacher is able to do this, because she does not need to control the world around her.

Finally, we see Mrs. Gillespie using herself as a role model for healthy eating. This can be a bit tricky. Teachers, because they can be substitute attachment figures, should encourage healthy lifestyle habits with their own behaviors. However, too much emphasis on weight and food can have unintended negative effects. Because of her autonomous-secure state of mind, we have to assume that Mrs. Gillespie is capable of mentalization and has a good deal of self-knowledge so as not to overemphasize issues of eating. If Mrs. Gillespie were a few pounds overweight, yet projected an air of self-acceptance and self-confidence about her appearance, she would be a very good role model for those students who feel they have to conform to societal pressure about weight.

Mrs. Gillespie from a Pedagogical Perspective

In sharp contrast with Mrs. Ballantine's pedagogical style, Mrs. Gillespie employs almost all of the components of our recommended pedagogical framework in her interaction with Anna. To be fair to Mrs. Ballantine, Mrs. Gillespie has a vested interest in understanding the etiology, characteristics, and treatment options involved in working with students who have an eating disorder. Her own daughter, as previously noted, has been diagnosed with bulimia and, as a result, Mrs. Gillespie has endeavored to learn all she can about that disorder. However, we sense that Mrs. Gillespie likely engaged in a student-centered approach even prior to her daughter's diagnosis.

We can simply review our recommended framework and identify evidence of most of the components in Mrs. Gillespie's pedagogical style. While it might be a bit speculative, it would seem very likely that she has taken the time to know herself (Palmer, 1998) and her raison d'etre as it pertains to teaching. Further, based on her interactions with Anna, Mrs. Gillespie displays an "authenticity of self," a marker of integrity (Austin et al., 2011; Korthagen, 2004; Loughran, 1997).

The evidence provided clearly suggests that Mrs. Gillespie is a self-reflective practitioner (Russell, 1997; Schön, 1983; Sellar, 2013), as demonstrated by her thoughtful attention to Anna's need for bathroom supervision, her research-based investigation of eating disorders, her understanding of Anna's need for some measure of control in her life, and her providing curricular options for Anna to choose from. Finally, she thoughtfully models good nutritional choices and healthy eating habits.

Next, in accordance with the recommendations of Noddings (2005) and Smith (2012) with respect to the importance of developing caring teacher–student relationships, Mrs. Gillespie is in compliance. We can affirm that based on her thoughtful, caring interventions in support of Anna. Furthermore, it would appear that Mrs. Gillespie has developed the "certainty, positivity, and unity of self and moral goals" recommended by Stout (2005, p. 194), as evident in her decisiveness in developing a viable behavioral intervention plan for helping Anna. Mrs. Gillespie also employs the fifth component of our recommended pedagogical framework, in that she empowers Anna to "take responsibility for her own learning" (Tompkins, 1996, p. xvi) by entrusting her to make sound choices relative to her assignment selections, as well as demonstrating how to make healthy nutritional choices and acquire good eating habits. Lastly, Mrs. Gillespie seems to incorporate the three elements Smith espouses: animation, reflection, and action. While we do not have sufficient evidence of the first two elements, based on our limited information, we can substantiate the last, action, as Smith defines it, since Mrs. Gillespie clearly seems to be working with Anna so that she will be able to "make changes" in her life (1994, p. 10).

We have provided a detailed analysis of Anna's case from both an attachment and pedagogical perspective. Because eating disorders manifest similarly in terms of observable classroom behaviors, we will now move on to discuss examples of students with anorexia nervosa and binge eating disorder, as well as sample teacher responses to avoid and to model.

Student Vignette: "Karen" (Anorexia Nervosa)

At first glance, Karen appears like many other 15-year-old girls. Despite being very slim, she is pretty, on-level academically, personable, articulate, and enjoys dressing fashionably. The thing that separates Karen from many of her peers is that, for the past two years, she has been receiving treatment for anorexia nervosa.

Family members first noticed the early stages of the disorder when Karen was in middle school. Karen's mother noted that she would comment about the thin and attractive bodies of models she observed on television and in magazine ads. She was also very envious of the body types of her thinner friends, to whom she constantly compared herself. Ironically, other girls and young women frequently complimented Karen on her "svelte" appearance. She refused to acknowledge these compliments, insisting that these people were simply being kind, since it was clear to her and them that she was grossly overweight. Despite encouragement from family members and friends, Karen's preoccupation became increasingly severe, which prompted her mother to seek out the help of a psychologist who specialized in the treatment of eating disorders.

While presently Karen's condition is not serious enough to require hospitalization, the school psychologist, as well as her therapist, have asked that a nutritionist supervise both the preparation and her consumption of meals to ensure that Karen is receiving sufficient nutrients to prevent severe weight loss. This latest treatment mandate has become a real bone of contention for Karen and her family. Some-

times caregivers must sit with and observe Karen's meal consumption for over an hour to ensure she has ingested the minimum number of calories. The supervised meal session can resemble the old-fashioned "eat everything on your plate before you're dismissed" exhortation, typically reserved for finicky young children. Understandably, Karen finds this process humiliating.

Karen's parents and therapist have appealed to her teachers to provide supervision during lunchtime to ensure that she consumes the required amount of food. This has become a real challenge for her teachers, who have only a 30-minute lunch period and must commit the services of the teacher assistant for this duty, which regularly exceeds one hour. This allocation of critical human resources has strained the relationship between school personnel and Karen, who is sometimes seen as attention seeking and self-absorbed. In addition, her extended lunch period has negatively affected Karen's academic progress in math, the class she attends immediately after lunch.

Karen from an Attachment Perspective

Research done on attachment and anorexia indicates overconcern about parental vulnerabilities resulting from unresolved loss (Barone & Guiducci, 2009; O'Shaughnessy & Dallos, 2009). It is generally recognized that secure attachment to the mother is one of the strongest protective factors against the development of anorexia. The "constraining rules" hypothesis (Gillett, Harper, Larson, Berrett, & Hardman, 2009) posits that those with anorexia tend to come from families where parental insecure attachment results in little expression of feelings, a muted response style to family difficulties, and a tendency to avoid conflict. Karen in the above vignette presents with the classic symptoms of anorexia. While we know little about her attachment history, one could only imagine the difficulties facing this family in having to monitor Karen's food intake, especially if the family members are conflict avoidant and noncommunicative. They are now faced with an emotionally charged issue of their daughter having a serious mental illness, along with having to spend inordinate amounts of time monitoring her food intake. It is very likely that such closeness is at odds with how Karen may have experienced her primary attachment figure throughout her earlier development.

Mr. Pulford: "We Are Devoting Far Too Much Time to One Student!"

Mr. Pulford, Karen's math teacher, is becoming very resentful of the time and resources allocated to her, to the detriment of other students who need help. He has expressed his concerns directly to Mrs. Baines, the assistant principal, who has asked that he simply comply with the behavioral intervention plan that has been developed for Karen, as a reasonable accommodation of her disorder. Mr. Pulford, a tenured teacher with 23 years of experience who is also the lead teacher in the high school math department, has threatened to "take this up with the union rep!"

Needless to say, he has not been too tactful around Karen, avoiding her outside of class and purposely ignoring her entreaties for help in class. Mr. Pulford has been quite vocal about his concerns relative to Karen's eating disorder, complain-

ing to colleagues that "We are devoting too much time and resources to one student! Karen's needs are beyond the capacities of a small suburban school district to address—she should receive treatment in an outpatient facility, in my opinion." Several other members of the teaching staff agree with him but are unwilling to confront the administration.

Mr. Schmidlein: "Anorexia Is a Very Serious Condition, and We Should Do All We Can to Help Karen"

Mr. Schmidlein has expressed real concern for Karen, confiding to others, "My niece is dealing with an eating disorder, and it has been very hard on her and her family. Once you read up on anorexia and the other eating disorders, you learn just how potentially serious they are. I think they might have among the highest morbidity rates of any emotional disorder. Anorexia is a very serious condition, and we should do all we can to help Karen!"

Mr. Schmidlein is Karen's health and gym teacher, and he knows a good deal about healthy nutrition and the importance of maintaining a normal-range body mass index. He has approached the school counselor and offered to help Karen achieve and maintain a healthy weight. He is always positive and affirming around Karen and doesn't discuss food or her appearance. Instead, he emphasizes a sensible exercise routine and good nutritional habits and finds meaningful ways to complement Karen when she makes healthy choices in these areas. He also occasionally engages her in a discussion of one of her passions: jazz music and dance. Mr. Schmidlein truly cares about Karen's health and well-being.

Mr. Pulford and Mr. Schmidlein from an Attachment Perspective

The contrast in styles and approaches to Karen between Mr. Pulford and Mr. Schmidlein is nothing new. It does, however, revive the question of where the relationship between students and teachers should begin and end, and what are appropriate boundaries for those relationships. There are no cookie-cutter answers to these questions. Mr. Pulford might represent the teacher who has more rigid boundaries in the relationship with his students, while Mr. Schmidlein might represent a teacher with more diffuse boundaries. Most humans, as determined by attachment histories, will tend toward one or the other. Problems arise when boundaries become overly rigid or overly diffuse. In the former, there is too much distance to allow for any warmth or caring; in the latter, not enough distance to allow for autonomy. A teacher with overly rigid boundaries would most likely have had an avoidant attachment style and a consequently dismissing state of mind as an adult. Mr. Pulford could be representative of this state of mind. He has a very clear idea of what his job should and should not be. He is most likely an excellent math teacher who cares about his students excelling in math, and that is where he feels the job should end.

Mr. Schmidlein seems to have a broader understanding of his responsibilities toward Karen and is willing to work with others in the school to promote Karen's optimal health and reduce the risk factors of a very serious mental illness. If not overinvolved, Mr. Schmidlein would represent a more secure-autonomous state of mind, as he is not afraid of the difficult emotions that an illness like anorexia could engender in a teacher who takes on the challenging and sometimes tedious task of caring for a student with the disorder. On the other hand, Mr. Schmidlein would represent a less secure state of mind, in the form of preoccupied (the precursor of which is a resistant attachment history), if he became overinvolved with Karen and took her case on as a personal charge, something we have seen in other teacher scenarios.

Mr. Pulford and Mr. Schmidlein from a Pedagogical Perspective

Mr. Pulford would benefit from the recommendation of Noddings (2005) and Smith (2012), who emphasize the importance of developing caring teacher–student relationships. From his comments and behaviors, it seems clear that he has developed resentment toward Karen, ostensibly based on his belief that she is receiving more than her fair share of the school's limited resources. As a result of this prejudice, Mr. Pulford is not likely to make an effort to learn about the causes, characteristics, and treatment of an eating disorder. He may resent the fact that Karen is frequently absent from his math class due to her extended lunchtime and is struggling to keep up as a result.

Mr. Schmidlein, on the other hand, has shown that he truly cares about Karen's well-being and has taken a real interest in her nutritional and physical health. Similarly, he has educated himself about eating disorders and has taken the initiative to speak with the school counselor to learn how he can best help Karen and support her behavioral intervention plan. In concert with the recommendations of Smith (1994; 2012) relative to our pedagogical framework, Mr. Schmidlein is clearly working with Karen so that eventually she may be able to make consistently healthful choices in her life.

STUDENT VIGNETTE: "GEOFFREY" (BINGE EATING DISORDER)

Geoffrey's case may be slightly unusual, since he is not an adult but a 16-year-old adolescent. Geoffrey's binge eating began much earlier, however. At the age of 13, Geoffrey's father found him rummaging through the kitchen waste container. He had eaten a significant amount of refuse that, fortunately for Geoffrey, had been recently discarded and therefore was not bacteria ridden.

Currently, Geoffrey's food intake is carefully monitored; his room and person are frequently checked for concealed food items, and, at least twice per day, the searches disclose prohibited foods. Although Geoffrey's parents are affluent and have the wherewithal to provide him with a substantial allowance, they must carefully dispense this money in order to prevent him from purchasing junk foods at the corner deli. Geoffrey's parents have even spoken with the deli owner and requested that he not sell food to their son without their express permission. In response to this new restriction, Geoffrey was recently intercepted in the act of attempting to bribe a friend to purchase food at the deli for him and secret it in a book bag that he would pass off to Geoffrey, who, if confronted, would insist it contained only school-related materials.

At 16, Geoffrey is morbidly obese and for health reasons has been placed on a cal-

orie-restricted diet. Geoffrey's obsession with food has begun to affect both his social life and academic progress. Classmates are repulsed by his poor table manners and gluttonous behavior in the school cafeteria and consequently refuse to socialize with or befriend him. He has become increasingly inattentive in school, clearly distracted by his obsession with food. Several times a day, teachers confiscate food items he has squirrelled away in class and subtly tried to consume without detection. Once confronted, he is very reluctant to surrender the food item to teachers and can become belligerent and even physically aggressive, causing him, on one occasion, to be removed from the classroom and placed in the in-school suspension room.

Geoffrey from an Attachment Perspective

Much of what has been said previously about attachment insecurity and eating disorders can also be applied to the relatively new diagnosis of binge eating disorder. In short, binge eating is compensatory behavior for attachment insecurity. The exact pathway is not known, but one could easily say that either depression or anxiety that results from attachment insecurity leads to addictive eating as an escape from negative feelings (Spoor, Bekker, Van Strien, & van Heck, 2007). Of course, the case can be made that those with binge eating disorder employ a deactivating strategy consistent with an avoidant attachment style. Most individuals who binge eat are severely overweight, which can easily foster scorn and rejection from others, and their physical appearance will often prevent intimacy and closeness. The lack of intimacy and closeness is characteristic of an avoidant attachment style.

Mrs. Gujaraji: "There Is Entirely Too Much Junk Food Advertised and Made Available to Children!"

Mrs. Gujaraji, Geoffrey's social studies teacher, has long been concerned with the increased incidence of childhood and adolescent obesity in the United States. She attributes this fact to the proliferation of television and Internet ads promoting fast-food like McDonald's. She has also expressed disdain for working parents who find it more convenient to give their children a few extra dollars to buy a couple of slices of pizza or a Big Mac rather than invest their time and energy in preparing a healthy meal. She disputes the claim of the school counselor and school nurse that Geoffrey's obesity is the result of an emotional disorder he cannot control without psychological and medical intervention. She has raised the ire of the school counselor and principal by assigning Geoffrey a detention every time she catches him with junk food in her classroom and has sent several notes home with Geoffrey admonishing his parents for giving him snack money and failing to monitor his snack purchases.

Mrs. Gomez: "Geoffrey Has a Real Obsession with Food and Truly Wants Help to Control his Compulsion to Eat"

After school last Monday, Mrs. Gomez noticed Geoffrey coming out of the detention room with his head down and a defeated look on his face. She greeted Geoffrey, who seemed startled to see a teacher walking the halls so late in the afternoon. "How's it going, Geoffrey?" she asked. Unable to control his suppressed emotions, Geoffrey began to sob. "Mrs. Gujaraji doesn't know what it's like," he stammered. "She doesn't believe me when I tell her I can't stop eating! Some of my teachers think that if they punish me, I'll stop, but I've tried and tried and I just can't!" Placing a hand on his shoulder, Mrs. Gomez guided Geoffrey to the cafeteria and sat beside him, listening patiently and intently as he poured out his heart to her. After several minutes, Geoffrey was able to compose himself, and Mrs. Gomez assured him that she believed that he had a condition that was beyond his control, just like any health-related issue, and that he needed medical and counseling intervention to help him overcome this very big challenge. She let him know she was there for him whenever he needed a sympathetic listener; her door was always open, and her classroom would provide a safe haven when he felt rejected and needed a friend.

Mrs. Gujaraji and Mrs. Gomez from an Attachment Perspective

Mrs. Gujaraji's approach to dealing with Geoffrey is somewhat perplexing. On one hand, she blames the environment for promoting unhealthy foods and implies that Geoffrey is yet another victim of an insidious campaign to harm children. On the other hand, she seems to blame Geoffrey when he eats these foods, and she thinks that a punitive approach (i.e., detention) is the answer for someone who should be more in control of his eating. The teacher seemingly blames both the environment and the student at the same time. Rather than take a more structural approach consistent with her philosophy and advocate for changes in the environment, she punishes Geoffrey. One would need a lot more information about Mrs. Gujaraji to understand her adult state of mind, but her approach does seem to be a bit harsh and maybe even abusive. This would point to a more unresolved adult state of mind that is linked to a disorganized attachment style. Of course, there is some room for speculation here, but the overly punitive approach and the seemingly complete absence of empathy (even though she blames the environment) would suggest an attachment style as a child that was punitive, controlling, hostile, and aggressive.

Mrs. Gomez, by contrast, shows compassion and empathy toward Geoffrey. She seems to understand that Geoffrey's behavior is beyond his control, which hints at the idea that binge eating is an addiction. Teachers can never go wrong by employing active listening with their students. If there is trust, many students will confide in them. The fact that Geoffrey is able to confide in Mrs. Gomez is an excellent example of how a teacher can provide attachment security to a student whose binge eating reveals a great deal of insecurity. More importantly, Mrs. Gomez's intervention goes beyond empathic listening, since this is not enough to intervene effectively with Geoffrey. He needs serious help, and Mrs. Gomez is not afraid to tell him so. His compensatory behaviors have been in place for a long time and will not be easy to change, but the hope is that Mrs. Gomez has provided a secure enough base from which to launch Geoffrey into professional help before he develops serious medical complications from overeating and obesity.

Mrs. Gujaraji and Mrs. Gomez from a Pedagogical Perspective

Mrs. Gujaraji clearly has her mind made up about Geoffrey. She has preconceptions about childhood obesity and its causes and feels that Geoffrey and his parents are largely to blame for his condition. As a result, she fails to develop a caring teacher–student relationship with Geoffrey, choosing to punish his compulsive eating by assigning him detention. She apparently cannot be bothered to investigate the etiology of eating disorders, because she doesn't consider them a credible explanation, at least with respect to Geoffrey's binge-eating problems. Mrs. Gujaraji's prejudice toward Geoffrey and his eating disorder precludes her ability to work with him and the school counselor and thereby facilitate a behavioral change.

Conversely, Mrs. Gomez is sufficiently knowledgeable about Geoffrey's condition to understand that it is not by choice that he is compelled to eat and has become obese. She acknowledges the emotional disorder that is driving his compulsive eating and does not blame him or his parents for his condition. As a result, she is able to express empathy and support for Geoffrey, offering her classroom as a safe haven and, more importantly, providing a sympathetic ear for him to share his challenges and frustrations. These gifts of time, space, and self demonstrate our pedagogical framework and its fundamental tenet: relationship building. Although Mrs. Gomez must ensure that she collaborates with the school counselor in providing emotional support for Geoffrey in his struggles with binge eating, she seems to have established a relationship with Geoffrey that engenders positive behavioral change.

Effective Teacher Responses

For students with anorexia nervosa, like Karen:

- Avoid commenting on the individual's thinness.
- Find things that you can genuinely compliment in the student (e.g., attractive dress, academic performance relative to a real accomplishment, pleasant demeanor).
- Give the student as much of your attention and positive reinforcement as possible; give generously!
- Model healthy eating practices—eat good food and consume healthy portions.
- Display pictures of "real" people in the classroom; these should include individuals who are full figured, of various shapes and sizes, doing everyday things. Avoid reinforcing the student's obsession with perfectionism.
- Accept less-than-perfect work. Remind everyone in your class that learning new skills takes time, and most of life consists of working through processes; ideally, we improve as we practice.
- Avoid bringing food for the individual or suggesting that she "needs to eat more" to look healthy (the student with anorexia will be unlikely to eat the food and will feel embarrassed at being the focus of attention). Remember that for the student with anorexia, eating is a very private ritual.

- Keep the student engaged in interesting, meaningful work, and hopefully she will discover avocations or activities that help her enjoy life more and be more accepting of herself as she learns that she can engage in rewarding activities and share these experiences with others.
- Stay in close contact with parents and the school counselor, dietitian, and psychologist, and be ready to support the treatment plan as appropriate and where feasible.
- Keep parents and clinicians informed of any significant behavior or changes in behavior observed in the classroom (e.g., melancholia or depression, lack of interest in others or schoolwork, a morbid preoccupation with death, expressed disgust with body weight or image).

For students with bulimia nervosa, like Anna:

- Praise the student for some legitimately laudable quality.
- Celebrate healthy body types. Avoid displaying pictures of ultra-slim celebrities or models.
- Model healthy eating and stress the importance of good nutrition.
- Compliment the individual's wardrobe or "look." You can say, "Those colors really make your eyes stand out," or "I like the way you've styled your hair."
- Be alert, but not overly reactive, to the student's requests to use the bathroom.
- Support the treatment plan developed by clinicians as appropriate and feasible within the framework of the classroom and school (e.g., don't let the student cajole you into letting her use the bathroom immediately after lunch if the treatment plan prohibits it, even if the student insists that she "really has to go," unless she can be provided one-to-one supervision).
- If the student's behavioral intervention plan calls for you or your assistant to supervise her during lunch, make it a pleasant experience for you both, and really enjoy your food.
- Make sure that the student is included in class discussions and activities, and provide frequent opportunities for her to choose assignments and projects. Having choices is empowering!
- Employ cooperative groups where possible, and ensure that the student is able to make relevant contributions to the group process.
- Ask for her input in class debates and discussions. Make her feel valued by reinforcing the importance you place on her contributions to the learning process and the classroom community.

For students with binge eating disorder, like Geoffrey:

- Avoid shaming the student for his impulsive eating.
- Substitute tactual or kinesthetic activities—such as a craft, like model building, or a board game such as chess—during breaks in the academic routine as a distraction from the compulsion to eat.

- Keep a container of dried fruit or sugar-free candy as a healthier, low-calorie substitute when the student craves a treat.
- Avoid making comments about the student's weight, and ensure that the student's classmates do likewise. Instead, invite him to go for a walk around the school grounds with you or a peer during lunch.
- Prohibit or restrict access to snack and soda machines, and lobby the administration to allow only ones that dispense healthy beverages and snacks, such as fruit juices, water, pretzels, popcorn, and trail mix.
- Avoid eating in the classroom; restrict food consumption to the cafeteria or staff room.
- Similarly, don't permit students to eat in the classroom; encourage them to eat in the cafeteria or outside the school building.
- Avoid discussing favorite foods and meals with the student, as this will only serve as a stimulus for the desire to snack. (excerpted from Austin & Sciarra, 2010 with permission, Pearson Education).

CONCLUDING THOUGHTS

Anna, an attractive high schooler, seemed at first to have a perfect life. Unfortunately, nothing could be further from the truth. The fact that approximately 30 million Americans have been diagnosed with an eating disorder and 11% of high school students in the United States have been similarly diagnosed should give teachers pause and encourage them to read this chapter closely, since there is a very good chance, based on these and other statistics, that they will be teaching some of these students.

The good news is that there is hope for students affected by this disorder, if it is identified soon and provided effective and intensive therapies. The sad truth that teachers and service providers must face is that there are some students they may not be able to help, despite their best efforts, as evident from the disturbing statistics on mortality rates for this disorder. Of similar concern is the comorbidity of eating disorders with mood and anxiety disorders and the potential for suicidal ideation.

Nevertheless, there are things teachers can do to mitigate the effects of this debilitating disorder and hasten remission and, hopefully, bring about a life-affirming behavioral transformation. The first step is understanding the student with an eating disorder from an attachment perspective, since a teacher's predispositions may interact with the maladaptive behaviors presented by the affected student.

To facilitate this understanding, we presented three relevant student vignettes and suggested ways to process the various problem behaviors associated with each of the cases they described. Next, we described the contrasting responses or interventions of two of the teachers involved in each case, from both an attachment and a pedagogical perspective. The analyses of these teacher responses from an attachment perspective provided valuable insights into the very antithetical ways these teachers processed and addressed their student's eating disorder. Likewise, an examination of their contrasting pedagogical approaches revealed both effective and ineffective techniques and provided an opportunity to offer remedial suggestions, based on the pedagogical framework we developed in Chapter 2.

Where Mrs. Ballantine expressed her belief that working effectively and therapeutically with Anna was not her job, and essentially abdicated an opportunity to develop a caring rapport with her student, Mrs. Gillespie was more than willing to provide Anna with the support and encouragement one associates with a role model. Readers should feel more empowered, after reading this chapter, to follow Mrs. Gillespie's example, and teach students like Anna courageously and effectively.

CHAPTER 7

Teaching Students Who Bully and Are Bullied

STUDENT BULLYING VIGNETTE: "KENNY"

Kenny, nicknamed "the Rat" by his classmates, is a bit of an agitator. He frequently sounds off at other students who cross him in some way or exhibit behavior that Kenny deems stupid. Such behavior is a bit foolhardy on Kenny's part, given his diminutive stature. Presently a 16-year-old, Kenny stands just a shade over 5'3" and weighs in at a very lissome 92 lbs!

Not surprisingly, most of Kenny's adversaries are much bigger than he and therefore capable of administering uncontested retribution in response to Kenny's verbal tirades. Kenny's response to this threat is usually the same: He uses his exceptional foot speed to distance himself from his adversary and then continues to harangue the now-infuriated student from afar.

Some of Kenny's classmates know that he has been diagnosed with an emotional and behavioral disorder that frequently causes his inhibitions to be suppressed, but that knowledge is small comfort given the frequency and intensity of his verbal abuse. Occasionally, one of the recipients of this abuse will ambush Kenny and inflict a few bumps and bruises, much to the delight of many of his classmates and even a few of his teachers, who are becoming unsympathetic toward his lack of control over these verbal outbursts. To make matters worse, Kenny frequently loses control and instigates a fight, then looks for a protector to intervene on his behalf, playing up the disparity in size and strength between himself and his adversary.

Nevertheless, a recent arrival seems to have changed everything for Kenny—and not for the better! In fact, the usually resilient "Rat" has become rather morose of late, ever since Billy J., a new student with a reputation as a real "tough guy," transferred to his school. Even those teachers who had been less than sympathetic toward Kenny have observed the change in his demeanor whenever Billy enters the room or passes by Kenny's desk. Kenny avoids eye contact with Billy and appears to be intimidated by Billy's size and aggressive behaviors. At first, Kenny's classmates were delighted that Kenny appeared to be "getting his just desert"; however, over time, they noticed that the indomitable "Rat" was uncharacteristically subdued and withdrawn, and they stopped gloating.

One day, while on lunchroom duty, Mrs. Jolivet, Kenny's algebra teacher, overhears a conversation between the two boys in which Billy threatens violence against Kenny if he doesn't agree to share his answers to an important take-home exam. When Mrs. Jolivet confronts Billy and Kenny privately about the incident, Billy laughs and insists he was "just playing" with Kenny: "I'm a good math student; I don't need anyone's help to pass a stupid little test. The math program at my other school was better than this one, anyway!" Kenny, glancing furtively at Billy, nods in agreement and supports Billy's contention.

Shortly after this incident, two of Mrs. Jolivet's most conscientious students approached her and reported that Billy was constantly threatening Kenny, occasionally punching him in the chest or arm or tackling him in the schoolyard. Kenny is really afraid of Billy—too afraid to tell his teachers or parents for fear of retaliation; and, unfortunately, he feels he's alienated everyone who might have offered him protection. He's the one kid in school who's had it coming, and he feels alone—and scared!

WHY DOES THE TEACHER NEED TO KNOW ABOUT BULLYING?

In the following paragraphs, we explain the impetus for understanding what constitutes bullying, how it is precipitated, who is victimized, and its consequences, as well as how to reduce its incidence in schools. But before substantiating the need for explicit knowledge about this topic, we need to provide the reader with a viable definition. The Centers for Disease Control and Prevention (CDC; 2014) defines bullying as

> any unwanted aggressive behavior(s) by another youth or group of youths who are not siblings or current dating partners that involves an observed or perceived power imbalance and is repeated multiple times or is highly likely to be repeated. Bullying may inflict harm or distress on the targeted youth including physical, psychological, social, or educational harm.

According to the CDC (2014), approximately 28% of high school students experience some form of bullying while on school property each year, and 16% report being bullied electronically (i.e., via social media, texting, or phone calls). Furthermore, an estimated one in seven students in K–12 in the United States is either a bully or a victim of bullying. That means, essentially, that approximately 2.7 million students are bullied, while another 2.1 million are their victimizers (Olweus Bullying Prevention Program, 2015).

Sadly, the roles of bully and victim are often recursive—students who are frequently victimized become victimizers. The effects of this victimization include missing school (160,000 students each day in the United States), "bullycide" (suicide prompted by being bullied), and the potential for the development of serious mental health issues (CDC, 2014). In addition, statistics provided by the CDC revealed that each month in the United States, an estimated 282,000 students are attacked in their high schools. Finally, over half of all U.S. students report having witnessed an act of bullying at school (Olweus Bullying Prevention Program, 2015). Consequently, it is imperative that teachers understand what constitutes bullying, what causes it, what incubates it, where it is most likely to occur, and, most importantly, ways that they can help reduce its occurrence.

WHAT THE TEACHER SHOULD KNOW ABOUT BULLYING

Bullying is best described as aggressive actions by a more powerful student or students toward a perceived less powerful student, sustained over a period of time. The world-renowned expert on bullying, Dan Olweus, identified a bullied student as one who is exposed, repeatedly and over time, to negative actions on the part of one of more other persons (Olweus, 1992). These negative actions are understood as intentionally inflicting or attempting to inflict injury or discomfort upon another. Behaviors perpetrated toward the victim may be physical (hitting, kicking, pushing, choking), verbal (name-calling, taunting, malicious teasing, threatening, spreading nasty rumors), or other actions such as giving obscene gestures, making faces, or keeping one isolated from a group (Olweus, 2004). These latter, more subtle forms are referred to as "indirect bullying," in contrast to "direct bullying" that denotes active attacks upon the victim. Bullying is found among both boys and girls, although among girls the forms of bullying tend to be more subtle.

As young people have become more connected, cyberbullying is a major concern; it occurs on electronic media such as e-mail, instant messaging, and social networking sites (Kowalski, Limber, Limber, & Agatston, 2012). Cyberbullying can be especially insidious because the bully can remain anonymous and the audience can take on global proportions (Mishna, Saini, & Solomon, 2009). Furthermore, the student may feel he cannot rely on the school to protect him from cyberbullying, since it is not taking place within the school environment, and he may also be reluctant to tell his parents out of fear of losing his Internet privileges (Cassidy, Jackson, & Brown, 2009; Doll et al., 2012).

When Is Bullying Not Just Teasing?

At times, it may be difficult for parents and school personnel to distinguish between normal teasing and bullying. If the agent's behavior is age inappropriate, negative, intense, and frequent, then it is better understood as bullying rather than teasing.

Roberts and Morotti (2000) identified four questions designed to help educators make this distinction:

1. **What is the nature of the behavior?** How age appropriate is the behavior? Who is the object of the behavior? Is the behavior gender-specific? Is the behavior directed toward those younger or older in age? How disturbing is the content of the behavior?

2. **What is the intensity of the behavior?** Is the main feature of the behavior verbal, physical, or psychological? What is the affect that accompanies the behavior? Does the actor manifest more anger, harshness, or maliciousness as opposed to acting in a more humorous fashion?

3. **What is the frequency of the behavior?** Is the behavior a one-time incident or does it occur in more regular fashion? Is the behavior more time and/or situation specific?

4. **How does the victim of the behavior respond?** How upset or offended is the victim by the behavior? Is there reciprocation on the part of the victim? What is the response of the agent to the victim's attempt at self-defense? (Based on Roberts & Morotti, 2000)

The effects of bullying upon the victim are both short- and long-term. The short-term effects include unhappiness, pain and humiliation, confusion, distress, loss of self-esteem, anxiety, insecurity, loss of concentration, and refusal to go to school. Some victims develop psychosomatic complaints like headaches and stomachaches. The psychological consequences of being bullied are serious: Victims begin to feel stupid, ashamed, and unattractive and see themselves as failures (Olweus, 2004). Long-term effects of bullying include difficulty forming relationships, poor integration in the workplace, and compromised economic independence (Wolke & Lereya, 2015).

Characteristics of the Bully

Bullies tend to possess certain individual characteristics. However, the seriousness and pervasiveness of their bullying will depend on environmental factors, such as the school's tolerance for such behaviors, teacher attitudes, and the arrangement of break periods. In addition, the influence of the early home environment cannot be underestimated. Bullies learn their behaviors early in life and tend to come from home environments that are quite harsh, where punishment is usually physical and capricious (Bibou-Nakou, Tsiantis, Assimopoulos, & Chatzilambou, 2013). Their home environment is filled with criticism, sarcasm, and put-downs, and there is a general absence of warmth and nurturing. As a result, the bully's personality is formed around the belief that intimidation and force are acceptable ways to deal with life's challenges (Roberts & Morotti, 2000). Through the dynamics of projective identification, the bully tends to prey on the less powerful, who remind the bully of his or her own vulnerability. "Bullies, through attacking the weaknesses of others, are striking out against the shame and humiliation they feel for their own inability to defend themselves against their abusers" (Roberts & Morotti, 2000, p. 151).

Unfortunately, the bully's behavior is often reinforced by parents, peers, and the media. The bully's parents will often defend their child's behaviors as sticking up for himself. Since the parents themselves have modeled such behaviors, they find it hard to disapprove of it. Some of the bully's peers may take delight in seeing another student victimized and encourage the bully to continue the victimization. The media is also guilty of portraying bullying behaviors as appropriate ways to deal with difficult and challenging situations.

Characteristics of the Victim

Because bullying affects a large number of students, it is somewhat difficult to profile the typical victim. Hanish and Guerra (2000) examined the variables of those children at risk for victimization along four dimensions: demographic characteristics, behavioral characteristics, peer group dynamics, and school structure influences.

Demographic characteristics. Younger children are more vulnerable to peer victimization than older children, since younger children are less apt to have developed protection skills. Bullying in elementary school, however, is more transient and relatively untargeted. The number of older children victimized is fewer, but when bullying does occur, it remains more stable over time (Hanish & Guerra, 2000). With regard to gender, there are differences in the type of victimization experienced. Boys are more likely to be physically victimized, while girls are more likely to be sexually and rationally victimized—gossiped about, excluded from activities, and sexually harassed (Zimmer-Gembeck, Pronk, Goodwin, Mastro, & Crick, 2013).

Behavioral characteristics. Some children are victimized because they are perceived as unable to defend themselves. They may be physically weak, submit easily to peer demands, be rejected by peers, and have few friends (Mishna, Khoury-Kassabri, Gadalla, & Daciuk, 2012; Olweus, 2013). Also, aggressiveness has been found to increase the likelihood of being victimized (Bjorklund & Hawley, 2014). Aggressive behaviors can cause annoyance and alienate others, leaving the student without support and therefore vulnerable to bullies. Those students who are socially withdrawn, shy, and unsure of themselves are also at risk for being victimized. Social withdrawal is more of a risk factor among older children (Pabian & Vandebosch, 2015).

Peer group dynamics. Peers can display a spectrum of reactions to bullying. Estimates are that peer protection occurs in less than 15% of bullying incidents (Atlas & Pepler, 1998). Peers may be distressed by the bullying, but active defense against the bully is relatively uncommon. On the contrary, peers may encourage the bullying. Bullying can be the result of wanting to attain or maintain a position of influence and power among peers in the school (Salmivalli, 2014). If the bullied student does not have an active support group, the victimization will remain more stable over time and therefore have more significant consequences for the victim.

School structure influences. Unfortunately, schools provide environmental influences that can be conducive to bullying. Unsupervised time allows the bully opportunity to prey on victims; most incidents happen in the hallways, during change of classes, and in the playground (Hong & Espelage, 2012). In addition, victims are reluctant to report the bully's behavior for fear of reprisal (Brandt et al., 2012). Bullying, therefore, can occur even on a large scale without the knowledge of school officials.

The Victim Turned Aggressor

Because bullying by its very definition is intense and sustained, the victim finds it impossible to be indifferent to the harassment. While many victims will manifest negative symptoms (withdrawal, depression, truancy, dropping out of school, and even suicide), some will turn into aggressors, and in rare instances may commit deadly school violence. A significant number of school shooters have a history of being bullied, and therefore the victim turned aggressor has become a concern in many schools. Several experts on violence have suggested that suicide and deadly revenge are the result of the same psychodynamics operating within the victim (Carney, 2000). In other words, the risk factors for the level of aggression against the self and against others are the same. Hazler and Carney (2000) have categorized these risk factors as biological, psychological, cognitive, and environmental.

Reaching the age of puberty increases the risk level for victims turned aggressors. Hormonal fluctuations along with rapid physical and psychological changes can increase the individual's level of hostility and desire for revenge. If the victim is severely depressed, a sense of hopelessness and negative self-evaluation increases the risk level for serious aggression. The victim may reason: Since life is not worth living, what's the difference if I kill myself and those who have been tormenting me? Accompanying depression is cognitive rigidity—for example, seeing revenge as the only option—which can lead a victim to serious aggression against others. It is not uncommon that the shooter, after killing several others, kills himself.

Both **family factors** and **poor peer relationships** can elevate the risk of violent aggression. Families with poor problem-solving skills that do not encourage assertiveness make it hard for the victim to learn alternate ways of dealing with conflict (Hazler & Carney, 2000). Isolation from peers also increases the risk for perpetrating deadly violence (Lovegrove, Henry, & Slater, 2012). Many school shooters could not rely on even one friend to provide a safety net and prevent tragedy from occurring.

UNDERSTANDING BULLYING FROM AN ATTACHMENT PERSPECTIVE

Research has examined bullying from four different perspectives: those who are pure bullies, those who are pure victims, those who are bully-victims, and those not involved (Ireland & Power, 2004). Kenny, from our case at the beginning of the chapter, would fall into the category of bully-victim. Rather than victim turned aggressor (the more common bully-victim), Kenny is a bully first and a victim second. Of course, it is possible that Kenny was bullied prior to becoming a bully.

As stated previously, bullying is a particular form of aggression, and according to attachment theory, aggression develops in one of three ways: (1) as a reaction to a negative relationship with the caregiver; (2) as attention seeking in reaction to a neglectful parent; and (3) as the result of resistant attachment and difficulty forming relationships, where aggression serves as a defense mechanism. We know little about Kenny's family background, but research indicates that family factors contributing to bullying include teasing, physical discipline, lack of supervision, and lack of role models (Ireland & Power, 2004).

It is quite possible that Kenny, because of his diminutive stature, was a victim of teasing early on in his development, and this was a contributing factor to his becoming a bully. Interesting research has shown that father involvement acts as a protective factor against bullying, and teasing by teachers has been shown to be a risk factor (Hansen, Steenberg, Palic, & Elklit, 2012). Denied power by his physical appearance, Kenny resorts to bullying others to gain a sense of power and importance. The vignette indicates that teachers are slow to defend Kenny, as they find him annoying. Since he is very provocative, teachers may have entered into collusion with other students against Kenny. Rather than serve as a protective factor, some teachers may have even contributed to the problem.

The second part of the vignette is intriguing because it is not clear why Billy, in particular, is able to inflict such fright in Kenny, and prior to Billy no one else seemed to have that capability. Billy seems to fit the profile of the aggressive bully capable of physically hurting another student. From an attachment perspective, Billy may have been the victim of harsh punishment and experienced the attachment figure as frightening, which would result in a disorganized attachment style. However, within the context of bullying, those children who have been victims of oppressive parental authority can easily become bullies. Victimized as children, they replicate the early trauma by victimizing others. The opposite would be true for victims, who tend to come from resistant attachment patterns, where the primary caregiver may have sheltered the child and been overprotective.

We know from the two students who report the bullying that Billy is physically hurting Kenny, and this causes Kenny to fear him. Billy's actions are enough to get at least some students to feel sorry for Kenny—as surprising as that might sound, since many of the students relished seeing Kenny get what was coming to him at first. The bystander effect is very real in bullying (Salmivalli, Voeten, & Poskiparta, 2011). Peers can be supportive of bullying behavior and take delight in seeing another student victimized, and may even encourage the bully to sustain the victimization. On the other hand, they may also intervene directly or indirectly to stop the bullying, as is the case with the two students in the vignette. They seem to have a certain amount of empathy for Kenny. The reader will remember that capacity for empathy is a sure sign of a secure attachment history. Students with secure attachment histories can be a real asset to a school's attempt to reduce bullying and other forms of violence.

UNDERSTANDING TEACHER INTERVENTIONS FOR BULLYING FROM BOTH ATTACHMENT AND PEDAGOGICAL PERSPECTIVES

Mr. Formisano: "If Kenny Thinks He Can Insult and Provoke Others with Impunity, He's In For a Rude Awakening!"

"Look, I understand that there are kids who have special needs in our classrooms, but we are doing a disservice to them and their families if we let them get away with rude and provocative behavior!" remarks Mr. Formisano. Mr. Formisano, Kenny's gym teacher and ice hockey coach, is considered by most to be a good judge of character and, as such, he is very concerned that Kenny might be alienating himself from his teammates and teachers. "Perhaps Kenny will get his lumps, and that might really help him to rein in his provocative behaviors," notes Mr. Formisano.

Mr. Formisano, who was a former professional hockey player before becoming a coach and gym teacher, understands the divergent personalities of successful athletes. Nevertheless, he compares Kenny and his hockey talents to those of Ken Linseman of the NHL. Linseman was similarly ostracized for inciting fights and engaging in controversial behavior on and off the ice. Accordingly, Mr. Formisano feels that Kenny might benefit from the physical and emotional challenges imposed by Billy. To justify this assertion, he cites Bob Nystrom's success over Dave Schultz in their 1980 Stanley Cup debut. Schultz, who was famous for his aggressive, intimidating play on the ice, was defused by the persistent speed and skills of Bobby Nystrom, a confident, assertive, and very talented player with the New York Islanders.

Mr. Formisano has emphasized that he doesn't play favorites and also doesn't believe in mollycoddling his players. "Hey, if you pick a fight with a bigger opponent, you've got to be ready for a beating. But, at the end of the day, you can look in the mirror and be proud of the man or woman who is looking back!" He feels that Kenny will ultimately benefit from the push-back exerted by "tough" classmates like Billy.

Mrs. Jolivet: "Billy's Threatening Behavior Needs to Be Addressed—Kenny Is the Victim Here!"

Mrs. Jolivet, a consummate professional, is most concerned about the incident in the cafeteria involving Billy and Kenny. She understands that Kenny's provocative temperament is alienating to most, including many of his teachers; nevertheless, she is able to identify a case of true bullying when she observes one, and she is convinced that Kenny is the victim of bullying behavior. Billy, she believes, is a real bully, who is using coercion, in the form of the threat of physical harm, to intimidate the more vulnerable Kenny.

While many of her colleagues are disaffected, citing Kenny's provocative behavior that alienates classmates and, in fact, provokes retribution on the part of some,

Mrs. Jolivet has expressed to her colleagues and to the administration that she feels Kenny's deficits in social skills do not condone or warrant the bullying behavior exhibited by Billy. Her persistent appeals have paid off, since the administration is investigating this most recent incident involving Billy and Kenny, as well as others involving Billy that have come to light as Mrs. Jolivet's complaints have garnered school district attention and credibility.

Mrs. Jolivet and Mr. Formisano from an Attachment Perspective

Mr. Formisano makes some formidable arguments as to the best way to deal with Kenny. A long history of competitive sports molds his worldview. He sees Billy's treatment of Kenny almost as an opportunity for Kenny to toughen up and become an even better hockey player. There is not a lot of room for the "warm and fuzzy" in his world. He sounds rather typical of an adult dismissing state of mind, where the self is described as being strong and independent, with little articulation of feelings of hurt or distress, which many in the world of competitive sports may see as an asset. Feeling sorry for your opponent is not a winning strategy. A dismissing adult state of mind is usually the result of an avoidant attachment style that employs the use of deactivating strategies that are seen operating in Mr. Formisano. He utilizes cold, hard logic: Pick a fight with someone, deal with the consequences. Some readers may find it hard to disagree—actions have consequences! In addition, Mr. Formisano sees the silver lining in all of this: a better hockey player.

Mrs. Jolivet, in contrast, is worried about Kenny. The little information we have makes it difficult to know how she might relate to students in general. She understands that Kenny has a disability, part of which manifests itself in social skills deficits. These deficits have resulted in Kenny being the victim of an aggressive bully, and the school should intervene. One could only imagine the conversation in the teacher's lounge between Mr. Formisano and Mrs. Jolivet, where they might exchange respective accusations of overprotection and lack of empathy. Is Mrs. Jolivet overprotective, resulting from a preoccupied adult state of mind, the precursor of which is a resistant attachment style? Could Mrs. Jolivet herself have a history of being bullied, and overidentifies with Kenny? One thing is for sure—in the world of Mr. Formisano, a teacher like Mrs. Jolivet is not helpful to the cause of forming strong, tough, independent hockey players. The contrast between their approaches is stark: Kenny has to learn the hard way, versus Kenny has a disability and needs help and protection.

If the two teachers were a couple and had children, they most likely would disagree on the best way to prepare their children for the real world. But as parents, they both could contribute something positive: toughness necessary for dealing with the challenges of the real world, along with caring and empathy necessary for forming intimate and loving relationships. Although the two teachers are not a couple, they nevertheless can learn to work together as colleagues and appreciate how the other's perspective can contribute to forming well-rounded students who can be productive and also have empathy toward others.

Mrs. Jolivet and Mr. Formisano from a Pedagogical Perspective

Mr. Formisano is clearly insensitive to Kenny's emotional needs in this instance, projecting his traditional values of manliness and courage on the relational crisis involving Kenny and Billy. He seems unable to appreciate the fear and intimidation that Kenny is experiencing at the hands of the much stronger boy. He is apparently unable to engage the fourth element in our pedagogical framework: the ability to empower his student (i.e., Kenny) to marshal his strengths and learn from his mistakes. Similarly, Mr. Formisano does not seem to be interested in developing a caring relationship with Kenny, which, according to Noddings (2005) and Smith (2012), is a critical element of sound pedagogical practice.

Furthermore, Mr. Formisano seems unaware of the impact of his own coaching philosophy on his students. As Kenny's gym teacher and coach, Mr. Formisano is in a unique position to be able to model and encourage prosocial behavior; nevertheless, he seems to feel that Kenny might truly benefit from the physical and emotional abuse inflicted by Billy, citing an example from the annals of sports to support this assertion. Indeed, Mr. Formisano's machismo, and his sincere belief that one can learn much from corporal punishment administered by a peer, run contrary to the principles of sound pedagogy described in this book. In stark contrast to the recommendation of Smith (2012), Mr. Formisano's attitude toward Kenny and his victimization will not facilitate meaningful prosocial change in Kenny and, in all likelihood, will only encourage Billy to continue to bully.

Mrs. Jolivet is able to see clearly the disparity between the two boys and the very real threat that Billy represents to Kenny. While acknowledging Kenny's provocative behavior, she is nevertheless able to contextualize this less onerous issue and focus on the more pressing concern: Kenny's victimization by Billy. She demonstrates the courage of purpose and integrity espoused by Loughran (1997) and Palmer (1998) as well as the true caring extolled by Noddings (2005), both tenets of a sound teaching pedagogy, as she vigorously pursues justice for Kenny and behavioral intervention to address Billy's victimizing behavior. Mrs. Jolivet seems confident in her role and certain of her responsibilities as a teacher, which embodies the third element in our pedagogical framework; namely, that good teachers cultivate "certainty, positivity, and the unity of self and moral goals" (Stout, 2005, p. 194). Unlike Mr. Formisano, Mrs. Jolivet seems equipped to facilitate prosocial change in both Kenny and Billy.

EFFECTIVE TEACHER RESPONSES

- "Do not tolerate bullying. Allowing seemingly harmless behavior to continue unaddressed can be viewed by children who bully as an indication of tolerance or acceptance.
- Set rules for behavior in your classroom, and ensure that students participate in developing and enforcing the rules and the specific consequences for breaking them.

- Learn and teach both conflict-resolution and anger-management skills" (New Jersey State Bar Foundation, n.d.).
- Learn and watch for the warning signs of violence; these include social withdrawal, feelings of rejection, rage, expressions of violence in writing or drawing, gang affiliation, and making serious threats of violence.
- Know your school resources for dealing with students who engage in threats or in violent behavior (e.g., school counselor, school psychologist, crisis intervention team and plan).
- Enforce school policies that seek to reduce the risk of violence (e.g., keep an eye on hallways between periods, check on students in the recess areas or school cafeteria during recess or lunch breaks).
- Help implement a safe school plan. If one doesn't exist, organize other concerned teachers and approach the administration about establishing one.
- Report safety threats or legitimate concerns about potential violence to the school administration immediately.
- Encourage and support student-led violence prevention programs. Examples of these programs include peer mediation, teen courts, and violence prevention training.
- Take time to get to know your students' parents or caregivers. It is possible that many lethal episodes of school violence might have been averted had teachers been alerted to the possibility by family members (adapted from Druck & Kaplowitz, 2005).
- "Learn what bullying is and what it is not. Many behaviors that look like bullying may be just as serious, but may require different response strategies. You can also learn about what to look for as warning signs that some of your students might be involved in bullying and who might be at more risk for being involved. Know about special considerations for specific groups. [. . .]
- Learn how to engage parents and youth in building a positive school climate. Learning how to talk about bullying with youth is a critical step.
- Know about your obligations under your state's anti-bullying law. Learn also about federal laws that require schools to address harassment based on race, color, national origin, sex, and disabilities. Work to establish rules and policies to help let the entire school community know the expectations around bullying and procedures to report and investigate when something happens. [. . .]" (Stopbullying.gov, n.d.).
- "Reframe Bullying Prevention. Bullying prevention shouldn't be just about solving another school problem. It's about improving how all members of the school community treat each other. People respond better to positive, inspirational goals than they do to a negative behavior. Bullying prevention is about strengthening community, so make that your goal!
- Start With And Stand On Principles. Bullying is more than a rule infraction. Bullying is about an abuse of power and the mistreatment of others. It's a violation of the values and social norms of the school. All members of the school

community should develop principles to guide how people treat each other in situations not 'covered' by the rules.

- Adults Should Go First. Bullying prevention shouldn't be just about changing student behavior. The adults in the school community need to model what they expect from students and make sure that their behavior is consistent with the school's guiding principles.
- Use The Community To Build Community. Change cannot be imposed on people from above. It should emerge from people learning together about what they want the change to be and about the process of changing" (Oklahoma Educators Credit Union, n.d.).
- "Develop, post, and discuss rules and sanctions related to bullying.
- Treat students and each other with warmth and respect. Demonstrate positive interest and involvement in your students.
- Establish yourself as a clear and visible authority with responsibility for making the school experience safe and positive.
- Reward students for positive, inclusive behavior.
- Take immediate action when bullying is observed and consistently use non-physical, non-hostile negative consequences when rules are broken.
- Listen to parents and students who report bullying in your classroom. Quickly and effectively resolve the issue to avoid perpetuation of bullying behaviors.
- Notify parents of all involved students when a bullying incident occurs, and resolve the problem expeditiously, according to discipline plans at school.
- Refer students affected by bullying to school counseling or mental health staff if needed.
- Protect students who are bullied with a safety plan.
- Hold class meetings during which students can talk about bullying and peer relations.
- Provide information to parents about bullying behaviors and encourage their involvement and support in addressing bullying issues" (Olweus Bullying Prevention Program, 2015).

CONCLUDING THOUGHTS

As we have pointed out in this chapter, bullying and its aftermath continue to represent a real challenge for students, teachers, and administrators. This destructive social phenomenon has always been prevalent among school-age children and adolescents, and the Internet and social media provide even more venues for bullies. Although much attention has been devoted to the bully, research has revealed that the victims of bullying might present an even greater challenge for teachers and administrators, since frequently they transition from victim to victimizer. Similarly, bullying in school is often incited by physical and emotional abuse at the hands of caregivers in the home, and many incidents of school shootings are believed to have been responses to long-term abuse in the home or community.

However, despite the increase in incidents of bullying and cyberbullying among school-age children and adolescents, there is hope for change. To that end, this chapter has provided the reader with ways to identify and understand the causes and development of bullying in school and the means to effectively address both the bully and the victim in and outside the school. While the costs of inaction are dear, the information and the frameworks of relationship building and effective pedagogical practices provided by the authors represent a potent countermeasure.

CHAPTER 8

Teaching Students Who Are Victims of Bias in the Classroom

STUDENT HATE CRIME VIGNETTE: "KULDEEP"

Kuldeep Singh and his family immigrated to Upstate New York in 1999, just two years before the 9/11 terrorist attack. Kuldeep was only 6 years old at the time. Although the Singhs clearly stood out because of their traditional clothing, the community was relatively kind and receptive. Dr. Singh, a trauma surgeon, worked at the regional hospital; his wife and parents shared the customary responsibilities of cooking, cleaning, and child rearing. Everyone took special care of Kuldeep, given his disability. The youngest of six siblings and the only male child, Kuldeep was diagnosed with cerebral palsy, a chronic orthopedic impairment, at the age of 5.

As practicing Sikhs, the men and boys in the Singh household did not cut their hair or beards and wore the traditional turban. The women and girls opted to wear colorful saris, along with matching headscarves, and sandals. Despite a few stares from classmates upon his arrival in the neighborhood school, the children and teachers proved very accepting of Kuldeep and his family. That is, until the tragic events of September 11, 2001.

The week following the tragedy marked the beginning of a very dark time for Kuldeep and his family. Mrs. Kaur, Kuldeep's mother, was accosted and threatened in the local grocery store by several "patriots" who assumed, based on her appearance, that she was an Arab and therefore "one of them." She fled the store, abandoning her shopping cart laden with the week's groceries and was too terrified to return to retrieve them. Dr. Singh was approached by a physician's assistant with whom he had never worked and was told to "Go back to Saudi Arabia—we don't want you people here!" He and his family, once accepted and welcomed, were now personae non gratae in their newly adopted community and country. Angry neighbors, outraged by the barbarity of 9/11, drafted a petition to try to force the Singhs to relocate. On another occasion, a group of teenage boys spray painted a message on the side of the Singhs' garage: "Go home rag heads and take Mohammad with you! Signed, The Infidels."

But the worst act of prejudice was meted out on little Kuldeep at, of all places, his school. Perhaps emulating their parents' prejudice, a group of Kuldeep's classmates surrounded him during recess and began pushing him, despite his physical disability, and calling him offensive names like "gimp" and "camel rider." Kuldeep fell several times during the assault, but was saved from further abuse by the playground monitors and the assistant principal, who observed the incident from her office window. In response to the actions of the offending students, the school's principal suspended them and called each of their parents, requesting a meeting to discuss the seriousness of their child's actions. Some of the parents seemed contrite and promised to address the issue of prejudice and tolerance with their child. Unfortunately, the parents of two of the offending children became defensive, accusing the principal of "siding with the enemy" and insisting that Kuldeep's teachers and family were grossly exaggerating the event. One of the parents said, "That's so typical of those people—they take advantage of our freedoms and opportunities and then have the gall to feel discriminated against because a few of our kids dared to feel outrage, when their people commit an atrocity like 9/11! You'll be talking to my lawyer if you suspend my kid over something like that!"

WHY DO TEACHERS NEED TO KNOW ABOUT BIAS AND RACISM?

According to the National Center for Education Statistics (2010), in the 2009–2010 school year, there were 16,270 reported incidents of bias or hate crimes committed in public schools in the United States. Furthermore, the FBI (2010) disclosed that, in 2009, 11% of all hate and bias crimes were committed on school and college campuses, and 50% of bias crime offenders were between the ages of 11 and 20. For example, in one state, New Jersey, the primary targets of those bias crimes were reportedly African Americans, Latinos, Asians, Native Americans, Jews, Muslims, other non-Christian religious practitioners, and LGBT-identified youth (New Jersey State Police, 2009). Furthermore, as reported by the CDC (Eaton et al., 2009), 61% of LGBT students reported feeling unsafe in school, 85% said they had been verbally harassed, 40% stated they had been physically harassed, and 19% reported having been physically assaulted. The foci of the bias crimes tend to fall into one or more of the following categories: race, ethnicity, religion, sexual orientation, and disability (Kosciw, Greytak, Diaz, & Bartkiewicz, 2010).

Clearly, then, as confirmed in these alarming statistics, since a disproportionate number of bias and hate crimes occur in school, it falls on the teachers and administrators to address this serious issue. Education is the principal weapon in eradicating bias and prejudice, which are born of ignorance and misinformation. However, in order for teachers to effectively deal with the prejudice displayed in their students, they too must do some soul-searching to ensure they are honest and courageous enough to both acknowledge and vanquish their own prejudice. In order to be successful educators, it is imperative that *all* teachers understand the root causes of bias, its detrimental effects on the learning environment, and effective ways to address it when it occurs among students in the classroom.

WHAT THE TEACHER SHOULD KNOW ABOUT BIAS AND RACISM

The increasing diversity of U.S. society has created an ongoing challenge for addressing bias in public schools. Unlike in years past, when the majority of immigrants to the United States were White Europeans, present immigration patterns reveal that the majority of immigrants arriving to the United States are from countries with visible racial and ethnic populations. In 2013, Mexican-born immigrants accounted for approximately 28% of the 41.3 million foreign-born population in the United States. India and China were the second most common countries of origin, both accounting for about 5%; the Philippines (4%) was the fourth most common. Vietnam, El Salvador, Cuba, and Korea sent 3% each, and the Dominican Republic and Guatemala accounted for 2% each. Immigrants from these 10 countries accounted for 60% of the U.S. immigrant population in 2013 (Zong & Batalova, 2015). When one considers in conjunction with these immigration patterns the significant number of African Americans and Native Americans in this country, our schools, created and managed for the most part by White Europeans, face the challenge of serving children and their parents whose racial and ethnic backgrounds are vastly different from those of teachers and administrators. According to the National Center for Educational Statistics (NCES), by the fall of 2015 the overall number of Latino, African American, and Asian students in public K–12 classrooms, projected to be 50.3%, is expected to surpass the number of non-Hispanic Whites (Maxwell, 2014).

How this challenge is perceived and reacted to will determine a school's degree of sensitivity and competence when working with students and their parents from diverse cultural backgrounds.

The purpose of this introduction is to help teachers and other school personnel meet the challenges of diversity in their classrooms by providing frameworks for understanding their own and their students' cultural backgrounds. In order to facilitate this understanding, the following is a list of definitions for commonly used terms in multiculturalism.

Multiculturalism	The philosophy of paying careful attention to and respecting all aspects of human diversity.
Culture	Beliefs, language, values, rituals, traditions, and other behaviors of a particular social group that one generation transmits to another (Helms, 1994).

Race	A social construct based on assumed biological traits and appearance designed to include some and exclude others from societal resources (Helms & Cook, 1999).
Ethnicity	Refers to cultural patterns of a group that is defined by a specific geographic region of the world (Helms & Cook, 1999).
Minority	Refers to the lower economic, legal, political, and social position of a particular group (Helms & Cook, 1999). Used synonymously with *non-dominant*.
Majority	Refers to particular groups in society that have a disproportionate share of power. Used synonymously with *dominant* and *mainstream*.
Based on Helms and Cook, 1999.	

It is impossible to write about multicultural counseling without serious sociopolitical overtones. While this chapter is not meant to offend anyone, it is meant to challenge members of dominant cultures (e.g., White, male, Eurocentric, heterosexual, Christian, high socioeconomic status) as to how they view membership in their own culture and the consequences of these views for working with those from nondominant cultural backgrounds. Conversely, members of nondominant cultures are also challenged to examine how they have internalized oppression by the dominant culture, and to what degree this internalization determines the teaching relationship with both members and nonmembers of their cultural group.

The definitions of *majority* and *minority* given above have nothing to do with numerical representation but with access to power. Writing about multiculturalism also means writing about unequal access to power in our society, especially among People of Color (POC), to maintain and influence societal structures that confer privilege. Whites will remain the dominant cultural group in this country for a very, very long time, and the present-day dynamic of some POC aspiring to membership and acceptance into White culture, while others continue to resent and struggle against the disproportionate share of power among people of color in this country, will continue. With their increasing diversity, schools cannot exempt themselves from an ongoing serious consideration and discussion of race, culture, and power.

Etic Versus Emic Debate

For many years, helping professionals have struggled with sameness and difference. Is it better to focus on what is the same in all human beings—what transcends culture and therefore is of "etic" quality; or on differences—what is culture specific and therefore of an "emic" quality? Critics of the multicultural movement argue that the emphasis upon cultural differences has caused people to lose sight of the sameness that unites all human beings. These critics argue that there are teaching strategies and interventions of etic proportion that can be applied to all students regardless of cultural background. Commonly referred to as the *universalist* position (see Qureshi, 1995, for a typology of approaches to multiculturalism), they do not deny cultural differences but clearly see them as secondary to similarities among individuals.

On the other side are multiculturalists who argue that looking for sameness really means looking for Whiteness in all human beings. Traditional teaching and helping theories, principles, strategies, and interventions have emanated from a particular cultural viewpoint, namely that of White, male, and Eurocentric. Most especially, the race-based theorists (those who consider primary the power differential between Whites and people of color and its intrusion into the helping relationship) criticize the universalists for ignoring issues of power and race and sometimes having an unconscious agenda of maintaining the status quo. In other words, failure to take into consideration societal forces of racism and other forms of oppression when teaching students from nondominant backgrounds promotes the status quo and maintains an unequal distribution of power.

At national conferences and other venues, enriching, spirited, and sometimes heated debates around these issues have taken place. Paying close attention to cultural differences seems absolutely necessary to successful teaching. How can teachers refrain from deleterious judgment if they do not understand how a student's culturally based values and behaviors differ from their own cultural socialization? Those who espouse an etic position might argue that a good relationship is necessary for all teaching, regardless of a student's cultural background. While few would argue against the etic quality of the helping relationship (even this book regards attachment as having an etic dimension), teachers have to recognize that how that relationship is formed—the strategies used to develop it—will vary depending on the students' and their parents' cultural backgrounds. For example, a recently arrived Asian student might feel uncomfortable with expressing his feelings, whereas a Latino might be put off by a teacher whom she perceives as cold and unfriendly. It is important to pay attention to **intergroup differences** (how cultural groups differ from one another), but it is equally important to pay attention to **intragroup differences** (how members of a particular cultural group differ among themselves) to avoid stereotyping.

Second Culture Acquisition

Teachers working across cultures need to ask themselves two things about a student: What are the broad cultural patterns of the student's salient referent group (intergroup and intercultural difference), and to what *extent* are this particular student and his family representative of such patterns (intragroup and intracultural difference). One of the primary methods for assessing intragroup difference is through the process of **second culture acquisition**—how and to what degree a person acquires another culture.

Second culture acquisition begins when two different cultures come into contact, and a process of adaptation begins. Cultural adaptation is the process through which a person learns to live in a culture that is different from his own. In most cases, it means adaptation to the dominant culture, which in the United States is clearly the White, Euro-centric culture. Berry (1997) conceived of the "other culture" as a stimulus that evokes a reaction of moving toward, moving against, or moving away. "Moving toward" assumes that a positive relationship to the dominant culture is sought.

More recently, the adaptation process has been conceptualized as either unidirectional, bidirectional, or multidirectional. *Unidirectional* implies that one adapts by moving in a single direction toward one culture and away from another. In contrast, a *bidirectional* adaptation implies moving back and forth between two cultures, allowing the individual to feel at home in both. *Multidirectionality* implies that individuals, while maintaining a positive identity with their culture of origin, are capable of participating in various and complex societal structures made up of multiple cultural groupings (Broesch & Hadley, 2012).

Often, immigrant children and their parents will assume conflicting forms of cultural adaptation, with the former moving toward the dominant culture and the latter either moving against the dominant culture or remaining marginal. The following is a list of various forms of cultural adaptation that are either unidirectional, bidirectional, or multidirectional.

- **Assimilation.** Individuals adapt by rejecting their native culture and trying as much as possible to become similar to the dominant culture.
- **Integration.** Individuals retain some aspects of their native culture and at the same time assume attributes of the dominant culture.
- **Alternation (Biculturalism).** A bidirectional, nonhierarchical relationship is formed between two cultures. Biculturalism is knowing and understanding two cultures, maintaining a positive relationship with both, and altering one's behavior to fit the particular cultural context.
- **Rejection.** One does not seek a positive relationship with the dominant culture and maintains a high identification with the nondominant culture.
- **Marginality.** There is identification neither with the dominant culture nor with the nondominant culture. (Adapted from Berry, 1990).

For members of nondominant racial and ethnic backgrounds, to learn and move with comfort in White dominant culture has enormous benefits for becoming upwardly mobile. Schools can help to facilitate the adaptation of students from nondominant cultural backgrounds. Failure to do so would keep them marginal, and they would be unable to benefit maximally from the opportunities in this country. When schools that have traditionally served a White population experience an influx of visible racial and ethnic students from nondominant cultural backgrounds, it should be looked upon as an opportunity for mutual enrichment. Teachers and administrators can benefit from the opportunity of becoming bicultural through work with their students and families. If this mutual biculturalism could become a reality, schools would be perceived as much more friendly and inviting to students and parents from nondominant cultures.

Formation of Worldviews

Though White is the most powerful and most dominant cultural group in the United States, Whiteness is simply another way of being in a world filled with cultural patterns. It is part of the mosaic of color that makes up American society. Few White people, however, are conscious of themselves as racial beings. Unlike people of color, who are confronted with their racial identity on a daily basis, Whites can easily go through their entire existence without reflecting on Whiteness: what it means to be White and the worldview that is clearly linked to being White (intra-group differences notwithstanding). "American" culture (acceptable ways of being in the world as defined by the Northern European Whites) has been the focus of many investigations. In their discussion concerning the formation of worldviews, Sue and Sue (2012) made use of the concepts of *locus of control* and *locus of responsibility* to draw comparisons between mainstream White Euro-American culture and other cultures. Locus of control and responsibility can be either internal or external. Figure 8.1 represents four worldviews based on different combinations of internal or external locus of control and responsibility. Quadrant I represents an internal locus of control (IC) and internal locus of responsibility (IR) that is thought to be most reflective of middle- and upper-middle-class White culture. Sue and Sue described this concept as follows.

> Perhaps the greatest exemplification of the IC-IR philosophy is U.S society. U.S. American culture can be described as the epitome of the individual-centered approach that emphasizes uniqueness, independence, and self-reliance. A high value is placed on personal resources for solving all problems: self-reliance, pragmatism, individualism, status achievement through one's own effort; and power or control over others, things, animals, and forces of nature. Democratic ideals such as "equal access to opportunity," "liberty and justice for all," "God helps those who help themselves," and "fulfillment of personal destiny" all reflect this worldview. The individual is held accountable for all that transpires. Constant and prolonged failure or the inability to attain goals leads to symptoms of self-blame (depression, guilt, and feelings of inadequacy). (p. 140)

Teachers, socialized by an IC-IR worldview, must be sensitive when working with students from nondominant cultures, whose worldview may be quite different. Some may come from countries with totalitarian regimes that have made it difficult to adopt an internal locus of control. Some people of color, having experienced institutional and societal racism, may not subscribe so easily to the philosophy of "If I want to, I can." Education in this country has always been considered a valuable means for achieving more control over one's destiny, and sometimes school

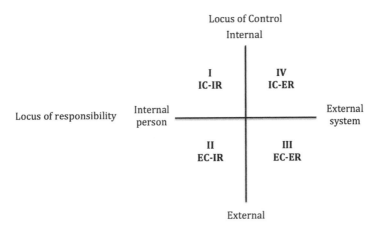

Figure 8.1: Locus of Control vs. Locus of Responsibility

From "Eliminating Cultural Oppression in Counseling: Toward a General Theory," by D.W. Sue, 1978, The Counseling Psychologist, 25, p. 422. Copyright 1978 by the American Psychological Association.

personnel simply assume that students and their parents buy into this philosophy. While education continues to be a gateway to upward mobility, teachers need to detect and be sensitive to those clients whose worldview may be more external in terms of control and responsibility. By listening to and validating some of the reasons why a student may not assume an internal locus of control or responsibility, teachers can begin to facilitate a better understanding of the clash of worldviews that their students may be encountering when immersed in a White, middle-class culture. Many times, a worldview more external in terms of control and responsibility can be perceived as a lack of motivation on the student's part, and some teachers, trained in ways of working that assume an internal locus of control, may question the student's appropriateness for learning.

Racial Identity Development

Helms (1984, 1990, 1994, 1995) theorized a process through which individuals develop a racial identity. According to Helms and Cook (1999), racial identity models are:

> psychological models because they intend to explain individuals' intrapsychic and interpersonal reactions to societal racism in its various manifestations. That is, they are descriptions of hypothetical intrapsychic pathways for overcoming internalized racism and achieving a healthy socioracial self-conception under varying conditions of racial oppression. (p. 81)

Helms suggested that, in the context of societal racism, where one race is judged "superior" precisely because another is implicitly or explicitly held to be "inferior," an individual's psychological experience of race necessarily includes attitudes toward one's own race as well as toward the other race with which one shares the dynamic of domination or oppression.

Racial identity development of Whites. Helms (1990, 1995) suggested six ego identity statuses for Whites' experience of race. Each status represents a cluster of attitudes, beliefs, and values that affect the ways in which an individual perceives the world and influences the way he or she processes information about race. According to Helms (1995), the statuses are arranged sequentially, with increasing complexity and flexibility in the processing of racially related information. According to Helms, at any given time, one status will predominate, although some characteristics of others may be present. The tasks and challenges of each lower status must be integrated in order to progress to the next. However, in a given situation, an individual may revert from his or her current predominant status to a lower one. Helms proposed two fundamental processes that underlie the development of increasingly more complex and integrated racial identity ego statuses: the abandonment of racism and the development of a positive White racial identity. Following is a description of each of the six statuses, the first three of which (contact, disintegration, and reintegration) are associated with the abandonment of racism, while the last three (pseudo-independence, immersion/emersion, and autonomy) are associated with the development of a positive White racial identity.

1. **Contact status.** Contact Whites are oblivious to issues of race and racism. There is little awareness as to how race as a sociopolitical construct determines one's place in society. Contact Whites are fond of their color-blind attitudes ("I don't see color; I look at the person"). They may even point to the fact that they have a friend of color as evidence of their nonracism. Since color doesn't matter, people of color only have to work hard, and they will get ahead like everyone else.
2. **Disintegration status.** There is an awakening to issues of racism in society, and the beliefs and attitudes of the contact status are dismantled. This can result in feeling anxious, guilty, lost, or helpless about racism in America. The disintegrated White will do something to reduce this state of conflict—frequently, avoiding contact with people of color and taking refuge in the comfort and acceptance of one's own racial group.
3. **Reintegration status.** There exists an achieved White racial identity with the explicit belief that Whites are superior and people of color inferior. Reintegration can be either passive or active. A passive reintegrated White tries to avoid people of color at all costs, in comparison to an active one, who engages in overt hostile and violent acts against people of color.
4. **Pseudo-independence status.** There is an acknowledgment of racism, an intellectual acceptance of people of color, and a desire to help people of color by imposing White standards and White culture. The pseudo-independent White sees the solution to racism as changing people of color, not Whites.

These Whites have "politically correct" views about racism but make little change in their lives to combat racism.

5. **Immersion/emersion status.** A positive White racial identity is being formed by learning about being White, the consequences of being White, and its relationship to the rest of society. The focus is no longer on changing people of color but changing Whites. This person seeks out others who have also struggled to achieve their own nonracist White identity.

6. **Autonomy status.** This status represents a continuation and consolidation of the identity process begun in the immersion/emersion status. The autonomous White seeks out contact with diverse cultural groups and experiences such contact as mutually enriching. Comfortable in their own evolved White identity, such people believe they have something to offer as well as something to learn. Committed to working for change, they may be willing to make life choices that reflect that stance (Adapted from Helms, 1995, with permission).

For White teachers to work effectively with a student population of varying races and ethnicities, they need to be aware of their own racial identity status and make every effort to achieve the highest developmental status, autonomy. Racial identity profiling is consistent with Helms's position that all statuses are present within an individual. However, given the situation and developmental level of the individual, one or more statuses will predominate. While Helms did not argue for a purely situational understanding of racial identity, she did allow for moving in and out of statuses depending on environmental circumstances. For example, a White individual at the autonomy status, if victimized in some way by someone of a different race or ethnicity, might re-cycle through the disintegration status. Helms's theory is dynamic rather than static.

Racial identity development of people of color. Drawing upon the Cross model (Cross, 1971), Atkinson, Morten, & Sue, 1998 developed a racial/cultural identity model that has been cited and used widely in the literature. Following are the racial identity statuses for people of color:

1. **Conformity.** Individual is oblivious to issues of race and their sociopolitical implications. Adheres to White standards of merit and success and tends to denigrate others of their own minority group.

2. **Dissonance.** Through an experience of some sort, the individual becomes confused and ambivalent about issues of race and their own socio-racial group. Begins to question Whiteness as the ultimate standard to judge himself and others.

3. **Resistance and immersion.** Contrary to conformity, this individual idealizes his own socio-racial group and denigrates Whiteness. Self-definition comes from his own racial group, and commitment and loyalty to the group is consid-

ered paramount. The person tends to be hypersensitive and hypervigilant to issues of race. There is a sense of well-being derived from solidarity with one's own racial group.

4. **Introspection.** Positive commitment to and acceptance of one's own socio-racial group, internally defined racial attributes, and capacity to objectively assess and respond to members of the dominant group.

5. **Integrative awareness.** Capacity to value one's own collective identities as well as empathize and collaborate with members of other oppressed groups. There is also an appreciation of the dominant culture's positive aspects not seen as necessarily in conflict with one's own culture. Life's decisions are often guided by the elimination of all forms of oppression. (Based on Atkinson, Morton, & Sue, 1998)

Much of what was said earlier about the dynamics of White racial identity development can be said about the racial identity development of people of color. The model is fluid, where all statuses to one degree or another are present in an individual, but one or more will predominate at a particular time or situation. An individual can re-cycle through less developed statuses because of a given circumstance. People of color must negotiate their relationship with the dominant culture, which can range from exaltation of White culture (conformity status), through outright and perhaps even hostile rejection (immersion), toward a healthy and enriching integration of their own racial culture with other oppressed groups and even the dominant culture (internalization and integrative awareness).

Racial identity development models for people of color also help teachers pay closer attention to intragroup differences and their impact upon the learning process.

Racial Identity and Teacher–Student Relationship

In her seminal article on people of color and White identity development, Helms (1984) classified four possible relationship types between a White helper and a non-White client (or vice versa): parallel, progressive, regressive, and crossed. A *parallel* relationship is one where the client and counselor are at the same level of racial identity development. For example, a White client at the contact status and a non-White client at the conformity status would be in a parallel relationship. A *progressive* relationship is defined as the helper being at least one level higher than the client. For example, a White teacher at the pseudo-independent status with a non-White student at the dissonance status would enjoy a progressive relationship. A *regressive* relationship is defined as the teacher being at least one level lower than the student. A White teacher at the reintegration status with a non-White student at the internalization status would be a regressive relationship. Finally, a *crossed* relationship is one in which the participants have directly opposite attitudes. For example, a person of color at the internalization status (feels positive about people of color, neutral about Whites) is in a crossed relationship with a White person at the pseudo-independent status (feels positive about Whites, neutral about people of color). The hypothesis that progressive relationships are beneficial to the helping relationship and regressive relationships are detrimental has received empirical support (Bradby & Helms, 1990; Helms & Carter, 1991 Carter, Helms, & Juby, 2004).

For teachers working with people of color, racial identity can help them understand the different attitudes and behaviors of both parents and children. For example, a non-White parent at the conformity status will acquiesce to a White teacher and be very willing to accept the school's suggestions for her child. However, the opposite would be true for a non-White parent who is at the immersion status. In this situation, the teacher may even be a target of hostility, since the parent feels that everything White is to be denigrated. If teachers can frame the various reactions of people of color within a racial identity framework, they can devise more appropriate interventions for establishing a collaborative relationship with parents. A non-White parent at the immersion status will not take kindly to a White teacher with an "I know better than you" attitude. On the other hand, a parent at the conformity status might welcome a more directive approach from a White teacher. Teachers need to listen carefully for racial themes in working with both children and parents of color, since it will help them assess racial identity status and effectuate a working relationship even with parents who are mistrustful and rejecting toward Whites. The same dynamics apply for non-White teachers when working with White parents.

Summary

This section has highlighted the changing racial and ethnic makeup of America's public schools. In order to appreciate the challenges of this change, the constructs of second-culture acquisition and racial identity development were presented to help teachers avoid stereotypes and understand intragroup differences. The etic versus emic debate also explained the various positionalities when it comes to dealing with sameness and difference. We now return to the case example from the beginning of the chapter, to apply some of these constructs in conjunction with attachment theory.

UNDERSTANDING BIAS AND RACISM FROM AN ATTACHMENT PERSPECTIVE

Attachment theory would posit that those with insecure attachment histories are more likely to behave in a racist fashion (Dalal, 2006). An individual operating from a secure base does not fear cultural difference. On the contrary, he is attracted to it. A secure attachment in childhood permits the activation of the exploratory system that in adulthood can take the form of exploring, understanding, and appreciating cultural difference. Simply put, an important indicator of an individual's attachment history can be his attitude toward cultural difference: Is it something to be avoided or embraced? Immersing oneself in another culture, while challenging and difficult, is enriching on many levels, but can only be achieved by someone who is capable of coming out of his secure world of sameness and live, at least for the time being, as an outsider. Attachment theory would have one believe that only people with secure histories can relinquish security to explore life beyond what is comfortable.

Schools should be places of learning that appreciate and promote diversity in spite of the challenges and difficulties that can often exist in such an endeavor. Keeping this in mind, let's examine two different teacher reactions to the Singh family after 9/11.

UNDERSTANDING TEACHER INTERVENTIONS FOR THE STUDENTS WHO ARE VICTIMS OF BIAS FROM BOTH ATTACHMENT AND PEDAGOGICAL PERSPECTIVES

Mrs. Chalmers: "Maybe They Should Just Relocate"

Mrs. Chalmers, a third-grade teacher in Kuldeep's school, was particularly affected by the events of 9/11—a close family friend perished in the terrorist attacks on the World Trade Center. While she understands that the Singhs are Sikhs from India and in no way affiliated with Islam or Islamic extremism, she has always been uncomfortable with their exclusive practices and distinctive appearance. A relative who visited India a decade ago told her that the Sikhs, who primarily inhabit the Indian state of Punjab, have at times sought political independence from India. He also said that there have been several recent violent assassinations and bombings attributed to Sikh extremists in India. Also, as part of their religious duty, Sikh men and boys are required to carry a kirpan, *or ceremonial dagger, to defend the religion and the helpless. This knowledge has helped to further estrange the Singhs in the eyes of Mrs. Chalmers and some of her colleagues. While Mrs. Chalmers does not condone the behavior of the students who harass and assault Kuldeep, secretly she feels that the presence of the Singhs in the school and the community has created unnecessary tension and anxiety at a time when "real" Americans need to come together, mourn their shared loss, and begin to heal. How can people newly arrived from another country, with such an alien culture and religion, possibly understand her fear and grief?*

To make matters even worse, Mrs. Chalmers will receive Kuldeep in her fourth-grade class in September. She finds the prospect distasteful for two reasons: She is uncomfortable teaching a child from such a radically different cultural and religious background, and she does not feel qualified to work with a child with such a profound orthopedic impairment, since she is not certified in special education. Recently, in a discussion with some of her neighbors and family members who are similarly uncomfortable with the Singhs living in their community, Mrs. Chalmers disclosed, "You know, I feel terrible saying this, but I'm just not comfortable having that family in the neighborhood or in our school. I'm not a prejudiced person, and I know we all came from somewhere else at some point, but the Singhs just aren't like us—who knows what they think about 9/11 and the terrorists who carried it out? Maybe they sympathize with them a bit because of their troubles with the Hindus in India—I just don't know. I wish they would reconsider staying here. Maybe they should just relocate; I think it would be in their best interests."

Mrs. Chalmers from an Attachment Perspective

Mrs. Chalmers has a passionate and challenging reaction to the Singh family, one that many others might identify with. First, she focuses on the "exclusive" practices of the Singh family in regard to their appearance. This is a very interesting commentary from the perspective of second culture acquisition. What is different is deemed exclusive and therefore bad. This dynamic is quite common between members of the dominant and nondominant cultures. A comment such as the following might be heard: "I don't mind having those people around, but I don't like it when . . ." The "when" usually refers to external culture expression that can take the form of things like dress, dance, or music. In other words, "You can stay here, but blend in and don't shove your culture in my face!" This comes from the assimilationist, melting-pot perspective. We should all look alike and act alike—and that usually means being like the members of the dominant culture. African Americans, for example, will often comment as to how they evoke very different reactions from coworkers when they wear their hair in cornrows or wear African dress. Mrs. Chalmers would probably not support a multicultural society, where different cultures are not only to be tolerated but celebrated, and where the metaphor of a mosaic replaces that of the melting pot. In a mosaic, the beauty of each piece is brought out by its juxtaposition with other pieces. The pieces are related without losing their identity. Harmony and beauty are created not by relinquishing cultural distinctions but by retaining them. Only securely attached individuals can accept that their own beauty is enhanced by those who are different.

Mrs. Chalmers does not simply spew out unsupported, biased, ethnocentric remarks against the Singh family. She has some facts to support her position, gleaned from a relative who visited India years ago and learned about Sikh extremism. No doubt, there may exist an extremist wing of the Sikh religion, as in every religion and as explained by the immersion phase of cultural identity development. Once again, the syllogism that prevents people from recognizing intragroup differences is: "I heard of a Sikh who was an extremist; therefore, all Sikhs are extremists." Once individuals form strong beliefs about a particular group, they see only the evidence that supports their beliefs and find a way to discard or ignore evidence that would challenge those beliefs. This is known as *scotosis*.

To her credit, Mrs. Chalmers does not condone the racist behavior of the students but sees the solution in having the Singhs disappear through relocation. It would very likely solve the immediate problem, but it would leave in place the insidious themes that drive the students' behaviors. To operate from a secure base, Mrs. Chalmers needs the community to restore its homogeneity. Security achieved in this fashion (by being with those who are culturally like oneself, the "real" Americans) is very fleeting, and it is only a matter to time before this prejudiced scenario repeats itself. If anything, Mrs. Chalmers seems to operate from a Resistant anxious state of mind, and she sees the anxiety and tension from encounters with the Singhs as harmful emotions to be avoided, not a potential learning and enriching opportunity to be embraced. She entertains the idea that the Singhs might even condone the 9/11 attacks and assumes that the Singhs are incapable of understanding her own fear. Her lack of empathy (always an indicator of an insecure base) prevents her from even considering the tremendous fear the Singh family must be experiencing as the result of being targeted by their community.

Mrs. Chalmers's feelings about having Kuldeep in class next year come as no surprise. He has triple minority status: religion, ethnicity, and a disability. In the world of the teacher, the greater the difference, the greater the anxiety, and even greater is the need to take refuge in what is known and familiar. No doubt, having Kuldeep in class would be a challenge and would require additional work and learning on the part of the teacher, along with engaging in a process of mentalization to understand and make sense of the feelings generated by having this student in her class. Regardless of what one thinks about Mrs. Chalmers's position, she does not engage in mentalization but is instead more reactive, driven by her Resistant anxious state of mind. This book posits that mentalization is required for teachers to form working alliances with their students, especially the ones they find most challenging and who may come from cultures different than their own.

Mrs. Chalmers from a Pedagogical Perspective

Mrs. Chalmers is, unfortunately, not alone in her prejudiced attitude toward the "other" (i.e., Kuldeep Singh and his family). However, in excusing her prejudice, she has failed to acquire a tenet of our pedagogical framework: the importance of understanding and respecting the cultural milieu of her students (Bruner, 1996; Freire, 1970). Although she purports to be a good and caring teacher, one who "feels terrible" for advocating the exclusion of the Singhs from the school and community, her disclosure of this sentiment to colleagues and friends belies her true feelings. In doing so, Mrs. Chalmers has abrogated one of our most important pedagogical tenets: the importance of developing caring teacher–student relationships that are unconditional and therefore blind to culture, race, sexual orientation, and difference (Noddings, 2005; Smith 2012; Solomon, 2012).

By advocating the exclusion of Kuldeep and his family, Mrs. Chalmers has also failed to embrace the fourth element in our proposed framework, the one that requires that effective teachers impart an understanding of the "value of cultural nuances"—the "hidden curriculums" of our social structures. Had she engaged this pedagogical tenet and worked to facilitate Kuldeep's inclusion in the school and classroom, his peers may have been far more likely to view him as part of the community, one of them, and not as an outsider. Finally, although Mrs. Chalmers has learned a bit about the Sikh religion and its history, her knowledge is incomplete and, as Alexander Pope famously observed, "A little learning is a dangerous thing" (1711). The sixth element in our pedagogical framework celebrates the notion that good teachers must cultivate a love of learning—not just about information that is sympathetic to their world view, but also that which challenges it. Mrs. Chalmers appears to be either unwilling or unable to embrace the truth about Sikhs like the Singhs, and instead has perpetuated the popular myths and misconceptions about them.

Mr. Wilson: "The Singhs Are Good People Who Contribute to Our Community"

Mr. Wilson, Kuldeep's third-grade teacher, was one of the first to intervene in the altercation on the playground. He has enjoyed teaching Kuldeep, finding him to be a very respectful, intelligent student. Despite his physical limitations, Kuldeep tries to participate in every class activity and gives his best effort in addressing each challenge that comes his way. Once, when one of the boys in his class made a rude remark about Kuldeep's turban and clothing, Mr. Wilson used the opportunity to educate his class about the contribution of different cultures to the United States. He also provided a follow-up lesson on Sikh culture and invited Kuldeep and his family to participate in a discussion of their heritage and religion. Mrs. Kaur, Kuldeep's mother, even baked jalebis, *a popular sweet treat in India, to be enjoyed by the class. The result of this cultural education was a significant improvement in the way Kuldeep was treated by his classmates. Mr. Wilson, who is certified in special education as well as general education, also took advantage of the opportunity to teach his students about physical impairments like cerebral palsy, with which Kuldeep has been diagnosed, and to demystify and debunk common misconceptions often associated with this disorder.*

Furthermore, Mr. Wilson has confronted the misperceptions and prejudices that have begun to circulate among his colleagues, especially in the teachers' lounge. He has been somewhat ostracized for this heroic intervention. Some of his fellow teachers have even suggested, behind his back, that he might be sympathetic to Islam and other "extremist" religions because of his unequivocal support for the Singhs. He has been their unwavering advocate, countering the naysayers and critics with facts about the family, such as Dr. Singh's pro-bono clinic work for the homeless and poor in the community and Mrs. Kaur's charity work, which, he said, was a hallmark of the Sikh religion. "The Singhs are good people who contribute unselfishly to our community. They are the kind of folks who make our community a better place to live," he contends.

Mr. Wilson from an Attachment Perspective

In many ways, Mr. Wilson's reaction to Kuldeep and his family is the opposite of Mrs. Chalmers's. That he operates from a secure state of mind is evident throughout the vignette. When a student makes a rude remark about Kuldeep's clothing, there is no mention of Mr. Wilson scolding or reprimanding the student. Because of his secure state of mind, Mr. Wilson may very well empathize even with a student who makes such a remark. He understands the part of human nature that can react negatively to cultural difference, and he therefore uses the student's remark as an opportunity to enhance the cultural learning and appreciation of his students. Mr. Wilson is not reactive! He mentalizes and capitalizes on his awareness of the classroom dynamics and the feeling provoked in him by the student's comment to convert what could have been a potentially volatile situation into a learning opportunity. Mr. Wilson takes charge not by yelling or reprimanding or punishing but by recognizing that everything can have an instructional purpose, even a prejudiced remark by one of his students. He understands the comment as providing the opportunity for diversity enhancement among his students with the hope that knowledge about the Sikh culture will help his students be less biased and more appreciative of cultural difference. Mr. Wilson takes charge by doing what he does best: teaching! He employs the same classroom dynamic in regard to Kuldeep's disability. In direct contrast to Mrs. Chalmers, Mr. Wilson understands Kuldeep's presence in his class as an asset that contributes to the diversity of his classroom and provides yet another opportunity for learning.

The second aspect of Mr. Wilson's secure state of mind is how he deals with the antagonism and objections of his colleagues. Based on the details of the vignette, we can posit that Mr. Wilson enjoys the autonomy status of White racial identity development that correlates with a secure state of mind. He seeks contact with diverse cultures and believes that he, along with his students, has something to learn from the Singhs, and he is committed to working for change. Mr. Wilson is trying to achieve a mutually enriching experience for himself and his class, and he sees the classroom as a potential laboratory for achieving a degree of biculturalism. The hallmark of the White individual at the autonomy status is advocacy and working for change to promote a more multicultural society. Mr. Wilson does not stand idly by when confronted with the insidious comments of his colleagues but continues his advocacy for the Singhs, perhaps even energized by the objections of his colleagues. Only a teacher operating from a secure state of mind could behave like this.

The hope is that Mr. Wilson will also have supporters, because it will be tough for him to go it alone. The best result would be for Mr. Wilson to have started a dialogue around cultural difference within a safe space where his colleagues can share their fears, many of which are very real and understandable. Mr. Wilson is most likely capable of empathy even for those who are his detractors. Just as he did not react to the student who made the rude comment about Kuldeep, one has to believe that he will not react to his colleagues but try to engage them in healthy dialogue about cultural difference. Only if people listen to each other without defensiveness is there a chance of achieving multiculturalism within schools.

Mr. Wilson from a Pedagogical Perspective

Mr. Wilson has evidenced his love of learning and a desire that his students understand all the facts about an issue before forming an opinion. He demonstrates this when he provides information to his students about the Sikh religion and its customs and about cerebral palsy. He also uses the teachable moment presented by Kuldeep's religious and cultural difference as an opportunity to provide information about the cultural origins of the other students in his classroom, to highlight the fact that everyone has come from somewhere else, and they should be proud of the contributions of their respective cultures to the mosaic that is the United States.

This initiative demonstrates his attunement with the fourth element of our pedagogical framework and his understanding of the value of cultural nuance as well as the "hidden curriculums" of social structures.

He is also clearly supportive of Kuldeep and his family, pointing out the valuable contributions of Dr. Singh and Mrs. Kaur to their community. In this way, he is affirming both his integrity (Palmer, 1998; Loughran, 1997) and the value of a caring teacher–student relationship (Noddings, 2005; Smith, 2012). Mr. Wilson's unequivocal support of the Singhs is also evidence of his integrity. By conveying the assertion that the Singhs "make our community a better place to live" to colleagues who are critical of his support, he stands by his own principles, which is in concert with the third element of our pedagogical framework: Good teachers must evidence "certainty, positivity, and the unity of self and moral goals" (Stout, 2005, p. 194). Finally, Mr. Wilson demonstrates, through practice, an awareness of the three features of a sound pedagogy recommended by Smith (1994); specifically animation, reflection, and action. The most important of these, action, is described by Smith (1994) as working with people to enable them to make meaningful changes in their lives. Through his efforts to educate his students about different cultures and worldviews, it is apparent that Mr. Wilson has achieved this goal.

Effective Teacher Responses

- *Creating an inclusive environment:* The following are some helpful strategies for teachers when addressing the subject of diversity in today's inclusive classroom: provide materials and displays that are representative of all the cultures, nationalities, and differences of the students in the classroom and school, provide teaching and resource materials that fairly represent all types of families, gender orientations, and belief systems, use the teachable moment to address issues of bias as they are experienced in the classroom, be aware of the subtle pitfalls of gender bias, such as attending to boys more than girls, using gender specific language; for example, stating "ladies and gentlemen, may I have your attention," rather than saying, "everyone, may I have your attention." (Plous, 2015).

- *Addressing children's questions and concerns:* Here are some helpful tips on effectively responding to children's queries about difference: address all such questions forthrightly and accurately, don't judge or qualify students' observations about difference, candidly acknowledge difference, be willing to defer from responding to questions which require self-reflection and consideration— suggest that you return to the question later, inform parents and caregivers about discussions of difference that occur in the classroom. (Plous, 2015).

- *Integrating children's own experiences* Use student experiences of diversity to teach tolerance and provide understanding; for example, encourage students to share their everyday cultural experiences, not limited to "ethnic" or "religious" holidays, use student differences within your classroom to teach about acceptance of diversity, and lastly, be inclusive of every child in your class, avoid stereotyping or "tokenism." (Plous, 2015).

- ***Dealing with discriminatory behavior:*** The following are some suggestions for responding to discriminatory behavior: first, address each incident in the moment and use it to teach the students about the misperception as well as the enlightened, prosocial response. Second, be patient with the offender-behavior—change takes time. Third, never humiliate or ostracize the student who displays prejudice. Provide ongoing education about tolerance and model the desired pro-social behavior. Finally, examine your own deep-seeded prejudices and seek to eliminate them through knowledge and understanding (Plous, 2015).

To prepare for successfully raising issues of diversity and bias in the classroom, teachers should attempt to make the following practices an integral part of their daily practice: integrate culturally diverse perspectives into the daily curriculum, be candid in examining and addressing personal bias, and acknowledge the fact that we all harbor prejudices that unconsciously affect our worldview and perceptions. Once we're apprised of these we can change these misperceptions, explore personal cultural bias and challenge their inaccuracies, begin a conversation that will advance tolerance and understanding, and in time address incidents of prejudice and bias directly. The goal is to educate, not punish, the offender, stay informed about new anti-bias programs and legislation, honor the life experiences of students and provide opportunities for conflict resolution (e.g., peer mediation), encourage the exploration and celebration of cultural diversity within the classroom and school and the community at-large, and finally, examine the cultural authenticity of classroom materials and use textbooks that reflect the truths and stories of all constituents and honor all peoples and their cultures. (Anti-Defamation League, 2015))

CONCLUDING THOUGHTS

The story of Kuldeep Singh is prototypical of many children and youths throughout the United States who are new to this country and whose culture, customs, and language are foreign to those who are established in various communities. The social-emotional and physical characteristics of an individual, both those viewed positively and negatively, help to distinguish him from others. Belonging to a social group may depend on one's specific values or traits. It is not unusual for people to deliberately try to exaggerate differences, or to conceal differences, for a variety of reasons. A few examples of this include tanning, hair straightening, skin bleaching, plastic surgery, orthodontia, and growth hormone treatment. On the other hand, male–female differences are enhanced in most societies (Augsburger, 1986; Smith et al., 2015).

Distinct societies may assign unique values to various differences. Various cultures may value certain qualities above others—for example, physical size, resourcefulness, beauty, skin color, and athleticism. Nonetheless, nearly all human differences possess some social value. In some cultures, physical imperfections can exclude a person from religious service; this was true for gaining admission to the priesthood of the ancient Hebrews.

In western culture there has been large-scale renegotiation of the social significance of "differences" that reduce the ability of a person to do one or more functions (Augsburger, 1986). Laws have been passed to ensure the protection of the rights of those deemed "disabled" (e.g., the Americans with Disabilities Act, 1990; IDEA, 2004; Section 504 of the Rehabilitation Act, 1973). "Differently abled" has been a preferred term used by those who are trying to persuade society to see limited capacities as a human difference with a positive value. On the other hand, one of the author's grandfathers, who was a paraplegic, along with those voices of the disabled featured in Joseph Shapiro's (1993) *No Pity*, prefer to be called "crips" or "crippled"; much like the deaf community, who don't like the term "hearing impaired" and prefer to be called "deaf." The folks one of the authors grew up with in Canada, whom the government refers to as "First Nations People," still prefer to be called "Indians" and don't see it as a pejorative. Indeed, Malcolm Gladwell's 2013 book *David and Goliath* reveals how the qualities society perceives as disabilities can, when viewed from a different perspective, be seen as abilities. Similarly, Andrew Solomon, in his award-winning bestseller *Far from the Tree*, noted, "Labeling a child's mind as 'diseased'—whether with autism, intellectual disabilities, or transgenderism—may reflect the discomfort that mind gives parents more than any discomfort it causes their child. Much gets corrected that might better have been left alone" (2012, p. 4).

There are many instances in which the degree of negative value of a human difference depends completely on the social or physical environment. For example, in a society with a large proportion of deaf people (e.g., Martha's Vineyard in the 19th century), it was possible to deny that deafness was a disability. Another example of social renegotiation of the value assigned to a difference is reflected in Jean Vanier's L'Arche Community. Essentially a society of developmentally disabled individuals, its philosophy is best described on Vanier's Web site (2015):

> In exploring what it means to be fully human, Vanier invites us to observe the tension in our world between the pressure to achieve mastery or control, and our longing to find ways to live at peace with our own, and others' imperfections. . . . Importantly, while acknowledging the humanness of our imperfection, Vanier also insists that we continually take responsibility to strive to grow towards freedom and serving others in spite of this. (n.p.)

The extreme exercise of social valuation of human difference is in the definition of *human*.

This chapter has provided one example of bias in a school and its community. Situations like this one and countless others provide teachers with a unique opportunity to address this all too common human frailty: the struggle to accept those who are different from us. The authors have provided the reader with the typical causes of bias, the antecedents that incubate it, and the behaviors that help to sustain it, as well as effective ways to address intolerance both in the classroom and in the school. We have also provided two prototypical therapeutic and countertherapeutic teacher responses, analyzed from both an attachment and pedagogical perspective, to serve as exemplars for the teacher. Our goal in providing this information is to help teachers combat bias and intolerance through education and understanding, helping the school community to acquire, in Abraham Lincoln's words, "the angels of our better natures" (Lincoln, 1861).

CHAPTER 9

Teaching Students Who Are Survivors of Suicide

Student Suicide Vignette: "Giselle"

Mrs. Hossa

I would like to share a personal experience involving the suicide of one of my students some years ago. Giselle was a student assigned to my 10th-grade English special education class in a rural school district. She was one of those students who easily slip under the radar because she was quiet, self-composed, and cooperative in a class of mostly boys who were anything but quiet and cooperative.

Giselle was diagnosed with dyslexia, but she was otherwise a model student. In fact, she was mainstreamed in all her courses except English. Nonetheless, because she worked hard and completed all her assignments, eagerly revising her written work to achieve a better grade, she was my most successful student.

She was so pleasant to have in class that she quickly became a favorite of mine, as I know she was of many of her other teachers. I think we all missed the tell-tale signs of impending suicide because she was so good—the least of our worries. In retrospect, I think we were all lulled into complacency by her congeniality and compliance.

However, tragically, at 6:00 A.M. on the last Friday of the marking period in June, I received the phone call that is every teacher's nightmare: a call from the principal informing me that Giselle had committed suicide in the early morning hours. I was asked to come in an hour early to help support students who may have already heard the news and to be prepared for the emotional fallout when the announcement of her loss was made by the principal during homeroom that morning.

The effect of the tragic news on the students was initially disbelief, followed by a deepening sorrow and sense of loss. Students and teachers who were affected by the news were invited to go to predetermined locations to receive grief counseling; clearly, I wasn't the only one who was blindsided by this unimaginable tragedy. Nevertheless, I kept asking myself how I had missed the cues, the warning signs. Surely, they must have been evident. The one question that plagued me for weeks and months afterward was, Could I have been instrumental in preventing Giselle's death if I had been more observant and identified the signs? But what were those signs? I was ashamed to admit I wasn't sure.

A few months after the tragedy, I attended a meeting with several of my colleagues as well as the principal to discuss the issue of adolescent suicide and risk assessment. Instead of an adversarial gathering of faculty, administrators, and parents that involved finger pointing and blame, the tone of the meeting was refreshingly cathartic. We came away determined to research the subject of adolescent suicide and develop effective in-service training as well as a fluid, responsive contingency plan.

Liam

Liam was Giselle's good friend and close confidante. Although she was a very attractive young lady and was pursued by several male students, Giselle's relationship with Liam was purely platonic. He was as happy to have Giselle's friendship as she was to have his. By all accounts, they were inseparable.

A conscientious student, Liam made it known that he had little time or interest in engaging in a romantic relationship. Similarly, Giselle found that her female classmates were disingenuous when they insisted that they wanted her to join their circle of friends. Behind her back they defamed her, jealous of her intellect and good looks. As a result of this alienation, a unique and formidable bond was formed between Giselle, who preferred the company of male classmates to "catty" female ones, and Liam, who really wanted a good friend in whom he could confide without the typical romantic entanglements.

Liam and Giselle seemed inseparable—always seen together walking into town, enjoying slices at the local pizzeria, or going to the movies. Both avid readers, they also liked to discuss the books they lent each other. So it was no surprise that Liam was devastated upon receiving news of Giselle's suicide.

In those first days after her tragic death, Liam vacillated between grief at the loss, anger that she hadn't shared what must have been her deepest secret and asked for his help, and guilt at not having read the signs and prevented her suicide.

As days became weeks, and weeks became months, classmates and teachers noticed a profound change in Liam's behavior. The imperturbable, always cheerful and upbeat Liam was withdrawing socially, becoming short-tempered, morose, and sometimes angry. An honors student every year throughout high school, Liam's recent grades, while still satisfactory, had dropped from As to Cs, and what's worse, he no longer seemed to care! Liam's classmates expressed concern over their friend and feared that he might be harboring a desire to follow his friend, Giselle.

WHY DOES THE TEACHER NEED TO KNOW ABOUT THE AFTERMATH OF SUICIDE?

Teachers must be prepared to deal with the aftermath of any number of tragic events that may affect them and their students, including natural disasters, such as floods, earthquakes, and cyclones; family tragedies that may involve the loss of a classmate, sibling, or parent to illness or accident; fire; episodes of school violence similar to those that occurred in 2012 in Newtown, CT, and in 1999 in Littleton, CO; and—one of the most impactful—student suicide. Students who experience more than one of these traumatic events are more prone to suicidal ideation and parasuicides due to the established effects of "collective trauma" (Garfin, Holman, & Silver, 2015). Because suicide is perhaps the most frequently experienced of these catastrophic events, it is the focus of this chapter.

Whereas teacher responses to student reactions in the aftermath of natural disasters (such as floods and tornadoes) and man-made disasters (such as fire) will vary given the different impacts of each of these phenomena, the teacher's response relative to her students in the wake of a suicide will require a more cautious and nuanced approach, which we will offer a model of in this chapter. Adolescent suicidal behavior seems to follow the same progression as that of a viral or bacterial epidemic, according to Gladwell (2000); thus, what teachers and related service providers do to mitigate such proclivities in the immediate aftermath of a student suicide can help prevent further, related tragedies.

According to the National Center for Education Statistics (2014), from July 1, 2010, through June 30, 2011, there were 31 school-associated deaths (occurring on school property): 25 homicides and 6 suicides. Furthermore, based on data compiled in the National Vital Statistics Reports for 2010, the most common causes of death for adolescents (ages 15–19) in 2010 were, in order of frequency, (1) accidents—41.7% or 4,537; (2) homicides (most typically gun violence)—16.8% or 1,832, and (3) suicides—15.2% or 1,659 (Heron, 2013). A more disturbing statistic is presented by the 2013 National Youth Risk Behavior Survey, distributed by the CDC (2015), which revealed that of the respondents in grades 9–12 nationwide, approximately 17.0% reported suicidal ideation, 8% actually attempted suicide, and 2.7% stated that they had been seriously injured in attempting suicide. Of those reporting ideation and serious attempts, females outnumbered males by a rate of approximately 2 to 1. Similarly, administrators of residential treatment facilities nationwide, reported that approximately 74% of the residents were admitted to their treatment facility due to self-injurious behavior (National Association for Children's Behavioral Health & National Association of Psychiatric Health Systems. 2008). According to the Minnesota Department of Human Services, residential treatment facilities in that state report that 42% of their students said they harbored suicidal thoughts, and 30% of female residents and 50% of male residents reported having attempted suicide at some point during their stay (Fulkerson, Harrison, & Beebe, 1997).

Teachers are not clinicians and are therefore not qualified to provide therapeutic interventions for students who have experienced a traumatic event; nevertheless, they are in a unique position from which to either mitigate or exacerbate student trauma in the aftermath of tragedies like suicide. The next section provides the reader with a deeper understanding of the causes and characteristics of this phenomenon, as well as some effective "postventions" that the teacher and therapist can employ to help students cope with the often debilitating sense of loss and sadness that follows in the wake of such tragedies.

WHAT THE TEACHER SHOULD KNOW ABOUT THE AFTERMATH OF SUICIDE

Just the word *suicide* can evoke strong feelings and result in avoidance. There is often survivor guilt that leads individuals to feel that they should have done something to prevent the death. A supervisor of one of this book's authors said, quite succinctly: "We do everything possible to prevent anyone in our charge from killing themselves; however, in the end, if they really want to do it, they will do it in spite of our best efforts." The author has been lucky—after almost 30 years of practice and having dealt with numerous suicidal clients, he has not lost one to suicide. He has had colleagues to whom it has happened, and the aftermath resulted in a great deal of turmoil.

From an attachment perspective, suicide is the ultimate rupture of all attachment bonds. One could argue that when the bonds of attachment are so seriously weakened, the risk of suicide is significantly increased. Suicide postvention is extremely important, but it is often exercised in schools in a haphazard fashion.

Facts About Suicide

More Americans die by suicide each year than by homicide: 31,484 versus 17,732. Suicide is the third leading cause of death among adolescents (Sheftall, Mathias, Furr, & Dougherty, 2013); an adolescent commits suicide every 2 hours and 5 minutes. American Indian and Alaskan Native males have the highest rates of suicide among people age 15–24, though Hispanic females have the highest rate of attempts in that age group. Among children ages 10–14, suicide rates increased 51% between 1981 and 2006. Most adolescents commit suicide after school hours and in their homes. Although there has been a significant increase in suicide among young African Americans, they still commit suicide at lower rates than Whites, and African American females have the lowest rates of all groups. Sexual minorities and persons with disabilities are at higher risk for suicide—for example, those with spinal cord injuries are more likely to commit suicide, especially immediately following the injury and in people who had almost complete recovery (McCullumsmith et al., 2015). For those with traumatic brain injuries, the suicide rate is 4 times that of the general population, and for those with epilepsy the rate is 5–10 times higher than the general population (Reeves & Laizer, 2012). In addition, those with HIV, multiple sclerosis, and sensory disabilities are at higher risk for suicide.

Suicide and Attachment

Several studies have supported the relationship between insecure attachment and suicide (Bostik & Everall, 2007; Sheftall et al., 2013). Suicide, in a sense, is the ultimate form of disengagement, a complete rupture of attachment bonds often preceded by a steady decline in attachment relationships and social relationships. An insecure attachment has been linked to several factors found to be significant contributors to suicide, such as difficulty in relationships, difficulty depending on others, depression, and fears of abandonment (J. P. Allen, Porter, McFarland, McElhaney, & Marsh, 2007). The literature does not appear to support one form of attachment insecurity as having greater significance over another when it comes to suicide. Resistant, avoidant, and disorganized have all been shown to have a relationship to suicide (Lizardi et al., 2011).

This may explain why adolescents are especially vulnerable to suicide and attempt suicide at higher rates than adults. For many, adolescence is a time of interpersonal confusion and turmoil in relationships with parents and peers, and for those with an insecure attachment style, this turmoil can feel unbearable and result in the desire to end one's life. Whereas secure attachment results in the confidence of available and supportive relationships, the opposite is true for those with an insecure attachment style, who perceive the world around them as uncaring and distant (Maio, Fincham, & Lycett, 2000). Although adolescents seek independence, they are still significantly dependent upon their parents, especially in times of difficulty and distress. If the attachment bond is not secure, the adolescent does not have a secure base from which to explore her emerging identities as well as newfound autonomy (Bostik & Everall, 2007). A protective factor against adolescent suicide is a supportive and secure connection with both parents and peers.

Suicidal ideas and gestures, seen through an attachment lens, can be understood as the communication of feelings of rejection and abandonment along with the need for attachment (Hunt & Hertlein, 2015). In other words, suicide is the result of an attachment injury, and it likewise causes attachment injuries among survivors—those who are coping with the loss. The next section discusses these attachment injuries as part of suicide postvention in school.

Suicide Postvention

Postvention is a term used to describe things that are done to address and help with the aftereffects of a trauma. Suicide will have traumatic effects upon the survivors, but the degree of trauma also depends on several factors. Eric Shneidman (1973) was the first to use the term *postvention* and gave the following definition:

> Those things done after the dire event has occurred that serve to mollify the aftereffects of the event in a person who has attempted suicide, or to deal with the adverse effects on the survivor-victims of a person who has committed suicide. (p. 385)

The principles of postvention discussed in this section can be applied to any trauma. Though recognized as an important part of suicidology, articles about it in professional journals lag significantly behind the number of articles dedicated to prevention and intervention (Andriessen, 2015). This is unfortunate, because trauma for the suicide survivors is very real, yet suicide is often not included in trauma literature. Though many survivors may not meet the diagnostic criteria for post-traumatic stress disorder, their beliefs and assumptions about how the world should work have been shattered by a death from suicide (Janoff-Bulman, 1985).

The terms *prevention, intervention,* and *postvention* derive from Caplan (1964), who talked about the concepts of primary prevention, secondary prevention, and tertiary prevention. *Prevention* refers to those activities designed to avoid a dire event from happening. For example, a school may have a suicide prevention program where students are screened for depression, and psychoeducation is given to all students about what to do if they hear about someone contemplating suicide. *Intervention* refers to those activities designed to help someone who is in crisis. For example, a school counselor or school psychologist will meet with a suicidal student to assess the risk of suicide and design an appropriate safety plan. *Postvention* refers to those activities after the dire event has occurred to help survivors deal with the traumatic effects or aftershock of a suicide. In schools, this would mean working with all those affected by the suicide: teachers, students, and parents. This chapter focuses primarily on postvention, since it is often underappreciated and often done in such a way that can cause more harm than good.

The characteristics of youth survivors can also confound the postvention environment and lead to some false conclusions. For example, children all the way up to age 13 usually have difficulty talking directly about their feelings. Very young children may act out their feelings through temper tantrums and separation anxiety, while older youth may suffer from sleep disturbance and other acting-out behaviors (Talbott & Bartlett, 2012). Adolescents ages 14–18 may be more able to talk about their feelings directly but also run the risk of internalizing their feelings and withdrawing from others, fearing that the expression of feeling may be misunderstood and leave them vulnerable. Research has found that high school survivors of suicide were more likely to smoke tobacco and marijuana; drink alcohol to excess; and engage in high-risk, aggressive behaviors (Cerel & Campbell, 2008). One of the biggest concerns in schools after a suicide is the contagion phenomenon, where other students will want to follow the student who died from suicide. Those most at risk for contagion are the students who have a history of contemplating suicide. Below, there is a discussion about strategies that schools can employ to minimize the contagion effect.

Principles of Suicide Postvention

Dealing with the aftermath of suicide is a difficult and sometimes messy endeavor, and there is no exact formula for doing so. The following guidelines are meant to help teachers avoid making a bad situation worse.

Reduce the risk of suicide contagion. As mentioned above, students who have thought about suicide in the past are most at risk. Added to this list are victims of bullying; teammates, classmates, or anyone who was romantically involved with the deceased or close in some other way; and those who perceive themselves as having things in common with the deceased (Juhnke, Granello, & Granello, 2010). The following suggestions are meant to minimize the contagion effect.

Never glamorize, romanticize, or glorify the student or the death. The deceased should not be portrayed as a hero or having died a noble or romantic death (Berkowitz, McCauley, Schuurman, & Jordan, 2011). But on the flip side, the student should also not be referred as a bad person for having died by suicide. Suicide is the result of a mental health disorder and impaired judgment.

Do not announce the student death over the intercom or other public address system. Information given to the student body should be done in small groups, such as homeroom. Teachers should be given a planned script for announcing the death and be on guard for extreme reactions that might indicate high risk and need for intervention.

Do not hold in-school memorials or cancel classes or school. School routine should be maintained as much as possible. In-school activities can lead to glorification and allow other students to overidentity with the deceased. Memorials in the school yearbook or on the school grounds and graduation speeches that reintroduce the suicide should also be avoided (Talbott & Bartlett, 2012). If the yearbook memorializes all student deaths in a fair and equitable way, then it may be acceptable. Schools must guard against treating death by suicide in some exceptional fashion. Some students may insist on a memorial and accuse the school of not caring by denying them the opportunity. Administration could suggest that the best way to memorialize a student who died from suicide is to encourage and support suicide prevention for local and national organizations (Berkowitz et al., 2011).

Never discuss suicide as a way to end pain. Suicide does not end pain. On the contrary—it causes pain among the survivors. Do not present the suicide as inexplicable or unavoidable. Suicide is avoidable! There are many alternatives to suicide for dealing with emotional pain. Suicide should be explained as a serious error in judgment (Berkowitz et al., 2011).

Minimize discussion of the details of the suicide death. In the age of social media, rumors, gossip, and sensationalization of the student's death can flourish almost instantaneously. In order to minimize this, the school should not provide too many details about the suicide, as it can give others who are contemplating suicide ideas about how they may end their own lives, which would exacerbate the contagion phenomenon. What should be emphasized is that the student who died from suicide made a serious mistake in believing that there were no other ways to get help.

Provide support. Postvention in the school setting should provide opportunities for students to sort out their complicated feelings around a death from suicide. Suicide, like any other loss, requires grief work, but the type of grief is often different, since many survivors have feelings of guilt and anger—not only toward the student who died but also toward those who they think did not do enough to prevent the suicide (Juhnke et al., 2010).

Many school systems will have a crisis plan in place and can rely on the support of a local crisis team to come in and provide grief counseling to the students. But often, schools are reluctant to seek help and believe in "not rocking the boat." Some naively believe that allowing students to talk about the suicide will contribute to contagion, but the exact opposite is true. If students have the appropriate opportunity to sort out their complicated feelings, it is less likely that they will resort to suicide as an acceptable way to deal with emotional pain.

It is also important to note that the aftermath of suicide does not disappear magically after a few days. While some students will recover quickly, for others the effects can linger or lie dormant for an extended period of time. School staff, especially teachers, should be on guard for changes in students' behavior after a peer's suicide, such as decreased academic performance, withdrawal, isolation, irritability, lethargy, and other signs of depression.

Dissemination and control of information. The control of information in the aftermath of a suicide is extremely important, especially in today's world of text messaging and social media. First, the school needs to verify the death, either from law enforcement or the family. The school should contact the family to express condolences and inform them how it plans to deal with the death among the student body. This initial contact will start the grieving process, in which the school can also serve as a valuable resource for the family. As mentioned previously, much of the initial information disseminated by the students may be inaccurate. The family may request secrecy around the cause of death, but the school must be careful in colluding with such secrecy. In many municipalities, cause of death is public knowledge, but this may also conflict with HIPAA medical privacy laws (Berkowitz et al., 2011).

The recommended way to disseminate information about a suicide is for the administration to prepare a written statement for staff and teachers to read to their students that contains factual information about the death, acknowledges the cause as suicide (if, indeed, that is confirmed), states the school's plan to provide support, and gives information about the funeral, which should always take place outside the school and preferably outside the normal school schedule to allow students to attend with the least interruption of their normal routine. Again, the announcement to students should always be made in a small setting, like a classroom.

Suicides are newsworthy events, and the media can be a help or a hindrance to the school's postvention plans. Human nature tends to simplify the causes of death, and suicide is no exception. People tend to want to know the precise reason why a student died from suicide. The media should be told that there is never any one cause; that suicide is the result of a perfect storm where multiple factors come together, and the student believed mistakenly that suicide was the only way out of the emotional pain. The goal is to make sure the media does not sensationalize the suicide. A media release by the school should include the general facts (avoid details) about the student's death, the school's postvention plan, a message that does not glorify the event, and information about where students can go to receive help (Juhnke et al., 2010). Staff should not talk to the media! The primary role of staff is to help disseminate controlled information and be alert for students who need additional help to deal with the suicide. Staff includes everyone employed by the school, from secretaries to bus drivers to teachers. It is important for everyone to be on the same page, with the same information.

Summary

The primary goal of suicide postvention is to restore equilibrium to the school and return to normal functioning not by circumventing the suicide but dealing with it in an honest, forthright, and nonsensational manner. Postvention also has to include grief counseling for those at risk, and should use the experience to educate staff and students about the contributing factors in suicide and the available resources to get help (Berkowitz et al., 2011). In other words, postvention can be used as prevention, to decrease the likelihood that others will use suicide and an acceptable means to end pain. Schools can play a crucial role in minimizing the deleterious effects of a student's death through suicide by having a solid postvention plan.

Suicide unsettles everyone, but some more than others, as we witnessed in the opening vignette. We now return to that vignette to help teachers gain a deeper appreciation for the aftermath of suicide so they can be helpful in restoring the school to normalcy, identify students who may be at risk, and use the suicide as a teachable moment.

UNDERSTANDING SUICIDE AND ITS AFTERMATH FROM AN ATTACHMENT PERSPECTIVE

The opening vignette deals with two survivors of suicide: a teacher (Mrs. Hossa) and a friend (Liam) of the deceased. The teacher describes Giselle as a student who was deeply internalized, "quiet, self-composed." Because she was a model student, she slipped under the radar, allowing those around her to believe there was nothing to worry about. As the saying goes, still waters run deep. Few teachers will cherish students acting out in the classroom, but they usually do not have to worry that such a student will kill himself. Externalization is negatively correlated with suicide. From an attachment perspective, it is somewhat difficult to classify Giselle; she could have been either avoidant or resistant. All subtypes of insecure attachment have been present in suicidal individuals. What we can say for sure is that she was insecurely attached, but, because we have very little background, it is difficult to posit the reasons for the lack of secure attachment. Liam was a close friend and may have provided some sense of security. However, as the previous section made clear, suicide is never the result of a single factor.

Mrs. Hossa

Mrs. Hossa's reaction to the suicide is rather typical based on the material presented previously. Her reaction is dominated by disbelief and feelings of guilt that she, along with others, missed the signs that Giselle was suicidal. One could only imagine Mrs. Hossa upon getting the phone call from the principal the morning after Giselle's death. And her task is challenging! The principal is asking her, along with the other teachers, to help support the students—while the teachers still have to deal with their own grief. The previous section talked about how information should be disseminated in smaller settings, like homeroom. This makes teachers an integral part of postvention. (The vignette says that the principal is going to make the announcement in homeroom. It is not clear whether this means he plans to do so over the PA system, but if that is his intention, it is inadvisable.) Teachers must be strong in order to support the students, and they should deal with their own grief in another setting. The end of the first part of the vignette seems to suggest exactly that. A meeting takes place months after the tragedy that is both cathartic and educational, in that the staff agree to use Giselle's death positively to learn more about suicide and thereby increase the school's suicide prevention protocol. This is the best way to memorialize Giselle.

Liam

As a very close friend and confidant of Giselle, Liam is an at-risk survivor who should be monitored carefully and receive mental health counseling. His world and his assumptions about that world have been shattered, and he has moved from a secure attachment bond to an insecure one as the result of the suicide. One feels deeply for Liam. His grief is real and complicated as he vacillates between sadness over the loss of a dear friend and anger that she could do such a thing. As stated previously, suicide does not end pain—it causes pain! Liam has a number of depressive symptoms, and his classmates are right to be worried about him possibly copying Giselle's suicide. A strong risk factor in suicide is the desire to join someone who is dead. Liam and Giselle may have built their close relationship around a mutual anxiety, which their friendship partially mitigated. Now, without Giselle, Liam is extremely vulnerable. Liam needs more than short-term crisis counseling. The vignette does not state his age, but it is assumed that he is a minor. In this case, the school should have a meeting with Liam and his parents, express their concerns, and recommend that he see a professional mental health worker. Once that is in place, someone from the school (a counselor or psychologist) can collaborate with the outside therapist (assuming permission to release information has been attained) by monitoring Liam for risk assessment while he is in school.

UNDERSTANDING TEACHER INTERVENTIONS FOR THE STUDENTS WHO ARE SURVIVORS OF SUICIDE FROM BOTH ATTACHMENT AND PEDAGOGICAL PERSPECTIVES

Mr. Delvecchio: "A Man on a Mission"

Mr. Delvecchio, a caring and empathic teacher who was close with both Giselle and Liam, and who was also greatly affected by Giselle's death, is determined to protect Liam and ensure his safety. In the weeks following the tragedy, Mr. Delvecchio reads everything he can about teenage suicide and suicide prevention and is convinced that Liam might be at risk for self-harm.

In response to this belief, he shares his concerns with the school counselor, the principal, and Liam's parents, whom he knows socially. He also persistently shares these apprehensions with Liam, disguising his fears by offering well-meaning but ill-advised counsel. For example, after class, Mr. Delvecchio pulls Liam aside and says, "Liam, it's natural that you would be grief stricken and traumatized by the loss of a dear friend. I felt the same way when I lost my dad two years ago, but trust me, in time it gets better, and the pain gradually subsides. You know I'm here for you, and my door is always open. Please don't do anything rash—promise me that if you feel especially sad, you'll come and talk to me. We can go for a walk or drive— get a change of scenery, get your mind off your loss for a while. OK?"

After noticing the excessive attention paid to Liam by Mr. Delvecchio, Dr. Schuster the school psychologist, and Mrs. Combs, the assistant principal, approach him and ask him to ease up on his surveillance of Liam and his almost obsessive concern for Liam's well-being. Mr. Delvecchio listens respectfully to their admonition; nevertheless, a man on a mission, Mr. Delvecchio is determined to continue providing oversight of Liam and to do everything in his power to protect Liam from self-harm. Liam will not *become another tragic statistic of teen suicide—he will see to that!*

Mr. Delvecchio from an Attachment Perspective

Although described as "caring and empathic," Mr. Delvecchio oversteps the proper boundary between teacher and student, especially a student who may be suicidal. It is perfectly acceptable that the teacher is concerned about Liam and feels the need to keep him safe—but there's a big difference between keeping him safe and protecting him. The latter implies more of a parent–child relationship, and it does appear that Mr. Delvecchio is playing the role of a parent more than a teacher.

Mr. Delvecchio does well by using the opportunity of Giselle's death to educate himself about teenage suicide and, as a result of that education, probably realizes that Liam, having been a close friend of Giselle and showing signs of depression, is at risk for suicide. Furthermore, the teacher does well by informing both the principal—ultimately responsible for keeping students safe; and the school counselor—professionally trained to deal with suicidal students. And this is where Mr. Delvecchio's efforts to protect Liam should have a boundary. He is not professionally trained, nor is it his responsibility to take on the liability of a suicidal student.

Proper procedure would be for the school counselor to follow up with Liam, do a suicidal assessment, and based on the results of that assessment develop a safety plan for Liam that includes his parents. It is not Mr. Delvecchio's responsibility to deal with Liam's parents. If the community has a mobile crisis team, the school counselor might want to call them and have a crisis worker come to the school to evaluate Liam and develop a safety plan with him, his parents, and the school.

Because he is not professionally trained, Mr. Delvecchio makes a number of ill-advised interventions with Liam. First, he puts the responsibility upon Liam to come and see him "if you feel especially sad." Few teenagers on their own will seek out help when they are feeling suicidal. A suicidal student is usually discovered by some other means, most likely through a third party. In the case of Liam, the school must be proactive, not reactive—that is what safety planning is all about. The second mistake is Mr. Delvecchio's self-disclosure about his own father's death two years ago. This is too much self-disclosure, especially to an at-risk student, and puts the focus now on the teacher. One could image Liam being intrigued by the death of the father and asking questions about how he died. What if Mr. Delvecchio's father committed suicide? The hypothesis is not far-fetched, given the teacher's obsession with keeping Liam safe. The third mistake is his inviting Liam to go for a walk or a drive, a clear indication that the teacher is overinvolved, as he feels it is his responsibility to "save" Liam.

From an attachment perspective, how can we explain the teacher's behavior? The behavior has a preoccupied attachment style that permits Mr. Delvecchio to violate boundaries and become enmeshed with the student. It is anyone's guess as to why the teacher feels this deep sense of insecurity that results in anxiously pursuing Liam. Whether it is caused by the lack of closure around Giselle's death and feelings of guilt or perhaps an experience of suicide within his own family, Mr. Delvecchio's insecure attachment style will do more harm than good, especially with a student who appears to have developed an avoidant attachment style. This combination has been described in earlier chapters: a preoccupied teacher and an avoidant student. It is not a good combination and will usually result in exacerbating the student's avoidance.

If he had a more secure attachment style, Mr. Delvecchio would be less reactive and more able to mentalize. He would ask himself: *What is driving these strong urges I have to pursue and protect Liam, pushing me to go beyond my role as a teacher?* Mr. Delvecchio should monitor Liam for any signs that might indicate the student is doing worse, and he should inform the appropriate personnel in the school if this is the case. Much beyond that, Mr. Delvecchio is venturing into waters that are too turbulent for someone not professionally trained to counsel suicidal students. The reading he did about suicide after Giselle's death does not qualify him to take on Liam as a client but should be used appropriately to refer Liam to those who can provide mental health counseling.

Mr. Delvecchio from a Pedagogical Perspective

It is clear that Mr. Delvecchio cares about Liam and his well-being, which comports with a critical aspect of our pedagogical framework: the importance of developing caring teacher–student relationships (Noddings, 2005; Smith, 2012). However, in his eagerness to ensure Liam's safety, Mr. Delvecchio has failed to empower Liam—he assumes responsibility that should rightly be ascribed to Liam and usurps the role of both the school counselor and school administrator.

Indeed, one of the skills our pedagogical framework encourages teachers to impart to their students is to help them "learn how to be with other people, how to love, how to take criticism, how to *grieve*, how to have fun, as well as how to add and subtract, multiply and divide" (emphasis ours; Tompkins, 1996, p. xvi). In shielding Liam from the grieving process, thereby assuming that he will be unable to process the loss of his close friend in a healthful manner, Mr. Delvecchio is simply impeding his emotional development. This unwarranted lack of confidence in Liam's ability to deal with the tragedy conveys a lack of trust on Mr. Delvecchio's part. As we know from experience and research on the subject, healthy relationships must involve mutual trust—without it, no positive growth can occur; no friendship can flourish.

Lastly, recommended by Smith (1994) as a critical component of a sound pedagogy, Mr. Delvecchio is encouraged to provide Liam, and all his students, with opportunities for reflection, thus creating opportunities to explore "lived experiences"—even sad ones. Accordingly, Mr. Delvecchio might look for ways to engage his students in order to facilitate their growth as responsible and self-actualized individuals, or, as Smith (1994) puts it, "to work with [students] so they are able to make *growthful* changes in their lives" (p. 10).

Mrs. Lafontaine: "Not a Qualified Counselor, but a Good Listener"

Mrs. Lafontaine, Liam's homeroom and physics teacher, has some experience with adolescent suicide, having lost one of her juniors to suicide six years ago. She subsequently learned, from the school and community crisis counselors, how teachers can best help their students in the aftermath of such a tragedy. In accordance with these recommendations, she asks to speak with Liam privately, and she tells him simply that she is someone he can always talk to about his feelings, or if he feels the need to seek professional help, she will ensure that he has the opportunity speak with the school counselor. She also offers her room as a safe haven for Liam during lunch or study hall, if he needs a place to think or just have some "peace and quiet."

A good listener, Mrs. Lafontaine assures Liam that she will be very receptive if he just wants to vent or express his feelings—she would never attempt to offer trite advice or duplicitous sympathy. Finally, Mrs. Lafontaine concedes that although she is not a qualified counselor, she can certainly help him obtain the support of one, should he ever feel the need for more involved support. She does tell him that there are a few ways that, as his homeroom teacher, she can provide assistance: First, she can reduce the magnitude of his assignments and request that his subject teachers do likewise; second, she can ask that Liam receive an extension on outstanding assignments in order to provide him adequate time to complete them, without the pressure imposed by time constraints; and last, Mrs. Lafontaine assures Liam that she understands that grief is a natural human process in response to real loss and, as such, is experienced differently by each individual and that it might take a while for him to start feeling better—that's why friends and family are so important in providing necessary support and understanding.

Mrs. Lafontaine from an Attachment Perspective

Like Mr. Delvecchio, Mrs. Lafontaine is trying to help Liam by keeping him from himself, but her approach is less intense. She, too, has learned from the experience of a past suicide and wants to support Liam in any way she can. The big difference between the two teachers is that Mrs. Lafontaine entertains the possibility of Liam needing professional help. She mentions the possibility of this, but still leaves it up to him, "if he feels the need."

Again, this "it's up to you" approach for getting mental health counseling is not necessarily recommended. If students are suicidal or showing signs of depression, they need professional help, regardless of whether they ask for it or not. As mentioned previously, most students will not be proactive in seeking professional help.

In the case of minors, parents have to be involved in giving informed consent for professional services either inside or outside the school. Parents have the obligation of getting their child necessary health care, and that includes mental health care. Though they may not seek it out on their own, most adolescents, after some initial resistance, welcome the opportunity to speak with a therapist with whom they can build a working alliance.

Mrs. Lafontaine recognizes she is not qualified to act as a therapist but sees her responsibility as helping Liam get the counseling he needs. This is the appropriate response for a teacher—not that of Mr. Delvecchio, who appears to want to counsel Liam. The only thing Mrs. Lafontaine could do differently is to be more forthright with Liam in regard to getting help if she is indeed worried about him based on her prior knowledge of suicide. She could say something like the following:

> Liam, I'm worried about you and about the possibility that you could harm yourself. The help you need is beyond what I can offer, although I will support you in any way I am professionally able to. I am going to speak with Mrs. Kelly [the school counselor] so she can meet you, get a better sense of how you are feeling, and hopefully work with you and your parents in getting you to see a professional counselor on a regular basis.

It is quite possible that Liam might resist such an intervention and even become upset with Mrs. Lafontaine for talking to the school counselor. However, if she is genuinely concerned and has some suspicion that Liam might be wanting to harm himself, she has an ethical and perhaps even legal obligation to keep him safe doing what is permitted within the boundaries of her profession. If the teacher is a secure-autonomous adult, she will not let Liam's resistance paralyze her, because she does not seek nor need Liam's approval. On the other hand, if Liam does have a good relationship with her, the safety plan could include Mrs. Lafontaine as an indicated person whom Liam could go to if he has thoughts of killing himself, and then she can follow the school's protocol for dealing with suicidal students, which for most schools is informing an indicated member of the school staff (e.g., a school counselor, psychologist, or social worker), who will proceed accordingly. This is how teachers can be helpful and yet remain within their professional role.

Mrs. Lafontaine appropriately extends this role by suggesting that Liam can use her classroom as a safe space when he's feeling overwhelmed, and also by making accommodations for his assignments. Though accommodations are an acceptable way to reduce the student's stress, Liam should still be monitored for the degree of interference in functioning—the greater the interference, the greater the risk!

To summarize, both Mr. Delvecchio and Mrs. Lafontaine have the same goal: They want to help Liam, and they want to prevent another suicide. However, the former's role is inappropriate for a teacher; the latter's is more appropriate. The inappropriate response results from a preoccupied adult state of mind and, as always is the case, the appropriate intervention results from a secure-autonomous adult state of mind.

Mrs. Lafontaine from a Pedagogical Perspective

Like Mr. Delvecchio, Mrs. Lafontaine has clearly established a caring relationship and meaningful rapport with Liam, conveying to him that she is someone he can always talk to about his feelings. However, in contrast with Mr. Delvecchio's overly attentive behavior, Mrs. Lafontaine quickly adds that she would gladly connect him with a counselor if he felt that he needed professional help, acknowledging the fact that she is not a qualified counselor. This self-awareness and candor are consistent with Loughran's (1997) insistence that effective teachers must strive to be honest with themselves about who they are and what they know and believe. Mrs. Lafontaine knows that she is a good listener but is not qualified as a counselor. She also shows respect for Liam by promising not to offer him trite advice or superficial empathy. In doing so, she demonstrates the authenticity of self, one of the tenets of effective pedagogy. In addition, Mrs. Lafontaine offers relevant and practical accommodations to help Liam develop his academic skills that are commensurate with her expertise as a teacher. In doing so, she demonstrates her integrity and self-efficacy, cultivating what Stout described as "certainty, positivity, and the unity of self and moral goals" (2005, p. 194).

In a similar fashion, Mrs. Lafontaine is helping Liam appreciate that grieving is a process—one that is very personal—and, in doing so, is exhibiting our fifth tenet of sound pedagogy: Teachers should empower students by helping them learn about themselves and their social milieu—learning "how to be with other people, how to love, how to take criticism, how to grieve, how to have fun"—in addition to the praxis of the academic curriculum (Tompkins, 1996, p. xvi). Mrs. Lafontaine is also actualizing what Smith (1994) describes as three essential elements of sound pedagogy: animation, reflection, and action. She accomplishes this feat by helping Liam learn about the process of grief and providing him a secure space in which to experience and explore this internal process, thereby helping him develop emotionally and so make changes in his life.

EFFECTIVE TEACHER RESPONSES

As Schlozman (2001) has observed, it is a sad fact that suicide occurs among students. In order to correct misinformation that often surrounds such tragedies, a related service provider, typically the school psychologist, might discuss with the suicide victim's family what to communicate to her classmates and then inform students in small groups about the tragic event. Teachers can help students process their grief, identify those students having difficulty with the loss, and provide them with a secure environment that acknowledges their grief but also allows for a return to normalcy..

Since the process of grieving is very individualistic, providing opportunities for various responses may be often helpful. Providing a book for students and staff to record their memories of the deceased may provide catharsis for them as well as the victim's caregivers. However, it is important to note that memorials are rarely helpful because they may be interpreted by the student's classmates as validating suicide. School counselors should check in on close friends of the student as well as students who have a history of depression or suicidal ideation (Schlozman, 2001, p. 82).

In the case of student suicide, postvention is the shared responsibility of students, teachers, related service providers, and administrators. All these school constituents need to work together to support each other and the student body to work through such shared crises. Doing so will help to reduce the chances that such a tragedy will be repeated. (Schlozman, 2001, n.p.)

CONCLUDING THOUGHTS

Every school and school district should (and more than likely does) have established and rehearsed crisis intervention and school emergency plans to help staff and students deal with natural and man-made disasters and threats to their safety and well-being. However, effective teacher response in the aftermath of a student suicide, a more frequently occurring tragedy, is seldom the topic of professional development workshops. As front-line staff, teachers are in a unique position to monitor student responses in the aftermath of a tragic event such as a student suicide. Knowing what to say and do to help reduce the potential for self-harm in the grieving and confused classmates of the student who has died may prevent further suicides. Teachers cannot predict or prevent natural and human-made disasters and tragedies such as school shootings and student suicides, but learning about and acquiring effective strategies designed to help student survivors in the wake of these crises is vital.

This chapter focused exclusively on student suicide, since it is one of the most frequently encountered school tragedies and it presents, arguably, the most pernicious residual effects for students, parents, teachers, and administrators. To this end, we discussed the characteristics and the most prevalent *perceived* causes of student suicides, along with some of the more effective, evidence-based therapeutic interventions. In addition, we sought to debunk some of the popular misconceptions surrounding suicide, always taking care to stress the importance of obtaining the assistance of qualified and trained professionals such as the school counselor, clinical psychologists, pastoral care counselors, psychiatrists skilled in working with children and adolescents, clinical social workers, and the appropriate medical personnel.

However, we also described ways that classroom teachers can help during postvention to mitigate the trauma experienced by their students in the aftermath of the suicide of a schoolmate. As we have done in each of the previous chapters, we examined the phenomenon of suicide and people's responses to it from an attachment perspective, and we presented teacher vignettes that provided the reader with examples and analyses of effective and ineffective pedagogical approaches in addressing student responses.

Finally, we offered evidence-based postvention practices that teachers can use to help their students deal with the traumatic effects of a crisis like student suicide. The information provided in this chapter will help prepare and equip teachers to effectively address a school tragedy or crisis—an event we earnestly hope never happens!

CHAPTER 10

Teaching Students with High-Functioning Autism and Social Skill Deficits

STUDENT VIGNETTE: "ALISON" (HIGH-FUNCTIONING AUTISM)

Everyone in the specialized high school for students with learning and emotional disorders knows Alison, or Ali, as she prefers to be called. She is a very talkative young woman, currently in her junior year, who is obsessed with everything about the 1960s, especially the music, sociopolitical issues, and revolutionary changes. Ali has a few friends at the school, primarily students who are also on the spectrum; however, she tends to alienate most of her classmates because she dominates conversations, perseverating on her favorite topics related to the '60s.

Ali's parents are both special educators, and she has one sibling, an older brother, who was also diagnosed with autism spectrum disorder (ASD) but is much lower functioning and is currently in a residential program for students evidencing more severe behaviors associated with the disorder, such as self-injury and physical aggression.

Like most individuals diagnosed with ASD, Ali experiences real difficulty in the area of social skills; specifically, turn taking, awkwardness in greeting and in beginning and ending a conversation, perseveration, and difficulty perceiving irony and sarcasm. Since she tends to be very concrete and literal in her interpretation of others' communication, this deficiency has been a real problem for her at school and presents a ready opportunity for teasing and harassment by some classmates who have openly expressed their dislike of Ali. For example, a few weeks ago, a male classmate whom Ali had expressed a fondness for asked her if she'd consider going out sometime. When Ali eagerly replied that she would, the student smiled and said,

"Well, why don't you consider going out from this class, or better yet, from this school?" He made sure that everyone in class could hear his reply, to which they all laughed uproariously. Ali was dumbstruck, not knowing how to respond and feeling humiliated at falling so easily for the student's cruel joke. Ali had misinterpreted an important social cue—part of the "hidden curriculum" most students acquire by osmosis while in school.

Further challenges associated with her disorder include a limited diet—Ali is very sensitive to the texture of certain foods and cannot tolerate them. Bread and pasta are two of her dietary staples. Ali is also very sensitive to loud noises such as applause, multiple simultaneous conversations, and fire alarms—any of which can induce a panic attack. Although nothing can prepare Ali for a fire alarm that signals a real-world emergency, the school administrators provide a warning to Ali several minutes prior to the sounding of the alarm prompting fire drills. In addition to harsh sounds, Ali is negatively affected by very bright lights and flashes, like those produced by strobe lights, lightning flashes, or fireworks displays. She also frequently experiences panic attacks when in crowded conditions for an extended period of time and therefore avoids attending indoor concerts and shows. Likewise, she has an aversion to being touched by others and refuses to even shake hands when introduced; such an aversion has significant social repercussions, as one might imagine.

Curiously, though, she doesn't seem to mind public speaking or performing for large groups of people. It would appear that she is able to tolerate these occasions, in part, because she is the center of attention and can share her passions and ideas with a captive audience. Finally, similar to her sensitivities to various textures, sounds, and lights, Alison cannot sleep on traditional mattresses or in a prone position, preferring to sleep upright in a reclining chair that has sides and helps her to feel secure and comfortable.

One of Ali's greatest passions is her love of music, particularly folk and rock music from the '60s and '70s that expresses a social message. Recently, Ali has begun to socialize with a few friends who have been similarly diagnosed with high-functioning autism (HFA). She has also been very proactive in joining a speaker's bureau, which connects individuals with an area of expertise with community organizations seeking a qualified speaker who can cogently present on a specific topic of interest. Ali has created several prezis (online slideshows) and prepared a 50-minute presentation that includes a 10-minute musical performance in which she sings two or three original compositions, accompanying herself on acoustic guitar.

Not everyone is supportive of Alison. Many of her classmates avoid her, complaining about her "rants" on obscure topics that are of little interest to anyone else. They also feel that Ali is "emotionally unavailable" as a friend—typically only engaging in unidirectional conversations and rudely ducking out when another classmate wants to share a relevant opinion or idea. Even a few of her special-education teachers seem to have lost patience with her "narcissistic" behavior, considering her to be willfully rude and insensitive.

Teaching Students with High-Functioning Autism and Social Skill Deficits • 189

WHY DOES THE TEACHER NEED TO KNOW ABOUT HIGH-FUNCTIONING AUTISM?

Because high-functioning autism (HFA), typically referenced as *Asperger syndrome*, is included under the rubric of autism spectrum disorder (ASD), and people diagnosed with it are incorporated in the prevalence estimates for autism, it is very difficult to provide an accurate diagnostic ratio.

According to the CDC MMWR Surveillance Summaries (2007), 1 in 150 individuals in the United States is diagnosed with ASD. Blumberg et al. (2013) estimated that 1 in 50 school-aged children in the United States have been diagnosed with ASD; Frombonne (2003; 2005) contended that ASD affects 1 in 65 U.S. children. Frombonne (2003) also suggested that a reasonable prevalence rate for Asperger's in the United States would be 0.26 per 1,000 persons. Finkelmeyer, Stewart, Woodford, and Coleman (2006) reported that out of every 10,000 persons broadly diagnosed with ASD, between 30 and 60 of them have Asperger's.

We also know from the literature on HFA that there are approximately four times as many boys diagnosed with the disorder than girls (Frombonne, 2005). Furthermore, the CDC estimates that 1 in 88 children in the United States has been diagnosed with Asperger's by the age of 8.

According to the National Center for Education Statistics in a report published in 2015, during the 2000–2001 school year, 93,000 school-aged children received special education services in public schools in the United States (in accordance with IDEA, 2004) for ASD. Alarmingly, by the 2011–2012 school year, that number had quadrupled to 440,592, representing 7.7% of all students that year who were eligible for and receiving special education services. Based on their investigation of this issue, Baron-Cohen et al. (2006) suggested that 1 in 100 students attending public schools in the United States may have ASD.

These and other data clearly suggest a trend toward the increased identification and inclusion of school-aged children with HFA in the regular classrooms of public schools nationwide. The statistical likelihood is that most, if not all, teachers working in public schools in the United States will have students with HFA in their classrooms. Therefore, it is imperative that all teachers become familiar with the defining characteristics, causes, and recommended behavioral and academic interventions in order to work more effectively with these students. The next section will provide the reader with that vital information.

WHAT THE TEACHER SHOULD KNOW ABOUT HIGH-FUNCTIONING AUTISM

The *DSM-5* made some major changes in regard to the diagnostic criteria for autism. It did away with the diagnoses of autism, Asperger's, childhood disintegrative disorder, and pervasive developmental disorder, and developed autism spectrum disorder (ASD) to encompass the four previously separate disorders. The reasoning behind this change was that the four separate disorders really presented a single condition with different levels of severity in two areas of dysfunction: (a) deficits in social communication and social interaction and (b) restrictive, repetitive behaviors, interests, and activities (APA, 2013).

This chapter deals primarily with the first area of dysfunction, social impairment, since it presents the most persistent and permeating challenge throughout development (Aduen, Rich, Sanchez, O'Brien, & Alvord, 2014). Though social impairment and restrictive, repetitive behaviors are both necessary for a diagnosis of ASD, it is the former that is more disruptive and challenging for teachers. With the ongoing emphasis on inclusion, those with HFA spend more time in larger, traditional classrooms, where the opportunities for socialization are greater and, consequently, their social impairment is more obvious and challenging (Stichter, O'Connor, Herzog, Lierheimer, & McGhee, 2012).

Social Communication and Interaction Deficits

When talking about HFA, it is important to define more clearly what is meant by *social impairment* or *social deficits*, since both of these terms are abstract and can be defined somewhat haphazardly. The *DSM-5* (APA 2013) lists three areas of deficits. The first is a lack of socioemotional reciprocity, characterized by a lack of back-and-forth conversation, reduced sharing of interests or emotions, and inability to initiate or respond to social interactions—in other words, social aloofness and the failure to respond to others' emotional verbal and nonverbal cues (Aduen et al., 2014). The second is a deficit in nonverbal communication, characterized by abnormal eye contact, abnormal body language and gestures, communication that is poorly integrated, and lack of facial expression and nonverbal communication. The third is difficulty in forming, keeping, and understanding relationships due to difficulty adjusting behaviors to various social contexts or a complete absence of interest in peer friendships. The *DSM-5* (APA, 2013) also lists three levels of severity for ASD. HFA would be Level 1, "requiring support," defined as:

> Without supports in place, deficits in social communication cause noticeable impairments. Difficulty initiating social interactions, and clear examples of atypical or unsuccessful responses to social overtures of others. May appear to have decreased interest in social interactions. For example, a person who is able to speak in full sentences and engages in communication but whose to-and-fro conversation with others fails, and whose attempt to make friends are odd and typically unsuccessful. (APA, 2013a)

Some with HFA will show greater interest than others in socialization and having friends. It is not really clear why this is, but one hypothesis is that areas of the brain responsible for social pleasure may be more or less impaired in different people. More discussion will take place about the brain and HFA later in this chapter. It may very well be that those with HFA suffer from social anhedonia, where seeking out and making friends brings little or no pleasure at all but rather the opposite

(Chevallier, Grèzes, Molesworth, Berthoz, & Happé, 2012). What may be at play here is the interaction between interest and skill. If the lack of social interest is innate, one does not develop the skills needed for socialization, since there is little interest in doing so. The longer this asocialization persists, the more pronounced the lack of social skills will be. Or the opposite may be true. The lack of social skill is innate and, consequently, there develops a loss of interest. This is true for most humans: People lose interest in things at which they are not skilled. This has consequences for the classroom, which often uses social rewards, like praise or extra playtime. For students with a lack of interest in socialization, such rewards are meaningless and have no reinforcement value. In order to help develop these skills, teachers may need to combine nonsocial incentives with social incentives for those with HFA (Aduen et al., 2014). Questions as to the causes of social deficits in those with HFA have resulted in an intense examination of the neuropsychological causes, to which we now turn.

What Is Behind the Social Deficits of Those with HFA? Theory of Mind

For the most part, research into social deficits for those with HFA has concentrated in the domain of theory of mind. *Theory of mind* is the ability to intuit one's own and another's mental state (i.e., beliefs, perceptions, knowledge, intentions, desires, and emotions) and to understand that others may have mental states different from one's own (Premack & Woodruff, 1978). In layperson's terms, one might refer to this ability as *folk psychology* or *mind reading* (Alic, 2009). How often do you find yourself saying to or about someone: "I know what you are thinking"; "I know how you feel"; "You were probably thinking that . . ." These reactions may be based on a gesture, a nonverbal cue, or simply an attempt to explain another's behavior that is not immediately apparent. Empathy is a related construct, because it refers to the ability to think or feel what another is thinking or feeling. The chapter on attachment theory discussed empathy as emanating from a secure attachment history where the primary caretaker was able to intuit the child's feelings and respond appropriately. In return, the child learns to intuit others' mental states. Knowing what oneself and others are feeling also helps with emotional regulation by enabling an individual to label emotion. When asked about their feelings, those with HFA often will say they feel nothing.

Emotional regulation has two components: suppression and reappraisal (Gross & John, 2003). *Suppression* involves learning to inhibit emotional behaviors, and *reappraisal* means changing the meaning of a situation in order to change its emotional impact. A mundane "She's having a bad day" thought is a form of reappraisal to lessen the emotional reaction when one is insulted. Those with HFA are better at suppression than reappraisal (Samson, Huber, & Gross, 2012). This makes sense, since reappraisal demands taking the mental perspective of another—a fundamental aspect of theory of mind, where deficits reside for those with HFA. This discussion of theory of mind may bring back memories of the concept of mentalization, also discussed in the chapter on attachment theory. *Mentalization* was defined by Slade (2008) as "the capacity to envision mental states in oneself and another, and to understand one's own and another's behavior in terms of underlying mental states and intentions" (p. 764). Sounds quite similar to theory of mind, and the two concepts are often used interchangeably. There is a subtle difference, however, in that mentalization connotes the processing of one's own and another's mental states. Theory of mind, on the other hand, is more of a "cold" concept, more limited to simply understanding another's mental state (Górska & Marszal, 2014).

The Development of Theory of Mind

Up until the ages of 3 or 4, children are quite egocentric and have difficulty under-standing that others can have mental states different from their own. But by the age of 5, almost all normally developing children can pass a first-order false-belief test. One of the most well-known of these tests is called the "Sally–Anne" test, where children are told a story about two characters: Sally, who has a basket, and Anne, who has a box. Sally also has a marble, which she puts in her basket and then leaves the room. While Sally is outside the room, Anne takes the marble from basket and puts in her box. Children are then asked where Sally will look for the marble when she returns. If children answer that Sally will look in her basket for the marble, they pass the false-belief test. Those with deficits in theory of mind do not pass, because they cannot recognize that someone has a belief different from their own. They know that the marble is in the box; therefore, Sally must also believe that the marble is in the box. Passing the false-belief test is considered a major milestone in the development of theory of mind (Alic, 2009). Another well-known false-belief test is the "Smarties" test, where the experimenter shows a child a box that looks like it contains Smarties candies. After the child guesses the contents of the box, the experimenter reveals that the box actually contains pencils. The child is then asked what she thinks another person who has not been shown the true contents of the box will think is inside. The child passes the test if she answers "Smarties" but fails if she answers "pencils."

By the age of 6 or 7, most children are able to pass a second-order false-belief task, a more complex theory of mind ability, which involves understanding that one character has a false belief about another character's belief. One such story is the "Surprise" story (Sullivan, Zaitchik, & Tager-Flusberg, 1994). In this story, a mother is going to surprise her son, Alex, by giving him a puppy for his birthday. She hides the puppy in the shed. When Alex says to his mother, "I hope you got me a puppy for my birthday," his mother tells him she did not—she got him a really nice toy instead. When Alex goes outside to play, he looks in the shed and discov-ers the puppy, and he realizes that his mother did get him a puppy for his birthday after all. While he is still outside, Alex's grandmother comes to visit and asks Alex's mother if Alex knows that she got him a puppy for his birthday. The experimenter then asks the children: "What does Mom say to Grandma?" If they answer "No," they pass the second-order false-belief test.

Those with ASD who have the most trouble passing basic theory of mind tasks also have an intellectual disability. However, once the verbal abilities of those with ASD are equivalent to those of an 11- or 12-year-old child, there is little difference between the ASD population and typically developing children (Fisher, Happé, & Dunn, 2005). Verbal ability seems to play a part in passing basic theory of mind tasks. Greater differences exist in more advanced theory-of-mind abilities such as second-order reasoning (inferences about someone else's thoughts and feelings— that is, their mental states). Studies of those with HFA, however, have shown conflicting results in regard to even more advanced theory of mind tasks, leading to the conclusion that "there is currently no consensus on whether adolescents and young adults with HFASD are impaired in their advanced ToM [theory of mind] understanding" (Scheeren, de Rosnay, Koot, & Begeer, 2013, p. 629). Age also seems to be a key factor, as adolescents do better than children do on theory of mind tasks. Also important is to realize that many of these studies are done under laboratory conditions, and everyday life is different from a controlled setting (Scheeren, de Rosnay, Koot, & Begeer, 2013). It is probably safe to say that those with HFA are good at passing false belief tests but not so good at intuiting another's state of mind. Connected with this is their difficulty in understanding intentionality. Those with HFA tend to see only the behavior and not the agent's intention (Moran et al., 2011).

This has important consequences in the area of moral judgment. For example, HFAs, when compared to typically developing children, did not differ in tasks involving false belief, but were less willing to pardon those who caused accidental harms based on innocent intentions (Moran et al., 2011). Understanding and appreciating intentionality is an even more mature theory of mind task than false beliefs, and herein seems to lie the enduring difference between HFAs and typically developing children. HFAs tend to focus on outcomes over intention, especially when the outcome is negative and even when the intention is neutral. Understanding someone's intentions is a critical aspect for understanding his mental state.

Neuroscience suggests that activation of the right-lateralized, temporo-parietal junction (rTPJ) of the brain is responsible for making moral judgments based on theory of mind (Saxe & Powell, 2006), and this may be compromised in HFAs. This brain structure seems to be critical for the development of theory of mind. Adults with HFA are less likely to activate rTPJ for mentalizing judgments when compared to physical judgments about the self and other (Lombardo et al., 2011). Furthermore, those whose rTPJ was more active for mentalizing were less socially impaired. A good deal of research has been done on the brains of those with ASD, but that goes beyond the scope of this chapter. Suffice it to say that rTPJ, the one area of the brain responsible for helping to intuit the mental states of others, is less activated in those with HFA, and this makes a difference in the whole area of social competency.

UNDERSTANDING HFA FROM AN ATTACHMENT PERSPECTIVE

Although children with ASD tend to exhibit less contact-seeking behavior with their mothers when compared to typical children, meta-analysis has shown that the majority of those with ASD do develop secure attachments with the primary caretaker (Rutgers, Bakermans-Kranenburg, van IJzendoorn, & van Berckelaer-Onnes, 2004). Overall, however, this same analysis showed that children with ASD are less securely attached than nonclinical children. The difficulties in attachment security of those with ASD have been discussed both from the child's impairments in social communication as well as lack of parental sensitivity.

One of the earliest studies on attachment and parental sensitivity found that mothers of securely attached children with autism showed more parental sensitivity than mothers of insecurely attached children with autism (Capps, Sigman, & Mundy, 1994). This study, however, did not distinguish between high- and low-functioning autism. Previously, parental sensitivity was defined as the parents' ability to intuit the child's attachment signals and respond to those signals in a prompt and appropriate fashion (Ainsworth, Blehar, Waters, & Wall, 1978). Parental sensitivity is very close to the concept of mentalization and results from a developed theory of mind. Children with ASD have more difficulty expressing their needs in explicit ways due to both social and language impairments that may make it difficult for the primary caretaker to intuit their child's needs. On the other hand, since autism has a strong genetic basis, the attachment figure may suffer from impaired theory of mind and therefore exhibit less social interaction ability compared to the attachment figures of typically developing children.

It may also be that children with ASD require different strategies for the development of attachment security. For example, Doussard-Roosevelt, Joe, Bazhenova, and Porges (2003) found that mothers of children with ASD used more physical contact and high-intensity behaviors and less social and verbal contact with their children.

In regard to the kind of attachment insecurity among those with ASD, a high percentage is classified as disorganized. In nonclinical samples, about 15% of children are classified as disorganized, compared to about 31% of children with ASD (Willemsen-Swinkels et al., 2000). Mentioned previously was the connection among nonclinical children between disorganized attachment style and parental behaviors that are frightening, highly intrusive, and neglectful. Research, however, has failed to establish this connection among those with ASD.

A later study found no main difference in parental sensitivity between parents of children with ASD and parents of children without ASD, and this included children who also suffered from mental retardation (van IJzendoorn et al., 2007). However, this same study showed more attachment disorganization among children with ASD than children without ASD, and children with mental retardation and autism displayed more attachment disorganization than did children with autism and without mental retardation. It does appear that a link between parental sensitivity and attachment security among children with ASD is not well established, in contrast to children without ASD, where the association between parental sensitivity and attachment security is robust. According to van IJzendoorn et al. (2007), "For children with ASD there is a biological constraint on the intergenerational transmission of attachment. Because of their inborn limited social information processing, children with ASD may challenge the established role of sensitive parenting obtained in studies on typically developing children" (p. 604). Impairments in the social domain often associated with HFA appear to have the strongest moderating effect upon attachment security—more than language impairment and stereotypic behaviors.

One of the implications of these findings is that the attachment figure and the child with ASD will need to make an informed effort to develop a well-synchronized interaction pattern, although the pattern may develop later than usual or maybe not all (van IJzendoorn et al., 2007). Such alternate strategies might include more explicit parental stimuli as well as more nonverbal input, which may look to the innocent observer as somewhat insensitive but is necessary to convey the subtleties of sensitive parenting that will often go unnoticed by the child with ASD. The use of alternate strategies could also have consequences for working with school-aged children who suffer from social impairment as the result of ASD. We now return to the case example.

UNDERSTANDING ALISON FROM AN ATTACHMENT PERSPECTIVE

The case of Alison represents many of the characteristics of HFA discussed in the previous section. The first paragraph of the vignette talks about her stereotypic interests, like the music of the '60s. Typically, students with HFA will know everything about a particular subject and have little interest in subjects they know little about. Because of her need to dominate conversations with her own peculiar interest, she has few friends. This is a good example of a deficient theory of mind: Alison is not able to understand or intuit the mental states of others. In this case, it means not understanding that others are not particularly interested all the time in the music of the '60s. For Alison, however, she believes that *If I'm interested in it, others have to be interested in it*. The third paragraph expands on theory of mind deficiency, talking about her difficulty in turn taking, perseveration, and difficulty perceiving irony and sarcasm. All these abilities are associated with a more developed theory of mind. A typical student, for example, would not have fallen for the cruel joke about "going out," because he or she would have picked up on the nonverbal cues embedded in how the student was asking and intuited that it was a setup for embarrassment.

The second paragraph briefly mentions Alison's brother, who suffers from a more severe form of autism and cannot function in a regular environment. This speaks to the genetic component of ASD. The vignette does not offer much about Alison's parents expect that they are both special educators. It is possible that one or both parents might have or have had a compromised theory of mind, but with proper interventions along the way went on to have careers as teachers of students with disabilities. Make no mistake about it—those with HFA can become very successful if they choose the right career that capitalizes on their abilities and interests, with the help of some intervention to improve their social skills. The vignette later on talks about how Alison can captivate an audience with her public speaking skills built around her need to be the center of attention. She combines this ability with presenting on a topic that is of particular interest to her, and the result is fantastic.

The vignette also talks about the many sensory processing issues that face a student like Alison. Her sensitivity to certain foods, loud noises, bright lights, and touch are rather typical of people with ASD and are related to neurological impairments other than theory of mind. Also mentioned is that Alison suffers from frequent panic attacks. Those with ASD tend to have a good deal of anxiety about many things. Sometimes, if the anxiety is extreme, a separate diagnosis of an anxiety disorder might be necessary to treat the anxiety as separate from ASD. It is not clear that this is the case with Alison, but "frequent panic attacks" are a serious symptom of anxiety and may also say something about her attachment history. Remember that there is not one attachment classification that dominates cases of ASD, and Alison might be more of the resistant type, as she seems to lose functionality when not in her comfort zone. Most people develop a level of anxiety when faced with a new task or environment, yet they manage the anxiety so as to take on the task. This is often not possible for those with ASD, and that includes those with HFA. Their rigidity and demand for sameness is a defense against anxiety. It makes their world more comfortable, but often at the expense of causing great turmoil and interference in the lives of those around them.

It is perfectly understandable that even some of Alison's teachers have lost patience with her "narcissistic" behaviors. Those with HFA can come across as narcissistic, since deficiencies of theory of mind allow them to live in their own world, unable to intuit the needs of others. They are obsessively concerned about their own interests and have little regard for the interests of others. They believe if something is important to them, it should be important to everyone.

A brief story about a boy with HFA illustrates this point well. The boy's mother was so happy when one day her son invited a friend over—something she had wanted for a long time. After playing outside for a while, the boys came in, and while the son went upstairs to do something, the friend asked the mother if he could turn on the TV and check the score of the baseball game. The mother said, "By all means." But when her son returned and saw the TV, he immediately switched it off, saying, "I don't like baseball."

However, there is an important difference between ASD and narcissism. ASD is a neurobiological disorder, as the previous section substantiated. Narcissism is more of an attachment disorder along the disorganized type, where the primary caretaker dealt an early psychological injury to the child. A deep sense of insecurity drives the narcissist to demand total and absolute obedience from others, and they see others as simply serving their own utilitarian purposes. Disagreement of any kind or confrontation is not allowed. The word *collaboration* is not in their vocabulary. This is quite different from someone with HFA. It is possible to work with them, point out their deficiencies, and help them to achieve better social skills by intervening with theory-of-mind activities. True narcissists would have none of this, because they consider themselves perfectly superior compared to those who form the world around them.

The vignette also mentions others' dislike of Alison because she is "emotionally unavailable." Many of those with HFA can come across as emotionally flat, disassociated from their affect. The previous section discussed the lack of emotional awareness in oneself and in others as part of a compromised theory of mind. Studies have shown that those with HFA have abnormal frontolimbic connectivity

(Zalla et al., 2014), and it is the limbic system of the brain that is primary responsible for emotion. The dislike of Alison, however, is not limited to her fellow students. She can easily push the buttons of teachers, who sometimes react in ways similar to Alison's peers. We now turn to one such teacher.

UNDERSTANDING TEACHER INTERVENTIONS FOR STUDENTS WITH HFA FROM BOTH ATTACHMENT AND PEDAGOGICAL PERSPECTIVES

Mr. Lyons: "There's Never an Excuse for Rude, Ill-Mannered Behavior—Disability or No!"

Mr. Lyons, Ali's language arts teacher, feels strongly that she is simply a "spoiled, self-centered girl who only cares about herself and her own interests." He has said to a few colleagues that he has no problem working with students with disabilities; he is, in fact, very sympathetic to their challenges and needs, but he cannot and will not tolerate rudeness of any kind in his classroom. "There is never an excuse for being rude," he remarks one day in class. "Being respectful of others and our social conventions is an expectation of every student, teacher, and administrator. Rude, insensitive behavior will not be tolerated in my class!"

Mr. Lyons finds Ali's behavior to be unacceptable. In support of this contention, he argues that in class discussions, she "hijacks" the conversation, often diverting the discussion to a topic that is of greater interest to her. Mr. Lyons has had to redirect her and curtail her "filibusters" on many occasions, and he has assigned her several detentions, citing her inflexibility and lack of compliance with his repeated requests that she remain on topic. Many times Ali has chosen to simply walk out of class when asked by Mr. Lyons to cede the floor to a classmate or to give others a chance to comment on a particular literary topic.

As mentioned before, Mr. Lyons firmly believes that many of Alison's maladaptive behaviors, attributed to her HFA, are really nothing more than manifestations of poor manners and social choices that are well within Ali's power to control. As a consequence, Mr. Lyons has decided to be less tolerant of Ali's narcissism, believing her to be capable of much better social behavior.

In accordance with his very negative appraisal of Alison and her poor social skills, Mr. Lyons and Alison have developed a very adversarial and nonproductive relationship. Ali has voiced on more than one occasion to her parents that she hates Mr. Lyons's class, despite the fact that English literature has always been one of her favorite subjects in school. For his part, Mr. Lyons has shared with his colleagues that he truly believes that Ali is capable of much better behavior and is she is "just clever enough to use her HFA diagnosis as an excuse to act out and behave selfishly." He and Ali are at an impasse and, in response, Ali's parents have asked for a change of teachers, a request the school administrators are very hesitant to support.

Mr. Lyons from an Attachment Perspective

Well, the title of the vignette about Mr. Lyons pretty much says it all: He feels there is *never* an excuse for Alison's behavior. Whenever a teacher uses such absolute language, it is pretty evident that the relationship between the student and the teacher is not going to end well. He experiences Alison as simply a "spoiled, self-centered girl." He is quite harsh in his opinion, most likely the result of longtime frustration with Alison. Mr. Lyons even dismisses Alison's disability, saying she uses it as an excuse for her self-centeredness. And dismissing is probably an attachment classification that would describe Mr. Lyons. He avoids the entanglements that can come from understanding the characteristics of a certain disability. For Mr. Lyons, the rules are the rules—disability or no disability.

But while there is never an excuse, there is always an alternate story. Mr. Lyons has told himself a story about Alison's behavior that can only result in anger, frustration, and maybe even hate for the student who has clearly been a disruptive presence in his classroom. He is not open to an alternate story—namely one that explains Alison's behavior in terms of theory of mind and compromised activity in certain parts of her brain that prevents Alison from engaging in normal, reciprocal, turn-taking relationships. One could just imagine Mr. Lyons saying, or at least thinking, that these explanations are a bunch of crap. The inability to entertain alternate stories and viewpoints is a function of compromised theory of mind. Could it be that Mr. Lyons himself suffers from this? His extreme negative view of Alison would make one wonder if Mr. Lyons sees in Alison something he does not like about himself.

For him, it is not a matter of "can" but of "want." According to Mr. Lyons, Alison is capable of controlling her poor manners—she is simply a rude girl who does not want to change her behavior and hides behind a disability. An alternate story would be that Alison can change her behavior, but she needs the appropriate interventions, because she does not learn social mores in the same fashion as typical students do. Mr. Lyons's story is that Alison is rude because she is spoiled. An alternate story is that Alison is unaware because of compromised activity in parts of her brain responsible for social skills. And because she is a "bad kid," the only remedy left to Mr. Lyons is a punitive one, detention, which apparently has had little or no effect.

On the other hand, it is not difficult to empathize with Mr. Lyons. Alison has been a nightmare in his class, seemingly upsetting at every turn an appropriate learning environment. The teacher's job is to maintain a healthy learning environment for all students, and Alison is a liability. Because of her, Mr. Lyons can't do his job. The fact that Alison sometimes walks out of class when Mr. Lyons redirects the discussion to someone else shows that he is not willing to let her grandstand. If she walks out of class, there ought to be consequences for leaving class. It may also be that Mr. Lyons and Alison are locked into a power struggle, a dynamic we have seen all too often between teachers and students. The power struggle is always the result of early nonintervention. Mr. Lyons might suffer from a lack of sensitivity in regard to Alison's disability. Yet he is in charge of making sure all students participate equally in the class discussion, and he clearly sees Alison as an obstruction to fairness.

The fact that Alison's parents have asked for a change of teachers does not help matters, because Mr. Lyons cannot count on parental support to manage Alison's behaviors. Mr. Lyons needs help in understanding and managing Alison. However, he is a dismissing type—which prevents him from being flexible, willing to entertain alternate viewpoints and opinions, and able to seek out help from colleagues who have, perhaps, have been more successful in working with Alison. He can't ask the question: How can I help Alison and maintain a proper learning environment? The problem with a dismissing attachment style is that there are no alternatives: What applies to all students should also apply to Alison. Unfortunately, Alison has the same problem. She, too, is inflexible and not able to consider alternatives because of her compromised theory of mind. It is little wonder, therefore, that Mr. Lyons and Alison seem to be a lethal combination.

Mr. Lyons from a Pedagogical Perspective

In his seminal work, *Thinking about Teaching and Learning*, Leamnson (1999) asserted the importance of "knowing the [student] clientele." Students must be known as they come to us, and not as we would like them to be. "Knowing them" includes knowing their culture, their level of preparedness, and their intellectual and emotional needs. This element of the author's philosophy of teaching resonates with that of Freire (1970) and Bruner (1996), both of whom stress the importance of appreciating one's own culture as the teacher, as well as that of one's students. Likewise, this philosophical tenet fits with our recommendations for a sound pedagogical foundation; specifically, that the teacher should be willing and able to work with his students in order to help them make meaningful changes in their lives. Mr. Lyons is convinced that he understands the complexities of Ali's diagnosis and has determined that she is faking in order to achieve selfish ends: to be the center of attention. However, if he allowed himself to consider the possibility that Ali truly might not appreciate the perspective of others due to a neurological dysfunction, he might be a bit more tolerant of her perseverating behaviors and, consequently, be more inclined to help her develop altruistic, prosocial ones.

Similarly, Leamnson (1999) suggests that "helping implies loving" (p. 8). Such "love" does not mean permissiveness and a lack of classroom discipline; it merely suggests, as he explains, that people will strive to help those they love through challenging, exhortation, cajoling, and with long-suffering patience. This ethos is reminiscent of the urging of Noddings (2005) and Smith (2012), who both encourage teachers to develop truly caring relationships with their students as integral to their pedagogical schema.

Perhaps, as alluded to earlier, Mr. Lyons is simply reflecting his lack of self-awareness—could he possibly be intolerant of the kinds of aberrant behavior displayed by Ali and be swift to judge others' "selfish" motives, as he perceives them? Might it be that he has been judged unfairly in life, or had a teacher or parent who was similarly cynical and based decisions on subjective prejudices or misperceptions? Possibly he was once duped by a manipulative student, colleague, or friend, and has become highly vigilant and defensive as a result. We cannot, of course, know any of this for certain. Nevertheless, what is certain is that his prejudice toward Ali and his subsequent disdain for her perceived motives have created an untenable chasm between them, resulting in an adversarial relationship.

Mr. Lyons needs to develop a fresh and unbiased perspective—maybe by talking to the school's counselor or to Mrs. Azulini, the speech-language pathologist, both of whom have a better understanding of Ali's atypical behaviors relative to her diagnosis of HFA.

Mrs. Azulini: "Ali has really benefited from my program"

Mrs. Azulini, the school's speech-language pathologist, runs several groups and individual sessions for students who, like Ali, have poorly developed social skills. Recently, Alison has begun participating in group counseling along with other students diagnosed with HFA. The focus of this counseling is to develop social communication skills and competence in interactions. Since people with HFA typically have strong verbal abilities, eliciting conversation is not a problem; the challenge is helping these individuals understand the emotional states and perspectives of others and recognize social conventions relative to context.

In addition, Mrs. Azulini has formed a "buddy skills training program" that helps nondisabled peers learn about HFA and its characteristics as well as effective communication interventions based on the use of concrete, unambiguous speech. As noted earlier, Ali and many individuals with HFA are very literal in their interpretation of language, missing the subtleties of irony and sarcasm. For them, it is important that people they are talking to use concrete language and avoid the ambiguities inherent in sarcasm and figurative speech. For example, Mrs. Azulini uses the anecdote about the father who observes his son lounging on the patio beside the overgrown lawn and idle lawnmower and remarks, "I guess I'll be saving some money this week!" The counselor then asks the group participants to explain the sarcasm represented in the father's remark.

In addition, Mrs. Azulini uses "social stories" to enhance Alison's understanding of social context, appropriate behavioral responses, and the perspective of a social partner. Ali's participation in the group sessions as well as her rehearsal and use of the skills taught by the counselor have succeeded in increasing her self-confidence in social situations and thereby reducing her depression. Helping Ali fit in and become more socially accepted is the ultimate goal of this cognitive approach. For students like Ali, successful social integration is the key to a productive, satisfying life.

Mrs. Azulini finds Ali to be a very eager participant and a cooperative group member. She believes that Ali truly cares about the well-being of her classmates, teachers, and family members. Furthermore, Mrs. Azulini feels that Ali has made great strides, as demonstrated in her recent creation of a presentation that she uses to "get the word out" about HFA, its characteristics, plausible causes, and effective interventions, such as the ones provided by Mrs. Azulini in group sessions. Mrs. Azulini feels that, since Ali receives little or no remuneration for providing this community service, she is acting altruistically and, in so doing, is displaying concern for others—particularly those, like herself, who have been diagnosed with HFA.

Likewise, Mrs. Azulini notes that Ali's conversational skills are also improving.

In support of that contention, she cites the fact that recently, in a group session, Ali was able to initiate, sustain, and tactfully close a conversation with a classmate. In doing so, Mrs. Azulini reports, Ali asked relevant questions of her partner that encouraged elaboration and also offered reflective responses that confirmed her accuracy in comprehending the speaker's intended message. She also was careful to restrict her comments and questions so that they were always relevant to the speaker's topic.

In short, Mrs. Azulini appreciates the great gains achieved this year by Ali and is hopeful that, in the near future, Ali will be able to engage with anyone socially and begin, sustain, and even advance that conversation successfully. She feels that soon, Ali's social and conversational skills will be sufficiently advanced so as to enable her to seek competitive employment and develop deeper, more meaningful relationships with others.

Mrs. Azulini from an Attachment Perspective

Mrs. Azulini appears to have done wonderful work with Alison in helping remediate her social deficits. The good relationship between the teacher and the student results from Mrs. Azulini's knowledge about HFA and her ability to impart that knowledge through effective strategies such as social stories. From an attachment perspective, there is not much to say about the dynamics of the relationship, but this implies an important point about working with students with HFA. What they need is to be taught social skills. As we have said many times before, ASD is a neurodevelopmental disorder that primarily affects areas of the brain responsible for social acumen. It is less about dynamics of personality, as Mr. Lyons would have his colleagues believe, and more about learning the necessary skills to function more appropriately in the social arena. Mrs. Azulini knows that she knows what Alison needs. This gives her the security necessary to help Alison and to understand and deal effectively with whatever resistance the student may display.

It would be interesting to know, however, exactly how Mrs. Azulini engaged Alison in counseling. Was Alison told she had to go? Did she go willingly? Did she first see it as an opportunity to once again be the center of attention, or did she understand that this experience would provide the help she needs? That Alison appears to be a very willing participant is not surprising, since many students with HFA want to please others. Their social deficits, however, get in the way. As mentioned previously, those with HFA are often not opposed to receiving help, which sets them apart from, for example, those who are narcissistically disordered. Students with HFA are aware that something is not right; they just don't know how to fix it.

When someone like Mrs. Azulini comes along, it really is a godsend. There is no judgment of the student except for the fact that the student, similar to any other student who is deficient in a subject area, needs to learn the subject, albeit with some alternate teaching strategies. The subject matter of Alison's deficiency is social skills. The techniques (concrete, unambiguous speech; the buddy system;

and social stories) used by Mrs. Azulini are all empirically supported for helping students with HFA. Social stories, in particular, are extremely useful and highly recommended. The first section of this chapter mentioned several stories used for first- and second-order beliefs: the Sally–Anne, Smarties, and Surprise stories. Stories for more advanced theory of mind functions are those involving emotional display (Begeer et al., 2011), double bluff, faux pas, and sarcasm (Kaland, Callesen, Møller-Nielsen, Mortensen, & Smith, 2008). Once Alison learns these skills, she is on the pathway to overall well-being.

The results of Mrs. Azulini's interventions seem almost magical. The skills allow Alison to feel more confident in social situations, less depressed about her ineptitude, and more able to show how much she truly cares about the welfare of others. This does not sound like narcissism! Furthermore, her newly learned skills allow her to build on her already innate qualities such as writing, developing presentations, speaking in public, and trying to make a difference in other people's understanding of HFA. With her social skill set as the seed, Alison blossoms into a caring, selfless, socially minded student—the opposite of Mr. Lyons's earlier description of her. Alison will continue to need help, but her willingness to receive that help and rehearse her social skills makes for an excellent prognosis. As we have seen many times in other vignettes, finding the right way of working with a student who presents with difficult behaviors allows that student to progress from an insecure to a secure state of mind. Insecurity is often behind many difficult behaviors. Mrs. Azulini, by providing Alison with a needed skill, also provides her psychological security and this, in the end, makes all the difference.

Mrs. Azulini from a Pedagogical Perspective

Mrs. Azulini, by way of contrast with Mr. Lyons, exhibits many of the pedagogical elements we describe in this book. First, she clearly provides her students (including Ali, of course), with the skills needed to become socially engaged and competent, as recommended by Alexander (2004). She accomplishes this through her "buddy skills training program," which facilitates pragmatic speech, reciprocity or turn taking in conversations, and "social stories" that teach appropriate prosocial behaviors through modeling and role-playing.

Furthermore, it seems apparent from the effective rapport she has established with Ali that she has developed the kind of caring teacher–student relationship that is the linchpin of a sound pedagogy (Noddings, 2005; Smith, 2012). Similarly, she understands that Ali's antisocial behaviors are truly a function of her HFA, and while these challenges may affect her throughout her life, she can acquire strategies that mitigate their effects on her socialization. Mrs. Azulini also seems to have a clear sense of her own identity as an educator—she knows what her tasks are and is confident in her ability to accomplish them, virtues extolled by Stout (2005).

In addition to this, she is distinctly aware of the importance of context to her students' social skills development and appears to be successful in imparting these critical skills to her students. This pedagogical skill is one of our recommended elements of an effective pedagogy. Also, in accordance with the suggestions of Tompkins (1996), Mrs. Azulini appears to empower or "entice" her students to take responsibility for their learning by helping them acquire the skill of how to be with others in a social context.

Finally, Mrs. Azulini's instructional skills reflect the three that Smith (1994) considers elemental to a sound pedagogy; specifically, "animation—introducing students to new experiences"; "reflection—creating opportunities to explore and practice new social skills"; and "action—working with students," like Ali, "to enable them to make positive life changes" (p. 10).

Thus, according to our proposed pedagogical framework, Mrs. Azulini demonstrates the essential elements of an effective teacher and mentor in that she serves as a prosocial role model for her students and, particularly, has established a productive rapport with Ali.

EFFECTIVE TEACHER RESPONSES

General supports:

- For students with HFA who experience difficulty in initiating or sustaining a dialogue with a social partner, use video instruction to provide nonthreatening "modeling" of successful behavior. Also, ensure that you comply with the strategies outlined in the student's behavior intervention plan that address social and interpersonal skills issues.
- Use prearranged "cues" to remind students with HFA when they are engaged in pedantic speech, are dominating a discussion, or fail to consider the perspective of a social partner.
- Be familiar with the "triggers" that incite a student with HFA and defuse the volatile situation by removing the affected student or antagonist or by redirecting the adversarial interaction.
- Use "social stories" where feasible in lessons or use the "teachable moment" to provide an opportunity to conduct a "social autopsy" on an ineffective or inappropriate social behavior and then teach the correct behavioral response (Austin & Sciarra, 2010 reproduced with permission, Pearson Education).

Cognitive-organizational supports:

- Across the curriculum, implement cognitive-organizational strategies in order to compensate for the individual's weaknesses, build on strengths, and use the individual's specialized interests.
- Use a broad range of structured teaching approaches to increase predictability and meaningfulness of the school environment for the student (e.g., use routines, create an organized and visually clear classroom environment, provide strategies for organizing materials, use picture schedules to smooth transitions, and clearly communicate work expectations).

- Present tasks in ways that increase the likelihood of understanding (e.g., present information visually, provide graphic organizers).
- Simplify tasks as appropriate by reducing workloads, breaking work into smaller units, and providing hands-on activities.
- Closely monitor student understanding and progress.

Social communication supports:

- Adjust communication to use shorter statements and avoid using figurative language.
- Make the social environment more meaningful and less overwhelming by providing appropriate structure (e.g., provide alternate activities, a less demanding classroom environment, fewer students, more structured routines).
- Provide students with HFA explicit explanations of social situations and expectations through a variety of techniques (e.g., social stories, cartooning, social scripts).
- Understand and respect students' social interests and preferences (i.e., allow some "alone" time).
- Promote social interaction by providing opportunities for structured social interactions, identifying peer activity partners, and identifying social activities that are of genuine interest to the student.

Behavioral-emotional supports:

- Proactively use cognitive-organizational and social communication supports.
- Identify key support people at school (e.g., a "safe" person such as a counselor or therapist to provide support with problem solving).
- Provide crisis plans and coping strategies (e.g., safe place, take-a-break routines) established in advance, practiced with the student, and followed by teachers.
- Help students develop self-esteem and confidence by providing daily opportunities for their success, pleasure, and interest.
- Choose your battles wisely; ask yourself: *What do I know about HFA that can help me understand this behavior? Is the behavior interfering with the student's learning?* (Prior, 2003) reproduced with permission, Guilford Press.

CONCLUDING THOUGHTS

As noted in this chapter, students with HFA are increasingly included in public school classrooms. They present unique challenges for educators because, while they can master subject matter, they struggle with both inference and irony. Moreover, they are very idiosyncratic in their interests and, because they can commandeer a discussion and behave oddly, are often socially isolated.

Due to the increase in the number of students diagnosed with HFA in public schools, teachers are encouraged to learn about the characteristics of students with HFA, the perceived scientific causes of the disorder, and the recommended interventions that seem helpful to these students in their quest to achieve academic and social success.

This information and unique perspective on the way one may understand students with this disorder will help prepare teachers and caregivers to work more effectively with them. Like anyone else, such students have encountered challenges that must be overcome to facilitate their success in school and in life!

CHAPTER 11

Teaching Students with Impulsivity

STUDENT VIGNETTE: "STEFAN" THE IMPULSIVE

Stefan is a 10th grader attending West Queens High School. Always a challenge for his teachers, his impulsive behaviors have become more intense and pervasive of late. Stefan's parents report that his teachers and principal call frequently to complain about his "acting out" behavior in school. They also have noted that his impulsivity is becoming more of a challenge at home as well as in his after-school activities. His friends have ostracized him because of his unpredictability and explosive temper. He recently punched one of his best friends because he accidentally tripped Stefan in a street hockey game. Stefan apologized profusely to his friend, who reluctantly accepted the apology, but, as his friend lamented afterward, "Stefan can't control his impulses—he just reacts!"

Academically, Stefan is struggling in all his subjects. Currently, he is receiving support in a resource room, because it was determined that he would not be provided sufficient help or structure to learn in general education classes. Even with the additional support, Stefan has received "incompletes" for his report grades in English and social studies. Behaviorally, he is also in jeopardy. Stefan has been suspended six times in the past year for physical aggression and insubordination. The principal has called for an emergency meeting with the chair of the Committee for Special Education as well as Stefan's parents to discuss more effective approaches for dealing with his impulsivity.

A recent incident is illustrative of Stefan's impulsive behavior. Following a class trip a few weeks ago, Stefan was horsing around with two of his friends when sud-

denly, and without apparent provocation, he slapped one of the boys very hard across the face. He then ran to his mother's car, which had just pulled up in front of the school to pick him up, and they drove away, leaving the slightly injured and humiliated student crying in the entranceway of the school building. An assistant principal, who witnessed the incident, ran outside to apprehend Stefan, but she was too late; the car had already turned onto the main highway. Upon his arrival at school the next morning, Stefan was called to the principal's office, and the incident was reviewed with him and the student whom he had struck. Stefan admitted to "playfully" slapping the student but claimed it was all in fun, and that the two of them frequently engaged in "play fighting." He insisted that he never meant to hurt his friend, and neither he nor his mother noticed the aftermath or the assistant principal's attempt to run after their car. Nevertheless, the principal, in accordance with school policy, once again suspended Stefan for two days and called home to inform his parents about his suspension and request a formal meeting with them about this incident and his frequent and troubling impulsive behavior.

His parents are convinced that some of Stefan's teachers—especially Mr. Jakubowitz, his global studies teacher, as well as the entire school administration—have it in for him because he is "spirited" and "stands up for himself." This perception has created an adversarial relationship between Stefan's parents and school administrators that has adversely affected the quality of their communication and willingness to work collaboratively to address Stefan's impulsivity.

Recently, Stefan's parents have taken him to an outside specialist, a psychiatrist who was recommended to them as an expert in diagnosing and treating students with ADHD. She has diagnosed Stefan with ADHD (combined type) and has recommended that, in addition to cognitive-behavioral therapy and family therapy, Stefan be prescribed a trial dose of Ritalin. Stefan's parents support the therapy, but they are uncomfortable with the pharmacological intervention recommended. They expressed concern about the adverse effects produced by the medication and the impact of long-term use. Stefan, they say, has the skill to become a professional athlete, and they fear that his long-term use of Ritalin might impair his chances for success in ice hockey. The school administration, however, is strongly urging that Stefan comply with the psychiatrist's recommendations and begin the medication trial, citing its beneficial effects for students with similar diagnoses. The alternative option if the recommended treatment plan is rejected, they caution, could be expulsion from the district, if Stefan's aggressive and impulsive behaviors continue unabated.

Presently, as a result of the meeting with school administration, Stefan is receiving his instruction in special-education classes in math and English. He participates in social studies, science, and gym in regular classes, and he has lunch in the cafeteria with all the students in his grade level at the school. Unfortunately, his behavioral problems continue despite the extra support he receives in the special classes; however, this support has helped him make modest academic gains in English and math. Stefan's school administrators as well as many of his teachers share legitimate concerns about his successful transition to postsecondary educa-

tion and the "world of work," due to his high degree of impulsivity. Teaching Stefan continues to be very challenging.

Why Does the Teacher Need to Know About Students with Impulsivity?

Impulsivity is a multifactorial construct that describes actions that are performed without due consideration of consequences and that clearly favor short-term gains over long-term ones. Impulsive behaviors occur in response to a perceived immediate gain and involve unplanned reactions. Examples of such behavior are abundant and include, for children, choosing a reward that can be enjoyed now over a better one that can be attained later—*delayed discounting*. Illustrations of adolescent impulsivity often involve more risk-taking behaviors and the potential for undesirable consequences. Such impulsive behaviors include engaging in unsafe sex, substance abuse, and driving an automobile at excessive speeds.

School-aged children, especially at the adolescent stage of development, naturally display impulsive behavior as a function of their neurological development—specifically, the growth and development of the prefrontal cortex, which is responsible for inhibition and executive function. Child and adolescent behaviors are functionally influenced by the limbic system of the brain, which is the region of the brain that governs emotion, memories, and stimulation: the "fight-or-flight" reactions.

There are several well-established causes attributed to impulsive behavior; specifically, these are "urgency," when a student is in a hurry to act, "lack of premeditation," when a student acts before thinking, "lack of perseverance," when a student gives up on a task, and "sensation seeking," when a student seeks a thrill without thought of the consequences. Most students engage in these behaviors on occasion, but they quickly learn that the consequences of acting on impulse are not advantageous or desirable in the long run. However, there is a subset of children and adolescents who behave impulsively most of the time and make decisions based on their whims in the moment.

Typically, the most common causes of chronic impulsivity are ADHD, conduct disorder, certain anxiety disorders such as OCD, and mood disorders including depression and bipolar disorder; less common factors may include brain injury as well as certain medical conditions such as hyperthyroidism, Parkinson's disease, fetal alcohol syndrome, and lead poisoning. Unfortunately, because impulsivity is a multifactorial construct, and is therefore expressed in many different ways to very different degrees of severity, it is almost impossible to provide a prevalence rate for impulsivity that is regarded as pathological. Nonetheless, since impulsivity is a defining characteristic of all three ADHD subtypes and, to a lesser degree, a component of conduct disorder, anxiety disorder, and mood disorder, we can gain some appreciation for its pervasiveness among school-aged children by examining the prevalence of these four disorders.

Currently, there are two respected reports of the estimates for the prevalence of ADHD (undifferentiated by type) among school-aged children in the United States.

One is offered by the APA and reported in the *DSM-5* (2013), in which it is estimated that 5% of all school-aged children have ADHD. The other estimate of the prevalence of ADHD among children is presented by the CDC Attention-Deficit/Hyperactivity Disorder (2014) from one of the largest community-based epidemiological studies of ADHD ever conducted in the United States. Based on this survey, they determined that, as of 2007, 7.2% or 4.1 million school-aged children in the United States had a diagnosis of ADHD. Prevalence rates have increased steadily since then (Wolraich et al., 2012). Relative to ADHD subtypes (i.e., predominantly inattentive, predominantly hyperactive-impulsive, and combined type), Akinbami, Liu, Pastor, and Reuben (2011), in conjunction with the National Research Center on ADHD, determined that for all children and adolescents in the United States aged 8–15, the distribution among the three subtypes was estimated to be 4.3% for inattentive type, 3.3% for combined type, and 2.5% for hyperactive-impulsive type. These are impressive numbers! Similarly, researchers at the National Institute of Mental Health determined that approximately 5.9% of adolescents 13–18 years of age in the United States had an anxiety disorder and 4.7% had a mood disorder (Merikangas et al., 2010). Investigators with the CDC, in a much larger study conducted in 2013, found slightly lower rates: For U.S. children and adolescents aged 12–17 years, the prevalence rate for conduct disorders was 3.5%, anxiety disorders 3%, and mood disorders (including depression) 2.1%.

These data suggest a high likelihood that teachers—even those in regular education or "inclusive" classrooms—will encounter students who exhibit chronic impulsivity. Since children and, to a greater degree, adolescents display impulsivity to some extent, and with the proliferation of inclusion, many students with one or more of the disorders that include chronic impulsivity will be educated alongside their nondisabled peers, it is *crucial* that teachers know about impulsivity and its behavioral manifestations in the classroom, along with effective interventions.

What the Teacher Should Know About Students with Impulsivity

Impulsivity is a construct that investigators have studied for many years using many different definitions. The reason for its popularity is that impulsivity is thought to be a factor in many problematic behaviors and psychiatric conditions, such as personality disorders (most especially borderline and antisocial), conduct disorder, substance abuse, ADHD, depression, suicide, bipolar disorder, post-traumatic stress disorder, autism, pathological gambling, aggression, eating disorders, and indiscriminate or risky sexual activity. The concept is part of the everyday vocabulary of most individuals. How often do you find yourself describing someone as "impulsive"? What exactly does this mean?

Usually, the construct is used to refer to someone who acts quickly and without thinking (Niv, Tuvblad, Raine, Wang, & Baker, 2012). In this definition there are two aspects to impulsivity: cognitive (acts without thinking) and motor (acts quickly). Those with impulsivity act on a whim without considering the long-term consequences of their behavior. A good example of this is a student with ADHD, combined type. This student in the classroom evidences impulsivity in two different domains: interpersonal and schoolwork. Interpersonal impulsivity is marked by interrupting other people, saying something rude, easily losing one's temper, and talking back when upset. Schoolwork impulsivity is evidenced by forgetting something needed for school, not finding something because of a mess, not remembering what one was told to do, and mind wandering (Tsukayama, Duckworth, & Kim, 2013). From many years of research, the science of human behavior has concluded that impulsivity is anything but a unidimensional construct.

The Multidimensionality of Impulsivity

Factor analyzing the construct of impulsivity has resulted in three-, four-, and five-factor models. Some studies support a three-independent-component structure of impulsivity: (a) acting without thinking, (b) reward sensitivity, and (c) novelty seeking (E. Miller, Joseph, & Tudway, 2004; Romer et al., 2011). Whiteside and Lynam (2001) developed perhaps the most comprehensive and most utilized multidimensional construct of impulsivity. The original model contained four factors: urgency, lack of premeditation, lack of perseverance, and sensation seeking. Urgency was later divided into two types, positive and negative, making it a five-factor model.

Urgency. Urgency reflects the tendency to act rashly in response to intense negative affect. After the addition of another factor, called *positive urgency*, the original urgency factor became known as *negative urgency*. Positive urgency refers to the tendency to act rashly when experiencing an unusually positive mood (Lynam, Smith, Whiteside, & Cyders, 2006). Negative urgency is often linked to aggression and positive urgency to activities like gambling.

Lack of premeditation. Premeditation is the tendency to delay actions in favor of careful thinking and planning. Lack of premeditation refers to the classic aspect of impulsivity: someone who acts hastily, without considering the consequences of his actions.

Lack of perseverance. Perseverance is the ability to remain with a task until its completion. Here, impulsivity is manifested in the school setting by the inability to finish papers and projects.

Sensation seeking. Sensation seeking is the tendency to pursue excitement by engaging in risky behaviors.

While all of the factors are somewhat correlated, they represent different dispositions (Franco-Watkins & Mattson, 2009). Lack of premeditation and lack of perseverance are more cognitive in nature, while urgency and sensation seeking are more emotion based. Premeditation and perseverance have to do with executive functioning, and that is why impulsivity along these lines is related to poor school performance. Sensation seeking, on the other hand, is related to activities designed to produce an emotional high such as alcohol, drugs, and driving at very fast speeds.

Working Memory and Impulsivity

Deficits in working memory have been linked to impulsive decision-making (Hinson, Jameson, & Whitney, 2003). Working memory is that part of the brain that holds and manipulates a small amount of information for a short period of time in order to complete a task, maintain an action, or reach a goal (Cowan & Morey, 2006). It is part of the frontal lobe system and allows for the maintenance of active memory representations even in the face of distracting stimuli (Jarrold & Towse, 2006). Working memory, along with cognitive flexibility and response inhibition (self-control, self-regulation to control or repress a response when the environment demands) are the core of executive functioning (Diamond & Lee, 2011). Working memory plays a critical role in decision-making, especially when the individual has to weigh benefits and costs of a particular decision. Those with deficits in working memory tend to have higher rates for the discounting of delayed rewards, defined as "the propensity to discount larger delayed rewards in favor of smaller immediate rewards" (Franco-Watkins & Mattson, 2009, p. 84). For example, delayed discounting might involve having to choose between accepting 100 dollars right away or waiting and accepting 500 dollars in five months. Given this task, the individual has to play with four pieces of information—two different dollar amounts and two different time frames—in order to decide the cost and benefit of waiting. All of this decision-making involves the use of working memory. Deficient working memory is more easily taxed. When working memory is taxed, the individual is more likely to resort to a simple strategy of choosing the more immediate reward, because trying to weigh the costs and benefits is too time-consuming (Hinson et al., 2003). How often do you find yourself saying, "I just want to get this decision over with"? What you are admitting cognitively is that your working memory is taxed, and waiting any longer is not a viable option. This could lead you to make a decision where you don't fully weigh the consequences of your actions. Of course, for unimportant things, some impulsivity may not be all that harmful. Those with good working memory will be able to assess whether an impulsive decision may not be all that bad. However, when working memory is deficient, there is more impulsivity, as well as an inability to distinguish the magnitude of the possible deleterious consequences of such impulsivity. From this perspective, impulsivity might be understood as existing along a continuum, with those with very deficient working memory located at one end of the continuum.

The discounting of delayed rewards has been implicated in substance abuse (Kirby & Petry, 2004). Drugs have benefits: they produce perceived physiological, emotional, behavioral, and social benefits for the individual. Of course, drugs also have a cost associated with each of these dimensions, as well as financial and legal costs. Drug abusers will tend to discount the negative effects, because they are delayed, and this allows them to reap the rewards of the immediate positive effects.

The behavior is maintained because the experiencing of the positive effects results in greater discounting of the negative effects. With adolescence comes the added factor of risk taking that contributes to impulsivity.

Early sexual initiation and its relationship to working memory and impulsivity has also been the focus of research (Khurana et al., 2012). This study found that acting without thinking and delayed discounting were significant mediators upon the effect of early sexual initiation. Sensation seeking, however, was not a significant mediator. The finding suggests that the two different dimensions of impulsivity, acting without thinking and sensation seeking, act independently of one another. This makes sense, since studies have shown that acting without thinking and delayed discounting both share an underlying weakness in working memory; but sensation seeking, as further explained below, is positively associated with working memory. Higher rates of delayed discounting result in the tendency to pursue immediate gratification, shown to be correlated with low socioeconomic status, which may explain why early sexual initiation is greater among certain racial and ethnic groups with disproportionate poverty rates. And the detrimental effects of poverty upon children's working memory has been well documented (Evans & Rosenbaum, 2008; Hackman & Farah, 2009).

Adolescent Development and Impulsivity

Adolescence is a period of development often marked by expanding boundaries and testing limits, which can result in impulsive and risky behaviors (Whelan et al., 2012). The brain continues to develop in adolescence, especially in the area of frontal cortical functioning that governs avoidance and self-control (Ernst et al., 2006), a critical part of executive functioning. However, during adolescence, the subcortical motivation system develops rapidly and results in an imbalance between the higher-order cortical functions (the residence of executive functioning) and the subcortical limbic system (the residence of reward processing and motivation). As a result, there is a rise in impulsivity and risk-taking during adolescence that is weakly governed by executive functioning (Romer et al., 2011). The imbalance between these two systems leads to risk taking and other externalizing behaviors.

Studies have shown that those with ADHD, chronic use of cocaine, and alcohol dependence all have longer stop-signal reaction times, considered a significant marker for impulse control (Whelan et al., 2012). The stop-signal task demands that an individual stop a motor response already initiated. The use of drugs during adolescence can produce long-lasting toxic effects upon the developing brain, especially in the frontal lobe area. Therefore, when an individual with weakness already in executive functioning arrives at adolescence, the imbalance between the cortical and subcortical systems is accentuated. This may be one reason why those with ADHD are at greater risk for substance abuse during adolescence and might explain the difference between problematic and nonproblematic drug use.

Sensation seeking and acting without thinking are two dimensions of impulsivity. The former is more about seeking novel and exciting experiences, while the latter is linked to deficits in executive functioning. Indeed, studies have shown sensation seeking to be positively related to IQ and acting without thinking negatively related to IQ and executive functioning (Horn, Dolan, Elliott, Deakin, & Woodruff, 2003). If, for example, risk-taking behavior in adolescence is the result of sensation seeking, it ought to decline with age as activation of the striatal-subcortical systems declines. On the other hand, if acting without thinking is a result of poor executive functioning, it will likely remain constant, and more problem-related behaviors will tend find their way into adulthood.

Experimenting with drugs as the result of sensation seeking is not the same as using drugs because one either cannot understand or minimizes the long-term consequences of their use. One long-term study found that adolescents high in sensation seeking experimented with alcohol in the adolescent years, but their alcohol use did not progress in frequency during the follow-up years; whereas those with preexisting weakness in working memory increased their frequency of alcohol use over the course of four years (Khurana et al., 2013). Put another way, sensation seeking can be considered a more controlled form of impulsivity due to its relationship with greater executive functioning and differentiated from a more dysfunctional impulsivity that results from deficits in executive functioning (Khurana et al., 2013; Romer et al., 2011). Not all adolescent risk taking is the result of poor executive functioning. Most important for those working with adolescents is to try and determine the cause of their impulsivity.

Adolescent impulsivity and suicidality. The pathway to adolescent suicide is not entirely known, but impulsivity is thought to heighten the risk, even in the absence of depression (Javdani, Sadeh, & Verona, 2011). Nevertheless, depression remains one of the major drivers for adolescent suicide. The neuroscience of depression shows that it reduces prefrontal cortex activation, previously emphasized as the area that governs executive functioning (Herrington et al., 2010). This is why depression can result in problems with memory, attention, and problem solving and consequently increase the risk of acting impulsively. Adolescents, whose prefrontal cortexes are still developing, suffer greater risks from depression, because a not-fully-formed prefrontal cortex is further compromised by the mood disorder and can lead to even greater emotional dysregulation.

Another suggested pathway is that adolescents with poor executive functioning engage in repeated risk taking with painful outcomes that increase their pain tolerance and make suicide a more tolerable option (Joiner, 2009). Many adolescents will say the major buffer against their committing suicide is that they are afraid to do it. This may be less true for those who have built up a tolerance against pain. In addition, frequent risk taking can lead to disappointing outcomes, which increases a sense of hopelessness, considered a major factor in the risk of suicide. Social support, however, has been shown to weaken impulsivity and serve as a protective factor in suicide (Kleiman, Riskind, Schaefer, & Weingarden, 2012).

Adolescent impulsivity and delinquency. Impulsivity has long been considered to play a pivotal role in juvenile offending. The dimensions of impulsivity that have received the most consideration are urgency, lack of premeditation, and sensation seeking. The first two are more often caused by reactive aggression, the kind often seen in schools. Those with negative urgency are prone to hostile attribution of neutral stimuli, believing, for example, that when someone makes eye contact with them, that person is really out to get them. Someone with a lack of premeditation is especially prone to criminal and aggressive acts, because such acts often provide immediate gratification and require little planning (Derefinko, DeWall, Metze, Walsh, & Lynam, 2011). Sensation seeking, on the other hand, is more related to proactive criminality, where certain acts are planned to give excitement and novelty. Punching someone in the school hallway because of a certain look that was perceived as hostile is not the same as planting a stink bomb in the school cafeteria. Lack of premeditation (acting without thinking) was found to be strongly related to intimate partner violence (Derefinko et al., 2011) and is a primary dimension of antisocial personality disorder (DeShong & Kurtz, 2013), the driving force behind chronic delinquency. Sensation seeking also plays a role in antisocial personality disorder, but it seems to have a weaker effect than lack of premeditation.

Trait Versus State Impulsivity

The role of impulsivity in the formation of antisocial personality disorder has raised questions about a trait-based theory of impulsivity and led to investigations of the person–context nexus for criminal behavior (Neumann, Barker, Koot, & Maughan, 2010; Zimmerman, 2010). Contextual factors such as neighborhood and family have long been thought to play a major role in the development of antisocial behavior (Leventhal & Brooks-Gunn, 2000). And the school is considered part of the neighborhood.

But in a trait-based theory of impulsivity and crime, contextual factors would play less of a role. In other words, the influence of a lack of self-control (impulsivity) would not vary across social contexts. A highly impulsive individual will tend to engage in criminal behavior regardless of whether his neighborhood and school offer greater or lesser opportunity for such behavior.

The other side of the argument is that environmental factors play a significant role in delinquency because they have an effect upon the formation of self-control. Previously mentioned was the effect of poverty on executive functioning. There is also a body of research that suggests lower levels of supervision also contribute to delinquency (Jones & Lynam, 2008). There is little doubt that those with lower levels of self-control have higher rates of offending.

The greatest effect, however, for adolescent delinquency seems to be the interaction between high levels of impulsivity and contextual factors that provide low levels of supervision and that offer greater opportunity for criminal activity. Here, delinquency is based neither purely on individual nor purely on neighborhood characteristics. Wikström (2004) put it most succinctly by saying: "[Crime] is always dependent on who is in what setting; it is not about the kinds of individuals or kinds of settings but about kinds of individuals in kinds of settings" (p. 19). To put it in real-world terms, highly impulsive adolescents in schools that are poorly managed and poorly supervised will tend to have the highest amount of externalizing behaviors such as aggression and other forms of delinquent behavior. The good news is that schools can work on both factors by teaching students ways to increase their working memory and overall executive functioning while at the same time engineering the school environment to create less opportunities for impulsive students to act out.

ADHD and Impulsivity

Nothing torments a teacher more than the hyperactive student. These students often produce feelings of frustration, as their behavior is constant and diminishes the learning environment. ADHD is highly comorbid with learning disability and other externalizing disorders such as oppositional defiant disorder and conduct disorder. When comorbidity exists, symptomatic behavior is worse and more resistant to interventions. The point has already been made that weakness in executive functioning, particularly in working memory, is a major cause of impulsivity. If there is more than one disorder impinging upon cognitive functioning, impulsivity will be heightened. ADHD, left untreated, interferes with learning, and the child develops a learning disability. Or the reverse—those with lower IQs will already have impaired executive functioning that manifests itself in impulsive and inattentive behaviors (Buchmann, Gierow, Reis, & Haessler, 2011). Those with ADHD are more likely to have tried nicotine and illicit substances (Whelan et al., 2012).

Earlier in the chapter, mention was made about how ADHD causes interference in two domains: the social and the academic. Teachers are faced with the challenge of working with those with ADHD on both impairments. Interventions have to target deficiencies in working memory and as well as social skills. The learning of prosocial skills and problem-solving skills has been shown to reduce conduct problems in those with ADHD (Andrade & Tannock, 2014). The same argument about learning disability and inattention can be made about peer difficulties and lack of social skills. It is quite true that those with ADHD develop early negative patterns of behavior toward peers, especially if comorbidity results in oppositionality, defiance, rule breaking and aggression. Early on, peers learn to avoid these students, and consequently there is diminished opportunity for social exchanges—not only with peers but also with teachers (Dodge et al., 2003). If inattentive and hyperactive students suffer from social exclusion, they are not exposed to positive peer interactions and do not have the opportunity to develop prosocial skills that could serve as a protective function against negative interactions with peers (Andrade & Tannock, 2014). From a social learning perspective, these students are not exposed to appropriate models of social interactions.

Schools, however, could provide such models with the hope that it serves as one form of learning for prosocial skills. More often than not, schools will pressure parents into medication that may be recommended if a student's impulsivity shows significant interference in learning. Medication may serve to diminish hyperactivity and increase attention, but it will not automatically cause someone to develop study and social skills. These will have to be learned like any other skill, through instruction, modeling, and practice.

Understanding Impulsivity from an Attachment Perspective

Understanding impulsivity from an attachment perspective is not so easy, since much of the literature has been dominated by neurophysiological theories about temperament. Indeed, the previous part of this chapter dedicated considerable space to understanding the neuroscience of impulsivity. There is a tension between temperament theory and attachment theory. Temperament theories tend to explain impulsivity and dysregulation of emotion and behavior as traits that make the behavior less context specific. Attachment theory, on the other hand, emphasizes interpersonal factors, especially the infant–caregiver dyad, as responsible for assembling IWMs that consequently determine the dysregulation of affect and behavior.

Simply put, an insecure early environment and the threat of loss will heighten emotional reactivity and will manifest in other environments (Vaughn, Bost, & van IJzendoorn, 2008). Attachment theory posits that the primary caregiver plays a crucial role in regulating arousal patterns in both the infant and the toddler. No doubt, a child is born with a certain temperament, the result of genetic inheritance and quality of the pregnancy, but the caregiver also determines temperament in how she reacts to and regulates the child's arousal patterns. In a study where children watched fear-inducing clips, highly reactive children (those who become motorically aroused and distressed when presented with unfamiliar stimuli) with secure relationships showed less skin conductance than less reactive children did, while highly reactive children with insecure relationships showed more skin conductance (Gilissen, Koolstra, van IJzendoorn, Bakermans-Kranenburg, & van der Veer, 2007) This is a very interesting finding and perhaps indicates that attachment security is more important for highly reactive children than for those who are less reactive. This book has consistently maintained the tension between person versus context, nature versus nurture, but also firmly posits that a secure environment, not only in infancy but later on even into adolescence, can make a difference. With this in mind, we turn our attention to Stefan, the impulsive student from our vignette.

It is not surprising that we are told at the very beginning of the vignette that Stefan's impulsive behaviors have become more intense and pervasive. He is now an adolescent. Previously, the chapter spoke about changes in the adolescent brain that will cause an increase in impulsivity, especially in those who suffer from impairment in executive functioning. Neuroscientifically, Stefan's subcortical striatal systems, responsible for reward processing and motivation, are significantly more activated than his prefrontal cortex, the home of working memory. Apparently, Stefan received little if any nonpharmacological interventions during his school years to reduce his impulsivity. At the beginning, the vignette seems to imply that Stefan's parents are in accord with the school—at least, they agree that Stefan has shown an increase in impulsivity. However, later in the vignette, it is clear that the school and his parents are at odds as to the cause of his problems and how to help Stefan. Even though the parents agree that his behavior has worsened at home, they blame the school for the deterioration, which suggests insecurity on the parents' part. Sometimes, schools are to blame, but this is more often true when behavior does not cross situations. Stefan has suffered from impulsive behavior for a long time, and it occurs in different settings. This dynamic has been present before, but it bears repeating. When parents constantly blame teachers, it is often a projection of the parents' own insecurity. Unfortunately, teachers tend to get defensive in such situations, and this is not very productive. A secure teacher can mentalize and understand that parents casting blame on the school is a manifestation of the parents' own insecure attachment history. In doing so, empathy would be the response, not defensiveness. If Stefan was a highly reactive infant in an insecure environment, then the path toward impulsivity was laid bare.

Punching one of his friends after he accidentally tripped Stefan is a good example of negative urgency, the tendency to act rashly in response to intense negative affect and to attribute hostile intentions to neutral stimuli. Getting tripped, accidentally or not, would cause negative affect in most people and create an impulse to act aggressively against the person who tripped them. Those with good impulse control are able to stop an already initiated motor response. Stefan is not. The reader will remember that those with ADHD have longer stop-signal reaction times. By the time Stefan stops, the damage has been done. The same dynamic is at work in the play-fighting incident. Play fighting is a bad activity in general, but especially for someone who is impulsive. Crossing the line is just too easy because of the inability to regulate emotion. Anyone working with Stefan should try and implement activities that are prosocial and can substitute for the pleasure he gets out of play fighting—perhaps something like karate. If one assumes that Stefan's apology after the tripping incident is genuine, then he is easily differentiated from a student who is more conduct disordered and would derive pleasure out of punching someone and, when confronted, would easily say the other student deserved it. The fact that his ADHD is not comorbid with another externalizing disorder makes for a better prognosis. Much of the vignette deals with interpersonal impulsivity. However, it should come as no surprise that Stefan has schoolwork impulsivity—his many incompletes are likely the result of a lack of perseverance.

Finally, a word about medication and other suggested interventions for Stefan. Stefan's parents took him to a specialist, who we have to assume was a child and adolescent psychiatrist. (As an aside, it is not easy these days to find a child and adolescent psychiatrist, let alone one who will take insurance.) The psychiatrist confirms the diagnosis of ADHD and recommends both pharmacological and nonpharmacological treatments. The recommendation of a psychostimulant (in this case, Ritalin) is standard practice. Psychostimulants are designed to release serotonin, the inhibitory neurotransmitter. Some people are confused as to why it is helpful to give stimulants to someone who is already hyperactive—but the intervention is designed to stimulate the release of neurotransmitters responsible for inhibition (serotonin) and attention (dopamine). Stefan's parents are not alone in their resistance to medication and seem to be weighing the benefits and long-term costs of his taking the drug. Their decision-making process seems anything but impulsive, in contrast to how their son makes decisions. Even though the heritability index for impulsivity is rather high, it seems in this case that Stefan's parents can serve as role models for how to make informed decisions. There is a cost and benefit to every drug. If there is a lot of interference in both the learning and interpersonal realms, medication is probably recommended in conjunction with other interventions. Some cognitive-behavioral therapy (CBT) skills could help Stefan, but without medication the effectiveness of those interventions may be minimal. Studies have shown mixed results for combined treatment (medication plus CBT) versus CBT alone versus medication alone (Mongia & Hechtman, 2012; Nathan & Gorman, 2015; Weiss et al., 2012). Perhaps a negotiating point between the school and the parents could be to first try nonpharmacological interventions, and if those don't work, then medication could be added. The challenge for the school is to work collaboratively with the parents, listen to their ideas, and design an intervention plan everyone can agree to. It will not be easy, but the school has at its disposal ways and means to help students with impulsivity. Let us now examine helpful and not-so-helpful approaches.

UNDERSTANDING TEACHER INTERVENTIONS FOR IMPULSIVE STUDENTS FROM BOTH ATTACHMENT AND PEDAGOGICAL PERSPECTIVES

Mr. Jakubowitz: "This Student's Antics Are Giving Our School a Black Eye!"

Mr. Sy Jakubowitz, a highly esteemed social studies teacher at West Queens High School, has been educating students successfully for over 30 years. "In all my years," he declared to colleagues, "I've never seen a kid so hyper and impulsive as Stefan. I think that his parents have instilled in him a sense of entitlement—he thinks he can do whatever he wants in this school and break any rule with impunity!" Many other teachers in the school, especially those who have taught Stefan, concur. The mere mention of his name sends a shudder through the teacher's lounge and soon enough, other teachers begin recounting Stefan's misbehaviors and impulsive acts.

One teacher, Mrs. Johansen, who had Stefan in math in 9th grade, related an incident that occurred during exam week in late June. She had placed a large floor fan in one corner of the room to help the students keep cool during the exam. Just before the lunch bell rang, Stefan jumped out of his seat, approached the fan and, before Mrs. Johansen could react, poked his index finger between the wires of the protective screen and into the path of the large rotating metal fan blades. As he was being prepared for transport to the emergency room, Mrs. Johansen asked, "Stefan, why did you do that?" To which Stefan replied, matter-of-factly, "I wanted to know what it would feel like, so I just did it."

Mr. Jakubowitz feels strongly that incidents like this confirm that Stefan needs a more secure environment and more intensive support than can be provided at West Queens. He feels that because Stefan has been recently classified as other health impaired, a disability category frequently selected for students who evidence symptoms of hyperactivity and impulsivity, Stefan's aggressive, antisocial behaviors will be excused. They will be ascribed instead to his disability and, as a consequence, Stefan will not be held accountable.

As Stefan's social studies teacher, Mr. Jakubowitz has firsthand experience with his impulsivity. He reports that several times each week, Stefan needs to be removed from the classroom for his provocative, disruptive behaviors: repeatedly mocking the teacher, demonstrating his jump shot and inadvertently knocking down several ceiling tiles, getting out of his desk and walking around the room without permission, interrupting other students and the teacher, telling inappropriate jokes aloud in class for the "shock effect," writing vulgar expressions on the white board, singing a pop tune aloud in the middle of a lesson, ripping up an assignment sheet and breaking his pencil—the list goes on!

Mr. Jakubowitz firmly believes that a teacher's job is to teach the subject matter, not to have to play the role of parent or therapist. He feels that he is being asked to change his teaching style, a style that has served him and his students well for 30 years, in order to accommodate the poor social skills and bad behavior of a few, like Stefan, who are "protected" by IDEA and the influence of wealthy parents who threaten to litigate if they don't get their way. Mr. Jakubowitz feels that Stefan could learn to control his impulsive tendencies if they were properly punished rather than excused. He believes that children learn to appreciate the consequences of their choices when they are held accountable for them. "Many adolescents behave impulsively—that's expected behavior, to a degree," he asserts. "That doesn't mean they have a psychological disorder. They learn best, as we all do, from their mistakes, and having to deal with the consequences. If we keep finding excuses for Stefan's poor choices and bad behavior, we are doing him and the school a disservice. Right now, his antics are giving the school a black eye!" Mr. Jakubowitz is adamant about not bending the rules for Stefan or providing extraordinary accommodations for his misbehavior. "If he acts out, he goes out!" he insists.

Mr. Jakubowitz from an Attachment Perspective

From Mr. Jakubowitz, we learn many more specifics about Stefan's impulsive behavior and how difficult he can be to manage in the classroom. The teacher seems like a reasonable man. When he says that Stefan is the worst he's seen in 30 years, it may be true, and, if true, would support the case for medication. Two comments by Mr. Jakubowitz are important for understanding further the psychological implications of Stefan's behavior: The student has a sense of entitlement and can break any rule with impunity. The sense of entitlement gives a clue to attachment issues. We have to assume that Stefan was a highly reactive child whose parents may have overindulged him in order to deal with his difficult temperament. In other words, a highly reactive child may have evoked a very intrusive kind of parenting that diminished the security of the early environment. Children whose parents overindulge them in order to deal with their problematic behaviors will generally grow up with a sense of entitlement. The fact that Stefan can break school rules without consequences is equally disconcerting. Research has shown that contingency management in the form of reward for good behavior and punishment for bad behavior along with response cost ("If you commit the crime, you pay the fine") is considered one of the most effective interventions for those with ADHD when compared to other CBT techniques such as self-instruction, problem solving, and self-reinforcement (Loren et al., 2015; Pfiffner & Haack, 2014; Power et al., 2012).

In previous scenarios where we have seen teachers who are very rule oriented, we have speculated that they had an avoidant attachment history that results in a dismissing classification as an adult. While Mr. Jakubowitz might fit this classification, his insistence that there need to be some consequences for Stefan's behavior should be taken seriously.

The incident with the fan in Mrs. Johansen's class is a good example of impulsivity that results from sensation seeking. Stefan is not the only boy to have wondered what it would be like to stick one's finger in a fan. However, most boys, unlike Stefan, would consider the possible consequences and decide that the sensation one could derive from such a risky behavior is probably not worth it, due to the possible harmful consequences. Stefan is not able to go through this decision-making process, but the incident could be used to help him make better decisions in the future.

What's the best way to deal with Stefan? For Mr. Jakubowitz, the solution is clear: "He's outta here." The teacher's solution deserves consideration. One could make the case that Stefan is a danger to himself and others and needs a more restrictive environment where he can be closely monitored. Besides, the school has tolerated the behavior for some time, possibly tried different ways to work with Stefan and his parents, and nothing has helped. Mr. Jakubowitz's description of Stefan's classroom behavior would make any teacher shudder. Yet, unless the argument can be made that Stefan poses a possible danger to himself and others, removal from the school will most likely be a huge hurdle, especially because of his diagnosis with a disability—though Mr. Jakubowitz sees this diagnosis as something of a ruse to excuse the student's disruptive classroom antics.

This is where the teacher comes closest to a classification of dismissing. He simply does not raise the question as to whether there is anything that can help him and the student to improve. Mr. Jakubowitz makes a cogent argument: He is a teacher, not a therapist. Hopefully, this book has made the distinction between a teacher who mentalizes and a therapist. Because they work intimately with children, teachers need as much self-awareness as humanly possible to gain insight into how their interactions with a particular student may make the situation better or worse. This is where Mr. Jakubowitz falls a bit short. The conflict is only about the student! One interesting piece of information would be to know if Stefan's behavior is any better in another classroom or environment. If so, that would enable Mr. Jakubowitz to learn from such difference, but he may not be open to it. On the other hand, if Stefan's behavior is no different in any other context, then Mr. Jakubowitz's solution that a contextual change, in the form of removing Stefan from the school, would carry more weight.

The vignette ends pretty much where it began, with the teacher's emphasis on not making excuses for Stefan, holding him to consequences, and not being beholden to his wealthy parents. The intricate issue here is that Stefan's disability results in diminished executive functioning that often prevents him from linking actions and consequences. If the school can develop a plan, perhaps through his individualized education program, to fortify working memory, there may be chance to then build on that with contingency management and other forms of behavioral control. One can imagine Mr. Jakubowitz arguing, "He's been given enough chances." But if you want Stefan to understand actions and consequences, then interventions are needed to strengthen the part of his brain that governs such connections.

Mr. Jakubowitz from a Pedagogical Perspective

Mr. Jakubowitz is plainly unsympathetic, almost contemptuous toward Stefan, which runs contrary to the notion that teachers should, above all else, develop caring relationships with their students (Noddings, 2005; Smith, 2012). Likewise, Mr. Jakubowitz seems to think he understands Stefan's culture or family structure with his suggestion that Stefan's parents have instilled in Stefan a sense of entitlement. This presumption is at odds with the recommendation of Freire (1970) and Bruner (1996), who both stressed the importance of truly understanding one's own culture as well as that of one's students. Mr. Jakubowitz does not seem willing to take the time to really get to know Stefan and his parents and their perspectives.

Furthermore, he challenges the notion that impulsive behaviors, like those displayed by Stefan, are evidence of a neurological condition. Most adolescents, he asserts, act impulsively from time to time. He seems to suggest that pathologizing these behaviors simply provides Stefan an excuse to continue to engage in them. Consequently, Mr. Jakubowitz is opposed to providing accommodations that Stefan's individualized education plan must invariably require. Having adopted this perception of Stefan and his impulsive behavior, Mr. Jakubowitz will certainly not empower Stefan to identify his academic strengths and weaknesses, advance his own learning, or to develop socially and emotionally, which is one of the tenets of our recommended pedagogical framework.

Unfortunately, in creating a schism between himself and Stefan, he is unable to help Stefan make meaningful improvements in his academic and social life. He has missed a unique opportunity to work effectively with Stefan, because he has decided to view Stefan as a willful, manipulative, and incorrigible child.

Mrs. Kugler: "Stefan Can't Help Acting on Impulse; It's Clearly the Cause of Something Beyond His Control"

Mrs. Kugler, Stefan's new 10th-grade "special" math teacher, has almost 28 years of experience working with students with disabilities similar to Stefan's. In fact, she has helped many students, mostly boys, diagnosed with ADHD combined type and hyperactive-impulsive type, to succeed in math, and even come to like it. She has already established an effective rapport with Stefan by welcoming him as a constituent in her classroom community and showing him that she genuinely cares about his learning and, more importantly, his well-being. As Kohn (1996) has encouraged, Mrs. Kugler thinks about Stefan's academic and social future—not just for the present academic year, or while she is his teacher, but where he will be in five or ten years. She finds that this "forward thinking" inspires her do more to help not just Stefan but all her students succeed in school and in life.

Because she is concerned about the success of all her students and wants to pro-

vide effective instruction and behavioral intervention, Mrs. Kugler has purpose-fully learned all she can about impulsive students. She has completed a graduate course that focused on emotional and behavioral disorders and has consulted with the school psychologist, who specializes in working with students who display inattention and impulsivity. As a result of her study and experience, she has learned to distinguish intentionality from impulsivity. In other words, she is able to differentiate a student who exhibits conduct disorders from one, like Stefan, who displays inattentive and impulsive behaviors. She truly believes that "Stefan can't help acting on impulse; it's clearly the cause of something beyond his control—perhaps it's biological, not intentional or malicious behavior!"

Consequently, Mrs. Kugler employs patience as she works with Stefan. She understands that he cannot sit for long periods of time or he will become anxious and fidgety. Likewise, he is unable to persevere and complete tasks of long duration that require sustained focus. To help Stefan benefit from her math class, Mrs. Kugler breaks longer tasks into smaller, more manageable ones, provides fewer problems for him to solve, changes her instructional methods to provide some variety, and allows him to move around in the class as long as he isn't disruptive. When Stefan was first introduced to Mrs. Kugler's class, some of the other students expressed their apprehension. To be sure, there was an adjustment period during which Stefan challenged his new teacher, but because she was so accepting and patient with him, Stefan began to focus on her instruction—and began to learn. As he experienced success in her math class, Stefan's attitude began to change, and he saw himself as a capable math student, not a "dummy" incapable of learning. Last month, Mrs. Kugler enlisted his help as a tutor, providing support to her struggling 9th-grade math students. This new responsibility seems to have produced a noticeable change in Stefan's tendency to behave impulsively. He has adopted Mrs. Kugler's model of teaching and exhibits patience and a caring attitude toward his younger tutees. When asked about the reason behind this recent behavior change, Stefan responded, "Mrs. Kugler took the time to really get to know me. I don't mean to act up. Sometimes I just can't help it. But she's helped me feel better about myself. Now I know I'm not dumb; I can learn math and I can help other kids learn, too!"

Mrs. Kugler from an Attachment Perspective

Mrs. Kugler's success with Stefan seems almost too good to be true. It does, however, support the basic premise of this book, that the attachment quality between student and teacher is the key to successful intervention, especially with students who exhibit difficult behaviors. One cannot underestimate the value of Mrs. Kugler's experience of working with student with disabilities. Unlike Mr. Jakubowitz, she does not expect conformity to an unchangeable environment but understands that disability is a part of diversity, a different way of being in the world. In order to allow students with a disability to flourish, certain accommodations to the learning environment can and should be made. This kind of flexibility allows the teacher to explore impulsivity through reading and then trying different ways for Stefan to feel comfortable in her classroom and become a productive learner.

She is the antithesis of a highly reactive individual. All of these qualities point to a teacher who is secure-autonomous in her attachment style. Unlike Mr. Jakubowitz, she does not feel threatened or a loss of control by experimenting with different methods and interventions to establish rapport with Stefan and, consequently, to have the influence that will guide him academically. What might look like loss of control to Mr. Jakubowitz is in reality the opposite. A teacher gains influence and control by ceding to the students' needs, not losing patience, never giving up, and always exhibiting a caring attitude. She may very well represent the attachment figure that Stefan always needed: someone who would regulate his impulsivity and dysregulation by responding calmly and with careful consideration of the underlying issues. She is able to mentalize and does not for a moment take Stefan's behavior personally, because she does not perceive it as intentional.

The establishment of genuine rapport with Stefan would be severely compromised if his ADHD were comorbid with conduct disorder. Because of her knowledge and experience, Mrs. Kugler is able distinguish a student like Stefan who wants relationships in spite of his impulsivity from a student who is sociopathic, manipulative, and lacking in empathy. Nevertheless, Stefan feels the need to "challenge" his new teacher. Why? Perhaps Bowlby's theory about the formation of IWMs can help explain this tendency. Stefan has a long history of rejection by both peers and teachers. It is quite possible that early on he formed an IWM that he is basically unlikable; that he will always be rejected. If so, he will behave in ways to evoke that response from others. Mr. Jakubowitz represents a "successful" encounter in the sense that he conforms to what Stefan expects. While this may lead Stefan to feeling that he has a certain power and control, the psychological consequences are devastating: his self-esteem is in the gutter.

Mrs. Kugler, however, is the exception. Her reactions to Stefan do not conform to his expectations, but rather she is accepting and patient in the face of his challenging behaviors. This is the turning point in the relationship. He begins to learn and starts on the path to self-confidence and positive self-esteem. The experience of being a tutor fortifies his belief in himself, and his IWM is shaken to the core. Mrs. Kugler's establishment of a secure relationship with Stefan allows him to have productive relationships with others. His impulsivity will always lurk in the background, but in the foreground will be his belief that he is capable of learning and helping others. To continue to do this, Stefan will have to find ways to moderate his impulsivity, and by doing so will reap long-term benefits over immediate gratification, a sign of increased executive functioning.

Mrs. Kugler from a Pedagogical Perspective

In stark contrast with Mr. Jakubowitz's pedagogical style, Mrs. Kugler has established an effective rapport with Stefan. To be sure, she has had training in working with highly impulsive, hyperactive students like Stefan; nevertheless, part of her success in working with Stefan must be attributed to her "certainty, positivity, and unity of self and moral goals" (Stout, 2005, p. 194), which is one of the critical elements in our pedagogical framework.

From the little we can glean from her vignette, we can deduce that she possesses a sense of her own identity; she is honest with herself about her lack of knowledge in how to work effectively with students who exhibit chronically impulsive, inattentive behaviors, and she has taken the initiative to learn from the school psychologist and through relevant professional development opportunities.

Based on this expanded knowledge, she feels confident that Stefan's impulsivity is not intentional but rather is most likely due to a biological disorder, and she responds accordingly. Certainly, Stefan "challenged" Mrs. Kugler, as he did all of his teachers, upon their first meeting, but she passed his test, understanding Stefan's need to do so. Her patient responses and consistent kindnesses affirmed her genuine caring for Stefan and her respect for him as a person. She fully accepted Stefan, from the very first day, as a viable member of her classroom community, and that acceptance proved to be a breakthrough in engaging Stefan as a math student.

This caring teacher–student relationship comports with our assertion that such a rapport is an essential component of any successful pedagogy (Noddings, 2005; Smith, 2012). Most assuredly, Mrs. Kugler employed our fifth element of a sound pedagogy as she helped Stefan identify his strengths and weaknesses in mathematics and provided strategies to address his deficits.

In accepting Stefan, and providing him with effective learning strategies, Mrs. Kugler enticed and motivated him to strive and finally succeed in math. Now he could see himself as someone capable of learning and mastering a challenging subject. Furthermore, he could even impart this knowledge to others, signaling a real breakthrough for Stefan (Tompkins, 1996, p. xvi)!

As noted earlier and in keeping with our sixth pedagogical element, Mrs. Kugler enrolled in courses and took advantage of opportunities to advance her knowledge of students who are impulsive and in so doing demonstrated that she is a lifelong learner and will cultivate her love of learning to stay relevant in her field.

Finally, unlike Mr. Jakubowitz, as a result of her relationship with Stefan, Mrs. Kugler was able to work with him successfully and thus enable him to make meaningful changes in his life (Smith, 1994, p. 10).

EFFECTIVE TEACHER RESPONSES

- "Whenever possible, avoid steps with more than one instruction and also avoid giving multipart assignments. Allow the child to finish one assignment or follow one direction at a time before offering him the next.
- Designate a specific location where the child should deposit completed assignments.
- If the child is capable at this stage, teach her to keep a daily homework journal. Or prepare a copy of the homework assignments to give to the child at the end of the day.
- Give shorter but more frequent assignments to increase success rates. Break long-term projects into short-term assignments. Reward the child for com-

pleting each step. Remember, confidence builds through repeated successful experiences.

- Ask parents to help the child get organized each night before school. Encourage them to develop a checklist so the child's clothes, books, assignments, and so on are ready for the next morning.
- If necessary, have the child finish all assignments at school.
- Require the child to clean out her desk each day.
- Use boxes, bins, or other organizers to help the child separate and store various items.
- Encourage the use of binders or individual folders to help keep schoolwork organized. Set up a special place for tools, materials, and books. Organization and routine are critical to success.
- If possible, do not place the student near distracting stimuli, such as an air conditioner, heater, high traffic areas, doors, or windows. Create a "stimuli-reduced" study area. Let all students be allowed to go to this area so that the student with ADHD will not feel self-conscious or singled out.
- Avoid planning numerous transitions and changes throughout the day. Clearly list and explain the daily schedule to help the child deal with change.
- Stand near the student while lecturing. This is called "proximity control."
- Try to preempt the child's behavior, especially during changes in the schedule. Inform the child of the change about 5 minutes beforehand and define your expectations for appropriate behavior.
- As appropriate to the age and situation, identify strengths in the child you can publicly announce or praise. This will help the other students develop a more positive perception of the child.
- If the child takes any mediation, protect her privacy (e.g., by avoiding publicly reminding her to go down to the nurse's office to take it).
- Encourage the use of word processing, typing, spell checking, and other computer skills.
- Create chances for peer interaction and cooperative learning for academic tasks that do not require sitting for long periods of time.
- An effective management system concentrates on a few behaviors at a time, with new behavior patterns added when the student masters the first ones. Reinforce appropriate behavior with something the student is willing to work for (or to avoid). For example, give or remove points immediately, according to the behavior, so the child understands why he is or is not being rewarded. While older children may be willing to work toward a deferred reward, younger children generally need more immediate reinforcement." (Pierangelo & Giuliani, 2001 pp. 30-32; 35, reproduced with permission, Research Press)

How to Help a Child Control Impulsive Behavior

"Avoid placing yourself in a power struggle with an impulsive child. Remember that impulsivity is like energy waiting for a catalyst (kind of like a landmine)—

don't make yourself the catalyst! Approach in a nonpunitive, nonthreatening, and nonadversarial manner. Try not to get into an "either/or" situation where you issue a request and immediately follow it up with the threat of a consequence. Don't get lulled into the belief that the harsher you sound the more they will comply; often times, it's just the opposite.

Give them room for healthy impulse discharge when they need it. One of the ways that students burn off their impulsivity is through physical activity, listening to music, playing video games, walking away when you are trying to have a conversation with them, and so on. Sometimes this can prevent a meltdown and preserve a channel of communication once they return. Try not to interfere with their access to these routes especially when you pick up signs of imminent impulse breakthrough.

The underlying issues are one of the keys to helping them control their impulsivity. As their world becomes more demanding, children experience more pressure and potential for impulsivity. Many times, impulse breakthrough follows a distinct pattern. Take note of these patterns and gently bring it to their attention. Suggest that they can take several deep breaths, give themselves time to cool down, or use relaxation exercises when they feel their impulses building.

Listen carefully and offer a little advice. Most students don't have patience for long and involved explanations about themselves. Teachers must strive to make sense out of their impulsive behavior without sounding like a know-it-all. No matter how ill-advised or irrational the behavior, there is some rational thread embedded in the story. Our job is to listen carefully, find the thread, and make our students aware of it in a nonthreatening manner. The more that we can designate the steps that lead to their acting out, the more able they will be to see it coming, and take preventive action before the point of no return." (Richfield, reproduced with permission, n.d.)

MANAGING IMPULSIVE BEHAVIORS

There are a number of coping strategies available to help students control impulsive behaviors. Gratz (2010) has provided four suggested strategies that therapists and teachers might impart to students who struggle with impulsivity.

1. Distract Yourself

"Urges to engage in impulsive behaviors may be very strong and hard to cope with. However, these urges generally pass fairly quickly. Therefore, if you can distract yourself when experiencing an urge, you may be able to sit with an urge until it passes. Fortunately, there are a number of healthy distraction strategies that may be helpful in riding out a strong urge or emotional experience.

2. Replace Your Impulsive Behavior with a Healthy Behavior

Even though impulsive behaviors may lead to long-term problems, in the moment, they are serving a purpose. For example, they may help you cope with emotional pain.

Therefore, one way of preventing impulsive behaviors is finding another, healthier behavior that may serve that same purpose. For example, you may seek out a friend or write about your emotions. Try to find a healthy way of relieving emotional pain that will not have long-term negative consequences for you.

3. Identify the Long-Term Negative Consequences of an Impulsive Behavior

We tend to be driven by the short-term consequences of a behavior. That is, people usually repeat behaviors that work well for us in the moment, regardless of what their long-term negative consequences are. Therefore, it can be useful to increase your awareness of the long-term negative consequences of a behavior. One way to do this is by identifying the short- and long-term pros and cons of a behavior.

4. Change the Consequences of a Behavior

People continue to engage in impulsive behaviors because they do something positive in the moment (for example, taking away anxiety or fear). One way to reduce the likelihood of an impulsive behavior is to take away its short-term positive effect. As soon as you engage in an impulsive behavior, immediately conduct a chain analysis to connect with why you engaged in that behavior in the first place. This will put you back in touch with all those emotions that you were trying to get away from in the first place and force you to face and cope with them in another, healthy way. It can also be very helpful to reward yourself when you don't engage in an impulsive behavior.

Impulsive behaviors can be very difficult to cope with; however, it is possible. Identify some impulsive behaviors that you would like to change, and next time you notice an urge to engage in those behaviors coming on, try one of the coping strategies above. It may be difficult at first; however, with every success, it will become easier and easier." (Gratz, 2010, n.p.)

Two Interventions for Impulsive Behavior

Teach Waiting and Self-Control Skills

"Impulsivity may be decreased by teaching students appropriate waiting behaviors, and by a reinforcement plan for appropriate responding behavior. For example, after an assignment has been given, a teacher may teach a student to place her hands on her desk, establish eye contact with the teacher, and listen for directions. The teacher should praise the student for demonstrating these waiting behaviors.

Students who manifest impulsive behavior will benefit from training in social skills such as self-control. At the same time, students may be taught relaxation techniques. Reinforcement will increase the possibility that a student will demonstrate behaviors that are alternatives to impulsivity. The student just described learned social skills through direct instruction and reinforcement for use of the skills to replace impulsive behavior. Schaub (1990) as cited in Zirpoli (2008), also found that targeting behaviors for intervention that were positive and incompatible with undesirable behaviors was effective with students who demonstrated impulsive behavior. Bornas, Servera, and Llabres (1997) as cited in Zirpoli (2008), suggest that teachers use computer software to assist students in preventing impulsivity.

The authors describe several software products that are effective in preventing impulsivity through instruction in problem solving and self-regulation.

Give Smaller and Shorter Tasks One at a Time

A student who hurries through an assignment without stopping to read the directions or to check for errors could be given smaller amounts of a task to accomplish at one time, rather than the whole task at once. This would give the student a smaller chunk of the problem to deal with and more opportunities for reinforcement since the student would be more likely to solve the problem correctly.

Sometimes, a student considered impulsive can handle solving only one problem at a time. In this case, the student should be allowed to solve the problem and receive feedback immediately. As the student becomes more confident and is able to pace him- or herself more efficiently, then he or she may be able to handle larger and larger portions of projects and assignments." (Zirpoli, 2008, pp. 458–461 reproduced with permission)

CONCLUDING THOUGHTS

We have established in the beginning of the chapter that impulsivity is a multidimensional construct that is caused by one of several factors. We described Whiteside and Lynam's (2001) five-factor model consisting of: (a) positive urgency, (b) negative urgency, (c) lack of premeditation, (d) lack of perseverance, and (e) sensation seeking. The first three factors—negative urgency, lack of premeditation, and lack of perseverance—appear to describe the causes for the impulsive behaviors exhibited by students with ADHD. These students are likely to be included in most regular classrooms and, as a result, teachers will probably encounter their impulsive behaviors, which are the product of a neurobiological disorder and are not generally premeditated or intended to satisfy a need for excitement and risk; rather, they are a response to a negative urgency and the additional distracted behaviors may be caused by a lack of perseverance suggestive of working memory deficits.

The next group of students who tend to engage in impulsive behaviors that teachers may encounter in the classroom are those with conduct or disruptive disorders. Less frequently encountered, the impulsive behaviors of these students are most likely caused by a need for excitement and a negative urgency to act out aggressively. In contrast with students with ADHD, their impulsivity is typically predicated on a need to exert a measure of power and control and is usually purposeful.

In addition, we have explained how adolescence represents a period of brain development in which the prefrontal cortex is given more responsibility for the oversight of behavior; but still, during this period, the limbic system contributes significantly to behavior, especially to impulsivity. There is an evolutionary purpose attributed to this "risk-taking" period of human development. Biologists and geneticists believe that a willingness to take certain risks during this stage of life ensured the survival of one's family and tribe. For example, the readiness to explore new and possibly more fertile hunting grounds, despite the risks posed by encounters with an enemy or a dangerous predator, might prove fruitful. So it is quite normal for today's adolescents to want to experiment with risks—sometimes even dangerous ones, such as risky sexual behavior, alcohol and drug use, and speeding in automobiles. However, these behaviors will typically not be observed in the classroom—save perhaps the occasional student who comes to school drunk or high, but these students are usually referred directly to the school administrator, who contacts the parent or guardian and has the student sent home. Where the teacher can provide help for students who engage in these types of impulsive behaviors is by modeling and encouraging engagement in prosocial, "reasonable" risk taking—such as the risks experienced in participating in athletic competition; adventure education; or regulated "thrill" adventures such as bungee jumping, parachuting, or dirt bike racing. Teachers can also plan trips to an amusement or water park, organize school dances, or arrange talent shows as well as encourage students to participate in performance arts like theater and dance—these help adolescents to satisfy that primal urge to take risks, but present reasonable ones that are supported, monitored, and well regulated.

We also discussed the correlative effects of impulsivity with suicidality and delinquency. There is a connection between depression and a reduction in emotional regulation due to its negative impact on the development of the prefrontal cortex. Students with depression would thereby be at greater risk of suicide because of their suppressed executive function. However, as we pointed out, social support can mitigate impulsivity and thus help prevent suicide.

Unfortunately, in regard to contributing to delinquent behaviors, impulsivity plays a major role. As expressed earlier in the chapter, highly impulsive adolescents in schools that are poorly managed tend to have the highest amount of externalizing behaviors, like aggression. Nevertheless, schools can both teach students ways to improve their executive functioning and create a school environment in which impulsive students have fewer opportunities to act out.

Students with ADHD, who typically evidence impulsive behaviors based on a positive urgency, lack of premeditation, and sensation seeking, are more likely to engage in delinquent behaviors than their nondisabled peers. On the other hand, students with conduct disorders are more likely to engage in delinquent behaviors due to negative urgency, a lack of premeditation—acting without considering the consequences—and sensation seeking. Teachers can help these students by establishing meaningful rules and providing consistent expectations and consequences for rule breaking. They can also help by modeling prosocial, respectful behavior in the classroom; adjusting the curriculum to accommodate working memory and cognitive deficits; and ensuring that these students, frequently excluded and isolated, feel that they are accepted as real members of the classroom community—a membership that comes with both privileges and reasonable expectations. As noted previously, interventions must target deficiencies in working memory as well as the development of social skills.

CHAPTER 12

Wrapping Up: A Review of the Framework

So much of the literature on teaching provides a unidirectional view—the problem is always seen as the student, whether the issue involves learning or behavior, and teacher issues are almost never discussed. This student-focused perspective ignores one half of the relational equation, which suggests that the teacher doesn't need to be self-reflective and honest about her or his strengths and weaknesses. The assumption is the student needs to be "fixed" with the application of just the right intervention—selected like the perfect wine to have with a dinner entrée—or with a medical treatment prescribed and administered by a physician. The very real problem with this perspective, as we see it, and as we have demonstrated throughout the chapters of this book, is that it fails to acknowledge the fact that the teacher and student are always in a relationship with one another, and since all relationships are recursive—that is, they affect each participant—the teacher's cultural influences as well as her emotional and psychological states are as important to the quality of the relationship as the student's. Without this understanding, the teacher's pedagogy suffers, her effectiveness is compromised, and her teaching is less than satisfying. What's more, her students will likely feel disconnected and unappreciated, and as a result, might be unwilling or unable to learn in her class.

What does it take to be the kind of teacher who treats her students with equanimity and care? It takes an intentional commitment to truly know yourself, as Palmer (1998) has expressed; to be honest about who you are and what you know and believe, and be courageous in that revelation. At the outset of the book, we introduced a structure for effective teaching—a strategic approach that will improve teacher–student relationships and, consequently, help to reduce problem behaviors in the classroom. We described a theory of attachment that we strongly believe is critical to working effectively and therapeutically with students who exhibit challenging behaviors.

We discussed the central tenet of the theory, which suggests that much of the way people interact with others is predicated on their relationship with the primary caretaker and the drive to connect with her in order to ensure their survival. Sometimes, through no fault of the child, the primary caretaker experiences an emotional crisis that causes her to withdraw and be unavailable to the child. At the other extreme is the primary caretaker who is overprotective and clings to the child, causing the child to push away. Regardless, whether healthy or unhealthy, the caretaker–child relationship is seen by the proponents of this theory as essential to the child's emotional survival and development.

ATTACHMENT THEORY: A WAY TO UNDERSTAND AND BUILD RAPPORT

Bowlby (1980), Ainsworth (1989), and others who developed and advanced attachment theory emphasized the importance of environment, context, and interaction with others in determining one's behavior, which proves very helpful in understanding the teacher–student relational dynamic. At its heart, attachment theory attributes greater value to the reaction of the teacher than to what the child says or does in the classroom, given the teacher's power and privilege. Another important tenet of attachment theory is that the quality of the attachment bond, established early on with an attachment figure, is a key determinant of future behavior patterns. Thus, when a teacher establishes a positive, prosocial relational bond with a student, very often this will influence the future behaviors exhibited by that child in the teacher's classroom.

While we acknowledge the impact of genetic predisposition on the development of a child, we also assert that environment, as represented in the bond established between teacher and student, contributes in an even more substantial way. Likewise, the teacher's capacity for empathy is an additional factor that contributes to the strengthening of this attachment bond.

Within the overarching principles of attachment theory are four distinct substrata: securely attached children, a product of parental oversight that provides security but also the freedom to explore; insecurely attached resistant children, often the result of anxious, hypervigilant parents and resulting in a very needy child who seeks close parental contact, but is not comforted by it; insecurely attached avoidant children, characterized as ones who do not pursue closeness with the mother and may, in fact, be more responsive to a stranger—these children typically avoid intimacy, maintain a negative view of others, and expect rejection; and finally, insecurely attached disorganized children, exemplified as seemingly "frozen" or "entranced" as a result of the fear caused by the behaviors of a caregiver. This latter type typically represents the greatest challenge for teachers, because children in this category have experienced a dichotomy with respect to their adult caregivers—that is, they see them both as protector and persecutor. Such children are often diagnosed with disruptive or conduct disorder.

In the classroom, resistant children are typically irritable and fussy; avoidant children appear to be more interested in the classroom materials than in the teacher; disorganized children seem apprehensive and fearful; and secure children display affection for the teacher and classmates, share their materials, follow the teacher's directions, and abide by the rules of the classroom and school.

These typologies of attachment affect a child's internal working model (IWM) of self and interpersonal relationships. For example, children who possess a healthy IWM view others as trustworthy and perceive themselves as valuable and effective when interacting with others. Closeness to the teacher can serve as a protective factor against the development of pathology. Teachers can contribute to revisions of their students' unhealthy IWMs by developing a prosocial, appropriate relationship with them. However, this endeavor becomes more challenging as children enter adolescence, because while children naively view their parents as infallible, adolescents learn that their parents have feet of clay; they are imperfect beings. Therefore, adolescence is seen through the lens of attachment theory as a time when children strive to balance the need for both autonomy and attachment.

Thus, our fundamental position is that the teacher–student relationship is both dynamic and interactive, and that understanding the various types of attachment styles displayed by both the student and the teacher will help the teacher respond effectively to challenging behaviors encountered in the classroom. Consequently, we urge teachers to consider their own attachment styles and address the potential impediments to relationship building they might present.

We introduced early on in the book the term *mentalization*, which really means "perspective taking," or understanding one's own behavior relative to another's, which promotes empathy. Secure teachers will be more likely to mentalize; insecure teachers, more prone to react. Students often project their attachment histories of parental figures onto the teacher, who, for them, comes to represent that figure. This projection helps the teacher identify his student's attachment style and address the student's behavior with empathy and understanding.

PRINCIPLES OF PEDAGOGY: MORE THAN AN ART AND A SCIENCE

The other key component of our framework for purposeful teaching is developing a sound pedagogy. More than a science or an art, pedagogy is really akin to a craft. In the beginning of the book, we provided some principles of effective pedagogy. We stressed, from the outset, the importance of establishing a teacher identity as well as developing personal and professional integrity through constant self-reflection and reflection on one's practice. We referred to the work of Korthagen (2004), Loughran (1997), Palmer (1998), and Austin et al. (2011) to underscore the value of these two pillars of the teacher's pedagogical framework. By *identity* we mean understanding oneself and others that is predicated on relationships, and by *integrity* we imply a teacher who is fair, authentic, and consistent. The kind of reflection we intend here is very broadly defined as deliberate, metacognitive thought that teachers engage in with the goal of improving their practice (Sellar, 2013).

Another important aspect of sound pedagogy that comports with the theory of attachment is the value of establishing caring relationships with students (Noddings, 2005), best demonstrated when teachers help their students see themselves as active and competent agents contributing to their own learning (Watkins & Mortimore, 1999). Likewise, Freire (1970) and Bruner (1996) discussed the importance of learning about the culture and social context of students and considering its influence on their behavior. Also, Alexander (2004) added to the elements of a viable pedagogy by pointing out the need for good teachers to possess the skill and commitment to make sound educational decisions.

Finally, based on an extensive review of the literature, we derived a list of six essential elements in a truly effective pedagogical framework, repeated as follows.

- Define *pedagogy* relative to teaching children.
- Ensure that the framework provides a schema for the development of a teacher's pedagogy and is not a prescriptive manual.
- Acknowledge and articulate the vitality of your role, as a teaching professional, in contributing to the development of children and adolescents.
- Recognize the importance of the culture and social context of your students.
- Be prepared and equipped to motivate, enthuse, entice, and inspire your students to learn, and accept your part in many aspects of your students' development, including body, emotions, and spirit as well as the intellect.
- Embrace the view that teachers are lifelong learners, and share your passion for learning.

We also really liked Smith's (1994) elements vital to a sound pedagogy; namely, (a) animation—introducing students to new experiences, (b) reflection—creating opportunities to explore lived experiences, and (c) action—working with students to help them make changes in their lives.

THE "NINES:" NINE OF THE MOST CHALLENGING BEHAVIORS FREQUENTLY ENCOUNTERED BY TEACHERS

Teaching Students with Disruptive Disorders

Most often considered the principal reason most teachers leave their jobs during their first three years of teaching, the two most commonly identified "disruptive disorders" are oppositional defiant disorder and conduct disorder. We learned in this book that students with oppositional defiant disorder typically have parental caregivers or models who are either lax and permissive or authoritarian and repressive. Conversely, students identified with conduct disorder tend to come from disorganized, dysfunctional homes in which one or both of the parental caregivers are abusive, life is chaotic, and parental behavior is unpredictable.

We also provided interventions that have demonstrated positive results in reducing antisocial behaviors for students with disruptive disorders. To review, the three most popular treatment programs for oppositional defiant disorder are parent-child interaction therapy, problem solving skills training together with parent management training, and the Incredible Years training series. Similarly, as noted in the book, for children and adolescents diagnosed with conduct disorder, multisystemic treatment has shown the greatest success.

Finally, we remind you of the importance of reflecting on the influences of your own parental caregivers as well as those of the disruptive student. Unaware of these influences, sometimes people can react in nontherapeutic ways.

Teaching Students with Anxiety Disorders

Chronic anxiety is one of the most common emotional disorders affecting students in today's schools. Each affected student displays an anxiety with different features and causes; some will display seemingly baseless fears, while others may display obsessions that compel them to engage in compulsive rituals. Still others may become traumatized by past events that are repeatedly experienced as though they happened yesterday. The teacher is responsible for keeping the anxious student safe and ensuring that the individual learns. Teachers who are possessed of a sound pedagogical foundation; have invested time in understanding themselves and their teaching purposes or philosophies; and who can step back from the anxious behavior and be mindful of their own prejudices, fears, and assumptions before offering an intervention will have a far better chance of success in relating to and understanding the child who exhibits these challenging behaviors.

Teaching Students Who Are Depressed or Bipolar

An alarming number of students in the United States are affected by depression. In fact, as we noted in our chapter on this topic, 2% of children and 5-8% of adolescents in the U.S. are currently struggling with depression (Rohde, Lewinshon, Klein, Seeley, & Gau, 2013). As their teachers, we need to be especially aware of the challenges these students face: poor academic performance, social isolation, low energy and lack of enthusiasm, low self-esteem, and, most critically, an increased risk for suicide. This latter risk-factor is of particular concern to teachers and caregivers because we know that suicide is the third leading cause of death for adolescents and young adults aged 15-24 (New York State Department of Health, 2011). Since 95% of suicides are committed by school-aged students previously diagnosed with a mental illness, typically a mood disorder, and because we know that about 95% of students with disabilities receive most of their education in inclusive classrooms, all teachers need to be familiar with the characteristics and recommended interventions for this population.

In this book, we examined the topic of mood disorders, their characteristic behaviors, their effects on students, and the best-practice interventions that can help affected students. We encourage you to take what you have learned from this book about working with students in your classroom who have a mood disorder and apply it to your teaching pedagogy and your relationships with your students.

Teaching Students with Eating Disorders

Approximately 30 million Americans have been diagnosed with an eating disorder, including 11% of high school students, so there is a very good chance, based on these and other statistics, that every teacher will encounter some of these students. There is hope for students affected by this disorder if it is identified soon and treated with the therapies described earlier in the book. In fact, there are things that teachers can do to mitigate the effects of this disorder. The first step is to strive to understand the student with an eating disorder from an attachment perspective, to ensure that your predispositions will not negatively affect your interactions with her or him. Next, engage your pedagogical framework as developed from the schema described in this book to help you develop remedial academic and behavioral options.

Teaching Students Who Bully and Are Bullied

Without a doubt, bullying, and its psychological effects, continues to represent a real challenge for students, teachers, and administrators. The Internet and social media have provided even more venues for its perpetrators. While the bully has always been a behavioral challenge for teachers, the victims of bullying might present an even greater problem since, frequently, they transition from victim to victimizer. However, despite the increase in incidents of bullying and cyberbullying among school-age children and adolescents there is hope, and this book has provided ways to identify and understand the causes and development of bullying in the classroom and strategies to work effectively with both the bully and the victim. The frameworks of relationship building and effective pedagogical practices represent a potent countermeasure to these pernicious behaviors.

Teaching Students Who Are the Victims of Bias in the Classroom

Racial, cultural, and religious bias is an urgent issue affecting many thousands of students in the United States. In response, it is important for teachers to learn about bias and racism as it affects both them and their students and to learn ways to effectively address these undesirable behaviors when they occur in the classroom. Numbers provided by the National Center for Educational Statistics (2010) present a very disturbing picture of the integration and acceptance of diverse groups in U.S. schools. For example, during the 2009-2010 school year there were 16,270 reported incidents of bias. Another unsettling fact is that 11% of all hate and bias crimes are committed in colleges and schools. The categories of difference targeted by the perpetrators of discrimination were most often religion, race, ethnicity, sexual orientation, and/or disability (Kosciw, Greytak, Diaz, & Bartkiewicz, 2010). Consequently, those typically affected by such crimes included minority and protected classes such as African Americans, Latinos, Asians, Native Americans, Jews, Muslims, and LGBT-identified youth (New Jersey State Police, 2009).

Situations like the one described in this book and countless others provide teachers with a unique opportunity to address this all too common human frailty: the struggle to accept those who are different. This section described typical causes of bias, the antecedents that incubate it, the behaviors that help to sustain it, and effective ways to address intolerance in the classroom and in the school. Two typical teacher responses, analyzed from both an attachment and pedagogical perspective, demonstrate possible reactions to situations of bias. Our goal in providing this information is to help teachers effectively address bias and intolerance through education and its corollary: enlightenment.

Teaching Students Who Are Survivors of Suicide

Students, teachers, and the entire school community are profoundly affected by the loss of a student through suicide. Such events produce what Garfin, Holma, and Silver (2015) refer to as "collective trauma." We also know that suicide seems to follow the same progression as a viral epidemic and can spawn an outbreak of suicidal ideation and attempts within the same school community (Gladwell, 2000).

Some students have even taken their lives on school property, during the school day, which can have devastating consequences on student and teacher morale. The National Center for Educational Statistics (2014) reported six suicides on school property in a twelve-month period and, as we have learned, according to the National Vital Statistics Report (2010), suicide was the third leading cause of adolescent death in the U.S. for youth aged 15-17. Similarly, the 2013 National Youth Risk Behavior Survey revealed that in high schools in the United States, 17% of the students polled reported having experienced suicidal ideation, 8% said they had attempted suicide, and 2.7% stated they had been seriously injured as a result of an attempted suicide.

Students in residential treatment facilities are at even greater risk for suicide. In a nationwide survey of administrators of these facilities, the respondents reported that 74% of their residents were admitted for self-injurious behavior (National Association for Children's Behavioral Health and the National Association of Psychiatric Health Systems, 2008).

Unfortunately, effective teacher response in the aftermath of a student suicide is seldom the topic of professional development workshops. As front-line staff, teachers are in a unique position to monitor student responses following a tragic event such as a student suicide. Knowing what to say and do to help reduce the potential for self-harm in the grieving and confused classmates of the student who has died may prevent further suicides. Thus, learning about and acquiring effective strategies designed to help student survivors in the wake of these crises is vital.

Student suicide presents pernicious residual effects for students, parents, teachers, and administrators. This book discussed the characteristics and most prevalent *perceived* causes of student suicides, along with some of the more effective, evidence-based interventions. In addition, it debunked some of the popular misconceptions surrounding suicide, always taking care to stress the importance of obtaining the assistance of qualified and trained professionals such as the school counselor, clinical psychologists, pastoral care counselors, psychiatrists skilled in working with children and adolescents, clinical social workers, and the appropriate medical personnel. It also described postvention and ways that the classroom teacher can help to mitigate the trauma experienced by students in the aftermath of the suicide of a schoolmate.

Teaching Students with High-Functioning Autism and Social Skills Deficits

As we have learned, 1 in 50 individuals in the United States has been diagnosed with Asperger syndrome or High-Functioning Autism (HFA) (Center for Disease Control and Prevention MMWR Surveillance Summaries, 2007). Likewise, researchers suggest that, conservatively, 1 in 50 school-aged children in the United States has been properly diagnosed with HFA (Blumberg et al., 2013). Furthermore, according to the National Center for Educational Statistics (2015), 440,592 or 7.7% of all students eligible for special education services were identified as having autism, which includes both Asperger syndrome and High-Functioning Autism.

These alarming statistics, together with the increase in the inclusion of students with High-Functioning Autism in the general education classroom, emphasize the importance of learning about its characteristic behaviors, as observed in students with the disorder, and effective strategies to employ when working with them in the classroom. Students with HFA present unique challenges for educators because, while they can master some subject matter, they struggle with both inference and irony. Moreover, they are very idiosyncratic in their interests and, because they can commandeer a discussion and behave oddly, are often socially isolated.

Teaching Students with Impulsivity

Impulsivity is a multidimensional construct that is caused by one of several factors: (a) positive urgency, (b) negative urgency, (c) lack of premeditation, (d) lack of perseverance, and (e) sensation seeking. The first three factors—negative urgency, lack of premeditation, and lack of perseverance—appear to describe the causes for the impulsive behaviors exhibited by students with ADHD. These students are likely to be included in most regular classrooms. Their impulsive behaviors occur when they act rashly due to negative affect; and their additional distracted behaviors may be caused by working memory deficits. Another group of students who tend to engage in impulsive behaviors are those with (less-common) conduct or disruptive disorders. The impulsive behaviors of these students are most likely caused by a need for excitement and a negative urgency to act out aggressively.

Adolescence represents a period of brain development in which the limbic system, which governs reward, contributes significantly to behavior, leading to impulsivity. The teacher can provide help by modeling and encouraging engagement in prosocial, "reasonable" risk taking, such as participating in an Adventure Education program that teaches teamwork and also provides the opportunity for personal challenge through the "high ropes" course, engaging in performance art such as music, dance, or theater, joining a debating team, running for student government, or playing an intramural sport such as volleyball or soccer. Impulsivity plays a major role in contributing to delinquent behaviors, particularly in schools that are poorly managed and supervised. Nevertheless, schools can help by teaching students ways to increase their working memory and by creating fewer opportunities for students to succumb to their impulses.

Teachers can also help these students by establishing rules and consequences for breaking them. Teachers can also adjust the curriculum to accommodate working memory and cognitive deficits, and can ensure that these students feel they are accepted as members of the classroom community.

A Recapitulation of Three Best-Practice Approaches in Addressing Challenging Behaviors

Positive Behavioral Intervention and Supports (PBIS)

PBIS is, essentially, the behavioral counterpart to response to intervention (RtI) and evolved almost simultaneously as a way to preempt behavioral problems among students. Like RtI, the model employs a three-tier framework.

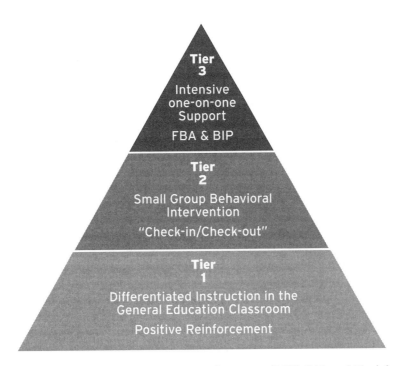

Figure 12.1. Positive Intervention and Support (PBIS)-3-Tiered Model

In this framework, students are awarded points for exhibiting key prosocial behaviors during each class period. Incentives or rewards are provided to students commensurate with their weekly point totals.

The first tier provides differentiated instructions and employs strategies that are scientifically based. Students are continually assessed to provide authentic data from which teachers and educational professionals can make informed decisions about how to provide students at risk for behavior problems with effective behavioral interventions to facilitate successful learning experiences.

The second tier of intervention is activated for students who do not respond successfully to Tier 1 interventions over time, as evidenced through assessment monitoring. The Tier 2 level of intervention typically involves the application of research-based strategies in a small group setting. Once again, students' performance is carefully assessed and monitored to determine whether the student is ready to return to the regular classroom curriculum, needs further intensive intervention, or might need to be screened for special-education classification.

The third tier of interventions are reserved for students who do not respond satisfactorily to Tier 2 interventions. These consist of more intensive, individualized approaches that may be applied for up to 12 weeks, during two or more 30-minute sessions weekly. Students who do not respond to Tier 3 intensive, individualized instructional techniques may qualify for screening for special education services (Fuchs & Fuchs, 2006).

In Tier 1, school-wide behavioral expectations are explicitly taught and reinforced by all school staff. These behavioral expectations are widely displayed and discussed, and positive reinforcement is consistently provided for compliance.

Tier 2 is designed to address the problem behaviors of students who are noncompliant with the school-wide behavioral expectations. Typically, a very simple functional behavioral assessment is implemented for noncompliant individuals, and a behavior intervention plan is developed. An example of a Tier 2 intervention is Check In, Check Out, in which the student's target behavior is monitored and his behavioral performance is recorded on a card by caregivers referred to as "checkers." This card is transmitted to guardians at home, who must sign it, thus ensuring home–school collaboration. Important aspects of this Tier 2 intervention are self-monitoring and scaffolding (Filter et al., 2007).

Tier 3 interventions are more intensive and employ individualized, evidence-based approaches, predicated on an effectively developed functional behavioral assessment and resulting in an actionable behavior intervention plan. Examples of Tier 3 interventions include individualized counseling sessions, daily report cards, and the implementing of self-monitoring skills. A concern expressed by stakeholders is that the Tier 3 interventions appear to be synonymous with those provided as related services in an individualized education plan for students receiving special education (Sugai & Horner, 2009).

PBIS can be used as a school-wide approach to obviate potential behavioral issues. Such an approach can substantially reduce behavioral problems throughout the school if the program is implemented with fidelity. Such a program, adopted by an entire school or school district, would be considered a Tier 1 behavioral intervention. As with RtI, designed to address academic performance issues, PBIS would likely preempt the majority of behavioral issues, as evidenced in office referral data provided by schools using PBIS models.

Mindfulness

Mindfulness, a form of meditational practice, has been used throughout history in various settings as a way to increase psychological well-being, improve cognitive performance, and reduce stress and anxiety. Mindfulness can also help enhance well-being in school settings. Through the use of mindfulness skills in the classroom, students and teachers learn to stay focused on the present and improve student attention in order to improve academic learning. An example of meditation, one technique used in the practice of mindfulness as it might be implemented in the classroom, follows.

Teacher: "This morning I'm going to teach you a way to help you improve your focus and reduce your stress and anxiety. First, I want you to sit comfortably in your chair with your back straight and both feet on the floor. Next, place your hands on your desk, open and palms up. Now, close your eyes and breathe normally in and out of your nose. As you do this, I want you to gradually shift the focus of your attention on your breathing and consciously breathe deeply and slowly, in and out. As you do this, thoughts will enter your mind, queries about the purpose of this exercise—'Why am I doing this?,' concerns about how you look, what you have to do next in your day, what you did earlier this morning and yesterday. Do not focus on these thoughts; simply acknowledge them and let them go. Try not to judge them or assign them a value—just stay focused on your breathing, being mindful of your body, from the soles of your feet to the top of your head." [This process continues for a few minutes, after which the teacher signals the conclusion of the session with a gentle word or sound.]

The implications for using mindfulness to address and reduce challenging behaviors in the classroom, like those discussed in this book, are obvious. Research supports its efficacy in reducing stress and increasing focus. In support of this contention, we recently conducted an investigation involving 20 high school students in a specialized school for students with emotional disorders, and preliminary results showed a significant increase in self-esteem and self-efficacy after only two months of participation in a routine mindfulness regime (Malow & Austin, 2016). The various diagnoses for these student participants ranged from internalizing disorders such as anxiety and mood disorders to externalizing ones like ADHD and conduct disorders.

The Life Space Interview (LSI) (Redl, 1966)

As we discussed earlier in our book, the Life Space Interview is a crisis intervention technique, developed for use by the classroom teacher, in which a student's behavior is discussed with her or him at the time of the problem's occurrence.

As we noted before, the process of implementing any of the Life Space Interviewing techniques involves first, intervening; second, listening to all parties involved in a nonjudgmental manner; third, analyzing the situation to determine whether the behavior is acute (an atypical or episodic occurrence) or chronic (frequently recurring); fourth, selecting a specific LSI approach; fifth, implementing the approach or approaches in a respectful, attentive, and professional manner; and finally, combining or modifying the relevant approach or approaches as required by the circumstances or context. We find this approach to be especially effective in addressing behavioral emergencies that occasionally arise in the classroom and always at the most inopportune times. After much practice with these techniques, so that they become habituated, the teacher can employ them strategically and effectively when the situation calls for a crisis intervention. However, to reiterate a word of caution, the interventions described above must be reviewed and practiced regularly to ensure their automaticity in use.

A FINAL WORD

So, then, what tools have we given teachers to help make them more confident and successful at their jobs? First, we have offered a bidirectional approach to more effective teaching—through improved teacher–student relationships and a proposed framework for a sound pedagogy. Second, we have provided examples through student and teacher vignettes that suggest a way of analyzing teaching to improve both its effectiveness and teachers' relationships with students whose behaviors pose a challenge to instruction and authority.

We identified the nine most common problem behaviors encountered in the classroom and then, through authentic vignettes, demonstrated the effective versus ineffective ways to address each of them. In addition, we offered teachers some "use-now" responses that have been successful in confronting and reducing the various problem behaviors described.

This book's goal was to provide teachers with a solid, research-based framework upon which to fashion a sound pedagogical model. We have repeatedly asserted that this book is not a best-practices manual but rather a framework for a system to approach purposeful teaching that accommodates various strategies and approaches unified by a common set of principles. It is our hope that readers will feel empowered to develop their own pedagogical styles within the structure provided by our framework, and from this solid foundation seek to build a relationship with each of their students—helping them succeed in changing their behaviors and their lives for the better.

References

Aber, L. (2012). Poor and low-income families, infant/toddler development, and the prospects for change: Back to the future. In S. L. Odom, E. P. Pungello, & N. Gardner-Neblett (Eds.), *Infants, toddlers, and families in poverty: Research implications for early child care* (pp. 3–18). New York, NY: Guilford Press. Retrieved from http://search.ebscohost.com/login.aspx?direct=true&db=psyh&AN=2012-25305-001&site=ehost-live

Abbott, M. M., & Goodheart, K. L. (2011). 19 Cognitive behavioral approaches for treating eating disorders. In K. L Goodheart, J. R. Clopton, & J. J. Robert-McComb (Eds.), *Eating disorders in women and children: Prevention, stress management, and treatment* (2nd ed., pp. 371–384). Boca Raton, FL: CRC Press.

Abrams, K. Y., Rifkin, A., & Hesse, E. (2006). Examining the role of parental frightened/frightening subtypes in predicting disorganized attachment within a brief observational procedure. *Development and Psychopathology, 18*(2), 345–361. doi:10.1017/S0954579406060184

Adler, A. (1964). *Social interest: A challenge to mankind.* New York: Capricorn.

Aduen, P., Rich, B. A., Sanchez, L., O'Brien, K., & Alvord, M. K. (2014). Resilience Builder Program therapy addresses core social deficits in youth with high functioning autism spectrum disorder. *Journal of Psychological Abnormalities in Children, 3*(2), 1-10.

Ainsworth, M. D. (1969). Object relations, dependency, and attachment: A theoretical review of the infant-mother relationship. *Child Development, 40*(4), 969–1025. doi:10.2307/1127008

Ainsworth, M. D., Bell, S. M., & Stayton, D. J. (1971). Individual differences in strange-situation behavior of one-year-olds. In H. R. Schaffer (Ed.), *The origins of human social relations* (pp. 17–58). Oxford, England: Academic Press.

Ainsworth, M. D. S., Blehar, M. C., Waters, E., & Wall, S. (1978). *Patterns of attachment.* Hillsdale, NJ: Erlbaum.

Ainsworth, M. S. (1979). Infant–mother attachment. *American Psychologist, 34*(10), 932–937. doi:10.1037/0003-066X.34.10.932

Ainsworth, M. S. (1989). Attachments beyond infancy. *American Psychologist, 44*(4), 709–716. doi:10.1037/0003-066X.44.4.709

Ainsworth, M. S., & Bowlby, J. (1991). An ethological approach to personality development. *American Psychologist, 46*(4), 333-341.

Ainsworth, M.D.S., & Wittig, B.A. (1969). Attachment and exploratory behavior of one-year-olds in a strange situation. In B.M. Foss (Ed.), *Determinants of infant behavior* (Vol. 4, pp. 111-136). London: Methuen.

Akinbami, L. J., Liu, X., Pastor, P.N., & Reuben, C.A. (2011). *Attention deficit hyperactivity disorder among children aged 5–17 years in the United States, 1998–2009.* Hyattsville, MD: National Center for Health Statistics.

Alexander, J. F., & Robbins, M. S. (2011). *Functional family therapy.* New York, NY: Springer.

Alexander, R. (2004). Still no pedagogy? Principle, pragmatism and compliance in primary education. *Cambridge Journal of Education, 34*(1), 7-33.

Alic, M. (2009). Theory of Mind. Retrieved July 3, 2015, from www.education.com/reference/article/theory-of-mind/

Allen, J. G., & Munich, R. L. (2003). Introduction. *Bulletin of the Menninger Clinic, 67*(3), 165–166. doi:10.1521/bumc.67.3.165.23436

Allen, J. P. (2008). The attachment system in adolescence. In J. Cassidy & P. R. Shaver (Eds.), *Handbook of attachment: Theory, research, and clinical applications* (2nd ed., pp. 419–435). New York, NY: Guilford Press.

Allen, J. P., Porter, M., McFarland, C., McElhaney, K. B., & Marsh, P. (2007). The relation of attachment security to adolescents' paternal and peer relationships, depression, and externalizing behavior. *Child Development, 78*(4), 1222–1239.

Allen, K. L., Byrne, S. M., & Crosby, R. D. (2014). Distinguishing between risk factors for Bulimia Nervosa, Binge Eating Disorder, and Purging Disorder. *Journal of Youth and Adolescence, 44*, 1580–1591.

Algozzine, B., Daunic, A. P., & Smith, S. W. (2010). *Preventing problem behaviors: School-wide programs and classroom practices.* Thousand Oaks, CA: Corwin.

Altman, S. E., & Shankman, S. A. (2009). What is the association between obsessive compulsive disorder and eating disorders? *Clinical Psychology Review, 29*(7), 638–646.

Al-Yagon, M. (2007). Socioemotional and behavioral adjustment among school-age children with learning disabilities: The moderating role of maternal personal resources. *The Journal of Special Education, 40*(4), 205–217. doi:10.1177/00224669070400040201

Al-Yagon, M. (2010). Maternal emotional resources and socio-emotional well-being of children with and without learning disabilities. *Family Relations: An Interdisciplinary Journal of Applied Family Studies, 59*(2), 152–169. doi:10.1111/j.1741-3729.2010.00592.x

Al-Yagon, M. (2012). Adolescents with learning disabilities: Socioemotional and behavioral functioning and attachment relationships with fathers, mothers, and teachers. *Journal of Youth and Adolescence, 41*(10), 1294–1311. doi:10.1007/s10964-012-9767-6

Americans With Disabilities Act of 1990. 42 U.S.C.A. § 12010 *et seq.* (West 1993)..

American Psychiatric Association. (2013). *Diagnostic and statistical manual of mental disorders* (5th ed.). Washington, DC: Author.

Amianto, F., Abbate-Daga, G., Morando, S., Sobrero, C., & Fassino, S. (2011). Personality development characteristics of women with anorexia nervosa, their healthy siblings and healthy controls: What prevents and what relates to psychopathology? *Psychiatry Research, 187*(3), 401–408.

Anderson, S. W., Bechara, A., Damasio, H., Tranel, D., & Damasio, A. R. (1999). Impairment of social and moral behavior related to early damage in human prefrontal cortex. *Nature Neuroscience, 2*(11), 1032–1037. doi:10.1038/12194

Andrade, B. F., & Tannock, R. (2014). Sustained impact of inattention and hyperactivity-impulsivity on peer problems: Mediating roles of prosocial skills and conduct problems in a community sample of children. *Child Psychiatry & Human Development, 45*(3), 318–328.

Andriessen, K. (2015). Suicide bereavement and postvention in major suicidology journals. *Crisis, 35*(5), 338-348.

Angelou, M. (n.d.). Maya Angelou Quotes. Retrieved from https://www.goodreads.com/author/quotes/3503.Maya_Angelou

Annie E. Casey Foundation. (2011, October 4). No Place for Kids. Retrieved from http://www.aecf.org/resources/no-place-for-kids-full-report/

Anti-Defamation League, 2015. Retrieved August 3, 2015, from http://www.adl.org/education-outreach/anti-bias-education/

Arcelus, J., Mitchell, A. J., Wales, J., & Nielsen, S. (2011). Mortality rates in patients with anorexia nervosa and other eating disorders: A meta-analysis of 36 studies. *Archives of General Psychiatry, 68*(7), 724–731.

Atkinson, D. R., Morten, G. E., & Sue, D. W. E. (1998). *Counseling American minorities.* New York, NY: McGraw-Hill.

Atlas, R. S., & Pepler, D. J. (1998). Observations of bullying in the classroom. *The Journal of Educational Research, 92*(2), 86–99. doi:10.1080/00220679809597580

Augsburger, D. W. (1986). *Pastoral counseling across cultures.* Louisville, KY: Westminster John Knox Press.

Austin, V., Barowsky, E., Malow, M., & Gomez, D. (2011, Winter). Effective teacher behaviors evident in successful teachers of students with emotional and behavioral disorders. *Journal of the American Academy of Special Education Professionals,* 4–27.

Austin, V. L. & Sciarra, D. T. (2010). *Children and adolescents with emotional and behavioral disorders.* Upper Saddle River, NJ: Pearson Education.

Bailer, U. F., Frank, G. K., Price, J. C., Meltzer, C. C., Becker, C., & Mathis, C. A. (2013). Interaction between serotonin transporter and dopamine D2/D3 receptor radioligand measures is associated with harm avoidant symptoms in anorexia and bulimia nervosa. *Psychiatry Research Neuroimaging, 211*(2), 160–168.

Baron-Cohen, S., Hoekstra, R.A., Knickmeyer, R., Wheelwright, S. (2006). The autism spectrum quotient (AQ)—adolescent version. *Journal of Autism Developmental Disorders, 36,* 343–50.

Barone, L. (2003). Developmental protective and risk factors in borderline personality disorder: A study using the Adult Attachment Interview. *Attachment & Human Development, 5*(1), 64–77. doi:10.1080/1461673031000078634

Barone, L., & Guiducci, V. (2009). Mental representations of attachment in eating disorders: A pilot study using the Adult Attachment Interview. *Attachment & Human Development, 11*(4), 405–417. doi:10.1080/14616730902814770

Beauchaine, T. P., Hinshaw, S. P., & Pang, K. L. (2010). Comorbidity of attention-deficit/hyperactivity disorder and early-onset conduct disorder: Biological, environmental, and developmental mechanisms. *Clinical Psychology: Science and Practice, 17*(4), 327–336.

Beck, A. T. (1967). *Depression.* New York, NY: Harper and Row.

Beck, A. T., Rush, A. J., Shaw, B. F., & Emery, G. (1979). *Cognitive therapy of depression.* New York, NY: Guilford.

Beck, J. S. (2011). *Cognitive behavior therapy: Basics and beyond.* New York, NY: Guilford Press.

Becker, S. P., Luebbe, A. M., Fite, P. J., Greening, L., & Stoppelbein, L. (2013). Oppositional defiant disorder symptoms in relation to psychopathic traits and aggression among psychiatrically hospitalized children: ADHD symptoms as a potential moderator. *Aggressive Behavior, 39*(3), 201–211.

Begeer, S., Banerjee, R., Rieffe, C., Terwogt, M. M., Potharst, E., Stegge, H., & Koot, H. M. (2011). The understanding and self-reported use of emotional display rules in children with autism spectrum disorders. *Cognition & Emotion, 25*(5), 947–956.

Behan, J., & Carr, A. (2000). Oppositional defiant disorder. In A. Carr (Ed.), *What works with children and adolescents? A critical review of psychological interventions with children, adolescents and their families.* (pp. 102–130). New York, NY: Routledge.

Belsky, J., & Fearon, R. M. P. (2008). Precursors of attachment security. In J. Cassidy, P. R. Shaver, J. Cassidy (Eds.), *Handbook of attachment: Theory, research, and clinical applications* (2nd ed., pp. 295–316). New York, NY: Guilford Press.

Belsky, J., & Jaffee, S. R. (2006). The multiple determinants of parenting. In D. Cicchetti, & D. J. Cohen, D. (Eds.), *Developmental psychopathology, Vol 3: Risk, disorder, and adap-*

tation (2nd ed., pp. 38–85). Hoboken, NJ, US: John Wiley & Sons Inc. Retrieved from http://search.ebscohost.com/login.aspx?direct=true&db=psyh&AN=2006-03609 -002&site=ehost-live

Berger, L. E., Jodl, K. M., Allen, J. P., McElhaney, K. B., & Kuperminc, G. P. (2005). When adolescents disagree with others about their symptoms: Differences in attachment organization as an explanation of discrepancies between adolescent, parent, and peer reports of behavior problems. *Development and Psychopathology, 17*(2), 509–528. doi:10.1017/S0954579405050248

Bergin, C., & Bergin, D. (2009). Attachment in the classroom. *Educational Psychology Review, 21*(2), 141–170.

Berkowitz, L., McCauley, J., Schuurman, D. L., & Jordan, J. R. (2011). Organizational postvention after suicide death. In J. R. Jordan & J. L. McIntosh (Eds.), *Grief after suicide: Understanding the consequences and caring for the survivors* (pp. 157–178). New York, NY: Routledge.

Berry, J. W. (1990). Acculturation and adaptation: A general framework. In W. H. Holtzman & T. H. Bornemann (Eds.), *Mental health of immigrants and refugees* (pp. 90–102). Austin, TX: Hogg Foundation for Mental Health.

Bibou-Nakou, I., Tsiantis, J., Assimopoulos, H., & Chatzilambou, P. (2013). Bullying/ victimization from a family perspective: A qualitative study of secondary school students' views. *European Journal of Psychology of Education, 28*(1), 53–71.

Biddulph, M. & Adey, A. (2004). Pupil perceptions of effective teaching and subject relevance in history and geography at Key Stage 3. *Research in Education, 71*, 1–8.

Biederman, J., Faraone, S. V., Milberger, S., Jetton, J. G., Chen, L., Mick, E., Greene, R.W., & Russell, R. L. (1996). Is childhood oppositional defiant disorder a precursor to adolescent conduct disorder? Findings from a four-year follow-up study of children with ADHD. *Journal of the American Academy of Child & Adolescent Psychiatry, 35*(9), 1193–1204. doi:10.1097/00004583-199609000-00017

Bierman, K. L., & Sasser, T. R. (2014). Conduct disorder. In M. Lewis & K. D. Rudolph (Eds.), *Handbook of developmental psychopathology* (3rd ed., pp. 467–485). New York, NY: Springer Science.

Bjorklund, D. F., & Hawley, P. H. (2014). Aggression grows up: Looking through an evolutionary developmental lens to understand the causes and consequences of human aggression. In T. K. Shackelford & R. D. Hansen (Eds.), *The evolution of violence* (pp. 159–186). New York, NY: Springer Science.

Blumberg, S. J., Bramlett, M. D., Kogan, M. D., Schieve, L. A., Jones, J. R., & Lu, M. C. (2013). Changes in prevalence of parent-reported autism spectrum disorder in school-aged US children: 2007 to 2011–2012. *National health statistics reports, 65*(20), 1–7.

Boden, J. M., Fergusson, D. M., & Horwood, L. J. (2010). Risk factors for conduct disorder and oppositional/defiant disorder: Evidence from a New Zealand birth cohort. *Journal of the American Academy of Child & Adolescent Psychiatry, 49*(11), 1125–1133.

Bögels, S. M., & Perotti, E. C. (2011). Does father know best? A formal model of the paternal influence on childhood social anxiety. *Journal of Child and Family Studies, 20*(2), 171–181.

Bokhorst, C. L., Bakermans-Kranenburg, M. J., Fonagy, P., Fearon, R. M. P., van IJzendoorn, M. H., & Schuengel, C. (2003). The importance of shared environment in mother–infant attachment security: A behavioral genetic study. *Child Development, 74*(6), 1769–1782.

Bolles, R. N. (2015). *What color is your parachute? A practical manual for job-hunters and career-changers.* New York, NY: Ten Speed Press.

Booth-LaForce, C., Rubin, K. H., Rose-Krasnor, L., & Burgess, K. B. (2005). Attachment and friendship predictors of psychosocial functioning in middle childhood and the mediating roles of social support and self-worth. In K. A. Kerns & R. A. Richardson (Eds.), *Attachment in middle childhood* (pp. 161–188). New York, NY: Guilford Press.

Borduin, C. M., Munschy, R. J., Wagner, D. V., & Taylor, E. K. (2011). Multisystemic therapy with juvenile sexual offenders: Development, validation, and dissemination. In D. P. Boer, R. Eher, L. A. Craig, M. H. Miner, & F. Pfäfflin (Eds.), *International perspectives on the assessment and treatment of sexual offenders: Theory, practice, and research* (pp. 263–285). Hoboken, NJ: Wiley-Blackwell.

Bostik, K. E., & Everall, R. D. (2007). Healing from suicide: Adolescent perceptions of attachment relationships. *British Journal of Guidance & Counselling, 35*(1), 79–96.

Bowlby, J. (1958). The nature of the child's tie to his mother. *The International Journal of Psychoanalysis, 39*, 350–373.

Bowlby, J. (1969). *Attachment and loss: Attachment*. London, UK: Hogarth.

Bowlby, J. (1973). *Attachment and loss: Separation: Anxiety and anger*. New York, NY: Basic Books.

Bowlby, J. (1982). *Attachment and loss*. New York, NY: Basic Books.

Bowlby, J. (1988). Defensive processes in response to stressful separation in early life. In E. J. Anthony & C. Chiland (Eds.), *The child in his family, Vol. 8: Perilous development: Child raising and identity formation under stress* (pp. 23–30). Oxford, UK: John Wiley & Sons.

Boynton, M. & Boynton, C. (2005). *Educator's guide to preventing and solving discipline problems*. Alexandria, VA: Association for Supervision and Curriculum Development.

Bracey, G. W. (2009, June). Identify and observe effective teacher behaviors. *Phi Delta Kappan*, 772–773.

Bradby, D., & Helms, J. E. (1990). Black racial identity attitudes and White therapist cultural sensitivity in cross-racial therapy dyads: An exploratory study. In J. E. Helms (Ed.), *Black and white racial identity: Theory, research, and practice* (pp. 165–175). Westport, CT: Greenwood.

Brandt, A., Zaveri, K., Fernandez, K., Jondoh, L., Duran, E., Bell, L., Benna, N., Guttierrez, J., & Cruz, D. (2012). School bullying hurts: Evidence of psychological and academic challenges among students with bullying histories. *Undergraduate Research Journal for the Human Sciences, 11*(1). Retrieved May 4th, 2015 from http://www.kon.org/urc/v11/bullying/brandt.html

Bretherton, I. (1985). Attachment theory: Retrospect and prospect. *Monographs of the Society for Research in Child Development, 50*(1-2), 3–35. doi:10.2307/3333824

Bretherton, I., & Munholland, K. A. (2008). Internal working models in attachment relationships: Elaborating a central construct in attachment theory. In J. Cassidy & P. R. Shaver (Eds.), *Handbook of attachment: Theory, research, and clinical applications* (2nd ed., pp. 102–127). New York, NY: Guilford Press.

Bridge, J. A., Iyengar, S., Salary, C. B., Barbe, R., Birmaher, B., Pincus, H. A., Ren, L., & Brent, D. A. (2007). Clinical response and risk for reported suicidal ideation and suicide attempts in pediatric antidepressant treatment: A meta-analysis of randomized controlled trials. *JAMA: Journal of the American Medical Association, 297*(15), 1683–1696. doi:10.1001/jama.297.15.1683

Broderick, P. C. (2013). *Learning to breathe: A mindfulness curriculum for adolescents to cultivate emotion regulation, attention, and performance*. Oakland, CA: New Harbinger Publications.

Broesch, J., & Hadley, C. (2012). Putting culture back into acculturation: Identifying and overcoming gaps in the definition and measurement of acculturation. *The Social Science Journal, 49*(3), 375–385.

Bruner, J. (1996). *The culture of education*. Cambridge, MA: Harvard University Press.

Buchmann, J., Gierow, W., Reis, O., & Haessler, F. (2011). Intelligence moderates impulsivity and attention in ADHD children: An ERP study using a go/nogo paradigm. *The World Journal of Biological Psychiatry, 12*(suppl.), 35–39.

Buskist, W., Sikorski, J., Buckley, T., & Saville, B. K. (2002). Elements of master teaching. In S. F. Davis & W. Buskist (Eds.), *The teaching of psychology: Essays in honor of Wilbert J. McKeachie and Charles L. Brewer* (pp. 27–39). Mahwah, N.J.: Lawrence Erlbaum Associates, Inc.

Buyse, E., Verschueren, K., & Doumen, S. (2011). Preschoolers' attachment to mother and risk for adjustment problems in kindergarten: Can teachers make a difference? *Social Development, 20*(1), 33–50. doi:10.1111/j.1467-9507.2009.00555.x

Buyse, E., Verschueren, K., Verachtert, P., & Van Damme, J. (2009). Predicting school adjustment in early elementary school: Impact of teacher-child relationship quality and relational classroom climate. *The Elementary School Journal, 110*(2), 119–141. doi:10.1086/605768

Calzo, J. P., Corliss, H. L., Blood, E. A., Field, A. E., & Austin, S. B. (2013). Development of muscularity and weight concerns in heterosexual and sexual minority males. *Health Psychology, 32*(1), 42-51.

Cambridge Dictionary Online. (2012). Pedagogy definition. http://dictionary.cambridge.org/us/dictionary/english/pedagogy

Canter, L. & Canter, M. (1997). *Assertive discipline: Positive behavior management for today's classroom.* Los Angeles, CA: Canter & Associates.

Caplan, G. (1964). *Principles of preventive psychiatry.* New York, NY: Basic Books.

Capps, L., Sigman, M., & Mundy, P. (1994). Attachment security in children with autism. *Development and Psychopathology, 6*(2), 249–261.

Carlson, E. B., Armstrong, J., Loewenstein, R., & Roth, D. (1998). Relationships between traumatic experiences and symptoms of posttraumatic stress, dissociation, and amnesia. In J. D. Bremner & C. R. Marmar (Eds.), *Trauma, memory, and dissociation* (pp. 205–227). Arlington, VA: American Psychiatric Association.

Carney, J. V. (2000). Bullied to death: Perceptions of peer abuse and suicidal behaviour during adolescence. *School Psychology International, 21*(2), 213–223. doi:10.1177/0143034300212007

Carter, R. T., Helms, J. E., & Juby, H. L. (2004). The relationship between racism and racial identity for White Americans: A profile analysis. *Journal of Multicultural Counseling and Development, 32*(1), 2–17.

Carter, R. T., & Qureshi, A. (1995). A typology of philosophical assumptions in multicultural counseling and training. In J. G. Ponterotto, J. M. Casas, L. A. Suzuki, & C. M. Alexander (Eds.), *Handbook of multicultural counseling* (pp. 239–262). Thousand Oaks, CA: Sage.

Cassidy, J. (2008). The nature of the child's ties. In J. Cassidy & P. R. Shaver (Eds.), *Handbook of attachment: Theory, research, and clinical applications* (2nd ed., pp. 3–22). New York, NY: Guilford Press.

Cassidy, J., & Kobak, R. R. (1988). Avoidance and its relation to other defensive processes. In J. Belsky & T. Nezworski (Eds.), *Clinical implications of attachment* (pp. 300–323). Hillsdale, NJ: Lawrence Erlbaum.

Cassidy, W., Jackson, M., & Brown, K. N. (2009). Sticks and stones can break my bones, but how can pixels hurt me?: Students' experiences with cyber-bullying. *School Psychology International, 30*(4), 383–402. doi:10.1177/0143034309106948

Cavanagh, M., Quinn, D., Duncan, D., Graham, T., & Balbuena, L. (2014). Oppositional defiant disorder is better conceptualized as a disorder of emotional regulation. *Journal of Attention Disorders, 20*, 1–20.

Cavin, C. (1998). Maintaining sanity in an insane classroom: How a teacher of students with emotional disturbances can keep from becoming an emotionally disturbed teacher. *Education and Treatment of Children, 21*(3), 370–384.

Centers for Disease Control and Prevention MMWR Surveillance Summaries. (2007). Prevalence of autism spectrum diorders: Autism and developmental disabilities monitoring network, 14 sites, United States, 2002, 56 (SS01), 12-28. Retrieved Ausgust 18, 2015 from http://www.cdc.gov/mmwr/preview/mmwrhtml/ss5601a2.htm

Center for Disease Control and Prevention. Attention-Deficit/Hyperactivity Disorder. (2014). Key findings of the prevalence of ADHD: Its diagnosis and treatment in a community based epidemiologic study. Retrieved Ausgust 18, 2015 from http://www.cdc.gov/ncbddd/adhd/features/adhd-key-findings-play.html

Centers for Disease Control and Prevention. National Youth Risk Behavior Survey. 2005. (2006). Retrieved August 15, 2015, http://www.cdc.gov/mmwr/preview/mmwrhtml/ss5505a1.htm

Centers for Disease Control and Prevention. Understanding Bullying—Fact Sheet. (2014). Retrieved May 14, 2015, from http://www.cdc.gov/violenceprevention/pub/understanding_bullying.html

Cerel, J., & Campbell, F. R. (2008). Suicide survivors seeking mental health services: A preliminary examination of the role of an active postvention model. *Suicide and Life-Threatening Behavior, 38*(1), 30–34.

Chamberlain, P., & Patterson, P. R. (1995). Discipline and child compliance in parenting. In M. Bornstein (Ed.), *Handbook of parenting* (Vol. 4, pp. 205–225). Mahwah, NJ: Lawrence Erlbaum.

Chevallier, C., Grèzes, J., Molesworth, C., Berthoz, S., & Happé, F. (2012). Brief report: Selective social anhedonia in high functioning autism. *Journal of Autism and Developmental Disorders, 42*(7), 1504–1509. doi:10.1007/s10803-011-1364-0

Clinical Advisor. (2013, May). Teen suicide prompts an investigation. Retrieved April 30, 2015, from http://www.clinicaladvisor.com/issue/may/01/2013/2244/

Cochran, M., & Niego, S. (2002). Parenting and social networks. In M. H. Bornstein (Ed), *Handbook of parenting: Vol. 4: Social conditions and applied parenting* (2nd ed., pp. 123–148). Mahwah, NJ: Lawrence Erlbaum.

Cochran-Smith, M., & Zeichner, K. (2005). *Review of research in teacher education.* Washington, DC: American Educational Research Association.

Cogill, J. (2008). *Primary teachers' interactive whiteboard practice across one year: Changes in pedagogy and influencing factors.* doctoral thesis, King's College, University of London. Available at www.juliecogill.com.

Cole-Detke, H., & Kobak, R. (1996). Attachment processes in eating disorder and depression. *Journal of Consulting and Clinical Psychology, 64*(2), 282–290. doi:10.1037/0022-006X.64.2.282

Collins, M. E. (1991). Body figure perceptions and preferences among preadolescent children. *International Journal of Eating Disorders, 10*, 199–208.

Conroy, M. A., Sutherland, K. S., Snyder, A., Al-Hendawi, M., & Vo, A. (2009). Creating a positive classroom atmosphere: Teachers' use of effective praise and feedback. *Beyond Behavior, 18*(2), 18–26.

Corbett, J. & Norwich, B. (1999). Learners with special educational needs. In P. Mortimore (Ed.), *Understanding pedagogy and its impact on learning* (pp. 115–136). London, UK: Paul Chapman Publishing.

Couros, G. (2010, April 24). What makes a master teacher [Web log post]. Retrieved June 3, 2014, from http://georgecouros.ca/blog/archives/267

Cowan, N., & Morey, C. C. (2006). Visual working memory depends on attentional filtering. *Trends in Cognitive Sciences, 10*(4), 139–141.

Croninger, R. G., Buese, D., & Larson, J. (2012). A mixed-methods look at teaching quality: Challenges and possibilities from one study. *Teachers College Record, 114*(4), 1-36.

Crosnoe, R., Johnson, M. K., & Elder, G. H. J. (2004). Intergenerational bonding in school: The behavioral and contextual correlates of student-teacher relationships. *Sociology of Education, 77*(1), 60–81. doi:10.1177/003804070407700103

Cross, W. E., Jr. (1971). The Negro-to-Black conversion experience. *Black World, 20*(9), 13–27.

Curry, J., Silva, S., Rohde, P., Ginsburg, G., Kratochvil, C., Simons, A., & March, J. (2011). Recovery and recurrence following treatment for adolescent major depression. *Archives of General Psychiatry, 68*(3), 263–270. doi:10.1001/archgenpsychiatry.2010.150

Dalal, F. (2006). Racism: Processes of detachment, dehumanization, and hatred. *The Psychoanalytic Quarterly, 75*(1), 131–161.

Damasio, A. (1999). *The feeling of what happens: Body and emotion in the making of consciousness.* Fort Worth, TX: Harcourt College Publishers.

Darling-Hammond, L. (2006). Constructing 21st-century teacher education. *Journal of Teacher Education, 57*(3), 300–314.

Davis, T. E. I., & Ollendick, T. H. (2011). Specific phobias. In D. McKay & E. A. Storch (Eds.), *Handbook of child and adolescent anxiety disorders* (pp. 231–244). New York, NY: Springer.

DeGraft-Johnson, A., Fisher, M., Rosen, L., Napolitano, B., & Laskin, E. (2013). Weight gain in an eating disorders day program. *International Journal of Adolescent Medicine and Health, 25*(2), 177–180. doi:10.1515/ijamh-2013-0027

DeKlyen, M., & Greenberg, M. T. (2008). Attachment and psychopathology in childhood. In J. Cassidy & P. R. Shaver (Eds.), *Handbook of attachment: Theory, research, and clinical applications* (2nd ed., pp. 637–665). New York, NY: Guilford Press.

Department of Health and Human Services. (n.d.) Attention deficit hyperactivity disorder among children aged 5-17 years in the United States, 1998-2009. Retrieved May 5, 2015, from children aged 5–17 years in the United States, 1998–2009. NCHS data brief, no 70.

Department of Health and Human Services. (n.d.). Eating disorders. Retrieved June 1, 2015, from http://www.mentalhealth.gov/what-to-look-for/eating-disorders/index.html

Derefinko, K., DeWall, C. N., Metze, A. V., Walsh, E. C., & Lynam, D. R. (2011). Do different facets of impulsivity predict different types of aggression? *Aggressive Behavior, 37*(3), 223–233.

De Ruiter, C., & van IJzendoorn, M. H. (1992). Agoraphobia and anxious-ambivalent attachment: An integrative review. *Journal of Anxiety Disorders, 6*(4), 365–381. doi:10.1016/0887-6185(92)90006-S

DeShong, H. L., & Kurtz, J. E. (2013). Four factors of impulsivity differentiate antisocial and borderline personality disorders. *Journal of Personality Disorders, 27*(2), 144–156.

Diamond, A., & Lee, K. (2011). Interventions shown to aid executive function development in children 4 to 12 years old. *Science, 333*(6045), 959–964.

Dodge, K. A., Lansford, J. E., Burks, V. S., Bates, J. E., Pettit, G. S., Fontaine, R., & Price, J. M. (2003). Peer rejection and social information-processing factors in the development of aggressive behavior problems in children. *Child Development, 74*(2), 374–393.

Doll, B., Swearer, S. M., Collins, A. M., Chadwell, M. R., Dooley, K., & Chapla, B. A. (2012). Bullying and coercion: School-based cognitive-behavioral interventions.

In R. B. Mennuti, R. W. Christner, & A. Freeman (Eds.), *Cognitive-behavioral interventions in educational settings: A handbook for practice* (2nd ed., pp. 339–375). New York, NY: Routledge.

Donovan, M. S., & Bransford, J. D. (Eds.). (2005). *How students learn: History in the classroom.* Washington, DC: National Academies Press.

Doussard-Rooosevelt, J. A., Joe, C. M., Bazhenova, O. V., & Porges, S. W. (2003). Mother–child interaction in autistic and nonautistic children: Characteristics of maternal approach behaviors and child social responses. *Development and Psychopathology, 15*(02), 277–295.

Dozier, M., Lomax, L., Tyrell, C. L., & Lee, S. W. (2001). The challenge of treatment for clients with dismissing states of mind. *Attachment & Human Development, 3*(1), 62–76. doi:10.1080/14616730010000858

Dozier, M., Stovall-McClough, K. C., & Albus, K. E. (2008). Attachment and psychopathology in adulthood. In J. Cassidy & P. R. Shaver (Eds.), *Handbook of attachment: Theory, research, and clinical applications* (2nd ed., pp. 718–744). New York, NY: Guilford Press.

Druck, K., & Kaplowitz, M. (2005). Preventing classroom violence. *Education Digest: Essential Readings Condensed for Quick Review, 71*(2), 40–43.

Dworkin, E., Javdani, S., Verona, E., & Campbell, R. (2014). Child sexual abuse and disordered eating: The mediating role of impulsive and compulsive tendencies. *Psychology of Violence, 4*(1), 21.

Dweck, C. S. (2008). *Mindset: The new psychology of success.* New York, NY: Ballantine Books.

Easter, M. M. (2012). "Not all my fault": Genetics, stigma, and personal responsibility for women with eating disorders. *Social Science & Medicine, 75*(8), 1408–1416.

Eating Disorder Information Sheet (2000). Public Health Service's Office in Women's Health. Retrieved August 12, 2015, from disorders/us/cjis/ucr/crime-in-the-u.s/2010/crime-in-the-u.s.-2010.

Eaton, D. K., Kann, L., Kinchen, S., Shanklin, S., Ross., J., Hawkins, J., . . . Wechsler, H. (2010). *Youth Risk Behavior Surveillance—United States, 2009.* Retrieved July 30, 2015, from CDC website: http://www.cdc.gov/mmwr/preview/mmwrhtml/ss5905a1.htm

Ehrensaft, M. K., & Cohen, P. (2012). Contribution of family violence to the intergenerational transmission of externalizing behavior. *Prevention Science, 13*(4), 370–383.

Eisenberg, J. F. (1966). The social organization of mammals. *Handbuch der Zoologie 8 (10/7),* Lieferung 39: 1–92.

Eisenberg, M. E., Berge, J. M., Fulkerson, J. A., & Neumark-Sztainer, D. (2012). Associations between hurtful weight-related comments by family and significant other and the development of disordered eating behaviors in young adults. *Journal of Behavioral Medicine, 35*(5), 500–508. doi:10.1007/s10865-011-9378-9

Erikson, E. H. (1964). *Childhood and society* (2nd Ed.). Oxford, England: W. W. Norton.

Ernst, M., Luckenbaugh, D. A., Moolchan, E. T., Leff, M. K., Allen, R., Eshel, N., London, E. D., & Kimes, A. (2006). Behavioral predictors of substance-use initiation in adolescents with and without attention-deficit/hyperactivity disorder. *Pediatrics, 117*(6), 2030–2039.

Essex, M. J., Klein, M. H., Slattery, M. J., Goldsmith, H. H., & Kalin, N. H. (2010). Early risk factors and developmental pathways to chronic high inhibition and social anxiety disorder in adolescence. *American Journal of Psychiatry, 167*(1), 40–46. doi:10.1176/appi.ajp.2009.07010051

Evans, G. W., & Rosenbaum, J. (2008). Self-regulation and the income-achievement gap. *Early Childhood Research Quarterly, 23*(4), 504–514.

Fahim, C., He, Y., Yoon, U., Chen, J., Evans, A., & Pérusse, D. (2011). Neuroanatomy of childhood disruptive behavior disorders. *Aggressive Behavior, 37*(4), 326–337. doi:10.1002/ab.20396

Farmer, C. A., Arnold, L. E., Bukstein, O. G., Findling, R. L., Gadow, K. D., Li, X., Butter, E. M., & Aman, M. G. (2011). The treatment of severe child aggression (TOSCA) study: Design challenges. *Child and Adolescent Psychiatry and Mental Health, 5.*

Fearon, R. P., Bakermans-Kranenburg, M. J., Van IJzendoorn, M. H., Lapsley, A., & Roisman, G. I. (2010). The significance of insecure attachment and disorganization in the development of children's externalizing behavior: a meta-analytic study. *Child Development, 81*(2), 435–456.

FBI. (2010). Crime in the U.S. Retrieved July 16, 2015, from https://www.fbi.gov/about-us/cjis/ucr/crime-in-the-u.s/2010/crime-in-the-u.s.-2010

Filter, K. J., McKenna, M. K., Benedict, E., Horner, R. H., Todd, A. W., & Watson, J. (2007). Check-In/Check-Out: A post-hoc evaluation of an efficient, secondary-level targeted intervention for reducing problem behaviors in schools. *Education and Treatment of Children, 30,* 69–84.

Finkelmeyer, A., Stewart, W., Woodford, J., & Coleman, M. (2006). Simulating social interaction to address deficits of autistic spectrum disorder in Children. *Cyberpsychology & Behavior, 9*(2), 213–217.

Fisher, N., Happé, F., & Dunn, J. (2005). The relationship between vocabulary, grammar, and false belief task performance in children with autistic spectrum disorders and children with moderate learning difficulties. *Journal of Child Psychology and Psychiatry, 46*(4), 409–419.

Fiske, S. T. (2004). *Social beings: A core motives approach to social psychology.* Hoboken, NJ: Wiley.

Fonagy, P. (2006). The mentalization-focused approach to social development. In J. G. Allen & P. Fonagy (Eds.), *The handbook of mentalization-based treatment* (pp. 53–99). Hoboken, NJ: Wiley.

Fonagy, P., Gergely, G., Jurist, E. L., & Target, M. (2002). *Affect regulation, mentalization, and the development of the self.* New York, NY: Other Press.

Fonagy, P., Leigh, T., Steele, M., Steele, H., Kennedy, R., Mattoon, G., Target M., & Gerber, A. (1996). The relation of attachment status, psychiatric classification, and response to psychotherapy. *Journal of Consulting and Clinical Psychology, 64*(1), 22–31. doi:10.1037/0022-006X.64.1.22

Fonagy, P., Target, M., Steele, M., & Steele, H. (1997). The development of violence and crime as it relates to security of attachment. In J. D. Osofsky (Ed.), *Children in a violent society* (pp. 150–177). New York, NY: Guilford Press.

Forman, S. F., Yager, J., & Solomon, D. (2012). *Eating disorders: Epidemiology, pathogenesis, and overview of clinical features.* Retrieved April 10th, 2015 from http://46.4.230.144/web/UpToDate.v19.2/contents/f28/5/28832.htm

Fraley, R. C. (2002). Attachment stability from infancy to adulthood: Meta-analysis and dynamic modeling of developmental mechanisms. *Personality and Social Psychology Review, 6*(2), 123–151. doi:10.1207/S15327957PSPR0602_03

Fraley, R. C., & Shaver, P. R. (2008). Attachment theory and its place in contemporary personality theory and research. In O. P. John, R. W. Robins, & L. A. Pervin (Eds.), *Handbook of personality: Theory and research* (3rd ed., pp. 518–541). New York, NY: Guilford Press.

Franco-Watkins, A. M., & Mattson, R. E. (2009). When working memory isn't effective: The role of working memory constraints on rates of delayed discounting and substance-use problems. In G.H. Lassiter (Ed.), *Impulsivity: Causes, controls and disorders.* Hauppauge, NY: Nova Science.

Franko, D. L., Keshaviah, A., Eddy, K. T., Krishna, M., Davis, M. C., Keel, P. K., & Herzog, D. B. (2013). A longitudinal investigation of mortality in anorexia nervosa and bulimia nervosa. *The American Journal of Psychiatry, 170*(8), 917–925. doi:10.1176/appi.ajp.2013.12070868

Freire, P. (1970). *Pedagogy of the oppressed.* New York, NY: Continuum.

Frick, P. J. (2012). Developmental pathways to conduct disorder: Implications for future directions in research, assessment, and treatment. *Journal of Clinical Child and Adolescent Psychology, 41*(3), 378–389. doi:10.1080/15374416.2012.664815

Frick, P. J., Blair, R. J., & Castellanos, F. X. (2013). Callous-unemotional traits and developmental pathways to the disruptive behavior disorders. In P. H. Tolan & B. L. Leventhal (Eds.), *Disruptive behavior disorders* (pp. 69–102). New York, NY: Springer Science.

Frick, P. J., & Nigg, J. T. (2012). Current issues in the diagnosis of attention deficit hyperactivity disorder, oppositional defiant disorder, and conduct disorder. *Annual Review of Clinical Psychology, 8*, 77–107.

Frombonne E. (2003). Epidemiological surveys of autism and other pervasive developmental disorders: An update. *Journal of Autism & Developmental Disorders, 33*, 365–382.

Frombonne, E. (2005). Epidemiological studies of pervasive developmental disorders. In F. R. Volkmar, R. Paul, A. Klin, & D. Cohen (Eds.), *Handbook of autism and pervasive developmental disorders* (3rd ed., pp. 42–69). Hoboken, NJ: Wiley.

Fuchs, D., & Fuchs, L. (2006). Introduction to response to intervention: What, why, and how valid is it? *Reading Research Quarterly, 41*, 93–99. doi:10.1598/RRQ.41.1.4

Fulkerson, J. A., Harrison, P. A., & Beebe, T. J. (1997). *Residential behavioral treatment facilities.* Retrieved August 14, 2015, from Minnesota Department of Human Services Report website: http://mn.gov/mnddc/past/pdf/90s/97/97-RBT-DHS.pdf

Gage, N. L. (1978). *The scientific basis of the art of teaching.* New York, NY: Teachers College Press.

Garfin, D. R., Holman, E. A., & Silver, R. C. (2015, April 20). Cumulative exposure to prior collective trauma and acute stress responses to the Boston Marathon bombings. *Psychological science.* doi: 10.1177/0956797614561043

Gauthier, C., Hassler, C., Mattar, L., Launay, J.-M., Callebert, J., Steiger, H., Melcior, J., & Godart, N. (2014). Symptoms of depression and anxiety in anorexia nervosa: Links with plasma tryptophan and serotonin metabolism. *Psychoneuroendocrinology, 39*, 170–178. doi:10.1016/j.psyneuen.2013.09.009

George, C., Kaplan, N., & Main, M. (1984). *Adult attachment interview.* Department of Psychology, University of California.

George, C., Kaplan, N., & Main, M. (1985). *Adult attachment interview.* Department of Psychology, University of California.

George, C., Kaplan, N., & Main, M. (1996). *Adult attachment interview.* Department of Psychology, University of California.

Gilissen, R., Koolstra, C. M., van IJzendoorn, M. H., Bakermans-Kranenburg, M. J., & van der Veer, R. (2007). Physiological reactions of preschoolers to fear-inducing film clips: Effects of temperamental fearfulness and quality of the parent–child relationship. *Developmental Psychobiology, 49*(2), 187–195.

Gillett, K. S., Harper, J. M., Larson, J. H., Berrett, M. E., & Hardman, R. K. (2009). Implicit family process rules in eating-disordered and non-eating-disordered families. *Journal of Marital and Family Therapy, 35*(2), 159–174. doi:10.1111/j.1752-0606.2009.00113.x

Ginsburg, G. S., & Walkup, J. T. (2004). Specific phobia. In T. H. Ollendick & J. S. March (Eds.), *Phobic and anxiety disorders in children and adolescents: A clinician's guide to effective psychosocial and pharmacological interventions* (pp. 175–197). New York, NY: Oxford University Press.

Goldhaber, D. D., & Brewer, D. J. (2000). Does teacher certification matter? High school teacher certification status and student achievement. *Educational Evaluation and Policy Analysis, 22*(2), 129–145.

Goldhaber, D. & Hansen, M. (2010). Race, gender, and teacher testing: How informative a tool is teacher licensure testing? *American Educational Research Journal, 47*(1), 218–251.

Górska, D., & Marszal, M. (2014). Mentalization and theory of mind in borderline personality organization: Exploring the differences between affective and cognitive aspects of social cognition in emotional pathology. *Psychiatria Polska, 48*(3), 503–513.

Gladwell, M. (2013). *David and goliath: Underdogs, misfits, and the art of battling giants.* New York, NY: Little, Brown and Company.

Gladwell, M. (2000). *The tipping point: How little things can make a big difference.* Boston, MA: Little, Brown and Company.

Gratz, K. L. (2010). An acceptance-based emotion regulation group therapy for deliberate self-harm. Unpublished therapy manual: University of Mississippi Medical Centre.

Greene, M. (1978). The matters of mystification: Teacher education in unquiet times. In M. Greene, Ed., *Landscapes of learning* (pp. 53–72). New York, NY: Teachers College Press.

Greene, R. W. (2006). Oppositional defiant disorder. In R. T. Ammerman (Ed.), *Comprehensive handbook of personality and psychopathology* (Vol. 3, pp. 285–298). Hoboken, NJ: Wiley.

Gross, J. J., & John, O. P. (2003). Individual differences in two emotion regulation processes: Implications for affect, relationships, and well-being. *Journal of Personality and Social Psychology, 85*(2), 348-362.

Grossmann, K., Grossmann, K. E., Kindler, H., & Zimmermann, P. (2008). A wider view of attachment and exploration: The influence of mothers and fathers on the development of psychological security from infancy to young adulthood. In J. Cassidy & P. R. Shaver (Eds.), *Handbook of attachment: Theory, research, and clinical applications* (2nd ed., pp. 857–879). New York, NY: Guilford Press.

Gushue, G. V. (2004). Race, color-blind racial attitudes, and judgments about mental health: A shifting standards perspective. *Journal of Counseling Psychology, 51*(4), 398–407. doi:10.1037/0022-0167.51.4.398

Gushue, G. V., Constantine, M. G., & Sciarra, D. T. (2008). The influence of culture, self-reported multicultural counseling competence, and shifting standards of judgment on perceptions of family functioning of white family counselors. *Journal of Counseling & Development, 86*(1), 85–94. doi:10.1002/j.1556-6678.2008.tb00629.x

Gundem, B. B. (1992). Notes on the development of the Nordic didactics. *Journal of Curriculum Studies, 24*(1), 61–70.

Gustafson-Larson, A. M., & Terry, R. D. (1992). Weight-related behaviors and concerns of fourth-grade children. *Journal of the American Dietary Association, 92*, 818–822.

Hackman, D. A., & Farah, M. J. (2009). Socioeconomic status and the developing brain. *Trends in Cognitive Sciences, 13*(2), 65–73.

Hagen, K. A., Ogden, T., & Bjørnebekk, G. (2011). Treatment outcomes and mediators of parent management training: A one-year follow-up of children with conduct problems. *Journal of Clinical Child & Adolescent Psychology, 40*(2), 165–178.

Hamre, B. K., & Pianta, R. C. (2001). Early teacher–child relationships and the trajectory of children's school outcomes through eighth grade. *Child Development, 72*(2), 625–638. doi:10.1111/1467-8624.00301

Hanish, L. D., & Guerra, N. G. (2000). Children who get victimized at school: What is known? What can be done? *Professional School Counseling, 4*(2), 113–119.

Hansen, T. B., Steenberg, L. M., Palic, S., & Elklit, A. (2012). A review of psychological factors related to bullying victimization in schools. *Aggression and Violent Behavior, 17*(4), 383–387.

Hargreaves, A. (2000). Mixed emotions: Teachers' perceptions of their interactions with students. *Teaching and Teacher Education, 16*, 811–826.

Harold, G. T., Elam, K. K., Lewis, G., Rice, F., & Thapar, A. (2012). Interparental conflict, parent psychopathology, hostile parenting, and child antisocial behavior: Examining the role of maternal versus paternal influences using a novel genetically sensitive research design. *Development and Psychopathology, 24*(4), 1283–1295.

Harris, A. (1998). Effective teaching: A review of the literature. *School Leadership & Management, 18*(2), 169-183.

Harrop, E. N., & Marlatt, G. A. (2010). The comorbidity of substance use disorders and eating disorders in women: Prevalence, etiology, and treatment. *Addictive behaviors, 35*(5), 392–398.

Hay, P. J., & Claudino, A. M. (2012). Clinical psychopharmacology of eating disorders: A research update. *International Journal of Neuropsychopharmacology, 15*(2), 209–222.

Hazler, R. J., & Carney, J. V. (2000). When victims turn aggressors: Factors in the development of deadly school violence. *Professional School Counseling, 4*(2), 105–112.

Helm, C. (2007). What's new in teacher dispositions affecting self-esteem and student performance. *The Clearing House,* 109–110.

Helms, J. E. (1984). Toward a theoretical explanation of the effects of race on counseling: A Black and White model. *The Counseling Psychologist, 12*(3–4), 153–165. doi:10.1177/0011000084124013

Helms, J. E. (1990). *Black and White racial identity: Theory, research, and practice.* Westport, CT: Greenwood Press.

Helms, J. E. (1994). How multiculturalism obscures racial factors in the therapy process: Comment on Ridley et al. (1994), Sodowsky et al. (1994), Ottavi et al. (1994), and Thompson et al. (1994). *Journal of Counseling Psychology, 41*(2), 162–165. doi:10.1037/0022-0167.41.2.162

Helms, J. E. (1995). An update of Helm's White and people of color racial identity models. In J. G. Ponterotto, J. M. Casas, L. A. Suzuki, & C. M. Alexander (Eds.), *Handbook of multicultural counseling* (pp. 181–198). Thousand Oaks, CA: Sage Publications.

Helms, J. E., & Carter, R. T. (1991). Relationships of White and Black racial identity attitudes and demographic similarity to counselor preferences. *Journal of Counseling Psychology, 38*(4), 446-457.

Helms, J. E., & Cook, D. A. (1999). *Using race and culture in counseling and psychotherapy: Theory and process.* Needham Heights, MA, US: Allyn & Bacon.

Helterbran, V. R. (2008). The ideal professor: Student perceptions of effective instructor practices, attitudes, and skills. *Education, 129*(1), 125–138.

Hendren, R. L., & Mullen, D. J. (2006). Conduct disorder and oppositional defiant disorder. In *Essentials of child and adolescent psychiatry* (pp. 357–387). Arlington, VA: American Psychiatric Publishing.

Henggeler, S. W., & Sheidow, A. J. (2012). Empirically supported family-based treatments for conduct disorder and delinquency in adolescents. *Journal of Marital and Family Therapy, 38*(1), 30–58.

Heron, M. (2013). Deaths: Leading causes for 2010. *National Vital Statistics Reports, 62*(6), 1-28.

Herrington, J. D., Heller, W., Mohanty, A., Engels, A. S., Banich, M. T., Webb, A. G., & Miller, G. A. (2010). Localization of asymmetric brain function in emotion and depression. *Psychophysiology, 47*(3), 442–454.

Hertsgaard, L., Gunnar, M., Erickson, M. F., & Nachmias, M. (1995). Adrenocortical responses to the strange situation in infants with disorganized/disoriented attachment relationships. *Child Development, 66*(4), 1100–1106.

Hesse, E. (2008). The Adult Attachment Interview: Protocol, method of analysis, and empirical studies. In J. Cassidy, & P. R. Shaver (Eds.), *Handbook of attachment: Theory, research, and clinical applications* (2nd ed., pp. 552–598). New York, NY, US: Guilford Press.

Hesse, E., & Main, M. (2006). Frightened, threatening, and dissociative parental behavior in low-risk samples: Description, discussion, and interpretations. *Development and Psychopathology, 18*(2), 309–343.

Hinshaw, S. P., & Simmel, C. (1994). Attention-deficit hyperactivity disorder. In M. Hersen, R. T. Ammerman, & L. A. Sisson (Eds.), *Handbook of aggressive and destructive behavior in psychiatric patients* (pp. 347–362). New York, NY: Plenum Press.

Hinson, J. M., Jameson, T. L., & Whitney, P. (2003). Impulsive decision making and working memory. *Journal of Experimental Psychology: Learning, Memory, and Cognition, 29*(2), 298-306.

Hjalmarsson, R. (2008). Criminal justice involvement and high school completion. *Journal of Urban Economics, 63*(2), 613–630.

Hoek, H.W., & van Hoeken, D. (2003). Review of the prevalence and incidence of eating disorders. *International Journal of Eating Disorders, 34*, 383–396.

Hong, J. S., & Espelage, D. L. (2012). A review of research on bullying and peer victimization in school: An ecological system analysis. *Aggression and Violent Behavior, 17*(4), 311–322.

Horn, N. R., Dolan, M., Elliott, R., Deakin, J. F. W., & Woodruff, P. W. R. (2003). Response inhibition and impulsivity: An fMRI study. *Neuropsychologia, 41*(14), 1959–1966.

Howes, C., Matheson, C. C., & Hamilton, C. E. (1994). Maternal, teacher, and child care history correlates of children's relationships with peers. *Child Development, 65*(1), 264–273. doi:10.2307/1131380

Howes, C., & Ritchie, S. (1999). Attachment organizations in children with difficult life circumstances. *Development and Psychopathology, 11*(2), 251–268. doi:10.1017/S0954579499002047

Howes, C., & Tonyan, H. (2000). Links between adult and peer relations across four developmental periods. In K. A. Kerns, J. M. Contreras, & A. M. Neal-Barnett (Eds.), *Family and peers: Linking two social worlds* (pp. 85–113). Westport, CT: Praeger/Greenwood.

Hruska, B. (2007). "She my friend": Implications of friend ideologies, identities, and relationships for bilingual kindergarteners. *Multicultural Perspectives, 9*(4), 3–12.

Hunt, Q. A., & Hertlein, K. M. (2015). Conceptualizing suicide bereavement from an attachment lens. *The American Journal of Family Therapy, 43*(1), 16–27.

Hyatt, C. J., Haney-Caron, E., & Stevens, M. C. (2012). Cortical thickness and folding deficits in conduct-disordered adolescents. *Biological Psychiatry, 72*(3), 207–214.

Imber, M. (2006, November). Should teachers be good people? *American School Board Journal*, 29–31.

Individuals With Disabilities Education Act, 20 U.S.C. § 1400 (2004).

Ireland, J. L., & Power, C. L. (2004). Attachment, emotional loneliness, and bullying behaviour: A study of adult and young offenders. *Aggressive Behavior, 30*(4), 298–312.

Ireson, J., Mortimore, P., & Hallam, S. (1999). The common strands of pedagogy and their implications. In P. Mortimore (Ed.), *Understanding pedagogy and its impact on learning* (pp. 212–232). London, UK: Paul Chapman.

Jackson, R. R. (2012). *Never work harder than your students & other principles of great teaching*. Alexandria, VA: Association for Supervision and Curriculum Development.

Javdani, S., Sadeh, N., & Verona, E. (2011). Suicidality as a function of impulsivity, callous–unemotional traits, and depressive symptoms in youth. *Journal of Abnormal Psychology, 120*(2), 400-413.

Johnson, W. A. (2001). Personality correlates of preferences for preprofessional training by special education and regular class trainees. *Education, 103*(4), 360–368.

James, A., Cowdrey, F., & James, C. (2012). Anxiety disorders in children and adolescents. In P. Sturmey, M. Hersen, (Eds.), *Handbook of evidence-based practice in clinical psychology, Vol 1: Child and adolescent disorders* (pp. 545–557). Hoboken, NJ: John Wiley & Sons Inc.

Janoff-Bulman, R. (1985). The aftermath of victimization: Rebuilding shattered assumptions. *Trauma and Its Wake, 1*, 15–35.

Johnson, S. M. (2008). Couple and family therapy: An attachment perspective. In J. Cassidy & P. R. Shaver (Eds.), *Handbook of attachment: Theory, research, and clinical applications* (2nd ed., pp. 811–829). New York, NY: Guilford Press.

Joiner, T. (2009). *Why people die by suicide*. Cambridge, MA: Harvard University Press.

Jones, V. F., & Jones, L. S. (1981). *Responsible classroom discipline: Creating positive learning environments and solving problems*. Boston, MA: Allyn and Bacon.

Jones, S., & Lynam, D. R. (2008). In the eye of the impulsive beholder: The interaction between impulsivity and perceived informal social control on offending. *Criminal Justice and Behavior, 36*, 307–321.

Juhnke, G. A., Granello, P. F., & Granello, D. H. (2010). *Suicide, self-injury, and violence in the schools: Assessment, prevention, and intervention strategies*. Hoboken, NJ: Wiley.

Kaland, N., Callesen, K., Møller-Nielsen, A., Mortensen, E. L., & Smith, L. (2008). Performance of children and adolescents with Asperger syndrome or high-functioning autism on advanced theory of mind tasks. *Journal of Autism and Developmental Disorders, 38*(6), 1112–1123.

Kazdin, A. E. (2010). Problem-solving skills training and parent management training for oppositional defiant disorder and conduct disorder. In J. R. Weisz & A. E. Kazdin (Eds.), *Evidence-based psychotherapies for children and adolescents* (2nd ed., pp. 211–226). New York, NY: Guilford Press.

Kazdin, A. E. (2011). Evidence-based treatment research: Advances, limitations, and next steps. *American Psychologist, 66*(8), 685–698. doi:10.1037/a0024975

Kendall, P. C., & Suveg, C. (2006). Treating anxiety disorders in youth. In P. C. Kendall (Ed.), *Child and adolescent therapy: Cognitive-behavioral procedures* (3rd ed., pp. 243–294). New York, NY: Guilford Press.

Kennedy, J. H., & Kennedy, C. E. (2004). Attachment theory: Implications for school psychology. *Psychology in the Schools, 41*(2), 247–259. doi:10.1002/pits.10153

Kennedy, M. M. (2008). Sorting out teacher quality. *Phi Delta Kappan, 90*(1), 59–63.

Kern, L. & Parks, J. K. (2012). Choice Making Opportunities for Students. Virginia Department of Education Division of Special Education and Student Services Web site. Retrieved August 14, 2015, from www.doe.virginia.gov/special_ed

Kerns, K. A. (2008). Attachment in middle childhood. In J. Cassidy & P. R. Shaver (Eds.), *Handbook of attachment: Theory, research, and clinical applications* (2nd ed., pp. 366–382). New York, NY: Guilford Press.

Kerns, K. A., Tomich, P. L., & Kim, P. (2006). Normative trends in children's perceptions of availability and utilization of attachment figures in middle childhood. *Social Development, 15*(1), 1–22. doi:10.1111/j.1467-9507.2006.00327.x

Khurana, A., Romer, D., Betancourt, L. M., Brodsky, N. L., Giannetta, J. M., & Hurt, H. (2012). Early adolescent sexual debut: The mediating role of working memory ability, sensation seeking, and impulsivity. *Developmental Psychology, 48*(5), 1416-1428.

Khurana, A., Romer, D., Betancourt, L. M., Brodsky, N. L., Giannetta, J. M., & Hurt, H. (2013). Working memory ability predicts trajectories of early alcohol use in adolescents: The mediational role of impulsivity. *Addiction, 108*(3), 506–515.

Kimonis, E. R., Fanti, K., Goldweber, A., Marsee, M. A., Frick, P. J., & Cauffman, E. (2014). Callous-unemotional traits in incarcerated adolescents. *Psychological Assessment, 26*(1), 227–237. doi:10.1037/a0034585

Kimonis, E. R., & Frick, P. J. . (2010). Etiology of oppositional defiant disorder and conduct disorder: Biological, familial and environmental factors identified in the development of disruptive behavior disorders. In R. C. Murrihy, A. D. Kidman, T. H. Ollendick, (Eds.), *Clinical handbook of assessing and treating conduct problems in youth* (pp. 49–76). New York, NY: Springer.

Kim, S., Thibodeau, R., & Jorgensen, R. S. (2011). Shame, guilt, and depressive symptoms: A meta-analytic review. *Psychological Bulletin, 137*(1), 68-96.

Kirby, K. N., & Petry, N. M. (2004). Heroin and cocaine abusers have higher discount rates for delayed rewards than alcoholics or non-drug-using controls. *Addiction, 99*(4), 461–471.

Kleiman, E. M., Riskind, J. H., Schaefer, K. E., & Weingarden, H. (2012). The moderating role of social support on the relationship between impulsivity and suicide risk. *Crisis: The Journal of Crisis Intervention and Suicide Prevention, 33*(5), 273–279. doi:10.1027/0227-5910/a000136

Kluck, A. S., Carriere, L., Dallesasse, S., Bvunzawabaya, B., English, E., Cobb, M., Borges, T., Zhuzkha, K., & Fry, D. (2014). Pathways of family influence: Alcohol use and disordered eating in daughters. *Addictive Behaviors, 39*(10), 1404–1407.

Kobak, R., Cassidy, J., Lyons-Ruth, K., & Ziv, Y. (2006). Attachment, stress, and psychopathology: A developmental pathways model. In D. Cicchetti & D. J. Cohen (Eds.), *Developmental psychopathology, Vol 1: Theory and method* (2nd ed., pp. 333–369). Hoboken, NJ: Wiley.

Kobak, R., & Madsen, S. (2008). Disruptions in attachment bonds: Implications for theory, research, and clinical intervention. In J. Cassidy & P. R. Shaver (Eds.), *Handbook of attachment: Theory, research, and clinical applications* (2nd ed., pp. 23–47). New York, NY: Guilford Press.

Kochanek, K.D, Murphy, S.L., Xu, J., & Arias, E. *Mortality in the United States, 2013.* (2014, December). NCHS Data Brief 178. Retrieved April 30, 2015, from the CDC website: http://www.cdc.gov/nchs/data/databriefs/db178.htm.

Kochanska, G., Kim, S., Boldt, L. J., & Yoon, J. E. (2013). Children's callous-unemotional traits moderate links between their positive relationships with parents at preschool age and externalizing behavior problems at early school age. *Journal of Child Psychology and Psychiatry, 54*(11), 1251–1260.

Kohn, A. (1996). *Beyond discipline: From compliance to community.* Alexandria, VA: Association for Supervision and Curriculum Development.

Kohut, H. (1971). *The analysis of the self: A systematic approach to the psychoanalytic treat-*

ment of narcissistic personality disorders. New York, NY: International Universities Press.

Koomen, H. M. Y., Verschueren, K., van Schooten, E., Jak, S., & Pianta, R. C. (2012). Validating the Student-Teacher Relationship Scale: Testing factor structure and measurement invariance across child gender and age in a Dutch sample. *Journal of School Psychology, 50*(2), 215–234. doi:10.1016/j.jsp.2011.09.001

Kopkowski, C. (2008). Why they leave. *NEA Today, 26*(7), 21–25.

Korthagen, F. A. J. (2004). In search of the essence of a good teacher: Towards a more holistic approach in teacher education. *Teaching and Teacher Education, 20*, 77–97.

Kosciw, J. G., Greytak, E. A., Diaz, E. M., and Bartkiewicz, M. J. (2010). *The 2009 National School Climate Survey: The experiences of lesbian, gay, bisexual and transgender youth in our nation's schools*. New York, NY: GLSEN.

Kowalski, R. M., Limber, S., Limber, S. P., & Agatston, P. W. (2012). *Cyberbullying: Bullying in the digital age*. Hoboken, NJ: Wiley.

Kowatch, R. A., Emslie, G. J., Wilkaitis, J., & Dingle, A. D. (2005). Mood disorders. In S.B. Sexson (Ed.), *Child and adolescent psychiatry* (2nd ed., pp.132–153). Hoboken, NJ: Blackwell.

Krishnakumar, A., & Buehler, C. (2000). Interparental conflict and parenting behaviors: A meta-analytic review. *Family Relations, 49*(1), 25–44.

Kurth, W. (2013). Attachment theory and psychohistory: Overview. *The Journal of Psychohistory, 41*(1), 14–38.

Kyriakides, L. (2005). Drawing from teacher effectiveness research and research into teacher interpersonal behavior to establish a teacher evaluation system: A study on the use of student ratings to evaluate teacher behavior. *Journal of Classroom Interaction, 40*(2), 44–66.

Ladd, G. W., & Burgess, K. B. (2001). Do relational risks and protective factors moderate the linkages between childhood aggression and early psychological and school adjustment? *Child Development, 72*(5), 1579–1601. doi:10.1111/1467-8624.00366

Landrum, T. J. & Sweigart, C. A. (2014). Simple, evidence-based interventions for classic problems of emotional and behavioral disorders. *Beyond Behavior, 23*(3), 3–8.

Latimer, K., Wilson, P., Kemp, J., Thompson, L., Sim, F., Gillberg, C., Puckering, C. and Minnis, H. (2012), Disruptive behaviour disorders: A systematic review of environmental antenatal and early years risk factors. *Child: Care, Health and Development, 38*, 611–628. doi: 10.1111/j.1365-2214.2012.01366.x

Lavigne, J. V., Gouze, K. R., Hopkins, J., Bryant, F. B., & LeBailly, S. A. (2012). A multi-domain model of risk factors for ODD symptoms in a community sample of 4-year-olds. *Journal of Abnormal Child Psychology, 40*(5), 741–757. doi:10.1007/s10802-011-9603-6

Lawson, E. A., Holsen, L. M., Santin, M., DeSanti, R., Meenaghan, E., Eddy, K. T., Herzog, D. B., Goldstein, J. M., & Klibanski, A. (2013). Postprandial oxytocin secretion is associated with severity of anxiety and depressive symptoms in anorexia nervosa. *Journal of Clinical Psychiatry, 74*(5), e451–e457. doi:10.4088/JCP.12m08154.

Leamnson, R. N. (1999). *Thinking about teaching and learning: Developing habits of learning with first year college and university students*. Sterling, VA: Stylus Publishing.

Lee, D. L., Belfiore, P. J., & Budin, S. G. (2008). Creating a momentum of school success. *Teaching Exceptional Children, 40*(3), 65–70.

Le Grange, D., & Lock, J. (2011). *Eating disorders in children and adolescents: A clinical handbook*. New York, NY: Guilford Press.

Lehmann, P., & Dangel, R. (1998). Oppositional defiant disorder. *Handbook of Empirical Social Work Practice, 1*, 91–116.

Leventhal, T., & Brooks-Gunn, J. (2000). The neighborhoods they live in: The effects of neighborhood residence on child and adolescent outcomes. *Psychological Bulletin, 126*(2), 309-337.

Lewis, C., & Carpendale, J. (2014). Social cognition. In P. K. Smith & C. H. Hart, (Eds.), *The Wiley Blackwell handbook of childhood social development* (2nd ed., pp. 531–548). New York: Wiley-Blackwell.

Lincoln, A. (1861, March 1) First inaugural address, Washington, DC.

Linville, D., Stice, E., Gau, J., & O'Neil, M. (2011). Predictive effects of mother and peer influences on increases in adolescent eating disorder risk factors and symptoms: A 3-year longitudinal study. *International Journal of Eating Disorders, 44*(8), 745–751.

Liotti, G. (2011). Attachment disorganization and the controlling strategies: An illustration of the contributions of attachment theory to developmental psychopathology and to psychotherapy integration. *Journal of Psychotherapy Integration, 21*(3), 232–252. doi:10.1037/a0025422

Lizardi, D., Grunebaum, M. F., Burke, A., Stanley, B., Mann, J. J., Harkavy-Friedman, J., & Oquendo, M. (2011). The effect of social adjustment and attachment style on suicidal behaviour. *Acta Psychiatrica Scandinavica, 124*(4), 295–300.

Lochman, J. E., Powell, N. R., Whidby, J. M., & Fitzgerald, D. P. (2006). Aggressive children: Cognitive-behavioral assessment and treatment. In P. C. Kendall (Ed.), *Child and adolescent therapy: Cognitive-behavioral procedures* (3rd ed., pp. 33–81). New York, NY: Guilford Press.

Lock, J., & le Grange, D. (2006). Eating disorders. In D. A. Wolfe, & E. J. Mash (Eds.), *Behavioral and emotional disorders in adolescents: Nature, assessment, and treatment.* (pp. 485–504). New York: Guilford Publications.

Lock, J., & Le Grange, D. (2012). *Treatment manual for anorexia nervosa: A family-based approach*. New York, NY: Guilford Press.

Loeber, R., & Burke, J. D. (2011). Developmental pathways in juvenile externalizing and internalizing problems. *Journal of Research on Adolescence, 21*(1), 34–46.

Loeber, R., Menting, B., Lynam, D. R., Moffitt, T. E., Stouthamer-Loeber, M., Stallings, R., Farrington, D. P., & Pardini, D. (2012). Findings from the Pittsburgh Youth Study: Cognitive impulsivity and intelligence as predictors of the age–crime curve. *Journal of the American Academy of Child & Adolescent Psychiatry, 51*(11), 1136–1149. doi:10.1016/j.jaac.2012.08.019

Lombardo, M. V., Chakrabarti, B., Bullmore, E. T., Consortium, M. A., & Baron-Cohen, S. (2011). Specialization of right temporo-parietal junction for mentalizing and its relation to social impairments in autism. *Neuroimage, 56*(3), 1832–1838.

Lopez, V., Corona, R., & Halfond, R. (2013). Effects of gender, media influences, and traditional gender role orientation on disordered eating and appearance concerns among Latino adolescents. *Journal of Adolescence, 36*(4), 727–736.

Loren, R. E., Vaughn, A. J., Langberg, J. M., Cyran, J. E., Proano-Raps, T., Smolyansky, B. H., Tamm, L., & Epstein, J. N. (2015). Effects of an 8-session behavioral parent training group for parents of children with ADHD on child impairment and parenting confidence. *Journal of Attention Disorders, 19*(2), 158–166.

Loughran, J. (1997). An introduction to purpose, passion and pedagogy. In J. Loughran & T. Russell (Eds.), *Teaching about teaching: Purpose, passion and pedagogy in teacher education* (pp. 3–9). London, UK: Falmer Press.

Loughran, J. J. (2002). Effective reflective practice: In search of meaning in learning about teaching. *Journal of Teacher Education, 53*(1), 33–43.

Lovegrove, P. J., Henry, K. L., & Slater, M. D. (2012). Examination of the predictors of latent class typologies of bullying involvement among middle school students. *Journal of School Violence, 11*(1), 75–93.

Lyke, J., & Matsen, J. (2013). Family functioning and risk factors for disordered eating. *Eating Behaviors*, *14*(4), 497–499.

Lynam, D. R., Smith, G. T., Whiteside, S. P., & Cyders, M. A. (2006). *The UPPS-P: Assessing five personality pathways to impulsive behavior.* West Lafayette, IN: Purdue University.

Lynch, M., & Cicchetti, D. (1992). Maltreated children's reports of relatedness to their teachers. In R. C. Pianta (Ed.), *Beyond the parent: The role of other adults in children's lives* (pp. 81–107). San Francisco, CA: Jossey-Bass.

Lyons-Ruth, K., Bronfman, E., & Parsons, E. (1999). Maternal frightened, frightening, or atypical behavior and disorganized infant attachment patterns. *Monographs of the Society for Research in Child Development*, *64*(3), 67–96. doi:10.1111/1540-5834.00034

Lyons-Ruth, K., & Jacobvitz, D. (2008). Attachment disorganization: Genetic factors, parenting contexts, and developmental transformation from infancy to adulthood. In J. Cassidy & P. R. Shaver (Eds.), *Handbook of attachment: Theory, research, and clinical applications* (2nd ed., pp. 666–697). New York, NY: Guilford Press.

Lyons-Ruth, K., Yellin, C., Melnick, S., & Atwood, G. (2005). Expanding the concept of unresolved mental states: Hostile/Helpless states of mind on the Adult Attachment Interview are associated with disrupted mother-infant communication and infant disorganization. *Development and Psychopathology*, *17*(1), 1–23. doi:10.1017/S0954579405050017

Main, M. (1991). Metacognitive knowledge, metacognitive monitoring, and singular (coherent) vs. multiple (incoherent) model of attachment: Findings and directions for future research. In C. M. Parkes, J. Stevenson-Hinde, & P. Marris (Eds.), *Attachment across the life cycle* (pp. 127–159). New York, NY: Routledge.

Main, M. (1999). Epilogue. Attachment theory: Eighteen points with suggestions for future studies. *Handbook of Attachment: Theory, Research, and Clinical Applications*, *1*, 845–887.

Main, M., & Hesse, E. (1990). Parents' unresolved traumatic experiences are related to infant disorganized attachment status: Is frightened and/or frightening parental behavior the linking mechanism? In M. T. Greenberg, D. Cicchetti, & E. M. Cummings (Eds.), *Attachment in the preschool years: Theory, research, and intervention* (pp. 161–182). Chicago, IL: University of Chicago Press.

Main, M., Hesse, E., & Goldwyn, R. (2008). Studying differences in language usage in recounting attachment history: An introduction to the AAI. In H. Steele, & M. Steele (Eds.), *Clinical applications of the Adult Attachment Interview.* (pp. 31–68). New York, NY: Guilford Press.

Main, M., & Solomon, J. (1990). Procedures for identifying infants as disorganized/disoriented during the Ainsworth Strange Situation. *Attachment in the Preschool Years: Theory, Research, and Intervention*, *1*, 121–160.

Maio, G. R., Fincham, F. D., & Lycett, E. J. (2000). Attitudinal ambivalence toward parents and attachment style. *Personality and Social Psychology Bulletin*, *26*(12), 1451–1464.

Malow, M. S. & Austin, V. L. (2016). Mindfulness practices with students classified with EBD: A pilot investigation. *Insights on Learning Disabilities: From Prevailing Theories to Validated Practices*, (March 2016 issue).

Manassis, K., Bradley, S., Goldberg, S., Hood, J., & Swinson, R. P. (1994). Attachment in mothers with anxiety disorders and their children. *Journal of the American Academy of Child & Adolescent Psychiatry*, *33*(8), 1106–1113. doi:10.1097/00004583-199410000-00006

Manassis, K., & Wilansky-Traynor, P. (2013). Special considerations in treating anxiety disorders in adolescents. In E. A. Storch & D. & McKay (Eds.), *Handbook of treating variants and complications in anxiety disorders* (pp. 163–176). New York, NY: Springer.

Manos, R. C., Kanter, J. W., & Busch, A. M. (2010). A critical review of assessment strategies to measure the behavioral activation model of depression. *Clinical Psychology Review, 30*(5), 547–561.

Marceau, K., Hajal, N., Leve, L. D., Reiss, D., Shaw, D. S., Ganiban, J. M., Mayes, L. C., Neiderhiser, J. M. (2013). Measurement and associations of pregnancy risk factors with genetic influences, postnatal environmental influences, and toddler behavior. *International Journal of Behavioral Development, 37*(4), 366–375. doi:10.1177/0165025413489378.

Marsee, M. A., Barry, C. T., Childs, K. K., Frick, P. J., Kimonis, E. R., Muñoz, L. C., ... Lau, K. S. L. (2011). Assessing the forms and functions of aggression using self-report: Factor structure and invariance of the Peer Conflict Scale in youths. *Psychological Assessment, 23*(3), 792–804. doi:10.1037/a0023369

Marsh, P., McFarland, F. C., Allen, J. P., Boykin McElhaney, K., & Land, D. (2003). Attachment, autonomy, and multifinality in adolescent internalizing and risky behavioral symptoms. *Development and Psychopathology, 15*(2), 451–467. doi:10.1017/S0954579403000245

Marzano, R. A. (2003). What works in schools: Translating research into action. Alexandria, VA: Association for Supervision and Curriculum Development.

Mascolo, M. F. (2009). Beyond student-centered and teacher-centered pedagogy: Teaching and learning as guided participation. *Pedagogy and the Human Sciences, 1*(1), 3–27.

Maslow, A. (1954). *Motivation and personality.* New York, NY: Harper.

Matthys, W., Vanderschuren, L. J., & Schutter, D. J. (2013). The neurobiology of oppositional defiant disorder and conduct disorder: Altered functioning in three mental domains. *Development and Psychopathology, 25*(1), 193–207.

Matthys, W., Vanderschuren, L. J., Schutter, D. J., & Lochman, J. E. (2012). Impaired neurocognitive functions affect social learning processes in oppositional defiant disorder and conduct disorder: Implications for interventions. *Clinical Child and Family Psychology Review, 15*(3), 234–246.

Maxwell, L. (2014). US school enrollment hits majority-minority milestone. *Education Week.* Retrieved May 26th, 2015 from http://libertyeducationgroup.org/yahoo_site_admin/assets/docs/US_School_Enrollment_Hits_Majority-Minority_Milestone.132151343.pdf

McCarty, C. A., Wymbs, B. T., King, K. M., Mason, W. A., Vander Stoep, A., McCauley, E., & Baer, J. (2012). Developmental consistency in associations between depressive symptoms and alcohol use in early adolescents. *Journal of Studies on Alcohol and Drugs, 73*(3), 444–453.

McCullumsmith, C. B., Kalpakjian, C. Z., Richards, J. S., Forchheimer, M., Heinemann, A. W., Richardson, . . . Fann, J. R. (2015). Novel risk factors associated with current suicidal ideation and lifetime suicide attempts in individuals with spinal cord injury. *Archives of Physical Medicine and Rehabilitation, 96*(5), 799–808.

McElroy, S. L., Kotwal, R., Keck, P. E., Jr., & Akiskal, H. S. (2005). Comorbidity of bipolar and eating disorders: Distinct or related disorders with shared dysregulations? *Journal of Affective Disorders, 86*,107–127.

McNeil, C. B., & Hembree-Kigin, T. L. (2010). *Parent-child interaction therapy.* New York, NY: Springer.

McWhirter, B. T., McWhirter, J. J., Hart, R. S., & Gat, I. (2000). Preventing and treating depression in children and adolescents. In D. Capuzzi, & D. R. Gross (Eds.), *Youth risk: A prevention resource for counselors, teachers, and parents* (3rd ed., pp. 137–165). Alexandria, VA: American Counseling Association.

Mendel, R. A. (2011). No place for kids: The case for reducing juvenile incarceration. Baltimore, MD: The Annie E. Casey Foundation.

Merikangas, K. R., He, J., Burstein, M., Swanson, S. A., Avenevoli, S., Cui, L., Swendsen, J. (2010). Lifetime prevalence of mental disorders in US adolescents: Results from the National Comorbidity Survey Replication–Adolescent Supplement (NCS-A). *Journal of the American Academy of Child & Adolescent Psychiatry, 49*(10), 980–989.

Mesa, F., Beidel, D. C., & Bunnell, B. E. (2014). An examination of psychopathology and daily impairment in adolescents with social anxiety disorder. *PloS One, 9*(4), e93668.

Metzler, J., & Woessmann, L. (2012). The impact of teacher subject knowledge on student achievement: Evidence from within-teacher within-student variation. *Journal of Development Economics, 99*(2), 486–496.

Miklowitz, D. J. (2012). Family treatment for bipolar disorder and substance abuse in late adolescence. *Journal of Clinical Psychology, 68*(5), 502–513. doi:10.1002/jclp.21855

Miles, S. B., & Stipek, D. (2006). Contemporaneous and longitudinal associations between social behavior and literacy achievement in a sample of low-income elementary school children. *Child Development, 77*(1), 103–117. doi:10.1111/j.1467-8624.2006.00859.x

Miller, E., Joseph, S., & Tudway, J. (2004). Assessing the component structure of four self-report measures of impulsivity. *Personality and Individual Differences, 37*(2), 349–358.

Miller, S., Chang, K. D., & Ketter, T. A. (2013). Bipolar disorder and attention-deficit/hyperactivity disorder comorbidity in children and adolescents: Evidence-based approach to diagnosis and treatment. *J. Clin. Psychiatry, 74*, 628–629.

Minuchin, S. (1974). *Families & family therapy.* Oxford, UK: Harvard University Press.

Minuchin, S., Rosman, B. L., & Baker, L. (1978). *Psychosomatic families: Anorexia nervosa in context.* Cambridge, MA: Harvard University Press.

Mischoulon, D., Eddy, K. T., Keshaviah, A., Dinescu, D., Ross, S. L., Kass, A. E., & Herzog, D. B. (2011). Depression and eating disorders: Treatment and course. *Journal of Affective Disorders, 130*(3), 470–477. doi:10.1016/j.jad.2010.10.043

Mishna, F., Khoury-Kassabri, M., Gadalla, T., & Daciuk, J. (2012). Risk factors for involvement in cyber bullying: Victims, bullies and bully–victims. *Children and Youth Services Review, 34*(1), 63–70.

Mishna, F., Saini, M., & Solomon, S. (2009). Ongoing and online: Children and youth's perceptions of cyber bullying. *Children and Youth Services Review, 31*(12), 1222–1228. doi:10.1016/j.childyouth.2009.05.004

Moberg, T., Nordström, P., Forslund, K., Kristiansson, M., Åsberg, M., & Jokinen, J. (2011). CSF 5-HIAA and exposure to and expression of interpersonal violence in suicide attempters. *Journal of Affective Disorders, 132*(1-2), 173–178. doi:10.1016/j.jad.2011.01.018

Mongia, M., & Hechtman, L. (2012). Cognitive behavior therapy for adults with attention-deficit/hyperactivity disorder: A review of recent randomized controlled trials. *Current Psychiatry Reports, 14*(5), 561–567.

Monk, D. H. (1994). Subject area preparation of secondary mathematics and science teachers and student achievement. *Economics of Education Review, 13*(2), 125–145.

Moran, J. M., Young, L. L., Saxe, R., Lee, S. M., O'Young, D., Mavros, P. L., & Gabrieli, J. D. (2011). Impaired theory of mind for moral judgment in high-functioning autism. *Proceedings of the National Academy of Sciences, 108*(7), 2688–2692.

Moss, E., St.-Laurent, D., Dubois-Comtois, K., & Cyr, C. (2005). Quality of attachment at school age: Relations between child attachment behavior, psychosocial functioning, and school performance. In K. A. Kerns & R. A. Richardson (Eds.), *Attachment in middle childhood* (pp. 189–211). New York, NY: Guilford Press.

Mowrer-Reynolds, E. (2008). Pre-service educator perceptions of exemplary teachers. *College Student Journal, 42*(1), 214–224.

Mufson, L., & Dorta, K. P. (2003). Interpersonal psychotherapy for depressed adolescents. In A. E. Kazdin & J. R. Weisz (Eds.), *Evidence-based psychotherapies for children and adolescents* (pp. 148–164). New York, NY: Guilford Press.

Nahas, D. (n.d.). Eating disorder fact sheet for educators. Retrieved August 15, 2015, from http://smhp.psych.ucla.edu/pdfdocs/edfactsheet.pdf

Nathan, P. E., & Gorman, J. M. (2015). *A guide to treatments that work.* Oxford, UK: Oxford University Press.

National Association of Anorexia Nervosa and Associated Disorders. (2015). ANAD Ten Year Study. Retrieved May 5, 2015 from www.anad.org

National Association for Children's Behavioral Health, National Association of Psychiatric Health Systems. (2008). *Characteristics of residential treatment for children and youth with serious emotional disturbances.* Retrieved August 14, 2015, from http://www.nacbh.org/PubDocs/Characteristics%20of%20Residential%20Treatment.pdf

National Autistic Society (2003). National autism plan for children. Retrieved July 23, 2015, from http://iier.isciii.es/autismo/pdf/aut_napc.pdf

National Center for Education Statistics. (2013). U.S. data on special education student placements. U.S. Department of Education, Retrieved April 30, 2015, from https://nces.ed.gov/

National Center for Education Statistics. (2014). School deaths, NCES, 2012. Retrieved August 14, 2015, from https://nces.ed.gov/

National Center for Education Statistics. (2015). Children and youth with disabilities. Retrieved August 14, 2015, from https://nces.ed.gov/

National Center for Education Statistics. (2010). School survey on crime and safety. Retrieved July 16, 2015, from https://nces.ed.gov/surveys/ssocs/

National Center for School Crisis & Bereavement. (n.d.). *Guidelines for Responding to the Death of a Student or School Staff.* Retrieved July 6, 2015 from the Coalition to Support Grieving Students website at http://grievingstudents.scholastic.com/wp-content/uploads/2015/02/Guidelines-for-Responding-to-the-Death-of-a-Student-or-School-Staff-Jan-5-2015.pdf.

National Commission on Teaching America's Future. (2005, August). The high cost of teacher turnover. Retrieved July 5, 2015, from http://nctaf.org/wp-content/uploads/2012/01/NCTAF-Cost-of-Teacher-Turnover-2007-policy-brief.pdf

Nelson, J. R., Maculan, A., Roberts, M. L., & Ohlund, B. J. (2001). Sources of occupational stress for teachers of students with emotional and behavioral disorders. *Journal of Emotional and Behavioral Disorders, 9*(2), 123–130

Neumann, A., Barker, E. D., Koot, H. M., & Maughan, B. (2010). The role of contextual risk, impulsivity, and parental knowledge in the development of adolescent antisocial behavior. *Journal of Abnormal Psychology, 119*(3), 534-545.

New Jersey State Bar Foundation. (n.d.). Working it out: A violence prevention program focusing on conflict resolution and peer mediation. Retrieved December 19, 2015 from https://www.njsbf.org/images/content/1/1/11205/working%20it%20out.pdf

New Jersey State Police. (2009). Bias Incidents in N.J., 2009. Retrieved July 30, 2015, from http://www.njsp.org/info/pdf/2009_bias_incident.pdf

New York State Department of Health. (Rev. April 2011). The epidemiology of suicide. Retrieved April 30, 2015, from http://www.health.ny.gov/regulations/task_force/reports_publications/when_death_is_sought/chap1.htm

Niv, S., Tuvblad, C., Raine, A., Wang, P., & Baker, L. A. (2012). Heritability and longitudinal stability of impulsivity in adolescence. *Behavior Genetics*, *42*(3), 378–392.

Noddings, N. (2005). *The challenge to care in schools: An alternative approach to education.* New York, NY: Teachers College Press.

Northfield, J., & Gunstone, R. (1997). Teacher education as a process of developing teacher knowledge. In J. Loughran and T. Russel (Eds.), *Teaching about teaching: Purpose, passion and pedagogy in teacher education* (pp. 48-56). London: Falmer Press.

O'Connor, E. E., Collins, B. A., & Supplee, L. (2012). Behavior problems in late childhood: The roles of early maternal attachment and teacher–child relationship trajectories. *Attachment & Human Development*, *14*(3), 265–288. doi:10.1080/14616734.2012.672280

O'Connor, T. G., & Croft, C. M. (2001). A twin study of attachment in preschool children. *Child Development*, *72*(5), 1501–1511.

Oklahoma Educators Credit Union. (n.d.). http://oecu.com/services/member-education/bullying-prevention-tips/

Olfson, M., Marcus, S. C., & Shaffer, D. (2006). Antidepressant drug therapy and suicide in severely depressed children and adults: A case-control study. *Archives of General Psychiatry*, *63*(8), 865–872.

Ollendick, T. H., & King, N. J. (1998). Empirically supported treatments for children with phobic and anxiety disorders: Current status. *Journal of Clinical Child Psychology, 27*, 156– 167.

Olweus, D. (1992). Bullying among school children: Intervention and prevention. In R. D. Peters, R. J. McMahon, & V. L. Quinsey (Eds.), *Aggression and violence throughout the life span* (pp. 100–125). Thousand Oaks, CA: Sage Publications.

Olweus, D. (2004). The Olweus Bullying Prevention Program: Design and implementation issues and a new national initiative in Norway. In P. K. Smith, D. Pepler, & K. Rigby (Eds.), *Bullying in schools: How successful can interventions be?* (pp. 13–36). New York, NY: Cambridge University Press.

Olweus, D. (2013). School bullying: Development and some important challenges. *Annual Review of Clinical Psychology*, *9*, 751–780.

Olweus Bullying Prevention Program. (2015). Retrieved July 6, 2015, from http://www.violencepreventionworks.org/public/index.page

O'Shaughnessy, R., & Dallos, R. (2009). Attachment research and eating disorders: A review of the literature. *Clinical Child Psychology and Psychiatry*, *14*(4), 559–574.

Pabian, S., & Vandebosch, H. (2015). An investigation of short-term longitudinal associations between social anxiety and victimization and perpetration of traditional bullying and cyberbullying. *Journal of Youth and Adolescence*, *45*(2), 328-339.

Palmer, P. J. (1998). *The courage to teach*. San Francisco, CA: Jossey-Bass.

Pantić, N., & Wubbels, T. (2010). Teacher competencies as a basis for teacher education– Views of Serbian teachers and teacher educators. *Teaching and Teacher Education, 26*(3), 694–703.

Pardini, D., & Frick, P. J. (2013). Multiple developmental pathways to conduct disorder: Current conceptualizations and clinical implications. *Journal of the Canadian Academy of Child and Adolescent Psychiatry*, *22*(1), 20-25.

Patrick, M., Hobson, R. P., Castle, D., Howard, R., & Maughan, B. (1994). Personality disorder and the mental representation of early social experience. *Development and Psychopathology*, *6*(2), 375–388. doi:10.1017/S0954579400004648

Patterson, G. R., Reid, J. B., & Dishion, T. J. (1992). *A social interactional approach: Antisocial boys* (Vol. 4). Eugene, OR: Castalia.

Pereira, A. I., Barros, L., Mendonça, D., & Muris, P. (2014). The relationships among parental anxiety, parenting, and children's anxiety: The mediating effects of children's cognitive vulnerabilities. *Journal of Child and Family Studies, 23*(2), 399–409.

Petersen, J. L., & Hyde, J. S. (2013). Peer sexual harassment and disordered eating in early adolescence. *Developmental Psychology, 49*(1), 184-195.

Pfiffner, L. J., & Haack, L. M. (2014). Behavior management for school-aged children with ADHD. *Child and Adolescent Psychiatric Clinics of North America, 23*(4), 731–746.

Piaget, J. (1952). Conclusions: "Sensorimotor" or "practical" intelligence and the theories of intelligence. In *The origins of intelligence in children.* (pp. 357–419). New York, NY: Norton.

Pianta, R. C., & Stuhlman, M. W. (2004). Teacher-child relationships and children's success in the first years of school. *School Psychology Review, 33*(3), 444–458.

Pichika, R., Buchsbaum, M. S., Bailer, U., Hoh, C., DeCastro, A., Buchsbaum, B. R., & Kaye, W. (2012). Serotonin transporter binding after recovery from bulimia nervosa. *International Journal of Eating Disorders, 45*(3), 345–352.

Pierangelo, R., & Giuliani, G. A. (2001). *What every teacher should know about students with special needs: Promoting success in the classroom.* Champagne, IL: Research Press.

Pierangelo, R., & Giuliani, G. (2008). *Classroom management techniques for students with ADHD: A step-by-step guide for educators.* Thousand Oaks, CA: Corwin Press.

Pink, D. H. (2011). *Drive: The surprising truth about what motivates us.* New York, NY: Penguin.

Piran, N., Levine, M., & Steiner-Adair, C. (2013). *Preventing eating disorders: A handbook of interventions and special challenges.* London, UK: Routledge.

Plous, S. (2015). Social Psychology Network, 2002–2015. Retrieved August 3, 2015, from www.understandingprejucdice.org

Plutarch (1992). *Essays.* (I. Kidd, Ed., R. Waterfield, Trans., p. 50) London, UK: Penguin Classics.

Polier, G. G., Vloet, T. D., Herpertz-Dahlmann, B., Laurens, K. R., & Hodgins, S. (2012). Comorbidity of conduct disorder symptoms and internalizing problems in children: Investigating a community and a clinical sample. *European Child & Adolescent Psychiatry, 21*(1), 31–38.

Polk, J. A. (2006). Traits of effective teachers. *Arts Education Policy Review, 107*(4), 23–29.

Pope, A. (1711). *Essays on criticism.* Oxford, UK: Clarendon Press.

Posada, G., Waters, E., Crowell, J. A., & Lay, K.-L. (1995). Is it easier to use a secure mother as a secure base? Attachment Q-sort correlates of the adult attachment interview. *Monographs of the Society for Research in Child Development, 60*(2-3), 133–145. doi:10.2307/1166175

Power, T. J., Mautone, J. A., Soffer, S. L., Clarke, A. T., Marshall, S. A., Sharman, J., Jawad, A. F. (2012). A family–school intervention for children with ADHD: Results of a randomized clinical trial. *Journal of Consulting and Clinical Psychology, 80*(4), 611-623.

Pratt, D. (2008). Lina's letters: A 9-year-old's perspective on what matters most in the classroom. *Phi Delta Kappan, 8*(7), 515–518.

Premack, D., & Woodruff, G. (1978). Does the chimpanzee have a theory of mind? *Behavioral and Brain Sciences, 1*(04), 515–526.

Prior, M. R. (Ed.). (2003). *Learning and behavior problems in Asperger syndrome.* New York, NY: Guilford Press.

Raevuori, A., Linna, M. S., & Keski-Rahkonen, A. (2014). Prenatal and perinatal factors in eating disorders: A descriptive review. *International Journal of Eating Disorders*, *47*(7), 676–685.

Rapee, R. M. (2012). Family factors in the development and management of anxiety disorders. *Clinical Child and Family Psychology Review*, *15*(1), 69–80. doi:10.1007/s10567-011-0106-3

Redl, F. (1966). The life-space interview: Strategy and techniques. In F. Redl, *When we deal with children*, pp. 35-67. New York, NY: Free Press.

Reeves, R. R., & Laizer, J. T. (2012). Traumatic brain injury and suicide. *Journal of Psychosocial Nursing and Mental Health Services*, *50*(3), 32–38.

Rehabilitation Act, 34 C.F.R. § 504, Part 104 (1973)

Rhodes, S. M., Park, J., Seth, S., & Coghill, D. R. (2012). A comprehensive investigation of memory impairment in attention deficit hyperactivity disorder and oppositional defiant disorder. *Journal of Child Psychology and Psychiatry*, *53*(2), 128–137.

Richards, D. A., & Schat, A. C. (2011). Attachment at (not to) work: applying attachment theory to explain individual behavior in organizations. *Journal of Applied Psychology*, *96*(1), 169-182.

Richfield, S. (n.d.). The parent coach: A new approach to parenting in today's society. Retrieved August 25, 2015, from http://www.parentcoachcards.com

Richfield, S. (n.d). Helping your impulsive ADHD child. Retrieved August 25, 2015, from http://www.parentcoachcards.com

Roberts, W. B. J., & Morotti, A. A. (2000). The bully as victim: Understanding bully behaviors to increase the effectiveness of interventions in the bully–victim dyad. *Professional School Counseling*, *4*(2), 148–155.

Rohde, P., Lewinsohn, P. M., Klein, D. N., Seeley, J. R., & Gau, J. M. (2013). Key characteristics of major depressive disorder occurring in childhood, adolescence, emerging adulthood, and adulthood. *Clinical Psychological Science*, *1*(1), 41–53. doi.org/10.1177/2167702612457599

Romer, D., Betancourt, L. M., Brodsky, N. L., Giannetta, J. M., Yang, W., & Hurt, H. (2011). Does adolescent risk taking imply weak executive function? A prospective study of relations between working memory performance, impulsivity, and risk taking in early adolescence. *Developmental Science*, *14*(5), 1119–1133.

Rose, M. (2000). Lives on the boundary. In M. Moller (Ed.), *The presence of others* (pp. 106–115). Boston, MA: Bedford/St. Martin's.

Rosenfeld, M., & Rosenfeld, S. (2004). Developing teacher sensitivity to individual learning differences. *Educational Psychology*, *24*(4), 465–486.

Rosenstein, D. S., & Horowitz, H. A. (1996). Adolescent attachment and psychopathology. *Journal of Consulting and Clinical Psychology*, *64*(2), 244–253. doi:10.1037/0022-006X.64.2.244

Rowa, K., Kerig, P. K., & Geller, J. (2001). The family and anorexia nervosa: Examining parent–child boundary problems. *European Eating Disorders Review*, *9*(2), 97–114. doi:10.1002/erv.383

Rowe, R., Costello, E. J., Angold, A., Copeland, W. E., & Maughan, B. (2010). Developmental pathways in oppositional defiant disorder and conduct disorder. *Journal of Abnormal Psychology*, *119*(4), 726.

Rowe, R., Maughan, B., Moran, P., Ford, T., Briskman, J., & Goodman, R. (2010). The role of callous and unemotional traits in the diagnosis of conduct disorder. *Journal of Child Psychology and Psychiatry*, *51*(6), 688–695. doi:10.1111/j.1469-7610.2009.02199.x

Rubia, K. (2011). "Cool" inferior frontostriatal dysfunction in attention-deficit/hyperactivity disorder versus "Hot" ventromedial orbitofrontal-limbic dysfunction in conduct disorder: A review. *Biological Psychiatry, 69*(12), e69–e87. doi:10.1016/j.bio-psych.2010.09.023

Rubia, K., Halari, R., Mohammad, A.-M., Taylor, E., & Brammer, M. (2011). Methylphenidate normalizes frontocingulate underactivation during error processing in attention-deficit/hyperactivity disorder. *Biological Psychiatry, 70*(3), 255–262. doi:10.1016/j.biopsych.2011.04.018

Russell, T. L. (1997). *The "No Significant Difference" Phenomenon as reported in 248 Research Reports, Summaries, and Papers* (4th ed.). Retreived from http://www2.ncsu.edu/oit/nsdsplit.htm

Rutgers, A. H., Bakermans-Kranenburg, M. J., van IJzendoorn, M. H., & van Berckelaer-Onnes, I. A. (2004). Autism and attachment: A meta-analytic review. *Journal of Child Psychology and Psychiatry, 45*(6), 1123–1134.

Salmivalli, C. (2014). Participant roles in bullying: How can peer bystanders be utilized in interventions? *Theory Into Practice, 53*(4), 286–292.

Salmivalli, C., Voeten, M., & Poskiparta, E. (2011). Bystanders matter: Associations between reinforcing, defending, and the frequency of bullying behavior in classrooms. *Journal of Clinical Child & Adolescent Psychology, 40*(5), 668–676.

Samson, A. C., Huber, O., & Gross, J. J. (2012). Emotion regulation in Asperger's syndrome and high-functioning autism. *Emotion, 12*(4), 659-665.

Sansone, R. A., & Sansone, L. A. (2011). Personality pathology and its influence on eating disorders. *Innovations in Clinical Neuroscience, 8*(3), 14–18.

Saxe, R., & Powell, L. J. (2006). It's the thought that counts: Specific brain regions for one component of theory of mind. *Psychological Science, 17*(8), 692–699.

Scharinger, C., Rabl, U., Sitte, H. H., & Pezawas, L. (2010). Imaging genetics of mood disorders. *Neuroimage, 53*(3), 810–821.

Scheeren, A. M., de Rosnay, M., Koot, H. M., & Begeer, S. (2013). Rethinking theory of mind in high-functioning autism spectrum disorder. *Journal of Child Psychology and Psychiatry, 54*(6), 628–635.

Schlozman, S. C. (2001). The shrink in the classroom: The suicidal student. *Educational Leadership (a publication of the Association for Supervision and Curriculum Development, ASCD), 59*(2), 81–82.

Schön, D. A. (1983). *The reflective practitioner: How professionals think in action* (Vol. 5126). London, UK: Temple Smith.

Schwitzer, A. M. (2012). Diagnosing, conceptualizing, and treating eating disorders not otherwise specified: A comprehensive practice model. *Journal of Counseling & Development, 90*(3), 281–289. doi:10.1002/j.1556-6676.2012.00036.x

Seligman, M. E. (1974). Depression and learned helplessness. In R. J. Friedman & M. M. Katz (Eds.), *The psychology of depression: Contemporary theory and research.* Oxford, UK: Wiley.

Sellar, S. (2013). Hoping for the best in education: Globalisation, social imaginaries and young people. *Social Alternatives, 32*(2), 31-38.

Shamir-Essakow, G., Ungerer, J. A., & Rapee, R. M. (2005). Attachment, behavioral inhibition, and anxiety in preschool children. *Journal of Abnormal Child Psychology, 33*(2), 131–143. doi:10.1007/s10802-005-1822-2

Shapiro, J. (1993). *No pity: People with disabilities forging a new civil rights movement.* New York, NY: Three Rivers Press.

Sheftall, A. H., Mathias, C. W., Furr, R. M., & Dougherty, D. M. (2013). Adolescent attachment security, family functioning, and suicide attempts. *Attachment & Human Development, 15*(4), 368–383.

Shenk, C. E., Dorn, L. D., Kolko, D. J., Susman, E. J., Noll, J. G., & Bukstein, O. G. (2012). Predicting treatment response for oppositional defiant and conduct disorder using pre-treatment adrenal and gonadal hormones. *Journal of Child and Family Studies, 21*(6), 973–981. doi:10.1007/s10826-011-9557-x

Shingleton, R. M., Richards, L. K., & Thompson-Brenner, H. (2013). Using technology within the treatment of eating disorders: A clinical practice review. *Psychotherapy, 50*(4), 576-582.

Shneidman, E. S. (1973). *Deaths of man.* Oxford, England: Quadrangle/New York Times Book Co.

Silberg, J. L., Maes, H., & Eaves, L. J. (2012). Unraveling the effect of genes and environment in the transmission of parental antisocial behavior to children's conduct disturbance, depression and hyperactivity. *Journal of Child Psychology and Psychiatry, 53*(6), 668–677.

Silove, D., & Manicavasagar, V. (2013). Let's not abandon separation anxiety disorder in adulthood. *Australian and New Zealand Journal of Psychiatry, 47*(8), 780–782.

Silverman, W. K., & Dick-Niederhauser, A. (2004). Separation anxiety disorder. In T. L. Morris & J. S. March (Eds.), *Anxiety disorders in children and adolescents* (2nd ed., pp. 164–188). New York, NY: Guilford Press.

Simon, N., & Johnson, S. M. (2015). Teacher turnover in high-poverty schools: What we know and can do. *Teachers College Record, 117*(3), 1–36.

Simpson, J. A., Collins, W. A., Tran, S., & Haydon, K. C. (2007). Attachment and the experience and expression of emotions in romantic relationships: A developmental perspective. *Journal of Personality and Social Psychology, 92*(2), 355–367. doi:10.1037/0022-3514.92.2.355

Slade, A. (2008). The implications of attachment theory and research for adult psychotherapy: Research and clinical perspectives. In J. Cassidy & P. R. Shaver (Eds.), *Handbook of attachment: Theory, research, and clinical applications* (2nd ed., pp. 762–782). New York, NY: Guilford Press.

Skirrow, C., Hosang, G. M., Farmer, A. E., & Asherson, P. (2012). An update on the debated association between ADHD and bipolar disorder across the lifespan. *Journal of Affective Disorders, 141*(2-3), 143–159. doi:10.1016/j.jad.2012.04.003

Skourteli, M. C., & Lennie, C. (2011). The therapeutic relationship from an attachment theory perspective. *Counseling Psychology Review, 26*(1), 20-31.

Smith, D. G. (1994). *Pedagon: Meditations on pedagogy and culture.* Bragg Creek, Canada: Makyo Press.

Smith, M. (2012). Social pedagogy from a Scottish perspective. *International Journal of Social Pedagogy, 1*(1), 46–55.

Smith, T. J., Henning, R.A., Wade, M. G., & Fisher, T. (2015). *Variability in human performance.* Boca Raton, FL: CRC Press, Taylor & Francis Group.

Smink, F. R., van Hoeken, D., & Hoek, H. W. (2013). Epidemiology, course, and outcome of eating disorders. *Current Opinion in Psychiatry, 26*(6), 543–548.

Solomon, A. (2012). *Far from the tree: Parents, children, and the search for identity.* New York, NY: Scribner.

Spangler, G., & Grossmann, K. E. (1993). Biobehavioral organization in securely and insecurely attached infants. *Child Development, 64*(5), 1439–1450. http://doi.org/10.2307/1131544

Spoor, S. T. P., Bekker, M. H. J., Van Strien, T., & van Heck, G. L. (2007). Relations between negative affect, coping, and emotional eating. *Appetite, 48*(3), 368–376. doi:10.1016/j.appet.2006.10.005

Sroufe, L. A. (1996). *Emotional development: The organization of emotional life in the early years.* New York, NY: Cambridge University Press.

Sroufe, L. A., Egeland, B., Carlson, E. A., & Collins, W. A. (2005). *The development of the person.* New York, NY: Guilford.

Steinberg, L. (2005). Cognitive and affective development in adolescence. *Trends in Cognitive Sciences, 9*(2), 69–74. doi:10.1016/j.tics.2004.12.005

Steele, M., Murphy, A., & Steele, H. (2015). The art and science of observation: Reflective functioning and therapeutic action. *Journal of Infant, Child & Adolescent Psychotherapy, 14*(3), 216–231. http://doi.org/10.1080/15289168.2015.1070558

Stichter, J. P., O'Connor, K. V., Herzog, M. J., Lierheimer, K., & McGhee, S. D. (2012). Social competence intervention for elementary students with Aspergers syndrome and high functioning autism. *Journal of Autism and Developmental Disorders, 42*(3), 354–366. doi:10.1007/s10803-011-1249-2

Stopbullying.gov. (n.d.). Prevention at school. Retrieved December 19, 2015 from http://www.stopbullying.gov/prevention/at-school/index.html

Stough, L. M., & Palmer, D. J. (2003). Special thinking in special settings: A qualitative study of expert special educators. *The Journal of Special Education, 36*(4), 206–222.

Stout, D. (2005). The social and cultural context of stone knapping skill acquisition. In V. Roux and B. Blandine (Eds.), *Stone knapping. The necessary conditions for a uniquely hominin behavior* (pp. 331–339), Cambridge, UK: McDonald Institute for Archaeological Research.

Strawn, J. R., Wehry, A. M., DelBello, M. P., Rynn, M. A., & Strakowski, S. (2012). Establishing the neurobiologic basis of treatment in children and adolescents with generalized anxiety disorder. *Depression and Anxiety, 29*(4), 328–339. doi:10.1002/da.21913

Sue, D. W. (1978). Eliminating cultural oppression in counseling: Toward a general theory. *Journal of Counseling Psychology, 25*(5), 419–428. doi.org/10.1037/0022-0167.25.5.419

Sue, D. W., & Sue, D. (2012). *Counseling the culturally diverse: Theory and practice* (6th ed.). Hoboken, NJ: Wiley.

Sugai, G., & Horner, R. H. (2009). Responsiveness-to-intervention and school-wide positive behavior supports: Integration of multi-tiered system approaches. *Exceptionality, 17*(4), 223–237.

Sullivan, P. F. (2002). Course and outcome of anorexia nervosa and bulimia nervosa. In C. G. Fairburn and K. D. Brownell (Eds.) *Eating disorders and obesity: A comprehensive handbook*, (2nd ed., pp. 226–232). Chichester: Wiley.

Sullivan, K., Zaitchik, D., & Tager-Flusberg, H. (1994). Preschoolers can attribute second-order beliefs. *Developmental Psychology, 30*(3), 395-402.

Swanson, J. M., Flodman, P., Kennedy, J., Spence, M. A., Moyzis, R., Schuck, S., . . . Posner, M. (2000). Dopamine genes and ADHD. *Neuroscience and Biobehavioral Reviews, 24*(1), 21–25. doi:10.1016/S0149-7634(99)00062-7

Swanson, S. A., Crow, S. J., Le Grange, D., Swendsen, J., & Merikangas, K. R. (2011). Prevalence and correlates of eating disorders in adolescents: Results from the national comorbidity survey replication adolescent supplement. *Archives of General Psychiatry, 68*(7), 714–723.

Szasz, T. S. (1974). *The myth of mental illness: Foundations of a theory of personal conduct.* New York, NY: HarperCollins.

Taborelli, E., Krug, I., Karwautz, A., Wagner, G., Haidvogl, M., Fernandez-Aranda, F., Castro, R. (2013). Maternal anxiety, overprotection and anxious personality as risk factors for eating disorder: A sister pair study. *Cognitive Therapy and Research, 37*(4), 820–828.

Talbott, L. L., & Bartlett, M. L. (2012). Youth suicide postvention: Support for survivors and recommendations for school personnel. *Alabama Counseling Association Journal, 38*(2), 104–119.

Tasca, G. A., Ritchie, K., Zachariades, F., Proulx, G., Trinneer, A., Balfour, L., Bissada, H. (2013). Attachment insecurity mediates the relationship between childhood trauma and eating disorder psychopathology in a clinical sample: A structural equation model. *Child Abuse & Neglect, 37*(11), 926–933.

Taylor, A. R. (1989). Predictors of peer rejection in early elementary grades: Roles of problem behavior, academic achievement, and teacher preference. *Journal of Clinical Child Psychology, 18*(4), 360–365. doi:10.1207/s15374424jccp1804_10

Terre, L., Poston, W. S. C. I., & Foreyt, J. P. (2006). Eating disorders. In E. J. Mash & R. A. Barkley (Eds.), *Treatment of childhood disorders* (3rd ed., pp. 778–829). New York, NY: Guilford Press.

Thapar, A., Collishaw, S., Pine, D. S., & Thapar, A. K. (2012). Depression in adolescence. *The Lancet, 379*(9820), 1056–1067.

Thompson, R. A. (1998). *Early sociopersonality development.* In W. Damon (Series Ed.) & N. Eisenberg (Vol. Ed.). *Handbook of child psychology: Vol. 3. Social, emotional, and personality development* (5th ed., pp. 25–104). New York, NY: Wiley.

Thompson, R. A. (2008). Early attachment and later development: Familiar questions, new answers. In J. Cassidy & P. R. Shaver (Eds.), *Handbook of attachment: Theory, research, and clinical applications* (2nd ed., pp. 348–365). New York, NY: Guilford Press.

Thornton, L. M., Mazzeo, S. E., & Bulik, C. M. (2011). The heritability of eating disorders: Methods and current findings. In R. A. H. Adan & W. H. Kaye (Eds.), *Behavioral neurobiology of eating disorders* (pp. 141–156). New York, NY: Springer-Verlag Publishing.

Tomlinson, M., Cooper, P., & Murray, L. (2005). The mother-infant relationship and infant attachment in a South African peri-urban settlement. *Child Development, 76*(5), 1044–1054. doi:10.1111/j.1467-8624.2005.00896.x

Tompkins, J. P. (1996). *A life in school: What the teacher learned.* Cambridge, MA: Perseus Books.

Topping, K., & Ferguson, N. (2005). Effective literacy teaching behaviors. *Journal of Research in Reading, 28*(2), 125–143.

Tortorella, A., Fabrazzo, M., Monteleone, A. M., Steardo, L., & Monteleone, P. (2014). The role of drug therapies in the treatment of anorexia and bulimia nervosa: A review of the literature. *Journal of Psychopathology, 20*, 50–65.

Trace, S. E., Baker, J. H., Peñas-Lledó, E., & Bulik, C. M. (2013). The genetics of eating disorders. *Annual Review of Clinical Psychology, 9*, 589–620.

Tsukayama, E., Duckworth, A. L., & Kim, B. (2013). Domain-specific impulsivity in school-age children. *Developmental Science, 16*(6), 879–893.

U.S. Department of Education. (2008). Data on U.S. Students with Emotional Disturbance, Office of Special Education Programs, 2008, Retrieved August 12, 2015 from https://www2.ed.gov/about/reports/annual/osep/2008/parts-b-c/30th-idea-arc.pdf

U.S. Department of Health and Human Services. (n.d.). Eating Disorders. The Center for Mental Health Services. Retrieved August 12, 2015 from http://www.mentalhealth.gov/what-to-look-for/eating-disorders/index.html

Van de Grift, W. (2007). Quality of teaching in four European countries: A review of the literature and application of an assessment instrument. *Educational Research, 49*(2), 127–152.

Van Ijzendoorn, M. H., Rutgers, A. H., Bakermans-Kranenburg, M. J., Swinkels, S. H., Van Daalen, E., Dietz, C., . . . Van Engeland, H. (2007). Parental sensitivity and attachment in children with autism spectrum disorder: Comparison with children with mental retardation, with language delays, and with typical development. *Child Development, 78*(2), 597–608.

Van Ijzendoorn, M. H., Schuengel, C., & Bakermans-Kranenburg, M. J. (1999). Disorganized attachment in early childhood: Meta-analysis of precursors, concomitants, and sequelae. *Development and Psychopathology, 11*(2), 225–249. doi.org/10.1017/S0954579499002035

Van Meter, A. R., Moreira, A. L., & Youngstrom, E. A. (2011). Meta-analysis of epidemiologic studies of pediatric bipolar disorder. *The Journal of Clinical Psychiatry, 72*(9), 1250–1256.

Vanier, J. (2015). Transformer les Coeurs. Retrieved August 3, 2015, from Jean-Vanier.org

Vaughn, B. E., Bost, K. K., & van IJzendoorn, M. H. (2008). Attachment and temperament: Additive and interactive influences on behavior, affect, and cognition during infancy and childhood. In J. Cassidy & P. R. Shaver (Eds.), *Handbook of attachment: Theory, research, and clinical applications* (2nd ed., pp. 192–216). New York, NY: Guilford Press.

Verschueren, K., & Koomen, H. M. Y. (2012). Teacher–child relationships from an attachment perspective. *Attachment & Human Development, 14*(3), 205–211. doi:10.1080/14616734.2012.672260

Vygotsky, L. S. (1987). *The collected works of L.S. Vygotsky: Vol. I: Problems of general psychology.* R. Rieber & A. Carton (Eds.), N. Minick (Trans.). New York, NY: Plenum Press. (Original work published 1934).

Wade, T. D., Keski-Rahkonen, A., & Hudson, J. (2011). Epidemiology of eating disorders. In M. Tsuang & M. Tohen (Eds.) *Textbook in psychiatric epidemiology* (3rd ed., pp. 343-360). New York, NY: Wiley.

Wade, T. D., Treloar, S. A., & Martin, N. G. (2001). A comparison of family functioning, temperament, and childhood conditions in monozygotic twin pairs discordant for lifetime bulimia nervosa. *The American Journal of Psychiatry, 158*(7), 1155–1157. doi:10.1176/appi.ajp.158.7.1155

Waters, E., & Cummings, E. M. (2000). A secure base from which to explore close relationships. *Child Development, 71*(1), 164–172. doi:10.1111/1467-8624.00130

Watkins, C. & Mortimore, P. (1999). Pedagogy: What do we know? In P. Mortimore (Ed.), *Understanding pedagogy and its impact on teaching* (pp. 1–19). London, UK: Chapman.

Webster-Stratton, C. H., Reid, M. J., & Beauchaine, T. (2011). Combining parent and child training for young children with ADHD. *Journal of Clinical Child & Adolescent Psychology, 40*(2), 191–203.

Webster-Stratton, C. (2011). *The Incredible Years: Parents, teachers, and children's training series: Program content, methods, research and dissemination 1980–2011.* Incredible Years.

Weinfield, N. S., Sroufe, L. A., Egeland, B., & Carlson, E. (2008). Individual differences in infant-caregiver attachment: Conceptual and empirical aspects of security. In J. Cassidy & P. R. Shaver (Eds.), *Handbook of attachment: Theory, research, and clinical applications* (2nd ed., pp. 78–101). New York, NY: Guilford Press.

Weiss, M., Murray, C., Wasdell, M., Greenfield, B., Giles, L., & Hechtman, L. (2012). A randomized controlled trial of CBT therapy for adults with ADHD with and without medication. *BMC Psychiatry, 12*(30), 1-8.

Weller, E. B., Weller, R. A., & Danielyan, A. K. (2004). Mood disorders in prepubertal children. In J. M. Wiener & M. K. Dulcan (Eds.), *The American Psychiatric Publishing textbook of child and adolescent psychiatry* (3rd ed., pp. 411–435). Arlington, VA: American Psychiatric Publishing.

Whelan, R., Conrod, P. J., Poline, J.-B., Lourdusamy, A., Banaschewski, T., Barker, G. J., . . . Spanagel, R. (2012). Adolescent impulsivity phenotypes characterized by distinct brain networks. *Nature Neuroscience, 15*(6), 920–925.

Whiteside, S. P., & Lynam, D. R. (2001). The five factor model and impulsivity: Using a structural model of personality to understand impulsivity. *Personality and Individual Differences, 30*(4), 669–689.

Wicks-Nelson, R., & Israel, A. C. (2003). *Behavior disorders of childhood* (5th ed.). Upper Saddle River, NJ: Prentice Hall/Pearson Education.

Wikström, P. O. H. (2004). Crime as alternative: Towards a cross-level situational action theory of crime causation. *Beyond Empiricism: Institutions and Intentions in the Study of Crime, 13,* 1–37.

Willemsen-Swinkels, S., Bakermans-Kranenburg, M. J., Buitelaar, J. K., van IJzendoorn, M. H., van Engeland, H., & others. (2000). Insecure and disorganized attachment in children with a pervasive developmental disorder: Relationship with social interaction and heart rate. *Journal of Child Psychology and Psychiatry, 41,* 759-767.

Wilson, S. M., Floden, R. E., & Ferrini-Mundy, J. (2001, February). *Teacher preparation research: Current knowledge, gaps, and recommendations: A research report prepared for the US Department of Education and the Office for Educational Research and Improvement.* Center for the Study of Teaching and Policy.

Wolke, D., & Lereya, S. T. (2015). Long-term effects of bullying. *Archives of Disease in Childhood, 100,* 879-885..

Wolraich, M. L., McKeown, R. E., Visser, S. N., Bard, D., Cuffe, S. P., Neas, B., . . . & Danielson, M. (2012). The prevalence of ADHD: Its diagnosis and treatment in four school districts across two states. *Journal of Attention Disorders, 18* (7), 563--575.

Wong, M.-L., Dong, C., Flores, D. L., Ehrhart-Bornstein, M., Bornstein, S., Arcos-Burgos, M., & Licinio, J. (2014). Clinical outcomes and genome-wide association for a brain methylation site in an antidepressant pharmacogenetics study in Mexican Americans. *The American Journal of Psychiatry, 171*(12), 1297–1309. doi:10.1176/appi.ajp.2014.12091165

Woodside, D. B., Bulik, C. M., Halmi, K. A., Fichter, M. M., Kaplan, A., Berrettini, W. H., . . . Kaye, W. H. (2002). Personality, perfectionism, and attitudes towards eating in parents of individuals with eating disorders. *International Journal of Eating Disorders, 31*(3), 290–299. doi:10.1002/eat.10032

Woolfolk, A. (2004). *Educational psychology* (9th ed.). Boston, MA: Pearson Education.

Yang, L., Qian, Q., Liu, L., Li, H., Faraone, S. V., & Wang, Y. (2013). Adrenergic neurotransmitter system transporter and receptor genes associated with atomoxetine response in attention-deficit hyperactivity disorder children. *Journal of Neural Transmission, 120*(7), 1127–1133. doi:10.1007/s00702-012-0955-z

Zabel, R., Kaff, M., & Teagarden, J. (2014, September 11). A good time: A conversation with C. Michael Nelson. *Intervention in School and Clinic,* published online. doi: 10.1177/1053451214546403

Zalaquett, C. P., & Sanders, A. E. (2010). *Major depression and dysthymic disorder in adolescents: The critical role of school counselors.* Vistas Online: American Counseling Association. Retrieved April 10th, 2015 from http://www.counseling.org/knowledge-center/vistas/by-year2/vistas-2010/docs/default-source/vistas/vistas_2010_article_77

Zalla, T., Sirigu, A., Robic, S., Chaste, P., Leboyer, M., & Coricelli, G. (2014). Feelings of regret and disappointment in adults with high-functioning autism. *Cortex, 58,* 112–122.

Zanarini, M. C., Gunderson, J. G., Marino, M. F., Schwartz, E. O., & Frankenburg, F. R. (1989). Childhood experiences of borderline patients. *Comprehensive Psychiatry, 30*(1), 18–25. doi:10.1016/0010-440X(89)90114-4

Zehm, S.J. & Kottler, J.A. (1993) *On being a teacher: The human dimension.* Newbury Park, CA: Corwin Press.

Zimmer-Gembeck, M. J., Pronk, R. E., Goodwin, B., Mastro, S., & Crick, N. R. (2013). Connected and isolated victims of relational aggression: Associations with peer group status and differences between girls and boys. *Sex Roles, 68*(5-6), 363–377.

Zimmerman, G. M. (2010). Impulsivity, offending, and the neighborhood: Investigating the person–context nexus. *Journal of Quantitative Criminology, 26*(3), 301–332.

Zimpher, N. L., & Howey, K. R. (2013). Creating 21st-century centers of pedagogy: Explicating key laboratory and clinical elements of teacher preparation. *Education, 133*(4), 409–421.

Zirpoli, T. J. (2008). *Behavior management: Applications for teachers.* Upper Saddle River, NJ: Prentice Hall.

Zong, J., & Batalova, J. (October 1, 2015). Green-card holders and legal immigration to the United States. Migration Policy Institute. Retrieved July 10th, 2016 from http://www.migrationpolicy.org/article/green-card-holders-and-legal-immigration-united-states.

INDEX

Note: Italicized page locators indicate figures.

aggression (*continued*)
   impulsivity and, 210
   negative urgency and, 211, 218
   reactive, impulsivity and, 215
aggressive behaviors, conduct disorder and, 51
agoraphobia, childhood, attachment history, and, 19–20
AIDS, depression and, 95
Ainsworth, M. D., xiii, 1, 3, 4, 232
   affectional bonds according to, 3
   classification system on infant attachment, 6
   joins Bowlby's research team, 4
   Strange Situation and, 5
Alaska Native males, suicide rate among, 174
alcohol use or abuse
   adolescent years, sensation seeking, and, 214
   eating disorders and, 111
   oppositional defiant disorder and, 48
Alexander, R., xiv, 33, 41, 65, 234
Algozzine, B., xii
"alone" time, high-functioning autism, effective teacher responses, and, 205
alternatiion (biculturalism), 155
ambivalent attachment, Strange Situation and, 5
American culture, individual-centered approach in, 156
American Indian males, suicide rate among, 174
anecdotal records, for students with mood disorders, 108
Angelou, M., xiv
anger
   avoidant attachment style and, 100
   externalized, poor attachment and, 18
   jealousy and, 104
   teachers' behaviors, Minnesota Study, and, 25
   unavailable caregiver and, 14
anger-management skills, learning and teaching, 147
anhedonia, 95
animation
   bias victim, teacher intervention, and, 167
   conduct-disordered student, teacher intervention, and, 61
   depressed student, teacher intervention, and, 104
   high-functioning autism, teacher intervention, and, 204

sound pedagogy and, 42–43, 234
   student with eating disorder, teacher intervention, and, 127
   survivor of suicide, teacher intervention, and, 185
   see also action; reflection
anorexia nervosa
   attachment perspective, and teacher interventions for, 129–30
   attachment style and, 20
   core characteristics of, 112–13
   developmental course of, 114
   DSM-5 typology, 112
   effective teacher responses and, 133–34
   genetics and, 116
   incidence of, 111
   medical problems related to, 114–15
   mortality rates for, 115
   OCD and, differential diagnosis, 116
   pedagogical perspective, and teacher interventions for, 130
   perinatal factors and, 117
   personality patterns and, 117
   prevalence of, 114
   student vignette for, 127–28
   teacher vignettes and, 128–29
anti-bias legislation, 168
anti-bullying law, knowing your obligations under, 147
anticonvulsants, for bipolar disorders, 99
antidepressants, eating disorders treatment and, 120
antisocial behavior, 17, 46
antisocial personality disorder, 20, 22
   development of, factors in, 21
   lack of premeditation and, 215
anxiety, 22
   conduct disorder and, 51
   fear *vs.*, 70
   maternal, disorganized behavior in infants and, 10
   as reaction to unavailable caregiver, 14
anxiety disorders
   attachment histories and, 19–20
   attachment perspective, and teacher interventions for, 77–79, 80–81
   attachment perspective and, understanding student with, 74–76
   comorbidities with, 94, 135
   depression comorbid with, 95
   eating disorders comorbid with, 111, 115
   effective teacher responses for students with, 88
   impulsivity and, 209
   insecure attachment and, 2

attachment theory, xiii, xvi
  academic development and, 16–17
  anxiety disorders and, 19–20
  biological basis of, 2
  classroom dynamics based on, 23–27
  development and, 14–22
  development of psychopathology and, 17–22
  disruptive behavior disorders and, 20–21
  dissociative disorders and, 21
  eating disorders and, 20
  emergence of, 4–6
  introduction to, 2–4
  mood disorders and, 19
  nature-*versus*-nurture argument and, 3, 4
  origination of, 1
  rapport building and, 232–33
  social development and, 17
  teaching difficult students and, 27–29, 232
attachment trauma, defensive exclusion and, 13, 100
attention deficit hyperactivity disorder (ADHD), 45
  bipolar disorders comorbid with, 98–99
  combined type, 208
  comorbidities with, 94
  conduct disorder comorbid with, 50–51, 52, 54–55
  executive skills deficit and, 49
  impulsivity and, 209, 210, 216, 229, 238
  insecure attachment and, 16
  oppositional defiant disorder comorbid with, 48, 49
  oppositional defiant disorder differentiated from, 47
  prevalence rate for, 209–10
  psychostimulants and, 218
  stop-signal reaction times and, 218
  substance abuse, stop-signal reaction times, and, 213
  subtypes, 210
Atwood, G., 21
atypical antipsychotics, for bipolar disorders, 99
Austin, V., 233
authenticity, suicide survivors, teacher intervention, and, 185
authoritarian model, conduct-disordered student, teacher intervention, and, 56
autism
  impulsivity and, 210
  prevalence estimates for, 190
autism spectrum disorder (ASD), 188
  attachment perspective for children with, 194–96
  DSM-5 and criteria for, 190–91

DSM-5 on three levels of severity for, 191
  genetic component of, 188, 196
  narcissism differentiated from, 197
  prevalence rate for, 190
  special education services for students with, 190
  see also high-functioning autism
autonomy, adolescents and need for, 15
autonomy status
  advocacy and White individual at, 166
  White racial identity and, 159
aversive classical conditioning, phobias and, 71
avoidance, anxiety disorders and, 70
avoidant attachment, 232
  anger and, 100
  binge eating disorder and, 131
  bullying, teacher intervention, and, 145
  deactivating and distancing strategies and, 8–9
  dismissing state of mind and, 106
  eating disorders and, 120, 121
  externalization and, 20
  Strange Situation and, 5
  suicide and, 175
  of teacher, anxious student and, 77–78
avoidant children
  bullying by, 17
  classroom dynamics and, 23–24, 233
  depression and, 19
  preoccupied teachers and, 28
  teacher ratings on, Minnesota Study, 26
avoidant personality disorder
  binge eating-purging type of anorexia and, 116
  restricting-type anorexia nervosa and, 115
avoidant teachers, classroom dynamics and, 26

Baron-Cohen, S., 190
Bazhenova, O. V., 195
Beck, A. T., 97
behavior, nature-*versus*-nurture argument and, 3
behavioral contract, oppositional defiant disorder, teacher response, and, 67
behavioral-emotional supports, high-functioning autism, effective teacher responses, and, 205
behavioral intervention plan
  anxiety disorders and, 89
  specific phobia and, 87
behavioral techniques, for eating disorders, 119

behavior in classroom, teacher-student relationship and, xiii

behavior inhibition, social anxiety and, 72

behaviorists, depression according to, 96

behavior momentum
anxious students and, 79
steps in, 41

behavior-specific praise
anxious students and, 79
principles underlying, 40–41

belongingness, xiii

Belsky, J., 4

bereavement, resistantly attached individuals and, 8

bereavement exclusion, removal from *DSM-5*, 93–94

Bergin, C., 12

Bergin, D., 12

Berry, J. W., 155

bias, successfully raising issues of diversity and, 168

bias victims
attachment perspective and, 161–62
attachment perspective and, teacher interventions for, 163–64, 165–66
combating intolerance and, 170
effective teacher responses and, 167–68, 236–37
pedagogical perspective and, teacher interventions for, 164–65, 166–67
teacher vignettes and, 162, 165
what teachers should know about, 152–61
why teachers need to know about, 151–52

biculturalism, 155, 166

Biddulph, M., 38

bidirectional cultural adaptation process, 155

binge eating disorder, 112
attachment perspective and, teacher interventions for, 132
attachment perspective and, understanding student with, 131
bulimia nervosa and, 115
core characteristics of, 113
effective teacher responses and, 134–35
group counseling and treatment of, 120
pedagogical perspective and, teacher interventions for, 133
prevalence of, 114
student vignette, 130–31
teacher vignettes and, 131–32

binge-eating episodes, bulimia nervosa and, 113

binge eating-purging type of anorexia nervosa
DSM-5 classification, 112
personality disorders associated with, 116

binging and purging cycle, student vignette, 110–11

biochemical models of depression, 96

biological factors
conduct disorder and, 51, 52
oppositional defiant disorder and, 48

biological models of depression, 96

bipolar disorder(s), 94
ADHD comorbid with, 98–99
attachment perspective, and teacher interventions for, 106–7
attachment perspective and, understanding student with, 105–6
characterization of, 98
impulsivity and, 209, 210
pedagogical perspective, and teacher interventions for, 107–8
student vignette, 105
teacher vignettes and, 106
teaching students with, 235
treatment of, 99
why teachers need to know about, 93

bipolar I disorder, diagnosis of, 98

bipolar II disorder, diagnosis of, 98

Blumberg, S. J., 190

body dysmorphic disorder, 116

body image, anorexia nervosa and, 112

body language
abnormal, high-functioning autism and, 191
awareness of, teacher effectiveness and, 40

body size, femininity, self-worth, and, 118

Bolles, R. N., 34

borderline personality disorder
attachment theory and, 21
binge eating-purging type of anorexia and, 116
disorganization and, 9
maternal, disorganized behavior in infants and, 10
restricting-type anorexia nervosa and, 115
"splitting" mechanism and, 15

Bornas, 228

boundaries
eating disorders, teacher intervention, and, 125, 129
oppositional defiant disorder, teacher intervention, and, 66
survivor of suicide and violation of, 181, 182

dependency, affective quality of teacher-child relationships and, 23
dependent personality disorder
  binge eating-purging type of anorexia and, 116
  restricting-type anorexia nervosa and, 115
depersonalization, disorganization and, 21
depression, 22
  adolescent, 19
  anorexia and, 115
  attachment perspective, and teacher interventions for, 101, 103–4
  attachment perspective and, understanding students with, 99–100
  biological models of, 96
  bullying victims turned aggressors and, 142
  causal factors of, 96–97
  classroom environment and students with, 108
  cognitive triad of, 97
  conduct disorder and, 51
  eating disorders comorbid with, 116
  events predictive of, 19
  familial anxiety disorders and, 74
  impulsivity and, 209, 210
  maternal, conduct disorder and, 52
  maternal, disorganized behavior in infants and, 10
  medical conditions and symptoms of, 95
  pedagogical perspective, and teacher interventions for, 101–2, 104–5
  prevalence rate for, 94, 95, 235
  student vignette for, 92–93
  suicide and, 214
  suicide prevention and screening for, 176
  teacher vignettes and, 100–101, 102–3
  teaching students with, 235
  treatments for children and adolescents with, 97–98
  underdiagnosis of, in childhood and adolescence, 94
  what teachers need to know about, 93–94
  why teachers need to know about, 93
depressive disorders, 94–96
  age of onset for, 94
  specific phobia comorbid with, 71
depressive episodes
  bipolar disorders and, 98
  predictable classroom routine and students with, 108
derealization, disorganization and, 21
despair, separation and, 17
detention facilities, incarceration costs for youth in, xii

developmentally disabled individuals, L'Arche Community and, 169
DHEAS, oppositional defiant disorder and levels of, 48
Diagnostic and Statistical Manual of Mental Disorders (5th edition). see DSM-5
Dick-Niederhauser, A., 73
diet, limited, high-functioning autism and, 189, 196
diet pills, anorexia nervosa and, 114
difficult students, attachment theory and teaching of, 27–29
direct bullying, 139
directivity, receptivity and, 102
disability(ies)
  bias crimes and, 151, 236
  suicide rate among people with, 174
discipline, spontaneity and, 102
discriminatory behavior, dealing with, 168
disintegration status, White racial identity and, 158
dismissing pattern of response, Adult Attachment Interview and, 5–6
dismissing states of mind, psychopathology and, 22
dismissing style (AAI)
  bipolar disorder and, 105–6
  bullying, teacher intervention, and, 145
  eating disorders and, 120
  of teacher, anxious student and, 77–78
  of teacher, student with eating disorder and, 123
  of teacher, student with high-functioning autism and, 199, 200
disorganized attachment, 9–11, 232
  bullying and, 143
  children with autism spectrum disorder and, 195
  conduct disorder and, 55
  coping mechanisms and, 10
  externalization and, 20
  frightened or frightening behavior subtypes and, 11
  gender differences and, 11
  narcissism and, 197
  psychopathalogy and, 11
  risk factors related to, 10
  Strange Situation and behaviors indicative of, 9–10
  suicide and, 175
  of teacher, student with binge eating disorder and, 132
disorganized behavior, parental, disorganized child and, 11

emotional first aid on the spot, Life Space Interview and, 40

emotional regulation
resistant children and, 16
two components of, 192

empathy
binge eating disorder and teacher's sense of, 132, 133
bullying, teacher intervention, and, 145
capacity for, early attachment relationships, and, 14, 232
insecure attachment and lack of, 164
mentalization and, 27, 28
multiculturalism in school and, 166
secure attachment and, 143, 165, 192
sociopath and lack of capacity for, 58

empowering students
bullying, teacher intervention, and, 146
high-functioning autism, teacher intervention, and, 204
student with eating disorder and, 124
survivor of suicide, teacher intervention, and, 185

encouragement, separation anxiety disorder in students and, 89

engagement
survivor of suicide, teacher intervention, and, 183
teachers' behaviors, Minnesota Study, and, 25

enlightenment, addressing bias and, 237

enthusiasm, for learning and learners, 34

entitlement issues, highly reactive children and, 220

environmental factors
anxiety disorders and, 72
attachment security and, 4
oppositional defiant disorder and, 48

environmental toxins, prenatal, conduct disorder and, 52

epilepsy, suicide rate among people with, 174

episodic memory, traumatic memories stored in, 13

ethnicity
bias crimes and, 151, 236
defined, 153

etic *versus* emic debate, 153–54, 161

Euro-centric culture, 155

executive functioning
impaired, impulsivity and, 212, 217, 221
increasing, role of schools and, 216
poverty and impact on, 215
quality of parent-child bond and, 13

executive skills, oppositional defiant disorder and lack of, 49

expectations for compliance, teachers' behaviors, Minnesota Study, and, 25, 26

expectations for students, effective pedagogy and, 33

exploration
attachment and, 2
resistant children and, 8
secure children and, 6

"extending a friendly hand," conduct-disordered student and, 59–60

externalization
conduct disorder, disruptive male presence in home, and, 56
eating disorders and, 121
parent-child attachment bonds and, 20–21
suicide and negative correlation with, 179

extracurricular activities, social phobia in students and, 89

eye contact
abnormal, high-functioning autism and, 191
teacher effectiveness and, 40

facial expression, lack of, high-functioning autism and, 191

false-belief test, theory of mind and, 193

family-based interventions, for conduct disorder, 53

family conflict, increased risk for violence and exposure to, 53

family counseling
depression treatment and, 97–98
eating disorders treatment and, 119–20

family dynamics, separation anxiety disorder and, 73–74

family dysfunction
eating disorders and, 118
oppositional defiant disorder and, 48

family environment, conduct disorder and, 52

family patterns
bullying and, 143
bullying victims turned aggressors and, 142
eating disorders and, 121

family systems theorists, depression according to, 97

family systems therapy, for conduct disorder, 53–54

family violence, 18

Far from the Tree (Solomon), 169

faux pas stories, high-functioning autism, theory of mind, and, 203

FBI, hate and bias crimes statistics, 151

fear
  anxiety disorders and, 70
  anxiety *vs.*, 70
  attachment and, 2
Fearon, R. M. P., 4
feedback, 34
  conduct-disordered student and teacher's
    need for, 59
  positive, formative, for all students, 34
femininity, body size and, 118
feminist group interventions, bulimia and
    binge eating treatment and, 120
Ferguson, N., 37
fetal alcohol syndrome, impulsivity and, 209
fight-or-flight reactions, 209
Finkelmeyer, A., 190
first-order false-belief test, theory of mind
    and, 193, 203
5-hydroxyindoleacetic acid, oppositional
    defiant disorder and, 48
flexibility
  impulsivity, teacher intervention, and, 223
  teacher effectiveness and, 40
folk psychology, 192
Fonagy, P., 20
food choices and healthy eating, teacher
    modeling of, 125, 126, 127, 133
Freire, P., 33, 42, 59, 107, 124, 200, 222, 234
Frick, P. J., 51
frightened or frightening attachment figure,
    conduct disorder and, 55, 56, 232
frightened or frightening behavior subtypes,
    disorganized attachment and, 11
Frombonne, E., 190
frontal lobe system
  substance abuse during adolescence and,
    213
  working memory and, 212
frontolimbic connectivity, abnormal,
    high-functioning autism and, 197–98
functional family therapy, conduct disorder
    treatment and phases of, 53–54

Gage, N. L., 30
gambling
  pathological, impulsivity and, 210
  positive urgency and, 211
Ganda families, Ainsworth's studies of
    infant-mother attachment in, 4–5
Garfin, D. R., 237
gender
  bullying and, 141
  conduct disorder and, 50
  disruptive behavior disorders and, 20
  eating disorders and, 111, 114

major depression and, 94
  oppositional defiant disorder and, 47
  parental frightening or withdrawal behav-
    iors and, 11
  traumatic grief and, 103
gender bias, inclusive environment and, 167
genetic model of depression, 96
genetics
  attachment security and, 4
  eating disorders and, 116
  phobic disorders and, 72
  separation anxiety disorder and, 73
gestures, abnormal, high-functioning autism
    and, 191
Gladwell, M., 169, 173
goals
  clarifying with students, 34
  effective pedagogy and, 33
Goldberg, S., 10
Goldhaber, D. D., xvi
Goldwyn, R., 77
good teaching framework, xii–xvi
  pedagogical skills, xiv–xv, 1
  relationship building, xii–xiv, 1
  subject knowledge, xv–xvi, 1
Gratz, K. L., 227
Greene, M., 102, 104
grief and grieving
  healthy, oscillation or alternation process
    and, 99–100
  suicide, at-risk survivor, and, 180
  suicide, guilt, anger, and, 177
  survivor of suicide, teacher intervention,
    and, 182, 185
  traumatic, 103
grief counseling, suicide postvention and, 177
group counseling, eating disorders treat-
    ment and, 120
growthful changes, survivor of suicide,
    teacher intervention, and, 183
Guatemala, immigrants from, 152
Guerra, N. G., 141
Gunstone, R., 31
gun violence, adolescent deaths and, 173

habituation, internal working models and,
    12–13
Hallam, S., 33, 42
Hanish, L. D., 141
Hargreaves, A., xiii
Harrop, E. N., 111
hate, externalized, poor attachment and, 18
hate crimes, 151, 236
  incidence of, 151
  student vignette for, 150–51

Hazler, R. J., 142
healthier behaviors, impulsive behaviors replaced with, 227–28
Helms, J. E., 157, 158, 159, 160
Helterbran, V. R., 36
Hesse, E., 10, 11, 21, 77
HFA. *see* high-functioning autism (HFA)
"hidden curriculum," 34
  bias victims, teacher interventions, and, 164, 167
  embedded in social contexts, student acquisition of, 34
  social cues and, 189
high-functioning autism (HFA)
  abnormal frontolimbic connectivity and, 197–98
  advanced theory of mind tasks and, 194
  attachment perspective, and teacher interventions for, 198–200, 202–3
  attachment perspective and understanding of, 194–98
  DSM-5 definition of "requiring support" for, 191
  effective teacher responses to students with, 204–5
  gender and, 190
  increased number of students in public schools with, 190, 206
  less activated rTPJ in students with, 194
  pedagogical perspective, and teacher interventions for, 200, 203–4
  prevalence rate for, 190, 238
  student vignette for, 188–89
  teacher vignettes and, 198, 201–2
  teaching students with, 188–206, 238
  theory of mind and social deficits of those with, 192–93
  unique challenges for educators and, 191, 205
  what teachers should know about, 190–94
  why teachers need to know about, 190
HIPAA medical privacy laws, suicide and, 178
Hispanic females, suicide rate among, 174
histrionic personality disorder, binge eating-purging type of anorexia and, 116
HIV, suicide rate among people with, 174
holistic approach to education, 35
Holma, E. A., 237
home background of student, mentalization and knowledge about, 64
homicides, adolescent deaths and, 173
honesty, good teachers and, 88, 185
Hood, J, 10
hopelessness, suicide and, 214

hospitalization, for eating disorders, 118–19
Howes, C., 23, 24
Howey, K. R., xv
Hruska, B., 102, 104
human behavior, tri-partite framework of, 57, *57*
human difference, social valuation of, 169
humor, teacher effectiveness and, 38
hyperactive impulsive behaviors, 45
hyperactivity, 2
hypersexuality, manic episodes and, 99
hyperthyroidism, impulsivity and, 209
hypervigilance, resistant attachment and, 8
hypomania, defined, 98
hypomanic episode, bipolar disorders and, 98

IDEA. *see* Individuals with Disabilities Education Act (IDEA)
idealization, cost of, 100
identity
  conduct-disordered student, teacher intervention, and, 61
  high-functioning autism, teacher intervention, and, 203
  impulsivity, teacher intervention, and, 225
  oppositional defiant disorder, teacher intervention and, 64
  sound teacher pedagogy and, 31, 41, 101, 102, 233
immersion/emersion status, White racial identity and, 159
immigration patterns, addressing bias in schools and, 152
implementing choice approach
  anxious students and, 79
  stages in, 41
impulse discharges, healthy, 227
impulsive behavior
  bulimia nervosa and, 115
  causes of, 209
  changing consequences of, 228
  controlling, helping child with, 226–27
  effective teacher responses to, 225–26, 230
  examples of, 209
  identifying long-term negative consequences of, 228
  managing, 227–28
  risk taking and, 213, 229–30
  two interventions for, 228–29
impulsivity
  ADHD and, 209, 210, 216, 229, 238
  adolescent development and, 213–15
  attachment perspective, and teacher interventions for, 220–22, 223–24

Lincoln, A., 170
Linseman, K., 144
listening
     careful, impulsive students and need for,
          227
     good teaching and, 102, 103, 132
Lithium, for bipolar disorder, 99
Littleton, Colorado (1999), 173
Llabres, 228
locus of control
     internal or external, 156, *157*
     locus of responsibility *vs.*, *157*
locus of responsibility
     internal or external, 156, *157*
     locus of control *vs.*, *157*
loss, resistantly attached individuals and, 8
Loughran, J., xiv, 31, 32, 41, 42, 64, 81, 88,
          102, 146, 185
love, high-functioning autism, teacher inter-
          vention, and, 200
LSI. *see* Life Space Interview (LSI)
lying, adolescents and, 15
Lynam, D. R., 211, 229
Lyons-Ruth, K., 21

Main, M., 6, 9, 10, 11, 21, 27, 77
mainstream majority, 153
major depression, age of onset for, 94
major depressive disorder
     comorbidities with, 94
     diagnosis of, 93
     DSM-5 and, 95
     eating disorders and, 111
     recurring, 95
majority, defined, 153
males, eating disorders underdiagnosed in,
          114
malnutrition, eating disorders and, 112
Manassis, K., 10
mania, ADHD and symptoms of, 98–99
manic episode, bipolar disorders and, 98
mantra or affirmation, separation anxiety in
          student and, 82
marginality, cultural adaptation and, 155
marital conflict, increased risk for violence
          and exposure to, 53
Marlatt, G. A., 111
Marzano, R. A., xii
Mascolo, M. F., 33
Maslow, A., 61
master teachers
     becoming, 43
     behaviors evidenced by, 37–38
master teaching, characteristics and quali-
          ties of, 38

maternal depression, childhood depression
          and, 16, 17, 19
meaningful learning tasks, good assessment
          procedures and, 34
meaning-making, internal working models
          and, 13
media
     bully's behavior reinforced by, 141
     suicide postvention plans and, 178
medications
     for bipolar disorders, 99
     for bulimia nervosa, 120
     for eating disorders, 120
     impulsivity and, 218–19
     for mood disorders, anecdotal records,
          and, 108
     see also psychopharmacological treat-
          ments
meditation, 241
Melnick, S., 21
Mendel, R. A., xi
menstruation, anorexia and cessation of, 114
mental health counseling, suicide, at-risk
          survivor, and, 180, 183
mental illness, myth of, questioning, 107
mentalization, 27
     bias victim, teacher intervention, and,
          165–66
     conduct-disordered student, teacher's
          intervention, and, 60
     defined, 192–93, 233
     impulsivity, teacher intervention, and, 224
     information about home background of
          student and, 64
     parental sensitivity and, 195
     student's eating disorder and teacher's
          antithesis of, 122
     survivor of suicide, teacher's intervention,
          and, 182
     teacher-student working alliances and, 164
     see also theory of mind
mental retardation, attachment disorganiza-
          tion and children with, 195
metacognitive monitoring, 27
Metzler, J., xvi
Mexican immigrants, 152
middle childhood, attachment theory and, 14
mindfulness, xiii, 241
mind reading, 192
Minnesota Department of Human Services,
          173
Minnesota Study of Risk and Adaptation
          from Birth to Adulthood (Sroufe, et al.),
          16, 17, 19, 20, 25, 56
minority, defined, 153

nonverbal communication skills
high-functioning autism and deficits in, 191, 196
social phobia in students and, 89
No Pity (Shapiro), 169
Northfield, J., 32
Norwich, B., 35
novelty seeking, impulsivity and, 211
nurturance/support, teachers' behaviors, Minnesota Study, and, 25
Nystrom, B., 144

obesity, binge eating disorder and, 113, 130–31, 132
obsessive-compulsive disorder (OCD)
anorexia and, differential diagnosis, 116
eating disorders and, 111
impulsivity and, 209
restricting-type anorexia nervosa and, 115
Olweus, D., 139
"one-size-fits-all' teacher pedagogy, 33
openness, conviction and, 102
operant conditioning, eating disorders treatment and, 119
oppositional defiant disorder, 20, 45, 67, 234
ADHD and, 216
attachment perspective, and teacher interventions for, 64
attachment perspective and, understanding student with, 62–63
causal factors in development of, 48–49
characteristics and symptoms of, 46–48
comorbidities with, 47–48, 94
DSM-5 and, 46, 47
effective teacher responses and, 66–67
gender and, 47
mood disorder distinguished from, 47
pedagogical perspective, and teacher interventions for, 64–65
prevalence rates for, 47
recommended treatments for, 49–50, 68, 234–35
student vignette for, 62
teacher vignettes and, 62, 63–64
oppression, nondominant backgrounds and forms of, 154
oppressive parental authority, bullies and, 143
orbital frontal cortex, internal working models and weaknesses in, 13
other health impaired disability category, impulsivity and, 219
overeating
bulimia nervosa and, 113
depressive disorders and, 116

overprotective parents, bullying victims and, 143
overstimulation, resistant children and, 20
overt aggression, conduct disorder and, 51

Palmer, P. J., xv, 31, 36, 37, 41, 43, 64, 79, 81, 88, 101, 102, 104, 146, 231, 233
panic attacks, high-functioning autism and, 189, 197
parallel process, attachment theory and, 24–25
parallel relationship, White helper, non-White client, and, 160
parasuicides, 173
parental psychopathology, 18
parental sensitivity
attachment and, 195
secure attachment in childhood and, 15
parent-child interaction therapy, oppositional defiant disorder and, 49, 68, 234–35
parenting styles, separation anxiety disorder and, 73–74
parent management training, conduct disorder treatment and, 53
parents
adversarial, teacher reactions, and, 87, 88
anxiety, separation anxiety disorder in child and, 74
anxiety-disordered, 72
bully's behavior reinforced by, 141
caregiving style of, child's attachment system and, 3
concordance between relationships with teachers and, 23
death of, depression in daughter, and, 92–93
dismissing, avoidant attachment in child and, 8
protection against suicide and, 175
racial identity and, 161
shy, social anxiety in child and, 72
suicide postvention and, 176
Parkinson's disease, impulsivity and, 209
passion, for subject matter, xv
PBIS. *see* Positive Intervention and Support (PBIS)-3-Tiered Model
pedagogical framework
cultural tools and, 33
six critical elements in, 42, 234
pedagogical knowledge, xiv, 31
pedagogical perspective
anorexia nervosa, teacher interventions and, 130
anxiety disorders, teacher interventions and, 79–80, 81–83
bias victims, teacher interventions and, 164–65, 166–67

race
   bias crimes and, 151, 236
   conduct disorder and, 50
   defined, 153
race-based theorists, 154
racial identity development, 157–60
   people of color and, 159–60
   teacher-student relationship and, 160–61
   Whites and, 158–59
racial identity models, defined, 157
racism, 154, 236
   attachment perspective and, 161–62
   what teachers should know about, 152–61
   White racial identity and, 158–59
   why teachers need to know about, 151–52
   see also bias victims
rapport
   building, attachment theory and, 232–33
   high-functioning autism, teacher interven-
      tion, and, 203, 204
   impulsivity, teacher intervention, and,
      222, 224, 225
   suicide survivors, teacher intervention,
      and, 185
   teacher-student, xii
reactive aggression
   conduct disorder and, 51
   impulsivity and, 215
reactive response, mentalization vs., 27
reality rub, separation anxiety in student
      and, 82
reappraisal, emotional regulation and, 192
receptivity, directivity and, 102
recidivism rate, for incarcerated youth in
      New York State, xii
Redl, F., 40, 104
refeeding, inpatient treatment for eating dis-
      orders and, 118–19
reflection
   bias victim, teacher intervention, and,
      167
   conduct-disordered student, teacher inter-
      vention, and, 61
   defined, 32
   depressed student, teacher intervention,
      and, 104
   high-functioning autism, teacher interven-
      tion, and, 204
   sound pedagogy and, 42, 43, 233, 234
   student with eating disorder, teacher
      intervention, and, 127
   survivor of suicide, teacher intervention,
      and, 183, 185
   see also action; animation
"reflective practitioner" (Schön), 32

regressive relationship, White helper, non-
      White client, and, 160, 161
reinforcement, impulsive students and, 226,
      228
reintegration status, White racial identity
      and, 158
rejection, cultural adaptation and, 155
relational aggression, conduct disorder and,
      51
relationship building
   binge eating by student, teacher interven-
      tion, and, 133
   good teaching and, xii–xiv
relationship difficulties, high-functioning
      autism and, 191
relationships, internal working models and,
      12
relaxation techniques
   conduct disorder and, 53
   impulsive students and, 228
religion, bias crimes and, 151, 236
resilience, 18–19
resistance and immersion status, racial
      identity of people of color and, 159–60,
      161
resistant anxious state of mind, of teacher,
      bias victim and, 163, 164
resistant attachment, 232
   adults with, 8
   aggression and, 143
   anxiety disorders and, 19
   anxious student, teacher's secure state of
      mind, and, 80–81
   children with, 7–8
   eating disorders and, 120
   separation anxiety and, 74
   suicide and, 175
resistant children
   academic development and, 16
   classroom dynamics and, 24, 233
   depression and, 19
   limits and, 18
   mentalization for teachers and, 28
   teacher ratings on, Minnesota Study, 26
   as victims of bullying, 17
respect
   relationship building and, xii, xiii
   toward students, 36
response delay, eating disorders treatment
      and, 119, 122
response prevention, eating disorders treat-
      ment and, 119, 122
response to intervention (RtI), Positive
      Behavioral Intervention and Supports
      and, 239, 240

restricting type anorexia nervosa
  DSM-5 classification, 112
  personality disorders associated with, 115
restrictive, repetitive behaviors, autism
    spectrum disorder and, 191
revenge, bullying victims and, 142
rewards, oppositional defiant disorder and,
    66
reward sensitivity, impulsivity and, 211
right-lateralized, temporo-parietal junction
    (rTPJ), of brain, moral judgments based
    on theory of mind and, 194
"risk-taking" period of human development,
    evolutionary purpose of, 229
Ritalin, 54, 208, 218
Ritchie, S., 23
Roberts, W. B. J., 140
romantic activity, bipolar disorder and, 106
Rose, M., xiii
Rosenfeld, M., 37
Rosenfeld, S., 37
rTPJ. *see* right-lateralized, temporo-parietal
    junction (rTPJ)
rules
  bullying prevention and, 146
  explicit and meaningful, 34
  fair and consistent application of, 58
  impulsivity and, 230, 239
Russell, T. L., 32, 42, 59, 104

safe place, high-functioning autism, effec-
    tive teacher responses, and, 205
safe school plan, implementing, 147
safety threats, reporting, 147
"Sally-Anne" test, 193, 203
SAMs. *see* situational accessible memories
    (SAMs)
sarcasm, high-functioning autism, and miss-
    ing subtleties of, 188, 201
sarcasm stories, high-functioning autism,
    theory of mind, and, 203
Saville, B. K., 38
Schaub, 228
Schlozman, S. C., 185
Schneidman, E., 175
Schön, D. A., 32, 42, 59, 104
school drop outs, conduct disorder and, 50
school environment
  bullying victims and, 142
  teacher advocacy, student with eating dis-
      order, and, 124
school performance
  mood disorders in students and, 108
  separation anxiety disorder in students
      and, 89

school refusal
  bullying victims and, 140
  separation anxiety and, 69–70, 75–76, 77
schools
  attachment and, 22–23
  impulsive adolescents and impact of, 215–16
  minimizing suicide contagion in, 176–77
  multisystemic treatment for conduct dis-
      order and, 54
  suicide postvention and, 176, 177–78
  see also parents; students; teachers
school shooters, history of being bullied and,
    142
school shootings, abuse in home or commu-
    nity leading to, 148
school violence, why teachers needs to know
    about aftermath of, 173
schoolwork impulsivity, 211
Schultz, D., 144
Scientific Basis of the Art of Teaching, The
    (Gage), 30
scotosis, 163
second culture acquisition
  attachment perspective, teacher interven-
      tion, and, 163
  intragroup difference and, 154–56
second-order false-belief task, theory of
    mind and, 193, 203
second-order reasoning, theory of mind and,
    194
Section 504 plans, eating disorders and, 112
secure attachment, 2, 6–7, 232
  appreciation of cultural difference and,
      161, 162
  available and supportive relationships
      and, 175
  bias victim, teacher intervention, and, 165
  children with ASD and difficulties with,
      194–95
  empathy and, 143, 165, 192
  internal working models of children with,
      12
  learning disabilities and lower rates of,
      16–17
  maternal characteristics related to, 7
  mentalization and, 27
  parental sensitivity and, 15
  revised internal working models and chil-
      dren with, 13
  social competency and, 16, 17
  of teacher, conduct-disordered student
      and, 60
  of teacher, impulsive student and, 218
  of teacher, specific phobia in student, and,
      87–88

Stough, L. M., 36, 37
Stout, D., 42, 61, 107, 127, 185, 203
Strange Situation, 17
    avoidant infants in, 8
    description of, 5
    dismissing state of mind correlated with
        avoidant in, 77
    disorganized children in, 9–10
    resistant children in, 7–8
    secure children in, 6
strengths, teaching students how to identify,
    34, 225
stress
    anxiety disorder and, 74
    resilience and, 18
stress reduction, mindfulness and, 241
STRS. *see* Student-Reacher Relationship
    Scale (STRS)
structural family therapy, for eating disor-
    ders treatment, 119
structured teaching approaches, high-func-
    tioning autism, effective teacher
    responses, and, 205
student-centered approach, eating disorder
    and teacher's use of, 126
student-centered focus, developing, 123
Student-Reacher Relationship Scale (STRS),
    23
students
    accountability and, 34
    attachment, and therapeutic bonds
        between teachers and, xiii
    counter-transference between teachers
        and, 1
    empowering, 34
    good teachers defined by, 36
    motivating and enthusing, 34
    peer's suicide and, 178
    positive formative feedback for, 34
    relationship building between teachers
        and, xii–xiv
    suicide postvention and, 176
    taking responsibility for own learning, 34,
        127
    teachers' respect for, 36
    transferable skills taught to, 34
    transference between teachers and, 1
    see also caring student-teacher relation-
        ship; schools; teachers
student teachers, development of sound ped-
    agogy and, 31
study buddies, social phobia in students and,
    89
subcortical striatal system, impulsivity and,
    217

subject-centered classrooms, xv
subject knowledge
    effective teachers and grasp of, 36
    good teaching and, xv–xvi
subject matter, passion for, xv
submissive behavior, parental, disorganized
    child and, 11
substance abuse, 22
    ADHD, stop-signal reaction times, and,
        213
    bipolar disorders and, 99
    bulimia nervosa and, 115
    depression comorbid with, 95
    discounting of delayed rewards and, 212–
        13
    eating disorders comorbid, 111, 115
    impulsivity and, 210
    maternal, disorganized behavior in
        infants and, 10
    prenatal, conduct disorder and, 52
success for students, transferable skills and,
    34
Sue, D., 156
Sue, D. W. E., 156, 159
suicidal assessment, safety plan and, 181
suicidal ideation, 173, 237
    conduct disorder comorbid with depres-
        sion and, 51
    eating disorders and, 135
suicidality
    adolescent impulsivity and, 214, 230
    school and vigilance for signs of, 104
suicide
    anorexia nervosa and, 115
    attachment and, 174–75
    attachment perspective, and understand-
        ing aftermath of, 179–80
    attempted, 173
    bipolar adolescents and, 99
    bullying victims and, 139, 142
    dissemination of information in aftermath
        of, 178
    effective teacher responses in aftermath
        of, 185–86, 237–38
    facts about, 174, 235, 237
    gender and, 173
    grief work and, 177, 237
    high school survivors of, profile, 176
    impulsivity and, 210
    insecure attachment and, 179
    mood disorders and, 93, 109
    pernicious residual effects of, 186
    statistics on, 173
    student vignette told by teacher, 171–72
    survivor guilt and, 174